Twenty-First-Century Gateways

JAMES A. JOHNSON METRO SERIES

The Metropolitan Policy Program at the Brookings Institution is integrating research and practical experience into a policy agenda for cities and metropolitan areas. By bringing fresh analyses and policy ideas to the public debate, the program hopes to inform key decisionmakers and civic leaders in ways that will spur meaningful change in our nation's communities.

As part of this effort, the James A. Johnson Metro Series aims to introduce new perspectives and policy thinking on current issues and attempts to lay the foundation for longer-term policy reforms. The series examines traditional urban issues, such as neighborhood assets and central city competitiveness, as well as larger metropolitan concerns, such as regional growth, development, and employment patterns. The James A. Johnson Metro Series consists of concise studies and collections of essays designed to appeal to a broad audience. While these studies are formally reviewed, some will not be verified like other research publications. As with all publications, the judgments, conclusions, and recommendations presented in the studies are solely those of the authors and should not be attributed to the trustees, officers, or other staff members of the Institution.

Also available in this series:

On growth and development

Boomburbs: The Rise of America's Accidental Cities
Robert E. Lang and Jennifer B. LeFurgy

Edgeless Cities: Exploring the Elusive Metropolis
Robert E. Lang

Growth and Convergence in Metropolitan America
Janet Rothenberg Pack

Growth Management and Affordable Housing
Anthony Downs, editor

Laws of the Landscape: How Policies Shape Cities in Europe and America
Pietro S. Nivola

Reflections on Regionalism
Bruce J. Katz, editor

Sunbelt/Frostbelt: Public Policies and Market Forces in Metropolitan Development
Janet Rothenberg Pack, editor

On transportation

Still Stuck in Traffic: Coping with Peak-Hour Traffic Congestion
Anthony Downs

Taking the High Road: A Metropolitan Agenda for Transportation Reform
Bruce Katz and Robert Puentes, editors

On trends

Redefining Urban and Suburban America: Evidence from Census 2000, vol. 1
Bruce Katz and Robert E. Lang, editors

Redefining Urban and Suburban America: Evidence from Census 2000, vols. 2–3
Alan Berube, Bruce Katz, and Robert E. Lang, editors

On wealth creation

Building Assets, Building Credit: Creating Wealth in Low-Income Communities
Nicolas P. Retsinas and Eric S. Belsky, editors

The Geography of Opportunity: Race and Housing Choice in Metropolitan America
Xavier de Souza Briggs, editor

Low-Income Homeownership: Examining the Unexamined Goal
Nicolas P. Retsinas and Eric S. Belsky, editors

Savings for the Poor: The Hidden Benefits of Electronic Banking
Michael A. Stegman

On other metro issues

Evaluating Gun Policy: Effects on Crime and Violence
Jens Ludwig and Philip J. Cook, editors

Revisiting Rental Housing: Policies, Programs, and Priorities
Nicholas P. Retsinas and Eric S. Belsky, editors

Twenty-First-Century Gateways

Immigrant Incorporation in Suburban America

Audrey Singer

Susan W. Hardwick

Caroline B. Brettell

EDITORS

BROOKINGS INSTITUTION PRESS
Washington, D.C.

Library of Congress Cataloging-in-Publication data

Twenty-first-century gateways : immigrant incorporation in suburban America / Audrey Singer, Susan W. Hardwick, and Caroline B. Brettell, editors.
p. cm.
Summary: "Focuses on the fastest-growing immigrant populations among 'second-tier' metropolitan areas. Examines the changes wrought by these new suburban settlement patterns and provides comparative analysis of immigration trends and local policy responses in these gateways. Case examples explore the challenges of newcomer integration, as well as immigration's impact on suburban infrastructure"—Provided by publisher.
Includes bibliographical references and index.
ISBN-13: 978-0-8157-7926-1 (cloth : alk. paper)
ISBN-10: 0-8157-7926-7 (cloth : alk. paper)
ISBN-13: 978-0-8157-7927-8 (pbk. : alk. paper)
ISBN-10: 0-8157-7927-5 (pbk. : alk. paper)
1. Immigrants—United States. 2. Social integration—United States. 3. Suburbs—United States. 4. Metropolitan areas—United States. 5. United States—Emigration and immigration—Social aspects. I. Singer, Audrey. II. Hardwick, Susan Wiley. III. Brettell, Caroline.
JV6475.T94 2008
305.9'069120973—dc22 2007048076

9 8 7 6 5 4 3 2 1

The paper used in this publication meets minimum requirements of the American National Standard for Information Sciences—Permanence of Paper for Printed Library Materials: ANSI Z39.48-1992.

Typeset in Sabon

Composition by Cynthia Stock
Silver Spring, Maryland

Printed by R. R. Donnelley
Harrisonburg, Virginia

Contents

Foreword

As has been the case at various points throughout our nation's history, the ability of the United States to sustain a vibrant economy, to develop a productive workforce, and to nurture a cohesive civil society through the years of this century will depend in substantial measure on the effectiveness with which we integrate immigrants. The percentage of foreign-born persons in the American population today approaches the proportions of the peak periods of immigration at the beginning of the last century. The numbers of immigrants are so substantial and their demographic attributes so significant—due to the larger size of immigrant families and the relative youthfulness of immigrant households—that they will assuredly influence the nation's most important social, economic, and educational indicators.

Immigrants will contribute their youthful energies, workforce capacities, and fiscal strengths at a time when the traditional American population is graying. The contrasts with the problems confronting other northern industrial nations are evident. Nations such as Japan, France, Germany, and Italy are either already declining or nearing steady-state levels of population because of low birth rates, aging populations, and troubled histories of immigrant integration. They are certain to confront challenges financing their health care and retirement systems, staffing institutions such as their armed forces, and growing their domestic markets. The United States will itself confront many problems, but the unavailability of youthful workers will not be one of them, thanks to our growing immigrant families.

Our nation's progress once depended on the strong arms and backs of immigrants from Italy, Ireland, Poland, Scandinavia, Germany, Mexico, and China, among other nations. Across several waves of immigration, the United States became an industrial power, populated its open spaces, built its great cities, and created a culturally diverse and inclusive society. Today the accents and last names are different, but the nation's progress will rely on the brainpower, entrepreneurial skills, and capacities for hard work of its newest immigrants. Among them are large numbers of immigrants from Mexico, Latin America, India, the Pacific Asian nations, the Caribbean, Africa, and steady streams from virtually every nation on earth.

Not only are the aggregate numbers of immigrants large, but the way they are dispersing across the geography of America will be helpful to the nation over the next decades. While many recent arrivals continue to live in the central neighborhoods of such well-established gateway metropolitan areas as New York, Los Angeles, Chicago, Houston, San Francisco, and Miami, many others have moved to the older inner suburbs, to newer, faster-growing suburbs, to moderate-sized heartland metropolitan areas, and increasingly to smaller communities.

The same push-pull effects that bring immigrants to the United States in the first place also influence their location decisions within the country. They are *pulled* by job opportunities to an older suburb such as Silver Spring, Maryland; to a new and quickly growing suburb such as Mesa, Arizona; to a heartland city such as Austin, Texas; and to smaller employment centers such as Rogers, Arkansas. At the same time immigrants are *pushed* out of the more established gateway cities by high prices, traffic congestion, and inhospitable living conditions for their families. This push-pull dynamic spreads people to areas where they are needed, beginning with immigrants already living within the United States, then drawing them directly from abroad. Industries receive the workers they need and communities receive the residents who can replace the civic energies and consumer spending of aging populations. From the standpoint of the immigrants, the new patterns of settlement may speed along the process of integration, enabling newcomers to ease their way into useful and remunerative roles outside the traditional enclaves where they often are separated from mainstream American society. Immigrant families benefit from locating in lower-cost suburban areas and may thereby shorten the time over which they can become homeowners and entrepreneurs. The need to learn English quickly and to fit into school settings in communities less accustomed to receiving immigrants accelerate the integration of the next generation.

While this process has positive dimensions both for the nation and for the immigrants, for many communities as well as for many immigrant families, these dynamics pose serious difficulties. Long-established residents may not be willing or capable of accepting newcomers. The pain for immigrants of functioning with limited English skills and the tensions between personal heritage and American practices can break the human spirit. But despite the hardships and controversies, the importance of integrating immigrants into our future makes it a paramount national interest to understand the new geography of immigration, to make integration as painless as possible, and to generate positive results for all involved.

The Brookings Institution and a team of knowledgeable editors—Audrey Singer, Susan Hardwick, and Caroline Brettell—have pulled together a group of contributors well qualified to chart the new spatial patterns of immigration and to describe the experiences of receiving communities across the nation. Their work describes how the massive redistribution of population under way, fueled by higher levels and new patterns of immigrant settlement, is reshaping the nation's prospects and teaching us about the contributions of immigrants. The next step for the twenty-first century is for us to translate the lessons of community experiences into a broader political will to sustain the good fortune that is America's immigrant tradition.

HENRY CISNEROS
Chairman, CityView
San Antonio

Acknowledgments

The idea for this book was launched in 2002 when several of the contributors convened to discuss the dramatic demographic and structural changes that were reshaping metropolitan America. No longer were immigrants confined to downtown neighborhoods as in the past. Instead, today's foreign-born populations more often were choosing life in the suburbs—places formerly viewed as the domain of white middle- and upper-class families.

The participants also took note of another equally surprising observation during that first discussion: not only were most immigrants choosing to live in the suburbs in the 1990s and the early years of the twenty-first century, many also were migrating to nontraditional immigrant gateways. While many new arrivals continued to settle in large-scale older immigrant gateways such as New York City, Chicago, and Los Angeles, others were taking up residence in unexpected places such as Atlanta, Georgia; Charlotte, North Carolina; Las Vegas, Nevada; and Portland, Oregon. But which sociospatial processes were shaping these two related new trends in immigrant settlement patterns in the United States? And what were some of the impacts of these increasingly large foreign-born populations on the communities in which they had newly chosen to reside? How were the longer-term, U.S.-born residents of these new suburban gateways handling the rapid changes in their neighborhoods brought on by the arrival of more diverse groups? Seeking answers to these and other related questions became our mission, and this book represents both an effort to document the trends and to raise awareness of the impact of immigration on the largest, newest destinations.

Having charged ourselves with this task, we assembled a multidisciplinary group of scholars engaged in research in specific metropolitan areas and in localities within those areas where the impact of immigration is most profound. Initial drafts of ideas for what were to become the chapters of this book were presented in many places along the way, most notably at two special sessions at the Social Science History Association meetings in Minneapolis in November 2006 and at the annual meetings of the Association of American Geographers in spring 2007 in San Francisco. These public discussions provided us with the opportunity to debate the processes shaping suburban gateways and to share ideas with a wider audience. We thank the participants in these sessions for insightful comments and suggestions.

We were fortunate all along the way to have the support of Living Cities, a partnership of financial institutions, private foundations, and government agencies established to improve urban neighborhoods and residents historically left behind.

We are particularly grateful to several individuals who have helped us shape the volume in one way or another. First, we all owe an enormous debt of gratitude to Jill H. Wilson of the Brookings Metropolitan Policy Program, who diligently worked through countless statistics and data sources, provided critical feedback, and who created many of the tables, graphs, and maps that appear in the book. Thanks are also due to the program's David Park, who contributed ideas that helped us think about broad changes across metropolitan areas and who read and critiqued sections of the draft manuscript. We thank many other colleagues at the Metropolitan Policy Program who offered advice and support, especially Alan Berube, Brooke DeRenzis, Bill Frey, Bruce Katz, Amy Liu, Mark Muro, and Rob Puentes, as well as the staff at the Brookings Institution Press for their enthusiasm and professionalism in moving the mass of electronic files into what you see here. We are tremendously grateful to Barbara Ray, who carefully read and edited the entire manuscript and improved the flow and clarity of each of the chapters to provide the finished book with a clearer and more consistent voice. And thanks should also go to Marty Gottron, who did the final copyedit.

Our biggest thanks are due to the contributors to this volume. They endured our suggestions and demands and did not balk when we asked for more. We learned a great deal from their on-the-ground experience living and working in these newest immigrant gateways. As co-editors we have been inspired by their contributions to our understanding of the processes unfolding before our eyes and by the newest Americans, who continue to settle in twenty-first-century suburban gateways.

PART I

The New Metropolitan Geography of Immigration

1

Twenty-First-Century Gateways

An Introduction

AUDREY SINGER

Straddling two centuries, the ten-year period between 1995 and 2005 came to mean dramatically different circumstances for immigrants residing in the United States. Immigrants arriving in the late 1990s were drawn to a soaring economy bolstered by growth in "new economy" jobs, especially in the information technology sector. This in turn spurred population growth in many urban and suburban communities. Attracted by the demand for workers in construction, manufacturing, and service sectors, immigrants began to locate in areas with little or no history of immigration. Although older industrial areas—the Detroits, Pittsburghs, and Clevelands of this country—have suffered job and population loss, metropolitan areas such as Phoenix, Washington, and Austin saw their new economy sectors boom, and their immigrant population along with them.

Thus, as the twentieth century came to a close, the United States experienced an extraordinary transformation of its population. More immigrants, legal and illegal combined, arrived during the decade of the 1990s than in any other decade on record. By 2000 the number of immigrants living in the United States was estimated to be 31 million.

In large part because of the strong economy of the 1990s, immigrants, legal and illegal, were, if not welcomed, at least tolerated in their new homes. This scenario abruptly changed, however, as the nation crossed over into the twenty-first century. The technology bubble burst, followed by a mild recession, resulting in a rise in unemployment from the historic lows of the late 1990s. Although employment levels are back up, other global and domestic events of the first years of the twenty-first century have fundamentally changed public attitudes toward immigrants.

First came the September 11, 2001, terrorist attacks. Because the attacks were undertaken by foreign nationals from various Middle Eastern countries, immigrants are now, more than ever, considered a security risk. Since March 2003 the United States has been engaged in a war in Iraq with no end in sight. Finally, the public's approval of the Bush administration is at a low point.[1] The uncertainty of the war, uneasiness over the economy, and the public's loss of confidence in the federal government have produced an insecure populace.

As the public deals with this diffuse set of fears, immigrants have been simultaneously cast under a more watchful eye. As this book goes to press, a national debate over reforming immigration policy, currently stalled in Congress—and stoked by talk radio and national anti-immigrant groups—has raised anxieties over the levels of unauthorized migration and the economic and social consequences of continued immigration.[2]

The result of these changing processes is that many new local areas of immigrant settlement are grappling with the fiscal costs of new streams of immigrants and the social costs of integrating them. Immigration debates—in recent decades limited to certain states such as California and New York—have spread along with the residential redistribution of immigrants. Local officials in many new settlement areas, in Georgia, North Carolina, Virginia and elsewhere, are under pressure to "do something" about immigration. In the absence of federal reform, state and local governments are facing an overwhelming sense of loss of control, and many are proposing (and sometimes passing) laws and ordinances that are designed to control immigrants. Often these policies are in the guise of local law enforcement, housing regulations, or employment policies. While most of the proposals and new policies are directed at undocumented immigrants, the public debates surrounding them are socially divisive and contribute to an unwelcome environment for all immigrants. Not all of the new local proposals are punitive, of course; some areas have longer-term goals of integrating immigrants and their children into communities. The backlash is the most intense, however, in many of the areas with the freshest and fastest-paced immigration.

The story of the United States, as it has been told many times over, is a story of immigration. That story typically begins on Ellis Island or the ports of California, with arriving immigrants heading immediately to ethnic enclaves in cities such as New York, Chicago, Philadelphia, or San

Francisco—to the Little Italys, Chinatowns, or Lower East Sides. There they set up businesses, build churches or synagogues, and send their children to the local public schools. The neighborhoods quickly become destination points for future waves of family and friends, as the newcomers relay their good fortune to friends and family in their home country. Eventually, following the American Dream, the first generation moves up and out to the suburbs, leaving room for the next wave.

Historically, these neighborhoods were primarily European in origin. Toward the end of the twentieth century, newer waves of immigrants from Latin America, the Caribbean, and Asia would locate in many of the same neighborhoods once occupied by the Slavs, Germans, Italians, and others in a process of ethnic succession. In more established immigrant cities, foreign-born newcomers simply settled in existing neighborhoods on the wane, transforming classic European enclaves such as Chicago's Bavarian Little Village into La Villita, a Mexican barrio, and New York's Lower East Side *shtetl* into the renamed Dominican and Puerto Rican Loisida neighborhood.

These areas—called in turn ghettos, barrios, or enclaves—have both negative and positive connotations. On the negative side, they are often viewed today as isolated areas with low-quality housing and services that restrict the incorporation of immigrants into the mainstream. They are seen as a defensive ethnic survival strategy and a destination of last resort for people with limited means. On the positive side, they offer new arrivals support, familiarity, and linguistic and cultural ease into a new society. Enclave neighborhoods represent both *stability* (that is, a constant presence that "institutionalizes" the immigrant experience) and *flux* as continuous waves of newcomers enter the neighborhood and use its services and structures at the same time that others are moving out to better opportunities elsewhere.

This story of ethnic enclaves in the heart of major gateway cities has been fundamentally altered with the restructuring of the U.S. economy, the decentralization of cities, and the growth of the suburbs as major employment centers. As industrial cities in the Northeast and Midwest began to lose population at mid-century, the lure of the suburbs enticed upwardly mobile, largely white families to relocate.[3] Thus, cities such as Buffalo, Cleveland, Detroit, and Pittsburgh have suffered continuous population and economic decline since 1950.[4] Other metropolitan areas with strong economic performance have grown during the same period, including the Sun Belt cities of Dallas, Fort Worth, Phoenix, Austin, and Charlotte. A third set of cities once in decline were revived during the 1980s and 1990s, due to strong metropolitan-wide economic growth. This group includes

Boston, Chicago, New York, and San Francisco, as well as Atlanta, Minneapolis, and Portland, Oregon.[5]

Therefore the economic fortunes of metropolitan areas are tied to population growth, and by the end of the century, local economies that were more diverse and included knowledge-based industries tended to attract the most migrants, both those who moved from within the United States and those who came from abroad.[6] Economic growth in certain sectors, and decline in others, has had an impact on where immigrants have located. Thus, while older industrial areas have suffered population loss related to the decline in manufacturing jobs (and no new jobs to replace them), metro areas like Phoenix and Austin saw their "new economy" sectors grow, and their immigrant populations along with it.

The patterns of economic growth of the 1990s are partly responsible for the shift in settlement patterns of immigrants. Another source of growth and change in the foreign-born population in recent decades is refugee resettlement. Since 1980, when the U.S. refugee resettlement program began, the leading refugee destinations have shifted away from traditional immigrant gateways to new areas. Although New York, Los Angeles, and Chicago still accommodate the most refugees among metropolitan areas, Seattle, San Jose, Washington, Minneapolis-St. Paul, Atlanta, Sacramento, and Portland resettled large numbers, fundamentally shifting their positions as immigrant gateways.[7]

The Rise of New Immigrant Gateways

As of March 2005 an estimated 35.7 million immigrants (legal and unauthorized) were living in the United States.[8] Map 1-1 shows the states with the highest immigrant shares and the most recent foreign-born growth across states for 2005. Most of the states with the highest proportion of immigrants also have the largest absolute numbers of immigrants. California has close to 10 million immigrants, the greatest number among all states, and it also has the highest percentage of immigrants, at 27 percent. New York, Florida, Illinois, and New Jersey follow, each with well over 1.5 million, and topped by New York with almost 4 million. Although Nevada ranks high on the proportion of its population that is foreign-born (17 percent), it is home to fewer than a half-million immigrants. Among states with a high percentage of immigrants arriving since 2000, there is a decidedly southeastern pull: Georgia and North Carolina each have well over a half-million immigrant residents, more than 30 percent of whom arrived between 2000 and 2005. In many southeastern states, agricultural jobs, as

Map 1-1. The Foreign-Born Population in the United States, 2005

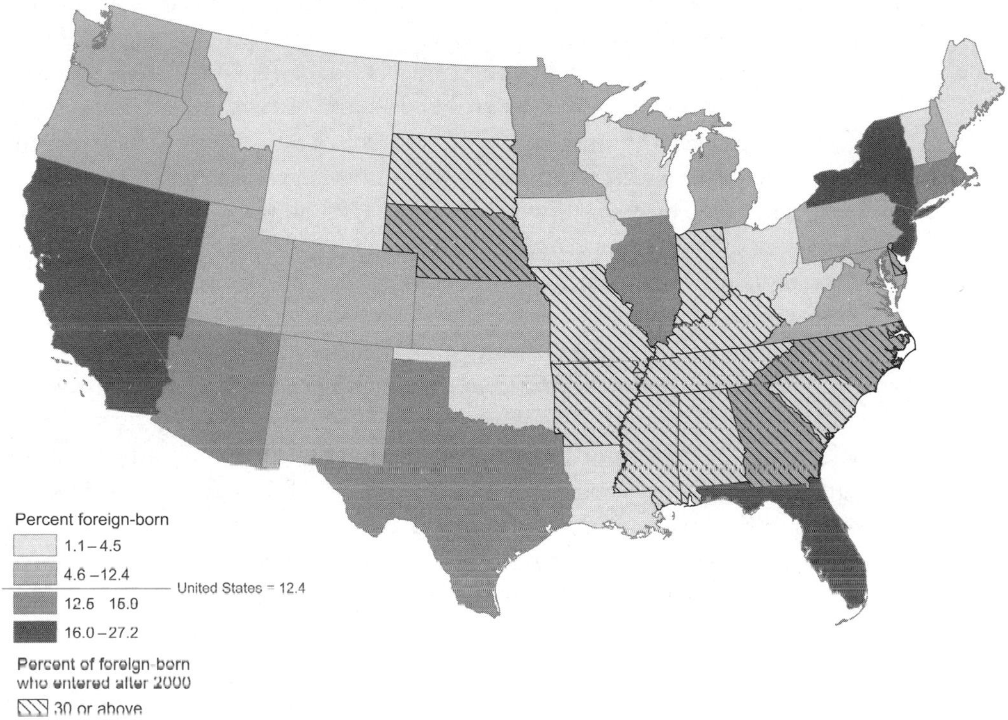

Percent foreign-born
1.1–4.5
4.6–12.4
United States = 12.4
12.6–16.0
16.0–27.2
Percent of foreign-born who entered after 2000
30 or above

Source: U.S. Census Bureau, *2005 American Community Survey.*

well as those in construction and meat and poultry processing and packing plants, attract immigrants, who are changing the face of rural communities.[9]

State trends are revealing and have relevance for policymaking; however, immigration is chiefly an urban phenomenon. In 2005 nearly 96 percent of all immigrants lived in a city or suburb within a metropolitan area. In that year 37 percent of America's immigrants were living in metropolitan New York, Los Angeles, Miami, and Chicago alone. However, these same four metro areas housed nearly half of all immigrants (46 percent) as recently as the 1990s.

As a consequence of historical patterns of immigrant settlement in a limited number of cities, social science immigration research has overwhelmingly been concerned with the economic and social impact of immigrants either at the national level or within the major cities of settlement. Thus, there is a large body of research on New York, Chicago, and Los Angeles, yet comparatively little is known about places like metropolitan Atlanta, Dallas, Fort Worth, and Las Vegas, all of which quintupled their foreign-born populations during the past twenty years.[10] As Roger Waldinger states, historically the study of cities was largely the study of immigrants; however, he notes, "how the particular characteristics of the immigrant-receiving areas impinge on the newcomers is a question immigration researchers rarely raise."[11]

A new wave of research has begun to focus on the patterns and related processes of immigrants in new destination areas.[12] Many of these studies tend to focus on recent dramatic change in rural areas or small towns, however, or on a specific immigrant origin group.[13] Moreover, *comparative* metropolitan studies are in short supply.[14] Several important works based on older census data describe trends during the 1980s, when the focus was still on just a limited list of cities and suburbs. These studies include Richard Alba and John Logan's explorations of metropolitan immigrant settlement in New York and Los Angeles and Waldinger and colleagues' comparative examination of immigrants in five cities.[15] Other in-depth studies of the suburbanization of immigrants tend to focus on a single place, such as John Horton's study of Monterey Park, a suburb of Los Angeles with a majority Chinese population, or Sarah Mahler's study of Salvadorans on suburban Long Island.[16]

This book contributes to this body of research by focusing on a new class of immigrant gateways that have changed—startlingly so—because of very recent immigration. These gateways have only recently emerged or re-emerged as major immigrant destinations. Many have seen their immigrant population triple or quadruple in size in recent decades. We name these metropolitan areas the *twenty-first-century gateways*. They are likely to be viewed as second-tier, since the size of their immigrant population is smaller than well-established gateways such as New York, Chicago, and Los Angeles. In the chapters that follow, we focus on nine new immigrant gateways: Atlanta, Austin, Charlotte, Dallas, Minneapolis-St. Paul, Phoenix, Portland, Sacramento, and Washington, D.C. Each of these places was nearly entirely native-born in 1970. Now, these nine metropolitan areas, along with 11 others, have emerged as some of the fastest-growing immigrant destinations among large metropolitan areas (map 1-2).

Our identification of twenty-first-century gateways for this book is based on a historical typology of urban immigrant settlement in the United States.[17] Based on trends in the size and growth of the immigrant population over the course of the twentieth century, this typology includes six immigrant gateway types.[18]

Map 1-2. Immigrant Gateway Metropolitan Areas

Source: Author.

—*Former gateways,* such as Buffalo and Pittsburgh, attracted considerable numbers of immigrants in the early 1900s but no longer do.

—*Continuous gateways,* such as New York and Chicago, are long-established destinations for immigrants and continue to receive large numbers of the foreign-born.

—*Post–World War II gateways,* such as Houston, Los Angeles, and Miami, began attracting immigrants in large numbers only during the past fifty years or less.

Together, the continuous and the post–World War II gateways will be referred to as *established immigrant gateways* here (map 1-2).

—*Emerging gateways* are those places that have had rapidly growing immigrant populations during the past twenty-five years alone. Atlanta, Dallas-Fort Worth, and Washington are prime examples.

—*Re-emerging gateways,* such as Minneapolis-St. Paul and Seattle, began the twentieth century with a strong attraction for immigrants, waned as destinations during the middle of the century, but are now re-emerging as immigrant gateways.

Figure 1-1. Distribution of the Foreign-Born, by Gateway Type, 1970–2005

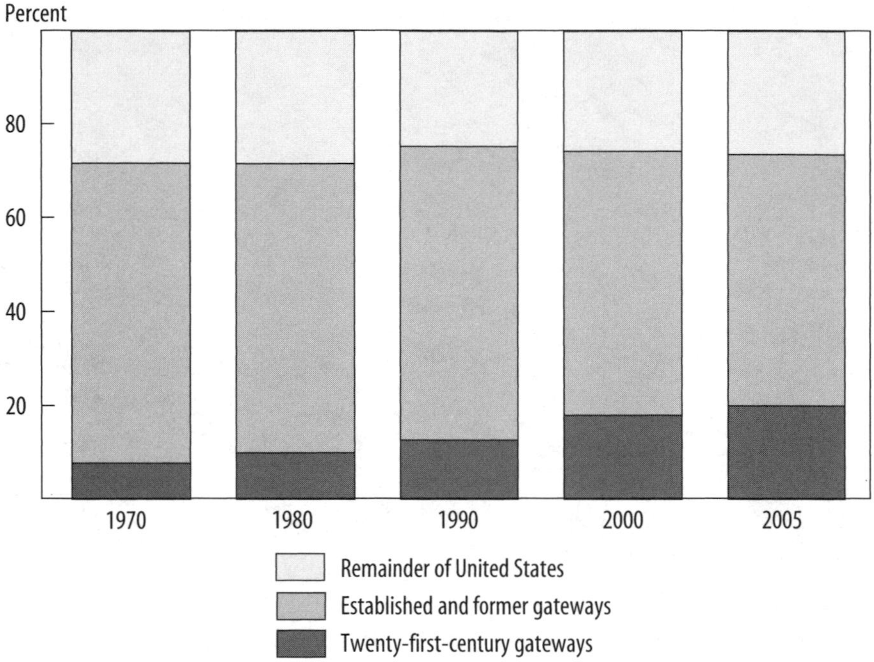

Percent

Remainder of United States
Established and former gateways
Twenty-first-century gateways

Source: Author's calculations based on data from the U.S. Census Bureau.

—*Pre-emerging gateways* are those places, such as Raleigh, Durham, and Austin, where immigrant populations have grown very rapidly starting in the 1990s and are likely to continue to grow as immigrant destinations.

The latter three categories make up the twenty-first-century gateways discussed in this volume (map 1-2).

In 2005 one-fifth of the U.S. foreign-born population—more than 7 million people—lived in a twenty-first-century gateway, up from less than 8 percent of the total in 1970, and ten times the number in 1970 in absolute terms (figure 1-1).[19] Meanwhile, even though the number of immigrants living in more established gateways tripled to 19 million, their share of the national total diminished throughout the period, falling ten percentage points from 64 to 54 percent of the total.

Immigrant Growth in New Gateways

Some of the most rapid rates of foreign-born population growth in metropolitan areas occurred in places with a very small base population of

Figure 1-2. Population Growth in Metropolitan Areas, by Gateway Type, 1980–2005

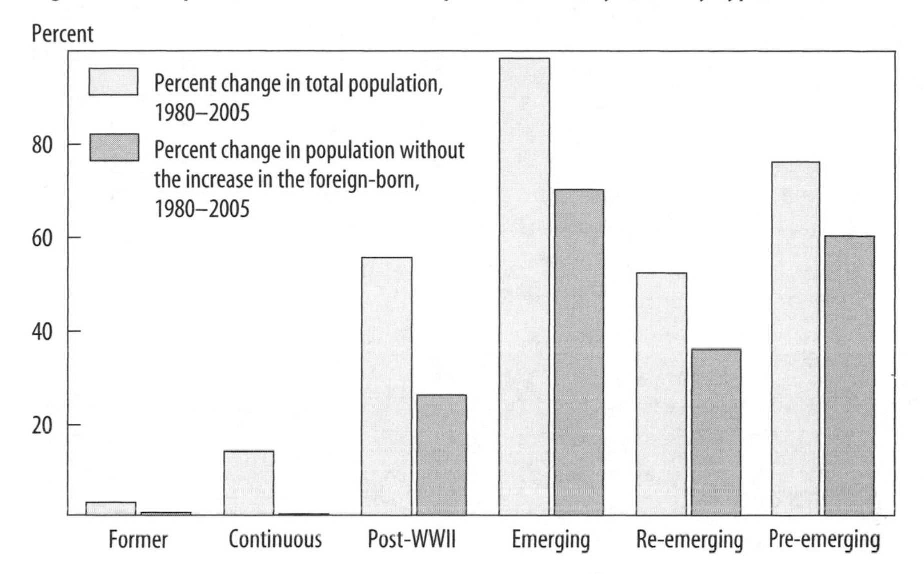

Source: Author's calculations based on data from the U.S. Census Bureau.

immigrants. At the same time, many large metropolitan areas saw a doubling or more of their foreign-born populations in the 1990s alone. The causes of shifting trends in settlement appear to be mixed. In the latter half of the 1990s, some metropolitan areas experienced economic growth, creating new job opportunities for immigrant newcomers that induced rapid change. In other places, refugee resettlement has contributed to an increase in the foreign-born population, spurring subsequent migration. Underlying this varied growth are social networks of information about jobs and housing that shape the decisions immigrants and refugees make on where to reside.

Despite total population decline or slow growth in metropolitan areas designated as former immigrant gateways, immigrants and refugees were sometimes the only source of growth in the population during the 1980s and 1990s. Figure 1-2 shows how each of the gateway types would have fared without the influx of immigrants they experienced between 1980 and 2005. (Appendix A provides metropolitan area statistics on the number and percentage growth in the foreign-born, 1980–2005.)

Overall, the continuous gateways grew modestly, on average by only 12 percent during that twenty-five-year period. The immigrant population nearly doubled, however, offsetting native-born loss in some metropolitan areas. Without the immigrant influx, these metropolitan areas would have experienced minuscule population growth, or even loss, as happened in New York. Although the total population in post–World War II gateways grew by 55 percent during the period, this growth too was largely driven by the movement of immigrants into those metropolitan areas, which otherwise would have grown only by 36 percent.

By contrast, all the twenty-first-century gateways—emerging, re-emerging, and pre-emerging—experienced rapid native-born population growth in addition to high inflows of immigrants, reflecting the strength of their economies. The emerging gateways together doubled their total populations. However, even without the rapid increase in immigrants, they still would have experienced a 70 percent growth in the total population. Several metropolitan areas that are classified as emerging are in fact fast becoming significant gateways on a grand scale. Metropolitan Washington and the Dallas-Fort Worth metroplex were estimated to have more than 1 million foreign-born residents each in 2005, on a par with metropolitan Houston and the Bay Area. Atlanta and Phoenix are each estimated to have reached more than 600,000 foreign-born, numbers that approach the levels of the more established Boston and San Diego metropolitan areas. In addition, the nascent metropolitan areas categorized as pre-emerging continue to register some of the fastest growth rates, especially since 2000.

The overall effect of immigration on the population in the metropolitan gateways is reflected in the growth of the share of the population that is foreign-born (see figure 1-3 and Appendix B for metro area statistics on the percentage of foreign-born in metropolitan areas, 1980–2005). In the 1970s, when the United States was at its lowest point of immigration in the century, the majority of large metropolitan areas were less than 10 percent foreign-born. There were some exceptions, for example, metropolitan Miami's population was 18 percent foreign-born, owing to the large wave of Cuban refugees who began arriving in the 1960s. Immigrant settlement peaked first in the post–World War II gateways, led by Miami, and followed closely by Los Angeles; the population of that group of gateways changed from 10 percent foreign-born in 1970 to 30 percent in 2005. The growth of the immigrant population was more subtle in the other gateways until the 1990s. During that decade, the emerging gateways collectively increased from only 8 percent to 14 percent foreign-born, with Washington on the leading edge. The re-emerging gateways experience a similar trend, with San Jose leading the pack in both absolute terms and share of foreign-born. The pre-emerging gateways witnessed an aggregate increase from 3.5 percent foreign-born to nearly 9 percent.

Figure 1-3. Percent Foreign-Born in Metropolitan Areas, by Gateway Type, 1970–2005

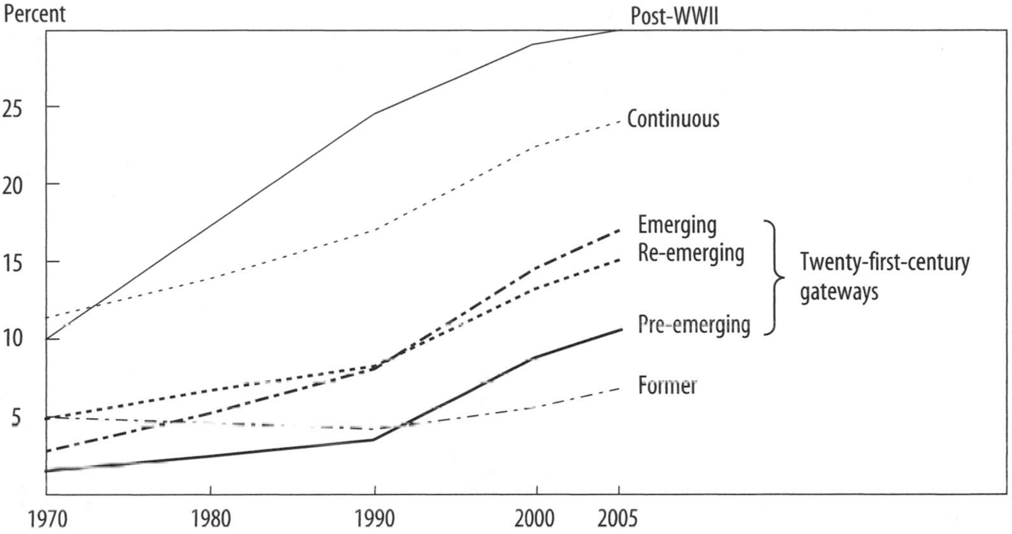

Source: Author's calculations based on data from the U.S. Census Bureau.

In the near term, the continuous and post–World War II gateways will maintain their large immigrant populations as well as the ability to attract newcomers through mature social networks. However, the pace of job creation and the expansion of newer metropolitan areas, particularly the emerging and pre-emerging gateways, are yielding rapid and simultaneous native- and foreign-born growth.

The growth of immigrants in new gateways has produced a mix of country origins among metropolitan areas that is more variable than it is uniform. In most of the twenty-first-century gateways featured in this book, the Mexican immigrant population is the largest origin group among the foreign-born population. (See figure 1-4 and appendix C for data on the top ten countries of origin for nine gateways.) In Austin, Dallas, and Phoenix, the Mexican-origin population constitutes more than half of the total foreign-born. However, in the Twin Cities and the nation's capital, the Mexican population is a much smaller share of the total. These places along with Atlanta, Portland, and Sacramento have a more diverse mix of national origins both because of refugee resettlement and because of their distance from the U.S.-Mexican border. In fact, all of the metropolitan areas located outside the Southwest have a greater mix of immigrant groups in their top ten because Mexico is not the dominant origin country.

Figure 1-4. Top Ten Countries of Origin for the Foreign-Born Population in Nine Twenty-First-Century Gateways, 2005[a]

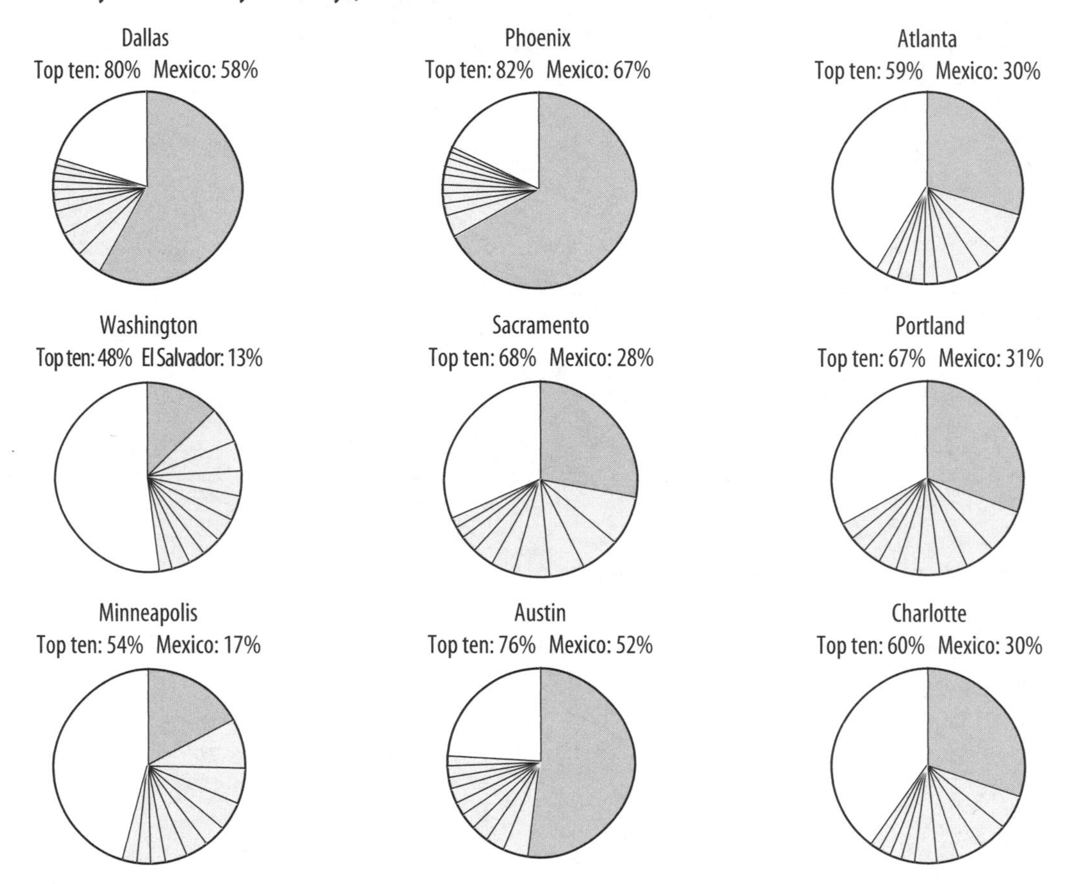

Source: Author's calculations based on data from the U.S. Census Bureau.
a. See appendix C for numeric data.

But the growing presence of the Mexican population in those places, for the most part very recent, also represents the leading edge of change. Recent Mexican immigrants represent one of the most flexible segments of the U.S. labor market, often the first to move to opportunities as they arise.

The Significance of Suburban Settlement

In addition to bolstering the populations in new and old gateways, immigrants are altering the urban landscape in other ways. As the chapters in this book show, they are often bypassing the inner city and moving directly

Figure 1-5. Number of Foreign-Born Settling in Central Cities and Suburbs in Twenty-First-Century Gateways

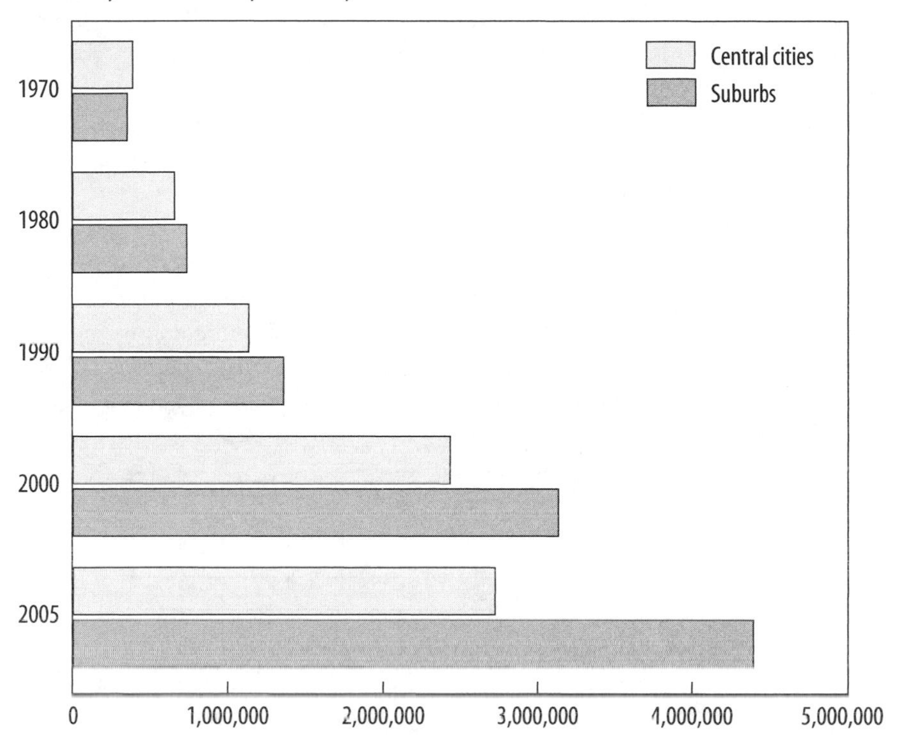

Source: Author's calculations based on data from the U.S. Census Bureau.

to the suburbs, and now more immigrants are living in the suburbs than in central cities (figure 1-5). Part of this relatively new trend is driven by the nature of the places themselves, particularly in the twenty-first-century gateways.[20]

These gateways are principally suburban metropolises—decidedly not cities, but for the most part large, loosely bounded, lower density, sprawling, auto-dependent metropolitan areas. Because these metropolitan areas developed largely after World War II, their growth patterns differ from those of the older cities where immigrants landed during earlier waves of immigration. Their suburban form is influenced by two distinctive development processes. In some cases, such as Atlanta and Washington, large suburban areas have developed while the central city has remained comparatively small. In other cases, such as Austin, Charlotte, and Phoenix, very large central cities are the result of annexation, which creates a sprawling suburban morphology.[21] (For more on suburban development, see chapter 2.)

Suburban settlement patterns among immigrants are also a cause and result of other common processes of growth and change. Among these is the role of new high-tech, knowledge-based industries that have drawn particularly Asian immigrants with high human capital (education, training, skills) to places such as Atlanta, Austin, Charlotte, Dallas, Phoenix, Portland, and Washington. These high-tech corporations, as well as other firms, have frequently established their headquarters not in central cities but in the suburbs, and their employees, many of them foreign-born, have chosen to settle near their places of work and in newer communities with good schools and affordable housing. Further, the economic and infrastructure growth in these suburbs, and in these twenty-first-century gateway metropolitan areas more generally, have also attracted immigrants with less human capital, many of them Mexican and Central American, to work in construction and landscaping. These job sites are often located in high-growth suburban areas.

In addition, the once-traditional ports of call have been transplanted by airports of call. Many of today's immigrants, in fact, fly directly from their place of origin to their new place of residence in the United States. The rise of global airports links cities in the United States with other places in the world to a degree unknown in the past, and these airports also provide local employment options for incoming groups. Two of our emerging twenty-first-century gateways (Atlanta and Dallas) have airports that are among the top ten busiest in the world (measured by volume of passengers). And Phoenix and Minneapolis are major domestic hubs.[22] Not only do these rankings say something about matters of scale and the positioning of these metropolitan areas in the global economy, but they also point attention to the kind of urban growth that necessarily occurs around transportation hubs and along transportation corridors.[23]

Finally, in some newer suburban destinations, immigrants are not necessarily self-segregating by language or national origin. As immigrants settle and sort out, many newer areas—admittedly not fully developed ethnic enclaves yet—are housing and catering to a multiethnic population. Yet in many ways the suburban destinations serve the same functions as did the early enclaves. In these more decentralized metropolitan areas, these suburbs are becoming identifiable places where goods and services catering to immigrants can be found in varying degrees, and perhaps more important, are places where housing, transportation, and jobs are available. Many suburban communities are just possibly forming as immigrant enclaves, and it is unclear how their role will play out over time and whether they will become identified with single origin groups or multiethnic groups.

What effect is immigration having on suburban infrastructure such as housing, transportation, schools, health care, economic development, and public safety? Conversely, what effect does the fragmented governance structure in suburban areas have on immigrant settlement and integration? The changes brought on by this new suburban settlement story remain largely unexamined. In contrast to more established central city destinations and patterns of settlement, these new trends constitute a new context for the social, economic, and political incorporation of immigrants. These are the central questions undertaken in this book.

Settling into the Twenty-First-Century Gateways

The chapters that follow provide case studies of these processes in gateways across the United States where immigrants have arrived in increasing numbers during the final decades of the twentieth century and the first decade of the twenty-first century. Although no overall, uniform framework of inquiry was applied to these case studies, several major themes surface that are important for understanding how immigration is playing out on the ground in the twenty-first-century gateways.

Among these are:

—the patterns of residence of the foreign-born in these new gateways, and the growing number of immigrants and refugees who are living in the suburbs

—the mixed attitudes and perceptions of receiving communities to immigrant and refugee newcomers

—the official response to new immigrant flows and attempts to "manage" immigration locally

—the role of social, political, and ethnic networks in migrant decision-making as shown in patterns of settlement, identity retention, and processes of adjustment.

The case studies that follow, beginning with the emerging immigrant gateways, take up many of these questions. Although many might consider Dallas and Phoenix, at first glance, to be historic gateways with large and historically significant Hispanic populations, the number of Mexicans, now the largest foreign-born population in both of these places, remained small throughout much of the twentieth century. These are cities that grew rapidly after World War II, and have become important centers of business and commerce. They grew up with the automobile, and expanded with the growth of the service and high-tech economies.

Caroline Brettell's chapter on Dallas, an emerging gateway in the Sun Belt, explores the rapidly changing composition of urban and suburban populations by focusing on four central counties in the Dallas-Fort Worth metroplex. Brettell addresses differences in immigration status and reasons for moving to the area among five distinct immigrant groups and thereby emphasizes how economic factors influence suburban settlement. Brettell directly takes up the question of how local suburban governments and other metropolitan institutions have responded to the fast growth in immigrant-led diversity. She contrasts the inclusionist approach of the Dallas suburb of Plano with the more exclusionist approach of Farmers Branch, a suburb that has been in the national news for its approval of harsh city ordinances directed at undocumented immigrants.

Alex Oberle and Wei Li compare the spatial and economic ramifications of the recently arrived Latino and Asian populations in Phoenix.[24] Although Mexicans and Chinese arrived in Phoenix early on, their presence was greatly diminished by the postwar influx of whites as part of the Sun Belt migration phenomenon. Oberle and Li focus on the differences in human capital among present-day immigrant populations, which result in different forms of economic integration. The authors address how these new immigrant populations are establishing their political and cultural identities, as well as their entrepreneurial impact, through stores that become community hubs; media outlets; and festivals, associations, and other cultural centers.

The third emerging gateway in the Sun Belt is heavily suburban Atlanta. In April 2006 many cities were sites for massive rallies in favor of immigrant rights, and those demonstrations in Atlanta, Dallas, and other unlikely locations took many by surprise. In her chapter on Atlanta, Mary Odem focuses on the Latin American presence in a metropolitan area that until quite recently was primarily composed of African Americans and whites. The legacy of segregation has played out in the residential choices that immigrant newcomers have made in Atlanta. Immigrants appear to be making inroads in the northern part of the metro area, which has traditionally been the whiter part of the racially divided region, and are less established in historically African American neighborhoods.

Closing the section on emerging gateways is the case of metropolitan Washington. Heading into the twenty-first century, it is fair to say that the nation's capital region has already emerged as a gateway, with more than

1 million foreign-born residents composing 20 percent of the total population. To capture the rapid transformation of native-born white suburbs surrounding Washington, Marie Price and Audrey Singer introduce the concept of *edge gateways* as identifiable local places where the foreign-born population has grown quickly in recent decades and where a diverse mix of immigrant groups cluster. Unlike Dallas, Phoenix, and Atlanta, no single immigrant population dominates in the region as a whole or in the edge gateways. Price and Singer explain the rapid suburban settlement of the foreign-born by pointing to housing affordability, access to major transportation corridors, social networks, and, as in Atlanta, a seeming avoidance of black neighborhoods. As do other authors in the volume, these authors find it useful to contrast differences in the local responses to immigrants. They describe suburban communities that either "accommodate" or "deflect" diversity and show that even in the very same metropolitan area, both tactics coexist, rooted in local governance structures.

Three metropolitan areas are examined in the section on re-emerging gateways: Sacramento, Minneapolis-St. Paul, and Portland. They have one major trend in common—a large portion of the foreign-born are refugees. In their chapter on Sacramento, long a place for refugee resettlement, Robin Datel and Dennis Dingemans explore the historical geography of immigrant and racial settlement, the region's role as a magnet for refugee resettlement, the availability of inexpensive suburban housing, and the demand for both high-tech workers and lower skilled agricultural and construction immigrant workers. Rather than focusing on how suburbs are responding to newcomers (as in the chapters on Atlanta, Dallas, and Washington), this chapter examines how newcomers have changed the visual landscape of the suburbs through the rejuvenation of commercial strips, the composition of suburban schools, and the formation of institutions such as religious congregations. Datel and Dingemans also describe the virtual and temporary immigrant spaces that have developed and raise questions about when and how political incorporation will proceed. "Can the suburbs," they ask, "with all their diversity, be genuine incubators for new leaders and new programs to further enhance the life chances of immigrants to America?"

Katherine Fennelly and Myron Orfield's chapter on Minneapolis-St. Paul draws attention to the fact that its refugees—in this case largely from Africa, Southeast Asia, and the former Soviet Union—have been settled in fiscally stressed areas that cannot easily facilitate economic integration and upward mobility but that do offer affordable housing, accessible transportation corridors, lower crime rates, and relatively more peaceful neighborhoods. This analysis addresses the housing and school segregation experienced by the foreign-born in the Twin Cities suburban context, although segregation is much less pronounced for Asian immigrants than for their Latino and black counterparts. Further, through the voices of U.S.-born Minnesotans, the authors address discrimination as an additional impediment to suburban integration. They reveal important differences in attitudes between urban, suburban, and rural residents, with suburban residents falling between the more liberal urban residents and the more conservative rural residents. Their findings focus on negative attitudes concerning language issues and the expenditures necessary to accommodate immigrants' needs.

In their chapter on Portland, Susan Hardwick and James Meacham offer a view of refugee and immigrant settlement in the context of a metropolitan area that makes conscious development decisions to level the socioeconomic playing field in outlying areas. Local housing and development policies stemming from the 1970s have encouraged Portland's foreign-born population to suburbanize along with other more modest-income U.S.-born families. As do other authors, Hardwick and Meacham note the significance of housing stock and income as broader contexts in explaining settlement patterns in the eastern and western parts of the larger metropolitan area. These authors emphasize that although economic and political processes have channeled immigrants to the suburbs, these are coincidental with personal preferences and choices and that some of the latter are influenced by the placemaking (including nodes of ethnic activity located around businesses) that has occurred in the suburbs.

The third set of case studies focuses on two pre-emerging gateways, Austin and Charlotte. Although these are both metropolitan areas composed of multiple counties, most of the immigrant settlement is taking place within the central county, in suburban-like settings. Austin's growth, like that of many of the other gateways discussed in this book, has been fueled by a technology boom that has attracted those with significant education and income, largely Asian, immigrants. At the same time, the growth in the Mexican population has been dramatic. Emily Skop and Tara Buentello address the bifurcation of experiences on the basis of national origins and education. The authors also point to some discriminatory local public policies that make incorporation difficult for nonwhite migrants. Finally, they address the displacement of Hispanics from very old neighborhoods, which has resulted from downtown gentrification.

The book's final case study presents a city of the "New South" that until recently had very little experience with immigrants. Against a backdrop of economic and metropolitan transformation, Charlotte's attraction for both domestic and international migrants has never been stronger. Similar to Odem's analysis of Atlanta, Heather Smith and Owen Furuseth focus their attention on the impact of Latinos on this North Carolina city by analyzing their patterns of settlement in three middle-ring suburban clusters. The authors identify housing stock as an important factor shaping patterns of settlement, but they also draw attention to the revitalization of neighborhoods by Latino-oriented businesses and entrepreneurs. These authors and the others in this volume illustrate that immigrant settlement in suburban areas across the country takes place on a variety of scales and local experiences. The outcomes are as diverse and varied as are the suburban settings.

As a corpus, these chapters explore the causes and consequences of the next tier of immigrant gateways, the twenty-first-century gateways. The ongoing spatial deconcentration and dispersal of residential and commercial land use and economic activities in metropolitan areas in the United States continue to reshape metropolitan America during the first decade of the twenty-first century. In almost every part of the country, the impacts and imprints of improved transportation and communication technologies, higher rents in gentrified parts of the downtown, intensified economic activities away from the central city, and the construction of new housing in both inner and outer suburbs are contributing to the ongoing expansion of the "outer city," home to diverse foreign-born groups and their children from many parts of the world. Unlike more traditional ethnic enclaves of the past that were located downtown, the majority of these newcomers are building their new lives in the suburbs even during their earliest years of settlement in the United States, and they are constructing their communities in different ways.

Many questions remain about the impact of suburban settlement on immigrant integration. Will the suburbs offer newcomers more opportunities for becoming part of the larger fabric of American life? Or might they develop into (more dispersed) zones of isolation and segregation? Do the suburbs of twenty-first-century gateways promise more multiethnic and multiracial neighborhoods and better access to jobs, and thus more rapid adjustment economically, socially, and linguistically? Or will the rates and pace of incorporation be slowed by dispersal in suburban areas? How will the reception of immigrants be influenced by how well equipped institutionally places are?

The chapters that follow provide answers to these and other questions on the dual processes of immigration and suburbanization in the United States during the past two decades. However, before moving into the case studies of these emerging gateways, chapter 2 explores the history of suburban evolution, focusing on economic and political changes that precipitated the emergence of the outer city, especially after 1945. Following the case studies, we propose some directions that federal, state, and local governments and community organizations might take to ensure that immigrants are successfully integrated into U.S. communities. It is clear that the future of these rapidly changing metropolitan areas, like the lives and livelihoods of the people who reside in them, will offer both challenges and opportunities in the coming years.

Notes

1. Megan Thee, "The Polls," *New York Times,* July 10, 2007.

2. Comprehensive immigration reform is stalled in Congress as of this writing in autumn of 2007. An overhaul of the way U.S. immigration laws function, including increasing border and interior enforcement, a legalization program, a temporary worker program, and visa reforms, was vigorously debated before being defeated.

3. Kenneth T. Jackson, *Crabgrass Frontier: The Suburbanization of the United States* (Oxford University Press, 1985); Dolores Hayden, *Building Suburbia: Green Fields and Urban Growth 1820–2000* (New York: Vintage Books, 2004).

4. Jennifer S. Vey, *Restoring Prosperity: The State Role in Revitalizing America's Older Industrial Cities* (Brookings, 2007); Myron Orfield, *American Metropolitics: The New Suburban Reality* (Brookings, 2007).

5. Jordan Rappaport, "U.S. Urban Decline and Growth, 1950 to 2000," *Economic Review,* Federal Reserve Bank of Kansas City (Third Quarter, 2003).

6. William H. Frey, "Metro America in the New Century: Metropolitan and Central City Demographic Shifts since 2000," Brookings Institution, 2005.

7. Refugee resettlement trends do not necessarily mirror other immigrant streams. With the exception of Washington, each of these metro areas placed higher in rank for refugee resettlement than for total foreign-born stock, indicating that refugees played a significant role in increased immigration. As discussed in several of the chapters that follow, the arrival of relatively large numbers of refugees in metropolitan areas with a small foreign-born population may prove challenging for both refugee newcomers and their new places of residence. See Audrey Singer and Jill H. Wilson, "From There to Here: Refugee Resettlement in Metropolitan America" (Brookings, 2006).

8. Demographer Jeffrey Passel has published the most widely respected and cited estimates of immigrant legal status. He notes that in March 2005, the U.S. foreign-born population fell into the following four categories: 35 percent naturalized U.S. citizens, 32 percent permanent legal status, 30 percent unauthorized to be in the United States, and 3 percent temporary legal residents. See Jeffrey S. Passel, *The Size and Characteristics of the Unauthorized Migrant Population in the U.S.* (Washington: Pew Hispanic Center, 2006).

9. William Kandel and John Cromartie, *New Patterns of Hispanic Settlement in Rural America* (U.S. Department of Agriculture, 2004); William Kandel and Emilio Parrado, "Industrial Transformation and Hispanic Migration to the American

South: The Case of the Poultry Industry," in *Hispanic Spaces, Latino Places: A Geography of Regional and Cultural Diversity,* edited by Daniel D. Arreola (University of Texas Press, 2004); Heather A. Smith and Owen J. Furuseth, eds., *Latinos in the New South: Transformations of Place* (Burlington, Vt.: Ashgate Publishing, 2006); and Greg Anrig Jr. and Tova Andrea Wang, eds., *Immigration's New Frontiers: Experiences from the Emerging Gateway States* (New York: Century Foundation, 2006).

10. Conditions in more traditional immigrant gateways are well represented, including the classic work of William I. Thomas and Florian Znaniecki, *The Polish Peasant in Europe and America* (New York: Alfred A. Knopf, 1927), along with more contemporary works such as Roger Waldinger and Mehdi Bozorgmehr, eds., *Ethnic Los Angeles* (New York: Russell Sage Foundation Press, 1996); Alejandro Portes and Alex Stepick, *City on the Edge: The Transformation of Miami* (University of California Press, 1993); Roger Waldinger, *Strangers at the Gates: New Immigrants in Urban America* (University of California Press, 2001); Nancy Foner, *From Ellis Island to JFK: New York's Two Great Waves of Immigration* (Yale University Press and New York: Russell Sage Foundation, 2000); Silvia Pedraza and Rubén G. Rumbaut, eds., *Origins and Destinies: Immigration, Race, and Ethnicity in America* (Belmont, Calif.: Wadsworth Publishing Company, 1996).

11. Roger Waldinger, "Immigration and Urban Change," *Annual Review of Sociology* 15 (1989): 211–32.

12. Elzbieta M. Gozdziak and Susan F. Martin, eds., *Beyond the Gateway: Immigrants in a Changing America* (Lanham, Md.: Lexington Books, 2005); Víctor Zúñiga and Rubén Hernández-León, eds., *New Destinations: Mexican Immigration in the United States* (New York: Russell Sage Foundation, 2005); Smith and Furuseth, *Latinos in the New South;* Anrig and Wang, *Immigration's New Frontiers: Experiences from the Emerging Gateway States.*

13. See, for example, Katharine M. Donato, Melissa Stainback, and Carl L. Bankston III, "The Economic Incorporation of Mexican Immigrants in Southern Louisiana: A Tale of Two Cities," in *New Destinations of Mexican Immigration in the United States,* edited by Zúñiga and Hernández-León, pp. 76–99; and Rubén Hernández-León and Víctor Zúñiga, "Making Carpet by the Mile: The Emergence of a Mexican Immigrant Community in an Industrial Region of the U.S. Historic South," *Social Science Quarterly* 81, no. 1 (2002): 49–66.

14. For international comparisons, see Takeyuki Tsuda, ed., *Local Citizenship in Recent Countries of Immigration* (Lanham, Md.: Lexington Books, 2006); Jeffrey Reitz, ed., *Host Societies and the Reception of Immigrants* (University of California, Center for Comparative Immigration Research, 2003); Blair Ruble, *Creating Diversity Capital: Transnational Migrants in Montreal, Washington, and Kyiv* (Washington: Woodrow Wilson Center Press and Johns Hopkins University Press, 2005).

15. Richard D. Alba and others, "Strangers Next Door: Immigrant Groups and Suburbs in Los Angeles and New York," in *A Nation Divided: Diversity, Inequality, and Community in American Society,* edited by Phyllis Moen, Henry Walker, and Donna Dempster-McClain (Cornell University Press, 1999); and Richard D. Alba and others, "Immigrant Groups in the Suburbs: A Reexamination of Suburbanization and Spatial Assimilation," *American Sociological Review* 64 (1999): 446–60; Waldinger, *Strangers at the Gates.*

16. Sarah J. Mahler, *Salvadorans in Suburbia: Symbiosis and Conflict* (Boston: Allyn & Bacon: 1996); John Horton, *The Politics of Diversity: Immigration, Resistance, and Change in Monterey Park, California* (Temple University Press, 1995).

17. In general, gateways are defined as metropolitan areas with Census 2000 populations over one million. The typology includes six immigrant gateway types (see Audrey Singer, *The Rise of New Immigrant Gateways* [Brookings, 2004]): *Former* gateways have a higher proportion of population foreign-born between 1900 and 1930 than the national average, followed by below-average foreign-born percentages in every decade through 2000. *Continuous* gateways have above-average foreign-born percentages for every decade, 1900–2000. *Post–World War II* gateways have low foreign-born percentages until after 1950, followed by higher-than-national-average foreign-born percentages in every decade through 2000. *Emerging* gateways have very low foreign-born percentages until 1970, followed by higher proportions from 1980 onward. *Re-emerging* gateways have foreign-born percentages exceeding the national average from 1900 to 1930, followed by below-average percentages until 1980, after which they experienced rapid increases. *Pre-emerging* gateways have very low foreign-born population percentages for most of the twentieth century, with rapid growth after 1990.

In addition, continuous, post–World War II, emerging, and re-emerging gateways must meet the following criteria: foreign-born populations greater than 200,000, and either foreign-born percentages higher than the 2000 national average (11.1 percent) or foreign-born growth rates higher than the 1990–2000 national average (57.4 percent), or both.

18. Since the original immigrant gateways analysis was conducted, metropolitan area definitions were overhauled by the Office of Management and Budget. Under the new classification system, adopted in 2003, many metropolitan areas have undergone changes in territory and population. The most common changes involved the addition of new counties to an existing metropolitan area, and the combination of two or more metro areas to form a new, larger metropolis, such as Dallas-Fort Worth. Other metropolitan areas were split, such as Raleigh and Durham, North Carolina. See William H. Frey and others, "Tracking Metropolitan America into the Twenty-First Century: A Field Guide to the New Metropolitan and Micropolitan Definitions," Brookings, 2004. Many of the forty-five metropolitan areas included in Singer, "The Rise of New Immigrant Gateways," have a new metropolitan definition. For the comparative metropolitan analyses in this chapter, the new definitions were used for a total of thirty-seven metropolitan areas.

19. The twenty-first-century gateways are metropolitan Atlanta, Dallas-Fort Worth, Las Vegas, Orlando, Phoenix, Washington, Denver, Minneapolis, Portland, Sacramento, San Jose, Seattle, Tampa, Austin, Charlotte, Greensboro, Winston-Salem, Raleigh, Durham, and Salt Lake City. See the appendixes for a full list of metropolitan areas considered in this study.

20. To be sure, suburban settlement is also rising in the more established gateways. Many continuous and post–WWII gateways have seen challenging inflows into their suburbs as well as into their central cities.

21. Thus the statistics on these places are not as cleanly defined as we would like, that is, suburban, and in some cases rural, areas are located inside the city limits (see the Austin, Charlotte, and Phoenix chapters).

22. Airports Council International (www.airports.org/cda/aci_common/display/main/aci_content07_c.jsp?zn=aci&cp=1-5-54-55_666_2__ [September 5, 2007]).

23. The highly diverse suburb of Herndon, discussed by Price and Singer in their chapter on Washington, is adjacent to Dulles Airport, for example, while the suburban community of Irving, discussed by Brettell, is near the Dallas-Fort Worth International Airport. It is no accident that the Dallas-Fort Worth Hindu temple is located in Irving, while a major Hindu temple, the Rajdhani Mandir, is located in Chantilly, another diverse suburban community adjacent to Dulles airport and just south of Herndon. Similarly, Portland's multicultural Gateway district is only two short freeway exits away from the busy Portland International Airport. This suburban node is home to a large and diverse population of new immigrants and refugees; it also houses the largest refugee resettlement agency in the state.

24. In the original framework that laid out the immigrant gateway typology (Singer, "The Rise of New Immigrant Gateways"), Phoenix was classified as a re-emerging immigrant gateway. However, subsequent analysis makes us confident that it resembles an emerging gateway more than a re-emerging gateway. Although the trends in the percentage of the population that is foreign-born follow the typical re-emerging gateway pattern, the absolute number of immigrants in the early part of the twentieth century was quite low.

Appendix A. Foreign-Born Population, by Gateway Type, 1980–2005[a]

Gateway type	Foreign-born population				Percent change in foreign-born population			
	1980	1990	2000	2005	1980–1990	1990–2000	2000–2005	1980–2005
Emerging								
Atlanta-Sandy Springs-Marietta, GA	47,815	117,253	424,519	612,759	145.2	262.1	44.3	1,181.5
Dallas-Fort Worth-Arlington, TX	125,157	317,977	782,995	1,016,221	154.1	146.2	29.8	712.0
Las Vegas-Paradise, NV	35,064	70,333	247,751	334,087	100.6	252.3	34.8	852.8
Orlando, FL	37,267	82,042	197,119	302,323	120.1	140.3	53.4	711.2
Phoenix-Mesa-Scottsdale, AZ	86,593	161,830	457,483	612,850	86.9	182.7	34.0	607.7
Washington-Arlington-Alexandria, DC-VA-MD	255,439	488,283	829,310	1,017,432	91.2	69.8	22.7	298.3
Total	587,335	1,237,718	2,939,177	3,895,672	110.7	137.5	32.5	563.3
Re-Emerging								
Denver-Aurora, CO	65,363	81,769	234,121	290,765	25.1	186.3	24.2	344.8
Minneapolis-St. Paul-Bloomington, MN-WI	71,697	88,093	210,344	267,368	22.9	138.8	27.1	272.9
Portland-Vancouver-Beaverton, OR-WA	66,627	88,217	208,422	250,955	32.4	136.3	20.4	276.7
Sacramento--Arden-Arcade--Roseville, CA	79,689	140,465	260,111	353,592	76.3	85.2	35.9	343.7
San Jose-Sunnyvale-Santa Clara, CA	179,833	353,468	583,156	614,304	96.6	65.0	5.3	241.6
Seattle-Tacoma-Bellevue, WA	150,152	201,982	383,824	479,913	34.5	90.0	25.0	219.6
Tampa-St. Petersburg-Clearwater, FL	108,059	146,003	233,907	294,848	35.1	60.2	26.1	172.9
Total	721,420	1,099,997	2,113,885	2,551,745	52.5	92.2	20.7	253.7
Pre-Emerging								
Austin-Round Rock, TX	24,220	56,154	152,834	192,738	131.8	172.2	26.1	695.8
Charlotte-Gastonia-Concord, NC-SC	13,830	22,677	91,990	134,749	64.0	305.7	46.5	874.3
Greensboro-High Point, NC	5,341	8,418	37,205	52,506	57.6	342.0	41.1	883.1
Winston-Salem, NC	3,783	5,257	23,296	29,501	39.0	343.1	26.6	679.8
Raleigh-Cary, NC	8,323	17,538	69,530	95,415	110.7	296.5	37.2	1,046.4
Durham, NC	5,394	11,949	39,721	52,706	121.5	232.4	32.7	877.1
Salt Lake City, UT	28,639	34,244	97,079	112,628	19.6	183.5	16.0	293.3
Total	89,530	156,237	511,655	670,243	74.5	227.5	31.0	648.6
Total 21st-century gateways	1,398,285	2,493,952	5,564,717	7,117,660	78.4	123.1	27.9	409.0
Former								
Baltimore-Towson, MD	74,225	87,653	146,128	184,439	18.1	66.7	26.2	148.5
Buffalo-Niagara Falls, NY	69,356	52,220	51,381	52,343	−24.7	−1.6	1.9	−24.5
Cleveland-Elyria-Mentor, OH	126,864	98,369	113,006	115,897	−22.5	14.9	2.6	−8.6
Detroit-Warren-Livonia, MI	282,766	235,285	337,059	387,027	−16.8	43.3	14.8	36.9
Milwaukee-Waukesha-West Allis, WI	58,422	54,043	81,574	93,562	−7.5	50.9	14.7	60.1
Philadelphia-Camden-Wilmington, PA-NJ-DE	259,814	270,817	391,829	485,800	4.2	44.7	24.0	87.0
Pittsburgh, PA	84,829	58,248	62,778	65,933	−31.3	7.8	5.0	−22.3
St. Louis, MO-IL	53,978	49,631	81,546	108,621	−8.1	64.3	33.2	101.2
Total	1,010,254	906,266	1,265,301	1,493,622	−10.3	39.6	18.0	47.8
Continuous								
Boston-Cambridge-Quincy, MA-NH	349,335	427,524	602,062	684,165	22.4	40.8	13.6	95.8
Chicago-Naperville-Joliet, IL-IN-WI	786,683	913,508	1,464,121	1,625,649	16.1	60.3	11.0	106.6
New York-Northern New Jersey-Long Island, NY-NJ-PA	2,729,216	3,424,413	4,846,322	5,117,290	25.5	41.5	5.6	87.5
San Francisco-Oakland-Fremont, CA	509,352	778,725	1,127,963	1,201,209	52.9	44.8	6.5	135.8
Total	4,374,586	5,544,170	8,040,468	8,628,313	26.7	45.0	7.3	97.2
Post-WWII								
Houston-Baytown-Sugar Land, TX	229,799	461,488	898,221	1,113,875	100.8	94.6	24.0	384.7
Los Angeles-Long Beach-Santa Ana, CA	1,921,987	3,470,174	4,299,343	4,407,353	80.6	23.9	2.5	129.3
Miami-Fort Lauderdale-Miami Beach, FL	749,401	1,178,146	1,755,004	1,949,629	57.2	49.0	11.1	160.2
Riverside-San Bernardino-Ontario, CA	134,998	360,650	612,359	827,584	167.2	69.8	35.1	513.0
San Diego-Carlsbad-San Marcos, CA	235,593	428,810	606,254	659,731	82.0	41.4	8.8	180.0
Total	3,271,778	5,899,268	8,171,181	8,958,172	80.3	38.5	9.6	173.8
Total established and former gateways	8,656,618	12,349,704	17,476,950	19,080,107	42.7	41.5	9.2	120.4
Total all gateway types	10,054,903	14,843,656	23,041,667	26,197,767	47.6	55.2	13.7	160.5

Source: 1980, 1990, and 2000 decennial censuses; *American Community Survey 2005.*

a. 2003 metropolitan area definitions used for all years.

Appendix B. Percent Foreign-Born in Metropolitan Areas, Cities, and Suburbs, 1970–2005

	Foreign-born in metropolitan area									
	1970		*1980*		*1990*		*2000*		*2005*	
Metro area	*Total*	*Percent*	*Total*	*Percent*	*Total*	*Percent*	*Total*	*Percent*	*Total*	*Percent*
Emerging										
Atlanta-Sandy Springs-Marietta, GA	17,889	1.0	47,815	2.1	117,253	3.8	424,519	10.0	612,759	12.7
Dallas-Fort Worth-Arlington, TX	38,897	1.6	125,157	4.1	317,977	8.0	782,995	15.2	1,016,221	17.7
Las Vegas-Paradise, NV	12,267	4.6	35,064	7.6	70,333	9.5	247,751	18.0	334,087	19.8
Orlando, FL	15,052	3.0	37,267	4.6	82,042	6.7	197,119	12.0	302,323	15.9
Phoenix-Mesa-Scottsdale, AZ	40,007	4.0	86,593	5.4	161,830	7.2	457,483	14.1	612,850	16.1
Washington-Arlington-Alexandria, DC-VA-MD	132,551	4.3	255,439	7.5	488,283	11.8	829,310	17.3	1,017,432	19.9
Total	256,663	2.8	587,335	5.1	1,237,718	8.0	2,939,177	14.4	3,895,672	16.9
Re-Emerging										
Denver-Aurora, CO	35,735	3.3	65,363	4.5	81,769	4.9	234,121	10.7	290,765	12.5
Minneapolis-St. Paul-Bloomington, MN-WI	55,506	2.8	71,697	3.3	88,093	3.5	210,344	7.1	267,368	8.7
Portland-Vancouver-Beaverton, OR-WA	41,634	3.9	66,627	5.0	88,217	5.8	208,422	10.8	250,955	12.2
Sacramento--Arden-Arcade--Roseville, CA	44,405	5.4	79,689	7.2	140,465	9.5	260,111	14.5	353,592	17.6
San Jose-Sunnyvale-Santa Clara, CA	86,449	8.1	179,833	13.6	353,468	23.0	583,156	33.6	614,304	35.6
Seattle-Tacoma-Bellevue, WA	106,711	5.9	150,152	7.2	201,982	7.9	383,824	12.6	479,913	15.3
Tampa-St. Petersburg-Clearwater, FL	69,292	6.5	108,059	6.7	146,003	7.1	233,907	9.8	294,848	11.4
Total	439,732	4.9	721,420	6.5	1,099,997	8.2	2,113,885	13.2	2,551,745	15.1
Pre-Emerging										
Austin-Round Rock, TX	8,330	2.2	24,220	4.1	56,154	6.6	152,834	12.2	192,738	13.7
Charlotte-Gastonia-Concord, NC-SC	5,743	0.8	13,830	1.6	22,677	2.2	91,990	6.9	134,749	9.0
Greensboro-High Point, NC	2,185	0.5	5,341	1.1	8,418	1.6	37,205	5.8	52,506	8.0
Winston-Salem, NC	1,429	0.5	3,783	1.1	5,257	1.5	23,296	5.5	29,501	6.7
Raleigh-Cary, NC	3,117	1.0	8,323	2.1	17,538	3.2	69,530	8.7	95,415	10.3
Durham, NC	2,200	0.9	5,394	1.8	11,949	3.5	39,721	9.3	52,706	12.1
Salt Lake City, UT	19,573	4.1	28,639	4.4	34,244	4.5	97,079	10.0	112,628	11.1
Total	42,577	1.5	89,530	2.5	156,237	3.5	511,655	8.8	670,243	10.5
Total 21st-century gateways	738,972	3.6	1,398,285	5.3	2,493,952	7.5	5,564,717	13.1	7,117,660	15.3
Former										
Baltimore-Towson, MD	58,894	2.9	74,225	3.4	87,653	3.7	146,128	5.7	184,439	7.1
Buffalo-Niagara Falls, NY	82,090	6.2	69,356	5.6	52,220	4.4	51,381	4.4	52,343	4.7
Cleveland-Elyria-Mentor, OH	147,318	6.5	126,864	5.8	98,369	4.7	113,006	5.3	115,897	5.6
Detroit-Warren-Livonia, MI	308,016	7.1	282,766	6.5	235,285	5.5	337,059	7.6	387,027	8.7
Milwaukee-Waukesha-West Allis, WI	62,528	4.5	58,422	4.2	54,043	3.8	81,574	5.4	93,562	6.3
Philadelphia-Camden-Wilmington, PA-NJ-DE	257,824	5.0	259,814	5.0	270,817	5.0	391,829	6.9	485,800	8.6
Pittsburgh, PA	111,989	4.1	84,829	3.2	58,248	2.4	62,778	2.6	65,933	2.8
St. Louis, MO-IL	49,393	2.0	53,978	2.2	49,631	1.9	81,546	3.0	108,621	4.0
Total	1,078,052	5.0	1,010,254	4.6	906,266	4.1	1,265,301	5.6	1,493,622	6.7
Continuous										
Boston-Cambridge-Quincy, MA-NH	344,134	9.0	349,335	8.9	427,524	10.3	602,062	13.7	684,165	16.0
Chicago-Naperville-Joliet, IL-IN-WI	604,073	7.8	786,683	9.8	913,508	11.2	1,464,121	16.1	1,625,649	17.5
New York-Northern New Jersey-Long Island, NY-NJ-PA	2,285,773	13.7	2,729,216	16.7	3,424,413	20.3	4,846,322	26.4	5,117,290	27.9
San Francisco-Oakland-Fremont, CA	339,314	11.2	509,352	15.7	778,725	21.1	1,127,963	27.4	1,201,209	29.5
Total	3,573,294	11.4	4,374,586	13.8	5,544,170	16.9	8,040,468	22.4	8,628,313	24.0
Post-WWII										
Houston-Baytown-Sugar Land, TX	57,255	2.7	229,799	7.3	461,488	12.2	898,221	19.0	1,113,875	21.4
Los Angeles-Long Beach-Santa Ana, CA	876,612	10.6	1,921,987	20.4	3,470,174	30.8	4,299,343	34.8	4,407,353	34.7
Miami-Fort Lauderdale-Miami Beach, FL	384,539	17.7	749,401	23.3	1,178,146	29.0	1,755,004	35.0	1,949,629	36.5
Riverside-San Bernardino-Ontario, CA	73,035	6.5	134,998	8.7	360,650	13.9	612,359	18.8	827,584	21.6
San Diego-Carlsbad-San Marcos, CA	96,444	7.3	235,593	12.7	428,810	17.2	606,254	21.5	659,731	23.4
Total	1,487,885	9.9	3,271,778	17.0	5,899,268	24.4	8,171,181	29.0	8,958,172	30.0
Total established and former gateways	6,139,231	9.0	8,656,618	11.9	12,349,704	15.7	17,476,950	20.1	19,080,107	21.6
Total all gateway types	6,878,203	7.7	10,054,903	10.2	14,843,656	13.2	23,041,667	17.9	26,197,767	19.5

(continued)

Appendix B (*continued*)

City	Foreign-born in central city									
	1970		1980		1990		2000		2005	
	Total	Percent	Total	Percent	Total	Percent	Total	Percent	Total	Percent
Emerging										
Atlanta-Sandy Springs-Marietta, GA	6,393	1.3	9,777	2.3	13,354	3.4	27,352	6.6	26,413	6.7
Dallas-Fort Worth-Arlington, TX	26,083	2.0	79,515	5.5	186,168	10.8	428,467	20.8	479,189	22.8
Las Vegas-Paradise, NV	6,811	4.5	21,617	8.7	40,917	10.7	132,706	20.0	153,216	20.0
Orlando, FL	3,735	3.8	6,641	5.2	11,436	6.9	26,741	14.4	38,989	17.6
Phoenix-Mesa-Scottsdale, AZ	26,834	3.8	55,570	5.4	106,860	7.6	321,173	16.7	395,938	19.4
Washington-Arlington-Alexandria, DC-VA-MD	51,812	5.0	73,764	8.2	113,401	12.8	158,854	17.9	149,955	17.8
Total	121,668	3.2	246,884	5.9	472,136	9.5	1,095,293	17.9	1,243,700	19.6
Re-Emerging										
Denver-Aurora, CO	24,322	4.1	39,064	6.0	47,234	6.8	141,293	17.0	161,155	19.3
Minneapolis-St. Paul-Bloomington, MN-WI	31,269	4.2	31,395	4.9	42,517	6.6	96,613	14.4	95,627	15.6
Portland-Vancouver-Beaverton, OR-WA	20,589	4.9	27,848	6.8	35,813	7.4	86,482	12.9	86,519	12.9
Sacramento--Arden-Arcade--Roseville, CA	18,217	7.2	27,708	10.0	50,569	13.7	82,616	20.3	99,162	22.3
San Jose-Sunnyvale-Santa Clara, CA	47,922	7.6	119,928	14.6	254,936	25.7	417,441	37.0	434,475	38.7
Seattle-Tacoma-Bellevue, WA	58,606	7.8	73,676	10.1	92,905	11.9	144,781	16.7	161,578	19.2
Tampa-St. Petersburg-Clearwater, FL	38,892	7.1	43,467	7.3	47,477	7.7	73,942	11.2	84,706	12.9
Total	239,817	6.1	363,086	8.8	571,451	12.5	1,043,168	19.9	1,123,222	21.7
Pre-Emerging										
Austin-Round Rock, TX	5,255	2.1	16,704	4.8	39,626	8.5	109,006	16.6	123,382	18.2
Charlotte-Gastonia-Concord, NC-SC	3,751	1.6	8,742	2.8	15,119	3.8	59,849	11.0	79,600	13.2
Greensboro-High Point, NC	1,190	0.8	2,712	1.7	4,839	2.6	18,146	8.1	24,491	11.7
Winston-Salem, NC	951	0.7	2,121	1.6	3,014	2.1	15,335	8.3	21,034	11.5
Raleigh-Cary, NC	2,550	2.1	5,321	3.5	10,434	5.0	32,410	11.7	42,050	13.3
Durham, NC	772	0.8	1,889	1.9	5,205	3.8	22,544	12.0	33,178	17.3
Salt Lake City, UT	11,546	6.6	12,473	7.7	13,258	8.3	33,252	18.3	32,019	17.5
Total	26,015	2.2	49,962	3.7	91,495	5.4	290,542	12.9	355,754	15.1
Total 21st-century gateways	387,500	4.3	659,932	6.8	1,135,082	10.1	2,429,003	17.8	2,722,676	19.6
Former										
Baltimore-Towson, MD	30,056	3.3	24,667	3.1	23,467	3.2	29,638	4.6	34,225	5.6
Buffalo-Niagara Falls, NY	33,940	7.3	22,025	6.2	14,741	4.5	12,856	4.4	13,990	5.5
Cleveland-Elyria-Mentor, OH	54,859	7.3	33,347	5.8	20,975	4.1	21,372	4.5	18,004	4.3
Detroit-Warren-Livonia, MI	141,292	7.8	90,887	6.2	53,141	4.2	66,408	5.6	74,001	6.9
Milwaukee-Waukesha-West Allis, WI	39,823	5.6	31,718	5.0	29,667	4.7	46,122	7.7	53,147	9.5
Philadelphia-Camden-Wilmington, PA-NJ-DE	129,109	6.6	107,951	6.4	104,814	6.6	137,205	9.0	155,961	11.1
Pittsburgh, PA	29,885	5.7	22,195	5.2	16,946	4.6	18,874	5.6	21,220	7.5
St. Louis, MO-IL	15,337	2.5	11,878	2.6	10,034	2.5	19,542	5.6	22,286	6.7
Total	474,301	6.1	344,668	5.4	273,785	4.7	352,017	6.5	392,834	8.0
Continuous										
Boston-Cambridge-Quincy, MA-NH	97,189	13.1	104,619	15.9	135,947	20.3	178,054	25.8	167,901	27.9
Chicago-Naperville-Joliet, IL-IN-WI	376,677	10.9	442,199	14.1	480,192	16.3	655,432	20.9	633,167	21.3
New York-Northern New Jersey-Long Island, NY-NJ-PA	1,457,394	17.6	1,717,938	23.2	2,134,354	28.1	2,937,089	35.5	2,991,395	36.4
San Francisco-Oakland-Fremont, CA	189,413	16.1	247,993	21.6	354,322	27.9	467,151	33.9	458,290	35.2
Total	2,120,673	15.5	2,512,749	20.4	3,104,815	24.9	4,237,726	31.4	4,250,753	32.5
Post-WWII										
Houston-Baytown-Sugar Land, TX	39,693	3.2	155,577	9.8	290,374	17.8	516,105	26.4	564,175	29.1
Los Angeles-Long Beach-Santa Ana, CA	446,659	13.4	918,388	26.0	1,590,260	37.8	1,824,821	40.6	1,801,618	40.1
Miami-Fort Lauderdale-Miami Beach, FL	153,945	32.4	201,508	40.3	240,091	47.3	248,677	48.3	236,277	47.0
Riverside-San Bernardino-Ontario, CA	17,456	5.7	32,906	8.7	90,779	17.3	137,845	23.1	173,508	26.5
San Diego-Carlsbad-San Marcos, CA	53,336	7.7	130,906	15.0	232,138	20.9	314,227	25.7	319,142	26.4
Total	711,089	11.8	1,439,285	20.9	2,443,642	30.6	3,041,675	34.6	3,094,720	35.1
Total established and former gateways	3,306,063	12.1	4,296,702	16.8	5,822,242	22.1	7,631,418	27.6	7,738,307	28.8
Total all gateway types	3,693,563	10.2	4,956,634	14.1	6,957,324	18.6	10,060,421	24.4	10,460,983	25.7

Suburb	Foreign-born in suburbs									
	1970		1980		1990		2000		2005	
	Total	Percent	Total	Percent	Total	Percent	Total	Percent	Total	Percent
Emerging										
Atlanta-Sandy Springs-Marietta, GA	11,496	0.9	38,038	2.0	103,899	3.9	397,167	10.4	586,346	13.2
Dallas-Fort Worth-Arlington, TX	12,814	1.2	45,642	2.9	131,809	5.8	354,528	11.4	537,032	14.8
Las Vegas-Paradise, NV	5,456	4.8	13,447	6.3	29,416	8.2	115,045	16.2	180,871	19.2
Orlando, FL	11,317	2.8	30,626	4.5	70,606	6.7	170,378	11.7	263,334	15.7
Phoenix-Mesa-Scottsdale, AZ	13,173	4.4	31,023	5.4	54,970	6.6	136,310	10.2	216,912	12.3
Washington-Arlington-Alexandria, DC-VA-MD	80,739	4.0	181,675	7.3	374,882	11.6	670,456	17.2	867,477	20.3
Total	134,995	2.6	340,451	4.6	765,582	7.3	1,843,884	12.9	2,651,972	15.8
Re-Emerging										
Denver-Aurora, CO	11,413	2.2	26,299	3.3	34,535	3.5	92,828	6.9	129,610	8.7
Minneapolis-St. Paul-Bloomington, MN-WI	24,237	1.9	40,302	2.6	45,576	2.4	113,731	4.9	171,741	7.0
Portland-Vancouver-Beaverton, OR-WA	21,045	3.3	38,779	4.2	52,404	5.0	121,940	9.7	164,436	11.8
Sacramento--Arden-Arcade--Roseville, CA	26,188	4.6	51,981	6.3	89,896	8.1	177,495	12.8	254,430	16.3
San Jose-Sunnyvale-Santa Clara, CA	38,527	8.9	59,905	12.1	98,532	18.2	165,715	27.3	179,829	29.8
Seattle-Tacoma-Bellevue, WA	48,105	4.6	76,476	5.6	109,077	6.1	239,043	11.0	318,335	13.9
Tampa-St. Petersburg-Clearwater, FL	30,400	5.8	64,592	6.3	98,526	6.8	159,965	9.2	210,142	10.8
Total	199,915	4.0	358,334	5.1	528,546	6.0	1,070,717	9.9	1,428,523	12.2
Pre-Emerging										
Austin-Round Rock, TX	3,075	2.3	7,516	3.1	16,528	4.3	43,828	7.4	69,356	9.5
Charlotte-Gastonia-Concord, NC-SC	1,992	0.4	5,088	0.9	7,558	1.2	32,141	4.1	55,149	6.2
Greensboro-High Point, NC	995	0.4	2,629	0.8	3,579	1.0	19,059	4.5	28,015	6.2
Winston-Salem, NC	478	0.3	1,662	0.8	2,243	1.0	7,961	3.4	8,467	3.3
Raleigh-Cary, NC	567	0.3	3,002	1.2	7,104	2.1	37,120	7.1	53,365	8.8
Durham, NC	1,428	1.0	3,505	1.8	6,744	3.2	17,177	7.2	19,528	8.0
Salt Lake City, UT	8,027	2.7	16,166	3.3	20,986	3.5	63,827	8.1	80,609	9.7
Total	16,562	1.0	39,568	1.8	64,742	2.4	221,113	6.2	314,489	7.8
Total 21st-century gateways	351,472	3.0	738,353	4.4	1,358,870	6.2	3,135,714	10.9	4,394,984	13.5
Former										
Baltimore-Towson, MD	28,838	2.5	49,558	3.5	64,186	3.9	116,490	6.1	150,214	7.6
Buffalo-Niagara Falls, NY	48,150	5.6	47,331	5.3	37,479	4.4	38,525	4.4	38,353	4.5
Cleveland-Elyria-Mentor, OH	92,459	6.1	93,517	5.8	77,394	4.8	91,634	5.5	97,893	5.9
Detroit-Warren-Livonia, MI	166,724	6.6	191,879	6.7	182,144	6.1	270,651	8.3	313,026	9.3
Milwaukee-Waukesha-West Allis, WI	22,705	3.4	26,704	3.5	24,376	3.0	35,452	3.9	40,415	4.4
Philadelphia-Camden-Wilmington, PA-NJ-DE	128,715	3.9	151,863	4.3	166,003	4.3	254,624	6.1	329,839	7.8
Pittsburgh, PA	82,104	3.7	62,634	2.8	41,302	2.0	43,904	2.1	44,713	2.2
St. Louis, MO-IL	34,056	1.8	42,100	2.1	39,597	1.8	62,004	2.6	86,335	3.6
Total	603,751	4.3	665,586	4.3	632,481	3.9	913,284	5.3	1,100,788	6.3
Continuous										
Boston-Cambridge-Quincy, MA-NH	246,945	8.0	244,716	7.5	291,577	8.4	424,008	11.5	516,264	14.1
Chicago-Naperville-Joliet, IL-IN-WI	227,396	5.3	344,484	7.0	433,316	8.3	808,689	13.6	992,482	15.8
New York-Northern New Jersey-Long Island, NY-NJ-PA	828,379	9.8	1,011,278	11.3	1,290,059	13.9	1,909,233	19.0	2,125,895	21.0
San Francisco-Oakland-Fremont, CA	149,901	8.1	261,359	12.4	424,403	17.6	660,812	24.1	742,919	26.8
Total	1,452,621	8.2	1,861,837	9.7	2,439,355	12.0	3,802,742	16.9	4,377,560	19.1
Post-WWII										
Houston-Baytown-Sugar Land, TX	17,562	1.9	74,222	4.8	171,114	8.0	382,116	13.8	549,700	16.9
Los Angeles-Long Beach-Santa Ana, CA	429,953	8.7	1,003,599	17.1	1,879,914	26.6	2,474,522	31.4	2,605,735	31.8
Miami-Fort Lauderdale-Miami Beach, FL	230,594	13.5	547,893	20.1	938,055	26.4	1,506,327	33.5	1,713,352	35.5
Riverside-San Bernardino-Ontario, CA	55,579	6.9	102,092	8.6	269,871	13.1	474,514	17.9	654,076	20.6
San Diego-Carlsbad-San Marcos, CA	43,108	6.8	104,687	10.6	196,672	14.2	292,027	18.4	340,589	21.1
Total	776,796	8.6	1,832,493	14.9	3,455,626	21.3	5,129,506	26.5	5,863,452	27.8
Total established and former gateways	2,833,168	7.0	4,359,916	9.3	6,527,462	12.4	9,845,532	16.7	11,341,800	18.5
Total all gateway types	3,184,640	6.1	5,098,269	8.0	7,886,332	10.6	12,981,246	14.8	15,736,784	16.8

Source: 1980, 1990 and 2000 decennial censuses; *American Community Survey 2005.*

Note: 2003 metropolitan area definitions used for all years.

Appendix C. Top Ten Countries of Origin for the Foreign-Born Population in Nine Twenty-First-Century Gateways, 2005

Dallas-Fort Worth-Arlington, TX		
1	Mexico	591,399
2	El Salvador	46,674
3	India	40,996
4	Vietnam	40,221
5	Korea	20,154
6	China*	18,135
7	Philippines	15,371
8	Pakistan	14,375
9	Guatemala	13,281
10	Honduras	12,242
Total foreign-born population		1,016,221

Phoenix-Mesa-Scottsdale, AZ		
1	Mexico	409,928
2	Canada	21,787
3	India	12,245
4	Philippines	11,262
5	China*	9,889
6	Vietnam	9,486
7	Germany	9,311
8	United Kingdom	8,002
9	El Salvador	6,558
10	Korea	6,081
Total foreign-born population		612,850

Atlanta-Sandy Springs-Marietta, GA		
1	Mexico	182,116
2	India	41,914
3	Korea	25,105
4	Jamaica	24,137
5	Vietnam	21,343
6	Colombia	14,773
7	China*	13,687
8	Brazil	13,414
9	El Salvador	12,563
10	United Kingdom	12,042
Total foreign-born population		612,759

Washington-Arlington-Alexandria, DC-VA-MD		
1	El Salvador	128,798
2	India	62,588
3	Korea	52,388
4	Mexico	45,049
5	Vietnam	42,758
6	Philippines	38,336
7	China*	33,740
8	Peru	30,085
9	Guatemala	29,238
10	Honduras	22,348
Total foreign-born population		1,017,432

Sacramento-Arden-Arcade-Roseville, CA		
1	Mexico	99,307
2	Philippines	28,857
3	Vietnam	22,122
4	India	21,106
5	Ukraine	20,911
6	China*	13,604
7	Russia	12,978
8	Laos	10,412
9	Thailand	6,352
10	United Kingdom	6,286
Total foreign-born population		353,592

Portland-Vancouver-Beaverton, OR-WA		
1	Mexico	77,634
2	Vietnam	17,644
3	Ukraine	12,679
4	Korea	11,968
5	China*	9,701
6	Canada	9,184
7	India	7,902
8	Russia	7,348
9	United Kingdom	7,316
10	Philippines	6,917
Total foreign-born population		250,955

Minneapolis-St. Paul-Bloomington, MN-WI		
1	Mexico	45,793
2	Laos	22,533
3	India	15,895
4	Vietnam	12,464
5	Korea	9,736
6	China*	9,721
7	Thailand	9,635
8	Canada	6,695
9	United Kingdom	6,544
10	Philippines	6,403
Total foreign-born population		267,368

Austin-Round Rock, TX		
1	Mexico	100,768
2	India	8,082
3	Vietnam	6,338
4	Korea	6,023
5	China*	4,913
6	El Salvador	4,586
7	Philippines	4,562
8	Canada	3,907
9	United Kingdom	3,834
10	Honduras	3,505
Total foreign-born population		192,738

Charlotte-Gastonia-Concord, NC-SC		
1	Mexico	40,740
2	India	7,500
3	El Salvador	6,407
4	Vietnam	5,607
5	Canada	5,021
6	Honduras	4,994
7	Guatemala	2,976
8	United Kingdom	2,666
9	China*	2,545
10	Korea	2,314
Total foreign-born population		134,749

*Excluding Hong Kong and Taiwan.

| 2

Toward a Suburban Immigrant Nation

SUSAN W. HARDWICK

When future scholars of immigration and urban studies look back at the last decade of the twentieth century and the first decade of the twenty-first century, they are likely to view this time period as a critical moment in the evolution of the American city, an era when a *suburban immigrant nation* first emerged. As urban geographer Peter Muller observed more than twenty years ago, after two decades of massive population shifts from the central cities outward in the years following World War II, an equally massive deconcentration of economic activity occurred in the late 1960s as businesses and other employment centers relocated to the suburbs.[1] These processes resulted in the emergence of post-1970s metroplexes where, as described by Andrew Hamer, "the suburbs [changed] from an amorphous, bedroom community status to an organized economy clustered around recognizable employment centers drawing on a fairly close commuting shed."[2] The result today is exactly what Muller and others predicted—the outer city is no longer "sub" to the "urb" in any traditional sense of the word. In fact, many American suburbs are replete with a wide range of employment opportunities; shopping districts, education, health care, and law enforcement systems; and a local sense of place that distinguishes them from other parts of the larger metropolitan area and makes them self-sufficient economically, culturally, and politically. Concomitant with these expanded services in the suburbs have come demographic changes; suburbs have emerged as rich sites of population diversity.

To lay a foundation for understanding more about this critical shift toward a suburban immigrant nation, this chapter presents a broad overview of the evolution of the suburbs and their role in regional urban economies and rapidly changing political and social systems in U.S. cities, especially since the mid-1970s. The goal is to provide a sociospatial and historical context for understanding some of the reasons why today's immigrant populations are often located in suburban areas, rather than in clustered immigrant enclaves in downtown neighborhoods as most were in the past. Following this historical overview is a description of the new models of spatial assimilation that have been developed to facilitate an understanding of the suburban immigrant nation to provide a foundation for their application in the case study chapters that follow.

Historical Evolution of Suburban Expansion in the United States

Despite popular misconceptions about the beginnings of suburban expansion in the United States, created at least partially by 1950s-era television series showing an idealized notion of life in the suburbs, the processes were set in motion a hundred years earlier. A combination of factors influenced the rise in suburban expansion: changes in transportation technologies, from streetcars to interurban railroads to automobiles; the construction of increasingly suburban residential, commercial, and industrial establishments along or near streetcar and rail tracks and later along roadways; and ongoing decentralization of economic and service activities away from the central city out to the suburbs.

Streetcar Suburbs

In the 1850s railroad connections began to link urban residents with places outside crowded downtowns. These transportation links to the outer city became accessible and affordable to middle-income city dwellers with the advent of horse-pulled streetcar technology, another innovation that helped make travel and subsequent residential and commercial expansion possible some distance from downtown for larger and larger numbers of people. These *horsecar suburbs,* as they have come to be known in the urban morphology literature, were especially timely given the onset of the Industrial Revolution and the resulting expansion of urban populations who sought employment in new factories and businesses. The continuing need for new housing for expanding urban populations was partially solved during this time period by developing large open tracts of land located outside the urban core.

The invention of the electric streetcar in the 1880s made it possible for middle-class workers and their families to relocate to the suburbs in larger and larger numbers. This period of urban evolution resulted in a whole new pattern of urban space along urban arterial lines that followed the streetcar tracks as they carried people home from their places of work downtown. At first, commercial buildings were constructed along both sides of these tracks—with residential districts gridded out behind them for a few blocks. Although these early suburbs were limited mainly to the emerging white middle class, many lower-income working-class residents from the inner city depended upon these same streetcar lines for weekend excursions to parks, fair grounds, or cemeteries located at the end of the line.

Several early scholars of the evolution of the suburb from a spatial perspective have pointed out that improvements in transportation technology helped create an entirely new urban form in American cities as concentric rings of growth evolved at ever greater distances from the downtown.[3] These new arterial developments defined a new social geography of the city. Blue-collar workers were forced to reside in an inner ring near the factories where they worked, while more affluent residents who could afford to use faster and newer steam railroads to travel to and from work each day chose housing farther away from the city's center. This *congregation by choice* of higher-income groups in the outer city laid the foundation for an early and enduring image of white exclusivity that continues to be associated with perceptions of life and landscape in suburbs today. Simultaneously, the model developed to describe the spatial assimilation of immigrants who came to the United States between 1880 and 1924 (when Congress curtailed immigration), commonly known as the Chicago School model, described ethnic ghettoes located near the center of the city as the places of settlement for the first generation. There immigrants found cheap housing that was located close to employment opportunities.[4] As these immigrants, and more particularly their children, became more economically prosperous, they moved away from inner-city neighborhoods to the surrounding suburbs, where they found better quality housing and a mainstream population into which they could integrate.

Automobiles and Suburban Expansion

The invention and subsequent widespread dissemination of automobile transportation in the early twentieth century provided the next impetus for change in a suburbanizing nation. As mass transit systems such as streetcars and urban railways increasingly became associated with crowding, discomfort, and inconvenience, automobile travel became the mode of

Figure 2-1. Suburban Growth and Automobile Ownership, 1900–70

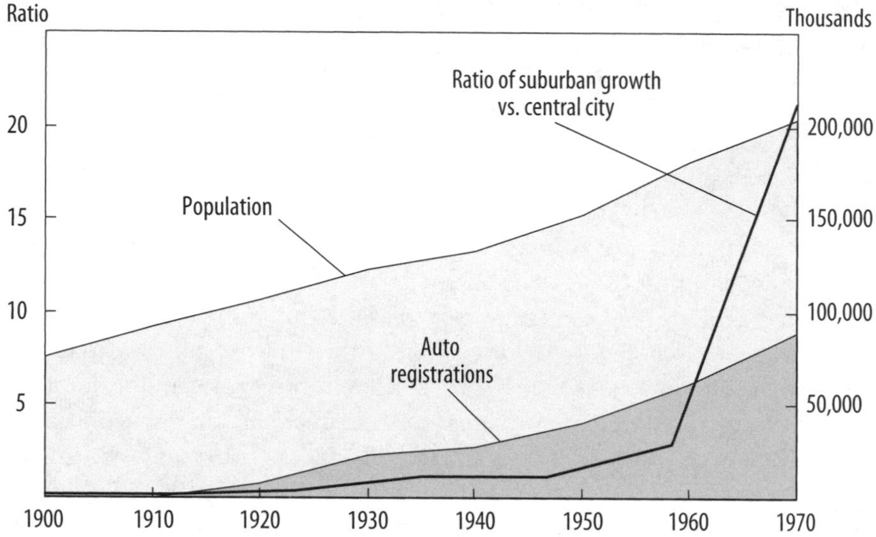

Source: U.S. Bureau of the Census, *Statistical Abstract of the United States, 1973*, pp. 5, 547; U.S. Census of Population, *Selected Area Reports, 1960;* U.S. Census of Population, 1970.

choice for those who could afford it. With Henry Ford's invention of mass-produced cars, the automobile became more accessible to a wider population. In addition, the availability of credit for the middle classes expanded in the 1920s as wages rose, adding to the number of people who could afford to purchase this newest form of urban transportation. As the number of auto registrations expanded exponentially between 1900 and 1970 (figure 2-1), a series of new interurban roads were established that made it possible to travel more easily between downtown neighborhoods and shopping districts and the city's outlying suburbs. Along with these improvements in urban connectivity came greater levels of personal mobility. This, in turn, "enabled increased choice in housing location, as people realized they could enjoy improved accommodation within convenient, and sometimes not-so-convenient, commuting distances from the city."[5]

Dependency on motor vehicle travel fueled other changes as well. Truck transport enabled producers to distribute raw materials and finished products more easily over wider areas. This freed industrial plants and distribution centers from dependency on their proximity to railroads and allowed companies to relocate factories and offices to the suburbs. Although this economic decentralization in American cities had been in motion since the 1850s, it accelerated dramatically with the evolution of the motor vehicle in the early and mid-twentieth century. Soon thereafter, the cheaper rents, lower taxes, and inexpensive land costs of vast areas of undeveloped land outside the city limits attracted new industries and other new types of economic development there. The widespread adoption of telephone communication systems and electricity in places far outside the city limits also contributed to the economic, residential, and commercial expansion of suburbs. By the early 1980s the suburbs had become home to about two-thirds of all manufacturing in the United States.[6]

New Roads and Highway Systems

Construction of new or improved roads and highways to accommodate the thousands of cars and trucks that were regularly traversing both urban and rural parts of the country added to the efficacy of intraurban linkages connecting central cities and suburbs. One of the primary forces behind road construction was the increasingly powerful auto industry. By the end of the 1920s most car and truck manufacturers already felt that they had saturated the rural market and so needed to expand into urban areas. Mounting pressure from this group as well as politicians and others who were eager to please their urban constituencies, led to the continued suppression of mass transit systems in cities and a push to build urban freeway networks. Numerous pro-highway groups such as the secretive "Road Gang," were led by powerful representatives from the auto industry, oil companies, the Teamsters Union, highway builders, truckers, and highway administrators who came together as strong advocates and lobbyists for the construction of new highways in the United States.[7]

Their efforts resulted in the passage of the Interstate Highway Act in 1956, providing for 42,500 miles of national highways, ostensibly to be constructed for defense purposes. Many journalists, historians, political scientists, and other scholars have since published critiques of this legislation and the highway system that resulted from it (citing especially the contrived military need for highways that had been pushed by the automobile lobby). Journalist Helen Leavitt, for example, noted that trucks carrying defense missiles in the 1950s were too high to pass under freeway overpasses since highway engineers never consulted the Defense Department before they started construction.[8] Other critics cited the overconfidence of highway designers who were insensitive to the leaders of communities that were being disrupted by road-building efforts.[9]

Despite these concerns and critiques however, road-building continued apace through the 1950s and 1960s—and along with it came the rapid expansion of American suburbs and financial benefits for national and local growth machines. According to Hayden, "road gangs" in every state "enriched automobile, truck, oil, construction, and real estate interests by providing infrastructure worth billions of dollars to open up new suburban land for speculation and development."[10]

Suburban Residential Expansion

Suburban land development (not national defense), therefore, was ultimately the most significant outcome of the Interstate Highway Act. And this newly connected land soon would become the preferred home for hundreds of thousands of Americans who wished to escape city life for an idealized and highly romanticized life that featured single-family homes, private yards, and clean and quiet streets. In a cover story featured in a 1950 issue of *Time,* life in the suburbs was celebrated as a revolution in American life: "Three years ago, little potatoes had sprouted from these fields. Now there were almost 10,600 houses inhabited by more than 40,000 people, a community almost as big as 96-year-old Poughkeepsie, N.Y., Plainfield, N.J. or Chelsea, Mass. . . . Its name: Levittown."[11]

Developer and public figure William Levitt had constructed the largest mass-produced housing in the United States in an effort to address the acute shortage of affordable housing following World War II. Levitt was supported not only by new factory methods of home construction and by new and generous home loan legislation for home builders (such as the Federal Housing Administration's Title VI, which for the first time in history encouraged developers to borrow money *before* finding buyers for their homes), but also by influential politicians like Senator Joseph McCarthy. After the passage of the Taft-Ellender-Wagner (TEW) Act, which was intended to eliminate slums in American cities by constructing high-density government housing downtown, McCarthy held a series of public hearings in cities across the country in 1947–48 to discredit this plan. The outcome of these hearings (and all the publicity they generated) was the emergence of a vociferous public outcry against the government's controlling the housing industry at the expense of private developers. The much publicized anti–TEW Act efforts of McCarthy, Levitt, and others also helped create a lasting perception in the general public that downtown living was to be avoided because of overcrowding, crime, dirt, and traffic—and that suburban life was the preferred lifestyle choice, especially for families who wanted their children to live in a safe, quasi-rural environment. In addition, new government mortgage insurance programs made standard for most home buyers the thirty-year mortgage with 5 percent down.

Under the GI Bill, returning veterans did not have to put any money down. A veteran and his family could buy a house in Levittown for $56 a month, making the American suburban dream a reality for average home buyers for the first time. By 1950 Levitt and Sons had become the General Motors of home construction and Levitt a national hero, all because of the affordability and availability of single family homes with yards and quiet streets in his massive Levittown suburban housing project.

The tarnishing of the American suburban dream has been documented by numerous critics, and a discussion of their major themes and concerns is well beyond the scope of this chapter.[12] Suffice it to say, however, that life and the landscape in Levittown and elsewhere in the outer city did not always result in an idealized existence, especially for immigrants and minority groups (who were barred from buying homes there) and women and children (who were left behind while their husbands were working in the office or factory). Homeowner-purchasing contracts made it clear that only residents of the Caucasion race were allowed to buy homes in Levittown, although persons of other races could work for the homeowners.[13] With 82,000 residents by 1960, Levittown had emerged as the largest all-white community in the United States.[14]

Sociologist Herbert Gans conducted a long-term study of Levittown in the mid-1960s and found that women's lives (although well-connected within their own neighborhoods) were often anti-intellectual and provincial. Putting a positive spin on these observations, Gans wrote: "Their major recreation is the care of home and children; their social life is focused on friends and neighbors, rather than on relatives; and they swell the membership rolls of churches and voluntary organizations. Their culture has always been anti-urban even when they lived in the city, and they made little use of city culture even when it was easily accessible."[15]

Gans' analysis of life in Levittown also mentioned how long it took him to meet his neighbors (a full year) and how much teenagers disliked life in the suburbs because of a lack of cultural and recreational amenities. As in more recent work on life in suburbia, this report on one of the oldest and most classic suburbs in the United States provides evidence that the American suburban dream often exhibits an anti-intellectualism and judgmental attitudes about the "other." These deep-seated and all-too-common suburban (read: white middle-class) value systems often make it difficult for immigrant groups from other cultures, races, ethnic, and socioeconomic backgrounds to penetrate the norms of suburban society without both internal and external support systems and networks—an issue discussed in later chapters of this book.

Postwar Suburban Commercial Development

Along with the construction of new houses and employment nodes in the suburbs, new roads and highways also led to opportunities for the construction of new or improved commercial districts. These shopping centers and malls, located at or near the interchanges of new highways for easy accessibility, drew consumers away from their habitual preference for shopping downtown. Assisted by tax breaks in the 1950s, as well as by subsidies from local and state governments in the form of economic development grants and other financial incentives, developers, including European immigrant Victor Gruen, laid out the country's first enclosed mall in 1956 outside Minneapolis. This innovation set the stage for the rapid proliferation of shopping malls, strip developments, regional malls, and supermalls all across the country in the next decades, with more than 43,000 commercial clusters constructed in the suburbs by the late 1990s.[16]

The evolution of suburban commercial and business centers in the United States may be conceptualized in a number of useful ways. One approach is Hartshorn and Muller's summary model listing some of the stages of urban change after 1950.[17] As shown in table 2-1, this approach captures some of the impacts of various events, technologies, and land use preferences. Each of the stages shown in this model summarizes some of the processes and patterns shaping today's suburbs and helps clarify how they have emerged in their current form. Understanding the sociospatial characteristics of each stage also lays a foundation for understanding the evolution of the emerging immigrant suburban nation discussed in the next section of this chapter and in the remainder of the book.

These continually changing relationships among commercial, business, residential, and other land use patterns in the central city and the suburbs in the postwar era gradually eroded the centrality of the downtown. With suburban expressway locations equally accessible to the entire urban area, offices, manufacturing plants, and other nonresidential activities became increasingly footloose and were able to relocate to what were perceived as more desirable outlying locations. As Muller observed, "With a rapidly growing number of manufacturers and office employers choosing deconcentration, a widely dispersed metropolitan economic network emerged in the 1970s as many suburbs came to perform singly a myriad of functions that hitherto had operated as a bundle in the central city."[18]

In sum, during the postwar years a redefined American dream centered in suburban living was promoted eagerly and positively by Hollywood, by governments, by Detroit, and by Wall Street. Affordable automobiles, federally

Table 2-1. The Evolution of Suburban Business Centers

1950s: Sprawl
- Bedroom communities
- Convenience retailing
- Arterial highway radial access
- Air conditioning

1960s: Independence
- Freeways
- Regional shopping malls
- Office and industrial parks
- Residential diversification

1970s: Magnet
- Mid-rise office buildings
- Hotels and conventions
- Corporate headquarters
- High-income residential areas
- Circumferential freeways
- Support services such as restaurants

1980s: High-rise and high-tech
- High-rise offices and hotels
- Low-rise, high-tech buildings
- Increased residential densities

1990s–present: Mature town center
- Cultural, social, recreational activity
- Maturing government functions
- Community mismatch
- Infrastructure and planning problems

Source: Based on T. A. Hartshorn and P. O. Muller, "Suburban Downtowns and the Transformation of Metropolitan Atlanta's Business Landscape," *Urban Geography* 10 (1989): 375–95; adapted from David Kaplan, James O. Wheeler, and Steven Holloway, *Urban Geography* (New York: John Wiley and Sons, 2004).

subsidized highways, cheap home mortgages, and sustained economic growth all meant that millions of families could have that dream house in the suburbs, with its quiet streets, nearby schools and shopping centers. By 1970 *urban America* clearly had become *suburban America* as more and more families chose to raise their children in low-density subdivisions located in suburbs rather than in high-density downtown neighborhoods

Figure 2-2. Relative Percentages of Urban Population Growth, 1900–70

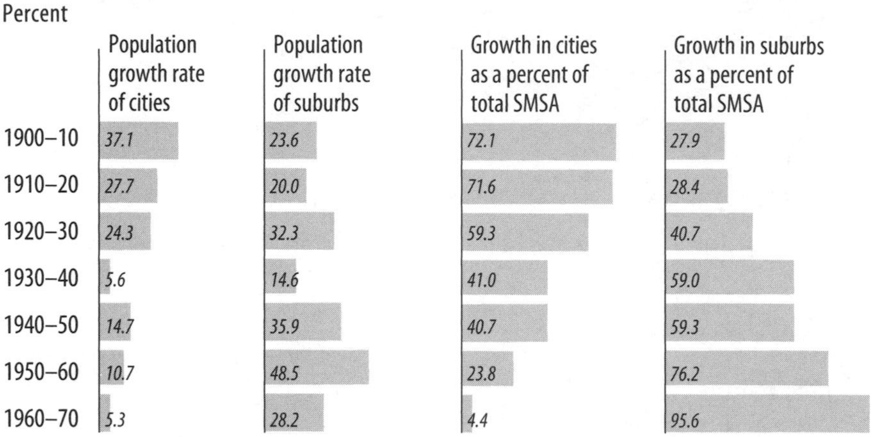

Percent

	Population growth rate of cities	Population growth rate of suburbs	Growth in cities as a percent of total SMSA	Growth in suburbs as a percent of total SMSA
1900–10	37.1	23.6	72.1	27.9
1910–20	27.7	20.0	71.6	28.4
1920–30	24.3	32.3	59.3	40.7
1930–40	5.6	14.6	41.0	59.0
1940–50	14.7	35.9	40.7	59.3
1950–60	10.7	48.5	23.8	76.2
1960–70	5.3	28.2	4.4	95.6

Source: U.S. Census of Population, 1960. *Selected Area Reports: SMSAs, Social and Economic Data for Persons in SMSAs by Residence inside or outside Central City, Final Report PC (3)-1D,* 1963, updated figures computed from the 1970 census by Muller; adapted from P. O. Muller, *Contemporary Suburban America* (Englewood Cliffs, N.J.: Prentice-Hall, 1981), p. 22.

SMSA = standard metropolitan statistical area.

(figure 2-2). Today, this pattern is truer than ever before as immigrant families join this suburban stream in ever greater numbers in the first decade of the twenty-first century.

Post-1970s Suburban Evolution and Change

The development of land located far from the city center continued in earnest after the 1970s. Commercially developed land outside the urban core, especially large regional shopping malls, set the stage for the expansion of developed land in edge nodes located beyond earlier suburban developments. In what Garreau called *edge cities,* land use is not geared to pedestrians but rather to automobile traffic as defined by commuting patterns.[19] Three distinctive types of edge developments seem to be most common in today's metropolis: booming areas around older strip developments and freeway interchanges like Virginia's Tyson's Corner near Washington; new developments that favor a mix of residential and commercial land located just beyond a city's outer suburbs, such as Orenco Station west of downtown Portland, Oregon; and developments that are located near a freeway exit on land that was formerly used for agriculture, such as the former agricultural community of Schaumburg, Illinois, located far from Chicago's downtown but still considered part of its urban sphere of influence.

More recently, Lang provided a convincing argument that counters many of Garreau's assumptions about edge cities.[20] Rejecting Garreau's claim that edge cities signal a return to high-density urban landscapes, Lang contends that today's expanding *postpolycentric* metropolitan areas are actually sprawling places with loose, unbounded outer edges. In addition, the business districts of these *edgeless cities* lack a high-density commercial core and therefore do not resemble older downtowns in either function or morphology (as the edge cities model claimed). This is an important observation for the chapters that follow because some of the case studies focus on the relationship between the residential and commercial patterns of new immigrants and refugees in these unbounded, edgeless outer rings of new foreign-born settlement. In suburban Portland, for example, Aloha is the most Vietnamese place in the state by percentage of total population. The visibility of this immigrant group in the suburban landscape is minimal, however, because of the sprawling nature of Aloha's unbounded commercial core. Although many of the restaurants, video stores, nail salons, and other businesses in Aloha are Vietnamese-owned, their location along a sprawling arterial that leads out to Portland's Westside *edge cities* renders them almost invisible in the suburban landscape.

In 1980 Pierce Lewis called this outer expansion at the city's edge the *galactic metropolis*.[21] The rising popularity of telecommuting for office workers and higher-income employees of software firms and other businesses continues to contribute to the growth of this edge development. The perception that these outer suburbs offer heightened safety, security, and beauty continues to attract the upper-middle and upper class to the edge as well. These new migrants helped create Wolf's *hot towns,* places that drew in residents from the creative class such as writers, technology designers, and artists; and Kotkin's *Valhallas,* urban places like Jackson Hole, Wyoming, that often possess environmental amenities and historical-looking village designs that are desired by even wealthier residents.[22]

Major changes in commercial land use at the edge have emerged since 1970 as well—notably, the construction of *big-box* stores in suburban and exurban landscapes in the 1990s and early 2000s. Some of these one-stop-shopping nodes are as large as 200,000 square feet. These massive structures located far from downtown shopping districts soon became major shopping destinations even for middle-class residents. Big-box developments also put many smaller businesses located in closer-in suburbs out of business and hastened the decline of commercial space in older suburbs.

Figure 2-3. The Evolution of Today's Suburban Nation

Percent of population

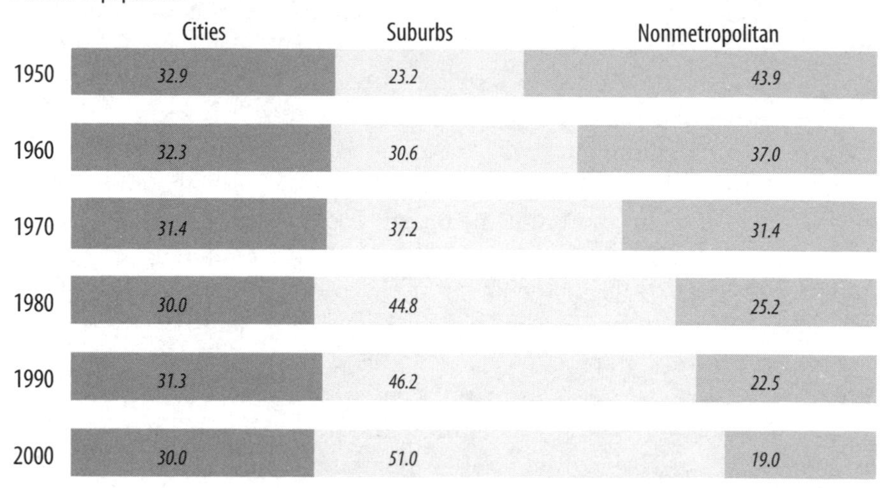

Source: U.S. Bureau of the Census, *Census of Population and Housing, 1950–2000.*

Not surprisingly, these large-scale commercial functions, new residential developments, and office parks and light industries have meant an explosive expansion of the American suburb and exurb. Consider these figures: In 1950, 69 million people lived on 12,715 square miles in the largest 157 urban areas in the United States. By 2000 these same 157 urban areas had 155 million residents who lived on 52,388 square miles—more than double the population and more than four times the land. Perhaps most telling, more than 80 percent of the population of these cities lived in suburbs located outside central cities. In addition, suburbanization of these 157 cities cut their population density by almost half, from 5,391 people per square mile in 1950 to 2,949 per square mile in 2000.[23] Census data for the years 1950–2000, shown in figure 2-3 provide a visual summary of the ever-expanding suburban nation during the past fifty years.

As suburban places in U.S. metropolitan areas expanded, the interplay of economic, cultural, political, and social processes reshaped place and space in the outer city, resulting in what Lang and Simmons have called *boomburbs*.[24] These suburban-dominated cities often develop along the interstate highways that ring large metropolitan areas and are most common in the Southwest. Boomburbs are made up of arterial suburban shopping districts dominated by regional shopping centers and big-box stores, office parks, and other businesses that are located close to highways and freeway off-ramps. Just behind these arterial, mixed-use developments are large residential subdivisions of single-family homes built on large lots. Boomburbs almost always lack a dense urban business core; therefore their spatial and economic structure resembles what Fishman has called the *technoburb,* a suburban area that "lacks any definable borders, a center or a periphery, or clear distinctions between residential, industrial, and commercial zones."[25] Although most of these boomburbs or technoburbs are home to upper-middle and high-income residents, many also have a few lower-income neighborhoods as well. Because of their large size, wide range of employment opportunities, accessibility along transportation corridors, and neighborhoods with differing income areas, these types of suburbs often feature more diverse populations than do smaller suburbs. In California, Florida, and elsewhere in the Sun Belt, for example, these outer suburban areas are now home to an increasingly large foreign-born population that has been steadily growing since the late 1980s.

This increase in foreign-born settlement far from the downtown does not fit common perceptions of life and landscape in suburban America as places most often dominated by white, middle-class families. Nor are all suburbs growing at the frantic pace many assume. Lucy and Phillips found that while U.S. suburbs as a whole continued to expand through the 1990s, this growth was not consistent across time and place.[26] Although recent census reports confirm that decentralized economic and residential space remained *the* dominant trend in the United States, many suburbs—especially those located in the Northeast and the Midwest—lost population during the 1990s. Pittsburgh, for example, had the greatest number of declining suburbs, with 84.4 percent of its 128 suburbs losing population in the 1990s.[27] Nonetheless, Puentes and Warren showed that nationwide, 29 percent of the foreign-born population lived in older, inner-ring, "first" suburbs in 2000.[28]

According to Singer, two large-scale major changes after the 1970s have irrevocably altered the form of metropolitan America. These dramatic and interrelated processes of change include the suburbanization, deindustrialization, and decentralization of economic and residential space that began after World War II and continue today; and the arrival of large and continuing flows of new immigrants from new places in Latin America, Africa, Asia, and elsewhere, many of whom settled in the suburbs instead of in traditional downtown immigrant enclaves.[29] The coming together of these two dramatic changes has resulted in new and ever more diverse suburban landscapes in the United States in the first decade of the twenty-first century.

Melting Pot Suburbs?

The somewhat surprising settlement of large numbers of immigrants in suburban neighborhoods is a result of an overlapping set of local, regional, national, and international processes. One of the causes of this shift is the ongoing densification of residential land in older suburbs. This process has created zones of *immigrant infill* caused by the construction of new apartments and other multiple-family housing in recent years, making suburban housing more affordable and available. Recent American Housing Survey data, in fact, indicate that 21.5 percent of all suburban immigrants live in multifamily housing, primarily in apartments, a very different image from the more common perception that housing choices in the suburbs are limited to single-family homes on large lots.[30] These expanded housing choices in the suburbs, along with the elimination of exclusionary zoning laws that prevented people of color or lower socioeconomic status from buying property in certain parts of the city, also opened the door to the settlement of larger numbers of nonwhite immigrant groups in suburban locales.

In tandem with the construction of this new and more affordable multifamily housing in the suburbs has been gentrification and new high-end residential construction downtown that has encouraged higher-income (and usually white) residents to relocate to the central city far from their former lives in the suburbs. The trend for older couples, single residents, and the "creative class" to prefer downtown condominiums to single-family homes is reinventing downtown landscapes in many of the nation's largest cities. This reverse flow of primarily white residents to upscale condominiums in places like downtown Chicago, St. Louis, the trendy Pearl District in Portland, and the Uptown District in Dallas is opening up housing for incoming foreign-born residents in the suburbs. This trend is thus not only changing the face of downtown neighborhoods but also leading to rapidly diversifying suburban landscapes.

At the national level, changes in immigration law in the 1960s opened the way for large numbers of new migrants from Latin America, Asia, and Africa to immigrate to the United States. Along with these changes, as chapter 1 outlines, a restructured global economy expanded transportation and communication technologies worldwide, and ongoing political changes continue to draw in ever more immigrants to U.S. metropolitan areas. In addition, the U.S. refugee resettlement program, which officially began in 1980 in response to the inflow of refugees from the Vietnam War, moved refugees into communities across the United States, encouraging certain groups such as the Vietnamese to settle in a range of smaller cities and suburban neighborhoods to avoid overloading local social service agencies. The dispersal of this group was orchestrated by the federal Office of Refugee Resettlement in an effort to help Vietnam War and other post-war migrants gain economic independence.[31] Along with these federal dispersal policies, local and state refugee resettlement agencies such as the Immigrant and Refugee Community Organization in Portland, prefer to settle new refugee arrivals in suburban neighborhoods largely because of the available and affordable multifamily housing there, the proximity of social services, and the economic opportunities for employment for refugee newcomers and other immigrants. Access to support services such as English language classes, employment skills training, and counseling services, as well as the availability of affordable housing in the suburbs, is drawing ever more immigrants to suburban neighborhoods to be close to each other and to the support networks they depend upon.

The increasing concentration of immigrants in the suburbs of new gateways is one of the most viable and visible characteristics of metropolitan areas in the United States. However, unlike the classic assimilation models developed by the Chicago School, which attributed the move out of crowded inner city immigrant enclaves to the suburbs as a process dependent on the improved socioeconomic circumstances of certain groups, many of today's immigrants settle in the suburbs immediately upon arrival in the United States. Immigrant groups with large amounts of human and social capital, such as Indians, Koreans, and Chinese, are coming to the United States in search of entrepreneurial or professional opportunities, and their settlement in the suburbs may be the result of their desire to create ethnic and racial enclaves in desirable parts of the city.[32] One example of this process is the ethnic *community of choice* of the Chinese in Monterey Park, California, a place geographer Wei Li has labeled an *ethnoburb*—a suburb dominated by one or more large groups of immigrants and their businesses, values, cultures, and politics.[33]

Suburban concentration and expansion is of particular note for certain Asian groups. At least half of all Filipinos, Indians, and Koreans reside in the suburbs, whereas a slight majority of Chinese reside in central cities (no doubt because of their long history of living in downtown urban enclaves in American cities).[34] Asians as a group (including both foreign- and native-born) are the most suburban of all minorities, with more than half of their population (58 percent) residing in suburbs in 2000. In addition, in metro areas where Asians are more than 4 percent of the total population, the average Asian now lives in a neighborhood that is 16 percent Asian, compared with only 12 percent in 1990. Overall, Asians are less segregated than other immigrant groups, and in some cities, they live where there are very few other Asians (for example, less than 3 percent of the population in Charlotte, West Palm Beach-Boca Raton, Milwaukee, and Indianapolis is Asian).[35] This is an important reminder that the ethnic diversity of the nation's suburbs and central cities is unevenly distributed in cities across the country. Further, the dispersal of Asian populations in particular has led some scholars to talk about *invisiburbs* where "the quintessential ethnic community fails to materialize in a necessarily recognizable manner as immigrants (and the organizations that represent them) construct ethnic spaces that are either externally anonymous or ephemeral in nature. The result is inconspicuousness and an ethnic community not easily discovered or delineated on the cultural landscape."[36]

Wilbur Zelinsky and Barrett Lee (1998) proposed a new theory, *heterolocalism,* to explain and predict the residential patterns of the majority of new immigrants during the past two decades.[37] Heterolocalism refers to the relationship between the dispersed spatial patterns of recent immigrants in U.S. cities and a group's ability to maintain its distinctive cultural and ethnic identify. Later, Zelinsky expanded on and further clarified this theory by emphasizing that dramatic improvements in urban transportation and communication systems in recent years have made it possible for new immigrants to settle in widely dispersed neighborhoods, while still holding onto their distinctive immigrant identities. Individuals in heterolocal groups may lack residential propinquity but find ways to connect regularly due to improved urban and suburban arterials and mass transit systems and the ubiquitous use of cell phones, e-mail, and other instant communications.[38] This heterolocal theory is referenced by several authors in this volume to capture the ways in which immigrant communities are constructed in the suburbs of places such as Charlotte and Portland.

Many authors in this book mention the impact of newcomers on the urban landscape in twenty-first-century gateways, in particular the revival of older commercial centers in the central city, in suburban strip shopping malls, and along older thoroughfares that are now lined with ethnic businesses. Immigrants across the spectrum have opened small enterprises, although there are important variations in the rate of self-employment from one group to the next.[39] Immigrant entrepreneurs in inner suburban communities, such as Sacramento's Florin Road suburban commercial area, cater not only to their own populations but also to a broader population that uses the services of dry cleaners, nail salons, greengrocers, and ethnic restaurants. This process of revitalization is happening in older neighborhoods within cities and their suburbs across the nation—surely a positive outcome and an important contribution of these new populations. Coupled with the range of institutions and activities that immigrant populations build and promote—clubs, congregations, sports teams, festivals—this revitalization not only has enriched urban life in both the old and new gateways but has also provided centers for the construction of community that are different from the more traditional ethnic enclaves of earlier waves of immigration. It is no accident that many of the authors in this book have looked to new models of integration such as heterolocalism or polynucleated settlement to characterize what is going on in twenty-first-century gateways.

New Hispanic populations also increasingly settle in the suburbs. Overall the Hispanic population in the United States grew 16 percent between 2000 and 2004.[40] Those with lower skills are choosing rapidly growing parts of the country such as Charlotte, Las Vegas, and Phoenix to seek jobs in retail, services, and construction. Higher-skilled Latino migrants are following the same professional opportunities that attract whites and other skilled immigrants, gravitating to larger cities where they are attracted by opportunities for professional-class employment and an improved lifestyle. Demographer William Frey found that the earliest centers of Hispanic settlement have become less important today in favor of more suburban locations.[41] For example, the heavily suburban Riverside-San Bernardino metropolitan area showed larger gains in its Spanish-speaking population between 2000 and 2004 than did Los Angeles. Likewise, cities such as Washington and Atlanta with strong employment markets continue to attract large numbers of Hispanic settlers.

Conclusion

The ongoing spatial deconcentration and dispersal of residential and commercial land use and economic activities in U.S. metropolitan areas continue to reshape the American metropolis during the first decade of the twenty-first century. The impacts and imprints of improved transportation and communication technologies, higher rents in gentrified parts of the downtown, intensified economic activities away from the central city, and the construction of new housing in both inner and outer suburbs are contributing to the expansion of the outer city in almost every part of the country. As this chapter has demonstrated, American suburbs are now home to immigrants and their children from many parts of the world. Unlike more traditional ethnic enclaves of the past that were located in dense central cities, the majority of these newcomers are building their new lives in the suburbs even during their earliest years of settlement.

The chapters that follow offer a series of rich case studies analyzing how immigrants are constructing new communities in the suburbs of nine metropolitan areas. This set of comparative case studies also provides evidence of some of the ways each of these distinctive places is receiving immigrants in the context of our evolving suburban immigrant nation.

Notes

1. Peter O. Muller, *Contemporary Suburban America* (Englewood Cliffs, N.J.: Prentice-Hall, 1981), p. 6.

2. Andrew M. Hamer, "Perspectives on Urban Atlanta," *Atlanta Economic Review* 28 (1978): 6.

3. See, for example, Muller, *Contemporary Suburban America*; John S. Adams, "Residential Structure of Midwestern Cities," *Annals of the Association of American Geographers* 60 (1970): 37–62; and J. E. Vance Jr., *Geography and Urban Evolution in the San Francisco Bay Area* (Institute of Governmental Studies, University of California Press, 1964).

4. Robert E. Park, Ernest W. Burgess, and Roderick D. McKenzie, eds., *The City* (University of Chicago Press, 1925); P. F. Cressey, "Population Succession in Chicago, 1898–1930," *American Journal of Sociology* 64 (1938): 364–74; David Ward, "The Emergence of Central Immigrant Ghettoes in American Cities: 1840–1920," *Annals of the Association of American Geographers* 58 (1968): 343–59.

5. Marc Clapson, *Suburban Century: Social Change and Urban Growth in England and the USA* (Oxford, U.K.: Berg Publishers, 2003), p. 25.

6. Howard P. Chudacoff, *Major Problems in American Urban History* (Lexington, Mass.: D.C. Heath, 1994), pp. 351–6.

7. James J. Flink, *The Automobile Age* (MIT Press, 1988), pp. 368–73; Dolores Hayden, *Building Suburbia: Green Fields and Urban Growth, 1820–2000* (New York: Pantheon Books, 2003), p. 165.

8. Helen Leavitt, *Superhighway–Superhoax* (Garden City, N.J.: Doubleday, 1970), pp. 187–8.

9. Mark H. Rose, *Interstate: Express Highway Politics, 1939–1989,* rev. ed. (University of Tennessee Press, 1990), p. 116.

10. Hayden, *Building Suburbia,* p. 167.

11. "Up from the Potato Fields," *Time,* July 3, 1950, pp. 67–8, 72.

12. See, for example, John Keats, *The Crack in the Picture Window* (Boston: Houghton Mifflin, 1957); James Howard Kuntsler, *The Geography of Nowhere* (New York: Simon and Schuster, 1993); and Lewis Mumford, *The City in History* (New York: Harcourt, Brace, and World, 1961).

13. Dolores Hayden, *Building Suburbia,* p. 135

14. Kenneth Jackson, *Crabgrass Frontier: The Suburbanization of the United States* (Oxford University Press, 1985), p. 241.

15. Herbert Gans, *People and Plans: Essays on Urban Problems and Solutions* (New York: Basic Books, 1968), p. 138.
16. International Council of Shopping Centers (2002) (www.icsc.com).
17. T. A. Hartshorn and P. O. Muller, "Suburban Downtowns and the Transformation of Metropolitan Atlanta's Business Landscape," *Urban Geography* 10 (1989): 375–95.
18. Muller, *Contemporary Suburban America,* p. 55.
19. Joel Garreau, *Edge City: Life on the New Frontier* (New York: Doubleday, 1991).
20. Robert Lang, *Edgeless Cities: Exploring the Elusive Metropolis* (Brookings, 2003).
21. Pierce Lewis, "The Galactic Metropolis," in *Beyond the Urban Fringe: Land Use Issues in Nonmetropolitan America,* edited by Rutherford H. Platt and George Macinko (University of Minnesota Press, 1980), pp. 23–49.
22. Peter Wolf, *Hot Towns: The Future of the Fastest Growing Communities in America* (Rutgers University Press, 1999); Joel Kotkin, *The New Digital Geography: How the Digital Revolution Is Reshaping the American Landscape* (New York: Random House, 2000).
23. U.S. Census Bureau, Population Estimates Program (www.census.gov/popest/counties/ and www.census.gov/popest/cities/).
24. Robert E. Lang and Patrick A. Simmons, "'Boomburbs': The Emergence of Large, Fast-Growing Suburban Cities," in *Redefining Urban and Suburban America,* vol. 1, edited by Bruce Katz and Robert E. Lang (Brookings, 2003), pp. 117–36.
25. Robert Fishman, *Bourgeois Utopias: The Rise and Fall of Suburbia* (New York: Basic Books, 1987), p. 25.
26. William H. Lucy and David L. Phillips, "Suburbs: Patterns of Growth and Decline," in *Redefining Urban and Suburban America,* vol. I, edited by Katz and Lang, p. 119.
27. Ibid., p. 120.
28. Robert Puentes and David Warren, "One-Fifth of America: A Comprehensive Guide to America's First Suburbs," Brookings, 2006.
29. Audrey Singer, "The Rise of New Immigrant Gateways: Historical Flows, Recent Settlement Trends," in *Redefining Urban and Suburban America: Evidence from Census 2000,* vol. 2, edited by Alan Berube, Bruce Katz, and Robert E. Lang (Brookings, 2004), p. 19.
30. Personal interview with Nico Larco, University of Oregon, Department of Architecture, based on his findings from the American Housing Survey, 2000.
31. Min Zhou and C. L. Bankston, *Growing Up American: How Vietnamese Children Adapt to Life in the United States* (New York: Russell Sage Foundation, 1998); Susan W. Hardwick and James E. Meacham, "Heterolocalism, Networks of Ethnicity, and Refugee Communities in the Pacific Northwest: The Portland Story," *Professional Geographer* 57 (2005): 539–57.
32. Alejandro Portes and Ruben G. Rumbaut, *Immigrant America: A Portrait* (University of California Press, 1996).
33. Wei Li, ed., *From Urban Enclave to Ethnic Suburb: New Asian Communities in Pacific Rim Countries* (University of Hawai'i Press, 2006); Wei Li, "Anatomy of a

New Ethnic Settlement: Chinese Ethnoburbs in Los Angeles," *Urban Studies* 35 (1998): 479–501.

34. Richard D. Alba and others, "Immigrant Groups in the Suburbs: A Reexamination of Suburbanization and Spatial Assimilation," *American Sociological Review* 64 (1999): 450.

35. John R. Logan, "The New Ethnic Enclaves in America's Suburbs" (Lewis Mumford Center for Comparative Urban and Regional Research, University of Albany, 2002).

36. Emily Skop and Wei Li, "From Ghetto to the Invisiburb: Shifting Patterns of Immigrant Settlement in Contemporary America," in *Multicultural Geographies: Persistence and Change in U.S. Racial/Ethnic Patterns,* edited by John W. Frazier and Florence Margai (New York: Academic Press, 2003), p. 118.

37. Wilbur Zelinsky and Barrett A. Lee, "Heterolocalism: An Alternative Model of the Sociospatial Behaviour of Immigrant Ethnic Communities," *International Journal of Population Geography* 4 (1998): 1–18.

38. Wilbur Zelinsky, *The Enigma of Ethnicity: Another American Dilemma* (University of Iowa Press, 2001).

39. See, for example, Chan Kok Bun and Ong Jin Hui, "The Many Faces of Immigrant Entrepreneurship," in *The Cambridge Survey of World Migration,* edited by Robin Cohen, pp. 523–31 (Cambridge University Press, 1995); Robert Kloosterman and Jan Rath, *Immigrant Entrepreneurs: Venturing Abroad in the Age of Globalization* (Oxford: Berg, 2003); and Ivan Light and Parminder Bhachu, eds., *Immigration and Entrepreneurship: Culture, Capital, and Ethnic Networks* (New Brunswick, N.J.: Transaction Books, 1993).

40. William H. Frey, *Diversity Spreads Out: Metropolitan Shifts in Hispanic, Asian, and Black Populations since 2000* (Brookings, Living Cities Census Series, 2006), p. 7.

41. William H. Frey, "Melting Pot Suburbs: A Study of Suburban Diversity," in *Redefining Urban and Suburban America: Evidence from Census 2000,* vol. 1, edited by Bruce Katz and Robert E. Lang (Brookings 2003), p. 170.

PART II

Emerging Gateways: The Leading Edge of Change

3

"Big D"

Incorporating New Immigrants in a Sunbelt Suburban Metropolis

CAROLINE B. BRETTELL

Texas is home to three of the ten largest cities in the United States: Houston (ranked fourth-largest in 2005), San Antonio (ranked eighth), and Dallas (ranked ninth). Unlike Houston and San Antonio, the proportion of Hispanics in the city of Dallas was small before 1980—4 percent of the total population in 1960 and 7.6 percent in 1970. Yet by 1990 Hispanics constituted nearly one-fifth of the population in the central city, and a decade later they represented more than one-third (table 3-1). By contrast, between 1960 and 2000, the African American population in the city declined moderately, and the non-Hispanic white population fell more dramatically. Indeed, had the overall increase in the number of Hispanics not been so significant, the city of Dallas would have lost population during the 1990s. Much of this growth in the Hispanic population was caused by immigration, both legal and undocumented. Overall, the foreign-born population in Dallas doubled between 1990 and 2000.

During this same decade, the Dallas suburbs exploded. Although some of this expansion was the result of internal migration, locally and nationally, it was also the result of the move of the foreign-born from Asia,

This research was supported by the Cultural Anthropology Program of the National Science Foundation (NSF/BCS 0003938). The co-principal investigators on the project were James F. Hollifield, Dennis Cordell, and Manuel Garcia y Griego. Some tables in this chapter were generated from survey data from 600 interviews across five different immigrant populations. Any opinions, findings, and conclusions or recommendations expressed in this chapter are those of the author and do not necessarily reflect the views of the National Science Foundation.

Table 3-1. Race-Ethnicity and Foreign-Born as Percentage of Total Population, Dallas Primary Metropolitan Statistical Area, Central City, and Suburbs, 1980–2000
Percent

Category	*Dallas PMSA*	*Dallas central city*	*Dallas PMSA suburbs*
White, non-Hispanic			
1980	73.4	61.5	87.2
1990	67.6	52.3	80.6
2000[a]	56.2	38.3	69.0
Black, non-Hispanic			
1980	16.1	25.4	5.3
1990	15.5	25.1	7.3
2000[a]	15.3	23.1	9.7
Asian			
1980	0.9	0.9	0.9
1990	2.5	2.5	2.5
2000	4.4	3.8	4.9
Hispanic (all races)			
1980	8.9	11.4	5.9
1990	14.0	19.7	9.2
2000	23.0	33.9	15.3
Foreign-born			
1980	4.5	6.1	3.0
1990	8.8	12.5	5.8
2000	16.8	24.4	11.7

Source: U.S. Census Bureau, *Census of Population 2000.*

a. For the 2000 data, only those persons identifying themselves as "White alone" and "Black or African American alone" are categorized as "White, non-Hispanic" and "Black, non-Hispanic," respectively.

Africa, and Latin America into suburban and exurban areas. The racial and ethnic composition of suburbia changed as dramatically as that of the central city during the last two decades of the twentieth century.

This chapter explores the impact of this rapidly changing composition of the urban and suburban populations in the Dallas-Fort Worth (DFW) Metropolitan Statistical Area (MSA) (map 3-1). The analysis draws on U.S. decennial census data from 1970 to 2000, the 2005 American Community Survey, ethnographic field research with five different immigrant populations (Mexicans, Salvadorans, Vietnamese, Asian Indians, and Nigerians), interviews with local community leaders, and media reports. This chapter focuses on the four central counties (Dallas, Collin, Denton, and Tarrant) that are at the heart of the Dallas-Fort Worth metroplex, and two local

Map 3-1. Dallas-Fort Worth-Arlington (DFW), Metropolitan Statistical Area, 2003

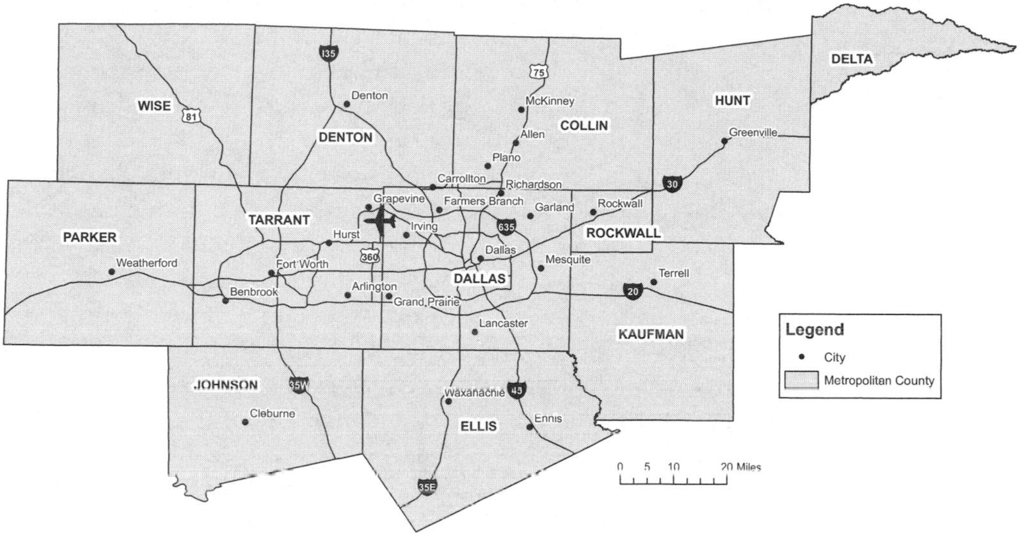

Source: U.S. Census Bureau, *Census of Population 2000*, SF3.

governments that took two different approaches to the rapid influx of newcomers.[1] The metroplex encompasses several suburban communities that have increasingly diversified since 1990. Specifically, the chapter explores how and why Dallas moved so rapidly from a biracial to a multiethnic metropolis; the patterns of urban and suburban settlement of different foreign-born populations; the characteristics of these newcomers—their immigration status and reasons for moving to the DFW metroplex; how these newcomers have claimed space and made place, particularly in suburban contexts; and how local suburban governments and other metropolitan institutions have responded to growing diversity.

From Biracial City to Multiethnic Suburban Metropolis

The city of Dallas was founded by John Neely Bryan in the early 1840s on a crossing of the Trinity River, a largely unnavigable river. By 1846 Dallas County was organized and the town was surveyed and platted; it was chartered in 1856. Early residents were farmers, many migrating to the area from states to the east—Alabama, Georgia, Missouri, and Tennessee. The city grew quickly, and by 1880 the population stood at more than 10,000, while the population of Dallas County had reached slightly more than

30,000. This growth was fueled by the cotton industry and the railroad. Cotton brought slaves who, in 1860, constituted 12 percent of the population.

The expansion of the railroad, which arrived in Dallas in 1872, led to further population growth, including the arrival of African American freedmen who came to the city to work as boilermen, trackmen, engineers, and common laborers.[2] In 1880 "Negroes" composed 19 percent of the Dallas population, and the foreign-born, largely of European ancestry, composed 12.8 percent. By 1910 Dallas had become a dominant city in north Texas, with a larger population and twice as many manufacturing firms as neighboring Fort Worth. The boomtown image was solidified in 1914 when a branch of the Federal Reserve was established.[3] During the first three decades of the twentieth century, individuals born in Mexico who were not "native indigenous" were included in the foreign-born category. Although their numbers were larger than any of the other foreign-born populations, the Mexican population was not sizable. In 1920 the U.S. census counted 3,378 Mexicans in the city of Dallas, most of whom were living in atrocious conditions.

Following World War II, Dallas became one of the fastest growing Sun Belt cities in the United States, offering jobs in aviation and electronics among other industries. Between 1940 and 1960 the city population more than doubled, to just under 680,000. In 1970 only 2 percent of the population was foreign-born and the city was highly segregated.[4] White flight to the suburbs had begun to increase dramatically after 1960, leading to the development of inner-ring commuter suburbs such as Richardson and Garland. By the early 1970s the population of Richardson had grown to more than 50,000, and 40 percent of its housing stock was new.

Richardson was one of the first suburbs to attract Asian Indian and Chinese immigrants. Indeed, the offices of the India Association of North Texas, founded in 1963, as well as Taj Mahal Imports, the signature store for the Indian population in the metroplex and a center of community life, are located in Richardson.[5] By 1990 the community's foreign-born population was just under 10 percent, but by 2000 it composed 18.1 percent, more than one-third of whom had entered the United States between 1995 and 2000.

According to the Greater Dallas Chamber of Commerce, the Dallas area ranked first in the nation for employment growth in the 1990s, creating 760,600 new jobs. As Mary Odem reports in this volume, Atlanta, another emerging gateway city, was second. The Dallas economy was growing at 4.8 percent annually in the late 1990s, outpacing the national average. The total gross domestic product for the DFW metropolitan area passed

$250 billion in 2001.[6] Several important companies moved to the area in the 1990s, including ExxonMobil to Irving, and JC Penney to Plano. The telecom corridor to the north of the city expanded as companies such as Alcatel, Nortel, Electronic Data Systems (EDS), and Erikkson built major facilities in Dallas and Collin counties. Nokia and Verizon built offices in Irving, an inner-ring suburb just to the west of Dallas. In 2000 Dallas had more information sector jobs than all but two other U.S. cities.

Other characteristics that fueled the economic boom were the airport, a low population density compared with other large metropolitan areas, and a low relative cost of living.[7] Residents of the Dallas area were spending, on average, 20 percent of their income on housing, compared with more than 40 percent in San Francisco and New York. By 2000 the population of Dallas Fort Worth exceeded 5 million and the city of Dallas had reached 1.1 million. The advantageous employment and housing markets were instrumental in attracting a diverse foreign-born population to the DFW metroplex during the 1990s.

The DFW Metroplex: Urban and Suburban Settlement of the Foreign-Born

Table 3-2 shows the spatial distribution of new immigrant populations. In Dallas County (which includes the suburb of Garland and most of the older suburb of Richardson), the foreign-born population doubled between 1980 (when it was 5.1 percent of the total population) and 1990, and it almost doubled again in the next decade to reach one-fifth of the population in 2000, and nearly one-fourth by 2005.

Tarrant County (which includes the cities of Fort Worth and Arlington, soon to be the new home of the Dallas Cowboys football stadium) experienced a similar doubling in the foreign-born population in the 1990s, and, on the basis of the proportion of foreign-born in 2005, this trend will likely continue through the first decade of the current century.

The change in suburban Collin County, which contains the very northern part of Richardson, was even more dramatic. There the foreign-born population was 2.9 percent in 1980, but by 2000 it was 13.3 percent. In fact, Collin County was one of the fastest-growing suburban counties in the United States during the 1990s, with one-half of its housing stock built during the decade. These trends have continued during the first years of the current century, with the foreign-born reaching 16.6 percent of the population by 2005. Collin is the only county in the metroplex where the proportion of the Asian foreign-born has steadily increased between 1990 and

Table 3-2. Changes in Foreign-Born Population in Central DFW Metroplex Counties, 1990–2000

County	*Total population*	*Foreign-born as a percent of total population*	*Percent foreign-born from Asia*	*Percent foreign-born from Latin America*	*Percent foreign-born from Africa*
Collin					
1990	264,036	5.9	39.0	33.6	2.9
2000	491,675	13.3	43.7	34.9	3.7
2005	655,994	16.6	48.3	36.3	n.a.
Dallas					
1990	1,852,810	10.6	21.6	61.5	3.4
2000	2,218,899	20.9	16.4	74.8	3.7
2005	2,267,080	24.6	15.0	78.1	n.a.
Denton					
1990	273,525	5.4	40.2	35.8	4.4
2000	432,976	9.4	34.2	50.1	3.1
2005	544,511	13.1	34.5	51.7	n.a.
Tarrant					
1990	1,170,103	6.8	29.0	51.3	3.4
2000	1,446,219	12.7	23.8	63.7	3.8
2005	1,595,715	15.0	20.5	67.7	n.a.

Source: U.S. Census Bureau, *Census of Population 2000;* U.S. Census Bureau, *American Community Survey 2005.*
n.a. = Not available.

2005. Finally, in more remote Denton County the foreign-born population has also risen steadily, with a particularly noteworthy increase in immigrants from Latin America during the 1990s.

Different immigrant groups are settling in different areas of the metroplex. In 2000 foreign-born Latin Americans outnumbered native-born Latin Americans only in Dallas County (51 percent). In Denton and Tarrant counties, the proportion of foreign-born Latin Americans is less than 40 percent; in Collin County it is 43 percent.

An examination of particular suburban places offers a more revealing and localized understanding of the settlement dynamics of the foreign-born. Unlike Houston and San Antonio, which incorporated neighboring suburbs into their greater metropolitan areas, the suburbs of Dallas have retained their autonomy. The DFW metroplex thus encompasses several suburban cities with populations in 2000 that exceeded 100,000. These cities include Garland, Grand Prairie, Irving, and Mesquite in Dallas

Table 3-3. Foreign-Born as Percentage of Total Population, Selected Suburban Places, 1970–2005

Place	*1970*	*1980*	*1990*	*2000*[a]	*2005*
Allen	n.a.	1.4	2.8	7.3 (43.3)	12.9
Arlington	1.9	3.9	7.6	15.3 (30.6)	17.2
Carrollton	1.7	5.9	11.4	19.9 (13.2)	26.4
Denton	1.3	5.7	7.1	11.2 (21.0)	14.0
Farmers Branch	1.6	5.2	13.6	25.1 (22.7)	n.a.
Frisco	n.a.	4.8	5.6	7.8 (26.6)	13.0
Garland	0.7	3.7	8.8	20.2 (28.3)	27.3
Grand Prairie	0.9	3.9	7.8	16.4 (31.6)	19.4
Grapevine	0.4	1.8	2.6	9.4 (23.6)	n.a.
Irving	1.1	4.2	12.6	26.4 (20.2)	33.0
Lewisville	0.7	2.1	4.8	12.7 (30.5)	18.0
McKinney	0.6	2.2	4.5	12.6 (16.9)	8.8
Mesquite	0.7	2.1	4.7	9.1 (36.5)	16.0
Plano	1.1	3.6	7.5	17.0 (35.7)	21.2
Richardson	1.7	4.9	9.8	18.8 (35.6)	21.3

Source: U.S. Census Bureau, *Census of Population 1970, 1980, 1990, 2000*; U.S. Census Bureau, *American Community Survey 2005*.

a. For 2000, the figures in parentheses represent the percentage of the foreign-born who are naturalized.

n.a. = Not available.

County; Arlington in Tarrant County; Plano in Collin County; and Carrollton in Denton County.

Table 3-3 shows that although those cities nearest the urban core (inner-ring suburbs) have some of the highest proportions of foreign-born (Farmers Branch, Garland, Irving, and Richardson), high proportions also exist in cities somewhat farther out that grew rapidly in the 1990s (Carrollton, Plano). The more remote, outer-ring suburbs (Allen, Denton, Frisco, Grapevine, Lewisville, and McKinney) are just beginning to witness increasing diversity. In most cases, however, the proportion of foreign-born grew quite significantly during the 1990s, no matter where the suburb was located in relation to the urban core. These growth trends, which have continued since 2000 except in McKinney, merit continued observation. Certainly some intriguing questions can be posed about why the pace of growth has varied and why some suburbs will continue to experience rapid growth in their foreign-born populations while others will not. Those where the rate of growth has continued apace during the first five years of the current decade are a combination of inner-ring (Garland, Irving, Mesquite) and outer-ring (Carrollton, Frisco, Lewisville) suburbs. The dynamism of local

Table 3-4. Distribution of Foreign-Born Chinese, Indians, Vietnamese, and Mexicans in Selected Suburban Places (as a Percentage of Total Foreign-Born in That Place)

	Foreign-born from			
Place	*China*	*India*	*Vietnam*	*Mexico*
Allen[a]	6.4	6.5	6.9	14.4
Arlington	4.3	3.2	14.3	44.3
Carrollton	1.9	9.9	8.6	37.8
Denton[b]	4.9	3.2	1.2	57.7
Farmers Branch[c]	0.7	1.1	4.8	58.3
Frisco	5.8	3.9	2.3	40.9
Garland	1.9	4.5	12.4	51.2
Grand Prairie	0.8	2.1	8.3	61.5
Grapevine	4.7	6.4	0.8	54.9
Irving[d]	2.1	8.5	2.7	44.1
Lewisville	2.2	6.9	3.9	53.2
McKinney	0.8	0.7	1.3	64.2
Mesquite	0.7	14.4	2.4	47.8
Plano	17.3	9.3	3.9	21.8
Richardson	12.9	9.7	8.2	21.9

Source: U.S. Census Bureau, *Census of Population 2000.*

a. The largest foreign-born population is Canadian.

b. Koreans outnumber Indians and Vietnamese in Denton.

c. Salvadorans are 17.5 percent of the foreign-born, and Koreans are larger than the Chinese and Indian populations.

d. Salvadorans are 11.8 percent of the foreign-born.

employment markets in suburban locations, lower-cost housing, the quality of schools, and improved transportation offer some explanation of these patterns, but the critical factors vary by suburban locality and by the major foreign-born populations attracted to particular areas.

Table 3-4 shows the concentration of foreign-born groups by various suburban communities. Although increasing diversity in all of these suburban places is largely the result of an expanding Hispanic (Mexican and Central American) immigrant population (something that may explain the variations in the pace of growth for the first five years of the current century), in some suburban places, the growth in the number of Asians is also noteworthy. Furthermore, in some of these places, the settlement patterns of Asians and Hispanics vary. For example, in the suburb of Irving, the large Mexican and Central American population, which includes a high proportion of Salvadorans (11.8 percent of the foreign-born in this city), lives in an older area closer to Dallas, while Indians, the largest Asian population, have settled further west along Highway 114, where many of the high-tech companies have built offices. In this part of Irving, dense rental and condominium housing has been built to accommodate the rapid demographic and economic growth. Similarly, in Plano, there is a division between east (where there are more Hispanics) and west (where there are more Asians). In Plano 22 percent of the foreign-born population is Mexican and 31 percent is Indian, Chinese, or Vietnamese. The proportion of foreign-born who are other than Mexican may have some impact on the proportion of naturalized citizens that were counted in 2000; that is, the naturalization rate may be higher in areas where there are higher proportions of Asian and other non-Hispanic populations among the foreign born. In general, Mexicans have the lowest naturalization rate of any major immigrant group in the United States.

Settlement Patterns of Mexicans

The settlement of Mexicans (map 3-2) is dense, widespread, and centered in and around the urban core. In 2000 immigrants from Mexico accounted for 71 percent of the foreign-born population in the city of Dallas, and 63 percent of the Mexicans in Dallas County lived in the city of Dallas itself. Another heavy concentration of Mexicans could be found in the midcities region between Dallas and Fort Worth south of Highway 183, one of two highways that pass by the Dallas-Fort Worth International Airport and connect the two cities. An even greater proportion of Mexicans were settled south of Interstate 30, which runs north of Arlington. Mexican settlement choices are influenced by the availability of low-cost housing and by kinship networks. The heavy concentration in south Dallas represents a legacy of segregation that still divides wealthy north Dallas from less wealthy south Dallas.

Several of the suburbs with higher median incomes have fewer Mexican foreign-born (Allen, Frisco, Plano, and Richardson). One interesting anomaly is McKinney, an outer-ring suburban city and the county seat of Collin County. McKinney has only recently been receiving the foreign-born, 64 percent of whom are Mexican. Nearly 70 percent of the total foreign-born population arrived in the 1990s. The median family income in McKinney, $72,133, is the sixth highest among the fifteen suburban places examined here. This suggests that McKinney may represent a new exurban pattern of simultaneous settlement of both high- and low-income immigrants, as well as native and foreign-born. Many of the lower-income Hispanic immigrants may be moving to the area for the ample jobs available in construction. Across from the McKinney courthouse is a day-labor site where contractors hire workers to help build the new homes that have been going

Map 3-2. Residential Distribution of Mexicans in the DFW Metro Area, 2000

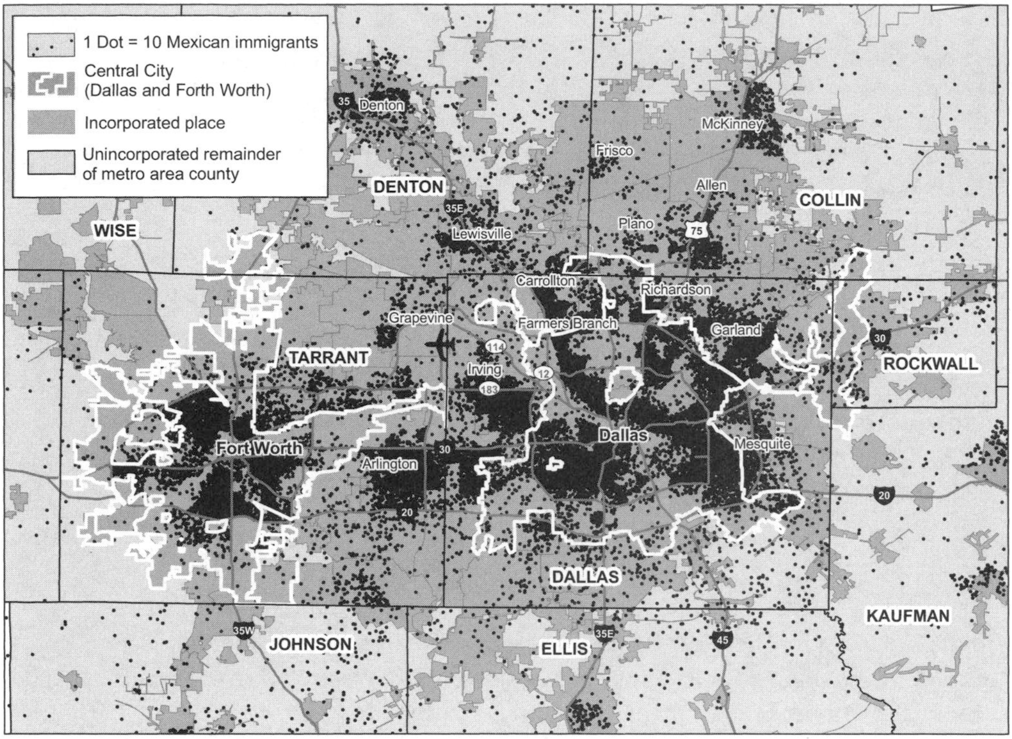

Source: U.S. Census Bureau, *Census of Population 2000*, SF3.

up at a rapid pace in the area. It is highly probable that some portion of these workers are undocumented immigrants from Mexico.

Settlement Patterns of Vietnamese

The Vietnamese first arrived in the area in the mid-1970s, but their population has recently been expanding. During the 1990s the foreign-born Vietnamese grew by 132 percent. In 2000 they concentrated in two areas (map 3-3). One is in Garland, an older inner-ring suburb that developed in the 1970s. Here the Vietnamese constituted 12 percent of the total foreign-born population in 2000. They have built a community center where first-generation Vietnamese immigrants—those with strong anticommunist sentiments—gather. Two important strip shopping malls catering to Vietnamese customers (and anchored by large food stores selling Vietnamese products) are also in this area. These strip malls along Walnut Street are some of the best evidence of place-making among suburban immigrants.[8]

Map 3-3. Residential Distribution of Vietnamese in the DFW Metro Area, 2000

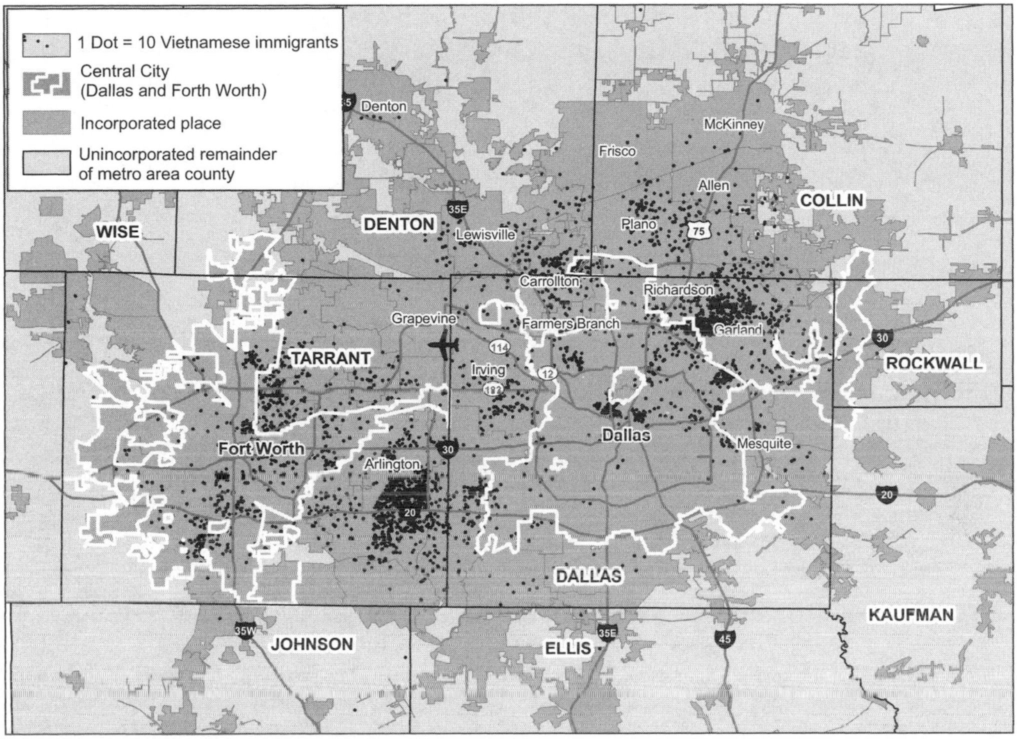

Source: U.S. Census Bureau, *Census of Population 2000,* SF3.

The other significant Vietnamese settlement is in South Arlington, a midcity with a lower cost of living and affordable housing. By contrast with some of the other large Asian groups in the Dallas area, the Vietnamese, who continued to arrive under refugee status in the 1990s, have lower income and lower human capital and are more insular, as reflected in their settlement patterns. In Arlington the Vietnamese made up 14 percent of the foreign-born population in 2000. It is certainly reasonable to conclude that the high rates of naturalization in these two cities (approaching or exceeding 30 percent) might be partly explained by the high proportion of Vietnamese among the foreign-born in these two communities. Unlike other immigrant populations, the Vietnamese, as refugees, cannot or do not wish to return to Vietnam and hence become citizens at a high rate. According to U.S. Census data for 2000, 44 percent of Vietnamese had become American citizens, the highest rate for all Asian immigrant populations.[9]

The proportion of Vietnamese living in the wealthier northern suburbs is small. Only 4 percent of the foreign-born in Plano is Vietnamese (compared with 17 percent for Chinese and 9 percent for Indians, both of whom have higher human capital). The Vietnamese tend to settle in suburbs with high proportions of Mexican immigrants (Garland and Grand Prairie, for example). Finally, many Vietnamese reside in the "Little Asia" area of East Dallas, where many of the initial refugee generation (Cambodians as well as Vietnamese) were settled and where they have remained, although recently this area has been undergoing gentrification.[10] The Vietnamese in 2000 were 2 percent of the foreign-born population of Dallas County, and 37 percent of this Dallas County population lived in the city of Dallas itself.

Indian Settlement Patterns

Indians (map 3-4), one of the fastest-growing minorities in the United States, are largely settled in the suburbs in a semicircle north of Dallas, from Highway 114, north of Irving in the west, through Carrollton and Lewisville in the northwest, to Plano in the north, and to Richardson and Garland in the east. Slightly more than one-half of all Indians in the area lived in Dallas County in 2000, which includes Richardson, where some of the first Indians who came to the area settled. As mentioned earlier, the major grocery store for this community, Taj Mahal Imports, is in Richardson on Beltline just west of Highway 75. It too is located in a strip shopping mall that has become a gathering point for a highly residentially dispersed population.[11]

Of those Indians living in Dallas County (which also includes Irving), only 40 percent lived in the city of Dallas itself. Nearly 20 percent of Indians lived in suburban Collin County (which includes Plano) in 2000. This settlement pattern reflects the higher mean income of Indians and their concentration in the high-tech sector. They live near where they work; EDS, Texas Instruments, and the headquarters of several major telecommunications companies are all to the north or in Irving near Las Colinas. Equally important to Indian families are the schools. Plano, for example, has one of the best public school systems in the DFW area.

A secondary node for Indian settlement is in Mesquite, a close-in suburban city in southeastern Dallas County. Many Indian Christians from the state of Kerala live here, and this is where the offices of the Kerala Association are located. The migration from Kerala has particular characteristics, in that it is often led by women, a high proportion of whom are nurses recruited by hospitals in the developed world.[12] These families were among

Map 3-4. Residential Distribution of Asian Indians in the DFW Metro Area, 2000

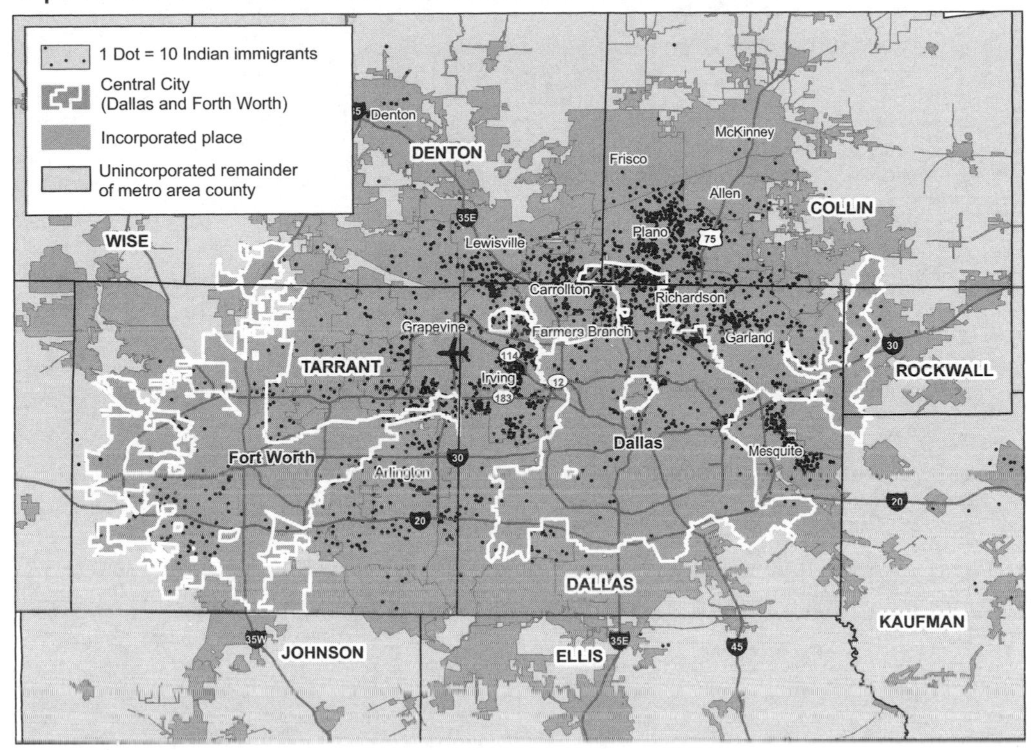

Source: U.S. Census Bureau, *Census of Population 2000*, SF3.

some of the early arrivals of Indians in Dallas and, because they are South Indians and often of darker complexion, they faced discrimination that made it difficult for them to settle in those early years in the whiter, northern suburbs. In addition, their incomes, at least initially, made it imperative to look for less expensive housing. Finally, being near the hospitals, most of which at the time were in the city of Dallas itself (Parkland, Baylor), was also an important consideration.

The pattern of Indian settlement in the metroplex offers an excellent example of what Wilbur Zelinsky and Barrett Lee have labeled "heterolocalism."[13] They are residentially dispersed and yet find ways to create community through place-making institutions, enterprises, and public events, such as India Nite held in an auditorium on the campus of Southern Methodist University or the Anand Bazaar, held every August at the Lone Star Park race track west of Dallas.[14]

Map 3-5. Residential Distribution of Salvadorans in the DFW Metro Area, 2000

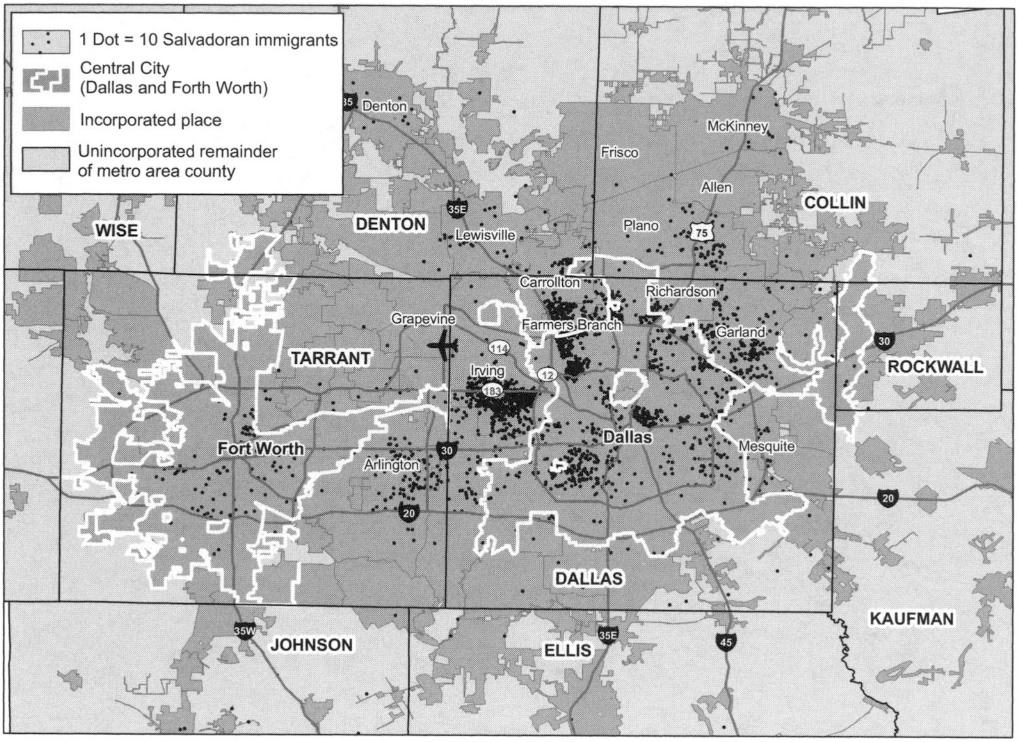

Source: U.S. Census Bureau, *Census of Population 2000,* SF3.

Salvadoran Settlement Patterns

Salvadorans (map 3-5), a population that grew by 172 percent during the 1990s to become the second-largest Hispanic group in the Dallas area, are concentrated in three inner-ring suburbs: Irving, Farmers Branch, and Garland, which are also areas of Mexican suburban settlement. In addition, and similar to Mexicans, Salvadorans have settled within the city of Dallas itself. Salvadorans made up 3.6 percent of the foreign-born in Dallas in 2000, and 47 percent of the Salvadorans in Dallas County resided in the city of Dallas. Indeed, a small but dense group of Salvadorans has settled in East Dallas, a very low-income area near some of the organizations that work with refugee resettlement and that also reach out to Salvadorans escaping political turmoil in their country. Many Salvadorans in the area are currently under Temporary Protected Status, which allows them to remain in and work legally in the United States. The Salvadoran consulate

Map 3-6. Residential Distribution of Nigerians in the DFW Metro Area, 2000

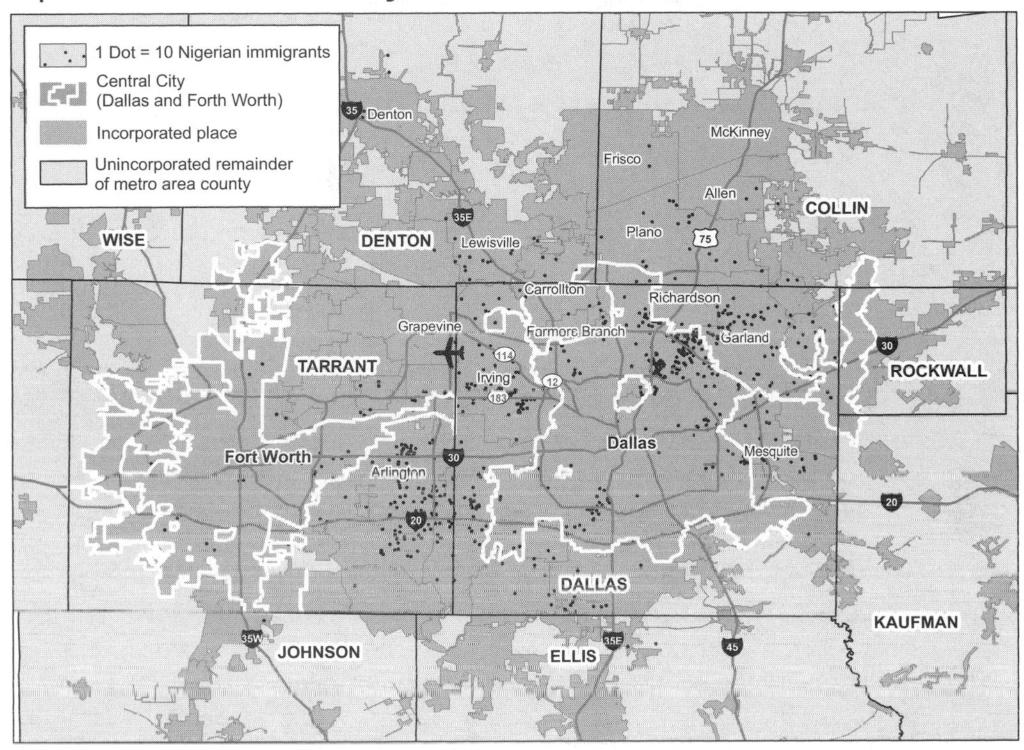

Source: U.S. Census Bureau, *Census of Population 2000*, SF3.

is in the heart of the city, not far from the inner-ring suburban nodes of settlement for this population. Like the Vietnamese, kinship and ethnic ties appear to provide the foundation for more clustered residential patterns, particularly compared with Indians.

Nigerian Settlement Patterns

The Nigerians (map 3-6) constitute a much smaller population, although the largest of the African groups settled in the DFW metroplex. Texas itself was the top state of settlement for Nigerians in 2000. Seventy-one percent of Nigerians in the DFW metroplex live in Dallas County, a proportion as high as the Mexicans, which may speak to the race issues that immigrants from Africa must confront in urban and suburban America. Of those in Dallas County, 49 percent live in the city of Dallas, especially in the near northeast just east of Highway 75. In this area, there is a market that caters to Nigerians and a popular restaurant. The area has ample rental housing and is also home to African Americans.

Comparing Five Different Immigrant Populations

Part of the research in the DFW metroplex involved interviews with slightly more than 600 immigrants in these five immigrant populations residing in the four central counties.[15] The respondents were not chosen randomly, and therefore generalizations are impossible from these results. However, the results do reveal some interesting patterns and comparisons.

These immigrants have entered the United States under very different circumstances. We asked respondents about immigration status at initial entry, about changes in immigration status, and about current status. The majority of Salvadorans (71 percent) and Mexicans (56 percent) entered as undocumented workers. Almost 15 percent of the Mexicans entered initially on a tourist visa and 8 percent entered with green cards. More than three-quarters of the Vietnamese (76 percent) entered as refugees. Forty-three percent of Indians entered initially on F-1 student visas, and another 22 percent with green cards. In addition, 9 percent of Indians entered with H-1B temporary worker visas, and 6 percent entered as H-4 dependents of H-1B visa holders. The Nigerians have entry patterns similar to the Indians, with 44 percent entering on student visas and 18 percent with green cards (including a few who received their green cards through the diversity lottery).[16] However, 19 percent of Nigerians said that they initially entered the United States on tourist visas. Only one Nigerian and no Indians in this sample entered without documentation.

Among the Vietnamese, 85 percent had become citizens of the United States, as had 58 percent of Nigerians and 45 percent of Indians. This figure drops to 22 percent for Salvadorans and 21 percent for Mexicans. Fewer Salvadorans (14 percent) than Mexicans (41 percent) were undocumented at the time of the interview because Salvadorans have been able to take advantage of Temporary Protected Status (25 percent of those interviewed). All groups have taken advantage of legalizing (that is, becoming a legal permanent resident), although fewer Mexicans (19 percent) were currently in this status than were Salvadorans (29 percent), Indians (25 percent), and Nigerians (27 percent). The number is low for Vietnamese (11 percent) because they have an extremely high rate of naturalization. Also noteworthy is the continued importance of the H1-B skilled worker visa as a mode of entry for Indians (15 percent).

We asked these individuals their reasons for migration and for coming to the DFW area. The responses were open-ended and then coded into categories. Among the men, Mexicans and Salvadorans (the groups with the least education and income) came primarily for work opportunities (59 percent and 43 percent, respectively), although 27 percent of the Salvadorans cited political turmoil as the reason for their departure. More than 50 percent of Nigerians and Indians (those with higher education and income) cited education as the major reason for coming to the United States initially (52 percent and 57 percent, respectively). Not surprisingly, the largest proportion of Vietnamese (42 percent) cited political reasons for their migration, followed by those who came with their parents (who were probably emigrating for political reasons) as young children (20 percent).

The female respondents reported slightly different reasons, reflecting women's greater tendency to emigrate as dependents among at least some immigrant populations. Although "work and opportunity" constitutes the largest proportion of responses for Mexican and Salvadoran women (35 percent and 29 percent, respectively), joining family is also important. Twenty-two percent of Mexican, 16 percent of Salvadoran, 15 percent of Indian, and 25 percent of Nigerian women noted this reason. Almost one-quarter of Salvadoran women cited political reasons, as did slightly more than one third of Vietnamese women. Nearly one-third of Vietnamese women also said they were accompanying parents, again suggesting that they entered the United States as young children. For Indian women, slightly more than one-quarter mentioned marriage as the reason for their emigration, reflecting a common pattern of men emigrating first and at some point returning to India to marry and bring their bride back to America.

The DFW metroplex was not always the first place of residence for these immigrants. Although a majority of Mexicans, Salvadorans, and Vietnamese moved immediately to the Dallas-Fort Worth area, fewer Indians and Nigerians came to DFW first. Only 18 percent of Indian males, for example, moved initially to Dallas, whereas 84 percent of Salvadorans did so (table 3-5). Most Mexicans and Salvadorans (male and female) said they chose DFW because they already had family in the area. The Mexican males who moved to DFW later came primarily because they heard it was a good place to find a job—something that reflects a growing pattern of secondary migration for Hispanics across the United States. The majority of Indian males move to DFW after living elsewhere in the United States because they were offered a job. Their original place of settlement was generally determined by where they were admitted to school or where they

Table 3-5. Initial Place of Residence in the United States

Country of origin	Percentage reporting Dallas-Fort Worth as initial U.S. residence: Males	Females
Mexico	63	75
Salvador	84	84
India	18	29
Vietnam	52	56
Nigeria	47	35

Source: Data collected as part of a research project on New Immigrants in the Dallas-Fort Worth Metropolitan Area, supported by the Cultural Anthropology Program of the National Science Foundation.

had family. The place of initial residence for Indian females was generally influenced by family (66 percent), but the responses were more varied with regard to moving to DFW: one-third said they moved for work (this could include their husbands' work), one-fourth for family reasons, and a little more than 10 percent for school or education. For Vietnamese, family contacts (36 percent of males and 39 percent of females, including children, for whom the place of initial settlement was determined by someone else) were common reasons for coming directly to DFW. Similar percentages (37 percent of males and 29 percent of females) noted that their initial place of residence was largely influenced by church or refugee organizations. For those who had not initially settled in the DFW metroplex, roughly equal numbers were drawn here by work and job opportunities and by family. For nearly half of Nigerian males (47 percent), the reason for moving directly to DFW was family, followed by where they were admitted to school (35 percent). The comparable proportions for Nigerian women are 55 percent (family considerations) and 20 percent (education). Most Nigerian men who had not settled initially in the DFW area were drawn there by job opportunities, while the majority of Nigerian women came for family reasons.

Kinship networks are clearly significant in determining where immigrants finally settle in the United States, but employment opportunities are also important. Although our interviews show that individuals change jobs quite frequently, table 3-6 shows immigrants' occupation at the time of the interview. Although the interviewees were not a representative random sample, the sample does indicate broad and not unexpected patterns in local labor market incorporation across different groups. Almost 20 percent of males in the two Hispanic populations reported working in the

Table 3-6. Current Occupation, as Percentage of Total for Each Ethnic Group, by Sex in the NSF Study Sample

Occupation[a]	*Mexicans*	*Salvadorans*	*Indians*	*Vietnamese*	*Nigerians*
Males					
Managers/small business owners	11.0	28.6	16.7	23.7	31.3
Professional and related occupations	5.5	7.1	61.7	42.4	30.0
Service	19.3	19.8	3.3	5.1	8.8
Sales and related occupations	2.8	5.4	1.7	3.4	2.5
Office and administrative support	0.9	1.8	0.0	3.4	0.0
Construction and extraction	29.4	7.1	0.0	0.0	0.0
Installation, maintenance, repair	8.3	10.7	0.0	0.0	0.0
Production, transport, materials moving	14.7	10.7	0.0	1.7	3.8
Military-specific	0.0	0.0	0.0	1.7	2.5
Unemployed/laid off	0.9	1.8	6.7	5.1	0.0
Economically inactive student	3.7	5.4	1.7	8.5	10.0
Economically inactive disabled and other	0.0	0.0	3.3	3.4	0.0
Retired	0.9	0.0	5.0	0.0	2.5
Student or part-time worker	2.8	1.8	0.0	1.7	8.8
Females					
Managers/small business owners	7.1	15.9	12.2	12.2	25.0
Professional and related occupations	13.1	11.4	31.7	36.6	20.0
Service	23.2	36.4	2.4	17.1	25.0
Sales and related occupations	7.1	4.5	2.4	2.4	0.0
Office and administrative support	4.0	0.0	0.0	14.6	5.0
Installation, maintenance, repair	1.0	0.0	0.0	0.0	0.0
Production, transport, material moving	4.0	13.6	0.0	7.3	0.0
Unemployed/laid off	4.0	6.8	7.3	2.4	0.0
Economically inactive housewife	31.3	4.5	31.7	2.4	5.0
Economically inactive student	1.0	2.3	7.3	2.4	10.0
Economically inactive disabled and other	0.0	0.0	2.4	0.0	0.0
Retired	0.0	0.0	0.0	0.0	0.0
Student or part-time worker	3.0	2.3	2.4	0.0	8.8

Source: Data collected as part of a research project on New Immigrants in the Dallas-Fort Worth Metropolitan Area, supported by the Cultural Anthropology Program of the National Science Foundation.

a. These occupational categories are adapted from U.S. Census categories. Professional services such as lawyer, doctor, and accountant are distinguished here from unskilled services such as domestic help, landscaping. Other categories were created to adapt to the survey population—for example, the inclusion of a category of student or part-time worker. "Current occupation" was occupation at the time of survey interview.

service sector, while the proportions of the other three groups working in this sector were small. Almost two-thirds of Indian males and slightly more than two-fifths of Vietnamese males were professionals. Small business owners and managers existed in all groups, but the proportion was small for Indians, and smaller still for Mexicans. Salvadorans, by contrast, seem to have some success in this area. Among Mexican males, 30 percent report working in construction. Indeed, as table 3-6 indicates, certain labor market sectors heavily involved the two Hispanic populations but employed no one from the other populations.

Nearly one-third of Mexican and Indian female respondents were housewives. Approximately one-third of Indian and Vietnamese females were professionals, significantly higher than the other groups. The total number of Nigerian female respondents was small (twenty), but they tended to be in small business, professional activities, or service activities. The high proportion of Salvadoran women in service activities is also worth noting.

Responses to Increasing Diversity: On the Road to a Multicultural Suburban Municipality

How have suburban communities in the DFW metroplex responded to the rapid growth in their foreign-born populations during the 1990s? I address this question by exploring one suburban place, the city of Plano in Collin County, and then comparing it briefly to a second suburban place, Farmers Branch, which has been much in the news since the fall of 2006.[17] In 1960 the population of Plano was 3,695, but by 1970 it had reached 17, 872, and by 1980, 72,000. In the late 1980s and early 1990s, several important corporations moved to Plano, including Frito-Lay and JC Penney. Other corporations that have made Plano their headquarters are Electronic Data Systems and Dr. Pepper/Seven-Up. Semiconductor and telecommunications companies such as Alcatel and Raytheon also have offices in the community. By 2000 the total population of Plano was 220,030. This population was 78 percent white, 5 percent African American, 10 percent Asian, and 10 percent Hispanic and Latino. In 2000, 17.1 percent of the population was foreign-born.

In an interview in October 2005, Plano Mayor Pat Evans observed that the growth of the immigrant population had taken Plano by surprise because it was very quick, but also understandable given the rapid increase in the number of companies that had moved into the area. "The Asian explosion was suddenly apparent," she said, "because there were families on your street and kids in your schools. Before their arrival, the largest diversity came from illegal workers and the stable black population." Evans said she ran her election campaign with the goal of embracing and building on the new diversity. For example, she drew on the support of a range of Muslim groups, making contacts and speaking at the Ismaeli cultural center, the new Shia Center, and at a Sunni mosque. She was forced to learn about and be mindful of the divisions within immigrant communities, such as the political divisions between Taiwanese and mainland Chinese. As she said, they all wanted her to be on *their* side. "I talked to them about not fighting foreign wars here and instead leaving the baggage they bring with them behind and focusing on their lives here, what they are experiencing here, what Plano can do for them and what they can do for Plano. I got them thinking about being pro-Plano and this is now the stand they take." In a post–9/11 world, the mayor made sure that the major instruments of government, particularly the police, worked closely with contacts in these communities, talking to them in their neighborhoods to build trust and to ensure that they were not afraid to report crimes regardless of their legal status. The Plano chief of police has made an effort to recruit Asian police officers, although with little success. In the eyes of Asian residents, the mayor suggested, policing "is not an honorable profession."

Plano sponsors a free Citizens Academy that teaches residents about the inner workings of local government. Several immigrants have participated in this academy. When asked what she thought the city and the participants got out of this program, the mayor replied, "More involved citizens who are sympathetic to what it takes to run a city. They are better ambassadors. They become more proud of their city. They also give good feedback and good ideas. They are real boosters. You create a devoted constituency through this. . . . It makes city government accessible to people. A lot of them do not think of city government as a service and that is what we want them to learn." She went on to say that from participants in the program, the city can identify individuals to serve on local boards and commissions. In Plano first-generation immigrants serve on the library board, the park board, and the senior citizens advisory committee. One Vietnamese man who has participated in the Citizens Academy and who is now serving on one of the Plano city boards described it as a leadership program and said he got a good deal out of it.

One of the more successful initiatives started by the mayor was a multicultural roundtable. She originated it to help the city council adopt methods, practices, and programs to serve the entire community and to help the council understand the objectives of all citizens. "While people are usually appointed to committees," she said, "this is something different—more open and more fluid. They can come to it on their own terms. There is little structure although the city sets up the time and place of meetings and offers support staff." At the first meeting, the group developed its mission statement ("to partner with the City Council and the diverse citizens of Plano, encouraging understanding and participation in the government process and fulfilling the needs and desires of its diverse citizens") and established a set of goals, among them to encourage inclusion of minority groups in the city government, to create opportunities for citizens to participate in a variety of multicultural activities that promote appreciation of diversity, and to encourage and facilitate communication between the city council and multicultural citizens of Plano. They also developed various subcommittees (recreation, facilities, and services; diversity and cultural affairs; provision of direct services to new residents; city government participation; and homeland security).

Several activities have emerged from the multicultural roundtable. A Chinese resident launched a World Peace table tennis tournament. Indians and Pakistanis have promoted cricket, and at their request the city has turned over two soccer fields for their matches. "Plano," the mayor observed, "has become the cricket capital of North America. On Sundays they are all out there and they have played teams from New York." Through these sports activities, immigrants are claiming space and visibility within the suburban landscape. Another activity launched by the roundtable that fulfills the same purpose is an International Festival. For two years before the festival, the Asian communities in Plano, through the Asian American Heritage Foundation, sponsored a Pan-Asian Cultural Festival with the support of the Plano city council. The purpose of the festival, according to an organizer, is to "bridge the culture gap" by illustrating to the mainstream how the Asian culture can be part of U.S. culture. For the larger international festival, the city provided seed money and some assistance from City Hall staff, but otherwise it was organized completely by volunteers within the immigrant communities and included African and Hispanic groups as well as Asian groups. Canadians also participated, and the chair of the event was an immigrant from Russia who had come to the United States with his wife—she had won the diversity lottery.

The first International Festival, held in the autumn of 2005, took place in the park across the street from City Hall. It began with a "parade of flags" carried by children from more than twenty countries, some of them dressed in regional costumes. The parade moved forward in two directions around the park. One branch was led by several "Anglo" men dressed in old military costume. The chair of the festival greeted everyone, as did a lively African American woman who served as the master of ceremonies for the day and called initially for a loud "Texas yelp." The purpose of the festival, she said, was to introduce "Plano to Plano." The national anthem, which launched the festivities and which was sung by a woman of Norwegian ancestry, was mirrored at the closing by a performance of "We Are the World," with new lyrics that mentioned the diversity (the rainbow) of Plano. After a moment of silence to honor the troops in Iraq, the mayor spoke. She described Plano as an "all-American city" and referred to its "gorgeous diversity." She read a proclamation that talked about showcasing diversity and educating the citizens of Plano about various cultures. "We can all be educated about each other," she said. "Diversity helps to make Plano an exciting place to work and play." In the audience were Anglos, many senior citizens, and a large turnout of Chinese. Several representatives of mainstream and government organizations and the business community were on hand, including Comerica Bank, the American Association of University Women, Girls Inc., the Plano Parent-Teacher Association, and the Plano Independent School District Diversity Group.

The International Festival is just one of many activities that occur in the metroplex throughout the year. These festivals, like the strip shopping malls that have cropped up throughout the area to cater to different immigrant groups, are a prime example of what feminist geographers have referred to as the public spheres of globalization.[18] They are also an excellent example of cultural citizenship. Renato Rosaldo and William Flores have defined cultural citizenship as "the right to be different (in terms of race, ethnicity, or native language) with respect to the norms of the dominant national community, without compromising one's right to belong, in the sense of participating in the nation-state's democratic processes."[19] If the festival and other activities sponsored by the multicultural roundtable represent the right to be different and to sustain a transnational identity, then participation in other urban programs discussed above, and the creation of associations that interact with urban government represent the right to belong, to claim an American identity that is embedded in citizenship practice.

Another critical urban institution that has had to adapt to increasing diversity is the public library. "Libraries are the vehicles for the entry of new immigrants—they help them to absorb the new culture," said the head librarian of a Plano branch library, where one staff member is Indian and two are Chinese.[20] She noted that many immigrants come from countries with no tradition of public libraries, but they soon learn that the library's services can help them to adjust to their new surroundings. In Plano the Asian and Hispanic groups use the library. The library, as mandated by the Plano city council, is required to make diverse cultures and all family generations welcome and to serve as a community gathering place. To that end, the library has developed several outreach programs for immigrants. One of these is bilingual story time—one in English and Spanish and another in Chinese and English. Indian parents, who often come to the United States fluent in English, bring their children to story time because they want them to hear and speak American English. "They want them to hear the other accent. They do not like readers who do not have an American accent, and they say so because they are goal-oriented for their children," the head librarian reported. Another program is the "Teens between Cultures" (funded by MetLife), which helps parents and their teenage children adjust to cultural differences. "These teens are very American," another librarian observed, "but the parents want them to know something about their own culture. So we get them talking about one thing—music, for example. The teen writes an essay on what he likes and so does the parent, and the essays are posted and people find it interesting, and between the parents and children a dialogue is created."

A third program is "Literacy for Life," an adult literacy program that helps Hispanics learn to read. This is supplemented by a program called "small talk," led by volunteers who encourage participants to learn English vocabulary according to life themes—such as doing the grocery shopping or applying for a mortgage. The waiting list for this program is long, and according to the librarian, the volunteers are very eager because they see their role as one of welcoming new Americans. The collections of the library have changed to supplement these programs. In one branch, an entire set of shelves is filled, top to bottom, with tapes and books related to learning English. Another branch features Chinese and Indian films, and on occasion the libraries sponsor foreign-language film festivals. The head librarian noted that some of the Chinese in the community donate their old books or they buy two copies of a book and donate one to the library. In this way they are participating in the improvement of one of their urban institutions. She recalled that a group of immigrant men who had just been to a seminar on how to do business in America came in looking for golfing videos. They had heard at the seminar that Americans do business on the golf course so they decided they needed to learn how to play. The Plano libraries have also built up their collection of books on citizenship with titles such as "Citizenship Made Simple," "Ethnic Routes to Becoming American," and "Citizenship: Passing the Test."

For many immigrant families, libraries also offer a safe place, a community living room, and a place to escape from a small apartment. The head librarian described one Muslim man whose pregnant wife was a newcomer and feeling isolated in their home. He brought her to the library and asked for a book that would make her laugh. Other immigrants bring their elderly parents and relatives to "hang out" during the day. "There are people who each day have the library on their walking circuit. They stop by, read the newspapers online, do e-mail and then go on," said a librarian. She noted that the Indian parents were signing up for Internet classes because they want to stay in touch with their children in the United States when they return to India. The library is also a town plaza, offering meeting rooms for various clubs and organizations, some of them formed by immigrants. For example, the Dallas Women's Lions Club is a new chapter whose members are largely women from India. The monthly meetings are held at one of the Plano branch libraries.

Suburban schools have also had to respond to increasing diversity. The Plano Independent School District (PISD) a few years ago appointed the first director of diversity programs. Among the issues that the diversity programs address are student conflict and resolution, parental conflict and resolution, leadership, religious diversity, bilingual and multilingual issues, and hiring procedures to emphasize diversity in staffing. In recent years, given the changing composition of the population, the program has made an effort to expand the number of Asian teachers. The program gives out diversity leadership awards to both students and faculty and promotes a Parade of Nations celebrated by the entire school district. The diversity programs director works closely with a multiethnic committee the PISD established in 1988. Made up of community members, this committee serves in an advisory capacity to the school board and plays an important bridging role between the schools and the community.

An Immigrant Program Coordinator employed by the PISD focuses on the needs of immigrant students. This program, which is largely supported by federal funds funneled through the state, serves students born outside the United States who have fewer than three complete years in a U.S. school. Among the initiatives launched from this program are full-time Spanish translators, family literacy classes, English classes for parents, after-school English reinforcement programs for students, annual oral and writing proficiency assessments, Spanish for school administrators, and school-readiness programs for younger siblings. These programs are mandated under Texas law, and the main goal is to foster English proficiency as quickly as possible.

Sociologist Michael Alexander has argued that "local government reflects the local host society which makes up its constituency, and this applies to its various reactions to the settlement of migrants."[21] Local authorities, he says, may largely ignore these migrants, on the assumption that they will not stay. They might see them as a threat to local economic, social, and political stability and act accordingly by restricting access to local institutions. Or they might view them as "positive potential" for the city and for local neighborhoods. Under the leadership of the current mayor, Plano has adopted this latter, pluralist perspective, recognizing the right of migrants "to retain their otherness while at the same time putting programs in place that facilitate incorporation." By introducing "Plano to Plano" at the International Festival, this community has clearly recognized that the process of transformation goes two ways, that Plano itself is changing as a result of the suburban settlement patterns of new immigrants. As Alexander writes, "The multicultural-minded municipality is sensitive to the particular needs and problems arising from the migrants' otherness. The positive potential of the migrants for the city is also acknowledged and their otherness is perceived as enriching the local host culture and economy."[22]

This was not always the case, however. Indeed, when the pioneering generation of Asian Indians in the DFW area decided to build their temple on land they had purchased in Plano, they were not warmly received. Eventually they sold this land and took their temple to Irving, where the mayor made them feel welcome. In the interim their numbers and those of other immigrant groups have increased in Plano, making a different and more inclusive approach necessary.

It is also worth noting that particular individuals in positions of leadership can make a difference in setting an inclusionary or exclusionary course. In August 2006, in Farmers Branch, a suburban community to the northwest of Dallas, Tim O'Hare, a member of the city council, proposed that the city adopt a set of local ordinances similar to those adopted in Hazleton, Pennsylvania, whose city council gained national attention for its anti-immigrant stance. Specifically, he proposed making it difficult for undocumented immigrants to live and work in Farmers Branch by barring landlords from leasing units to them and penalizing employers who hired them. Also under discussion were proposals to make English the official language of the city and to make local law enforcement officers acting immigration officers who could ask people to demonstrate that they were in the country legally. O'Hare's proposals drew the attention of both the local and the national press, as well as street protests by groups of immigrants, largely Hispanics. Organizations such as the League of United Latin American Citizens (LULAC) and the International Coalition of Mexicans Abroad eventually entered the fray, calling for a recall of O'Hare and a boycott of local businesses. The letters to the editor from local citizens in Farmers Branch reflected some of the underlying hostility to migrants in this largely middle-class community. Several writers, objecting to accusations of racism, noted that undocumented immigrants were breaking the law. Others reflected discomfort with change ("I grew up there and it saddens me to see what it has become. I am tired of hearing Spanish in the streets and trying to figure out if someone understands what I'm saying," or "The only thing [Mr. O'Hare] forgot to mention is that a single-family home is for a single family, not a hotel for six or seven families").[23]

After two weeks of heated debate the city council put the entire matter on hold, but city attorneys set to work on the ordinances. In November 2006, English was declared the city's official language. Among other things, signs in Spanish were removed from the public library and the city stopped printing fliers in Spanish announcing park and recreational activities. A month later, the city council passed employer and housing ordinances affecting undocumented workers, and by late December, the Mexican American Legal Defense and Educational Fund, the American Civil Liberties Union, and several individual residents, including some apartment complex owners, had filed several lawsuits against the city. In addition, petitions were submitted to try to force the city to put the ordinances to a citywide vote. The city had set up its own legal defense fund, although funding by mid-December was minimal. In January 2007 the city council decided to put the housing ordinance on a May 2007 ballot but to proceed with its implementation in the interim. A judge temporarily blocked the ordinance from taking effect, and the Farmers Branch City Council subsequently reexamined all the ordinances pertaining to illegal immigrants.[24] On May 12, 2007, 68 percent of the voters in Farmers Branch supported the ordinances targeting illegal immigrants. City Council member O'Hare suggested that the people of Farmers Branch were "saying loud and clear they want change. . . . People recognize we have a problem, and they are proud we stood up."[25]

The Farmers Branch controversy certainly offers an example of intense local politics revolving around immigration. Even the Bishop of Dallas weighed in, telling worshipers at the Cathedral of Guadalupe on Sunday, January 14, 2007, that although the United States should control its borders, "immigration policy should be tempered with justice and mercy."[26]

The mayor of Irving, a community where about two-thirds of the public school students are Hispanic, said in response to the Farmers Branch events: "Given current demographics, we'll have this diversity forever. . . . It is never going to be reversed. And since that's the case . . . then let's embrace it."[27] In contrast to Farmers Branch, city officials in Irving announced in October 2006 that they would not participate in the federal initiative that would train local law enforcement to detain illegal immigrants. However, by the fall of 2007 Irving was itself in the news and the DFW area Mexican consul was issuing a warning to Mexican immigrants to avoid the community because the number of deportations had increased dramatically. In 2007 the Irving City Council adopted the Criminal Alien Program. Local police, who were routinely stopping people for traffic violations or public intoxication, turned them over to Immigration and Customs Enforcement if they had no proper identification.[28] In late September 2007 more than a thousand people assembled at the Irving City Hall to protest the deportations and the unfair targeting of Hispanics. The mayor responded by claiming that the city of Irving was simply following the law.[29]

Farmers Branch was the locus for another incident that drew media attention earlier in 2006. In January, the police chief was suspended without pay and required to attend counseling for making an inappropriate remark regarding a Vietnamese police recruit. The Southeast Asian community in the DFW area responded by asking for a public apology. Some of those interviewed by the media noted that these kinds of incidents only confirmed the distrust of law enforcement that many had brought with them to the United States.[30] Others noted that this kind of racism was inappropriate in public institutions. The police chief finally retired and the city manager, engaged in the search for a new chief, went on record saying, "Our demographics are changing. [The new chief] would need to be someone who has effective leadership skills in a diverse community."[31] Farmers Branch is a suburban community that continues to wrestle with its growing diversity. In October of 2007 a new controversy erupted over the bright colors that some residents were using to paint their homes and their impact on home values.[32] By contrast, a few weeks earlier the Plano Multicultural Roundtable hosted a reception to celebrate diversity and foster global thinking.[33]

Certainly there is more work to be done in determining why there is such variation in how these suburban communities respond to immigrations. Why has Farmers Branch developed such a strong anti-immigrant position, while Plano has established a day laborer pick-up center near the city bus station? How important is the size and composition of the foreign-born population? In Farmers Branch, the foreign-born represented

25 percent of the total population in 2000, compared with 17 percent in Plano. Mexicans made up close to 60 percent of the foreign-born in Farmers Branch but only 22 percent in Plano, where the major immigrant population is Asian. In the main feeder schools to the main high school in Farmers Branch, 91 percent of the students are minority, and of these, 86 percent are Hispanic and 71 percent are from low-income families.[34] How important are class issues in shaping local responses? In 2000, 27.2 percent of the Farmers Branch population had a bachelor's degree or higher, compared with 53.3 percent in Plano. The median household income in Farmers Branch in 1999 was $54,734, compared with $78,722 in Plano. These income differences further suggest that the tax base may be an important factor shaping how local communities respond to immigrants in their midst.

"Eruptions" like those in Farmers Branch reflect the frustrations in local places with the foot-dragging at the national level over immigration reform. Even Texas senator Kay Bailey Hutchison weighed in on the Farmers Branch issue, calling for calm and emphasizing that the development of immigration policy was a federal responsibility. However, federal policy will not solve the burdens on local places in the short term. Immigration policy is one thing; local incorporation is another. A report on illegal immigration issued by the Texas State Comptroller in December 2006 estimated that although illegal immigrants cost the state $1.16 billion in services, they pay $1.58 billion in taxes and fees. Yet, at the city and county levels, expenditures for indigent care and law enforcement are $1.44 billion, while revenues from illegal immigrants for city, county, and special district sales and property taxes amounted to only $513 million.[35] And these figures do not take education expenditures into account. As geographer Mark Ellis has suggested, these are questions of the politics of scale. "Too often," he argues, "immigration dynamics are conceptualized in homogenizing national terms with . . . insufficient sensitivity to the degree of local versus central government responsibility for the social costs and incorporation of newcomers."[36]

Conclusion

At the end of 2005, a reporter for the *New York Times* noted that America was "growing at its fastest in places like [Frisco]," an exurb of Dallas. Life in such places, he concluded, is framed by time spent in the car.[37] But, as this chapter has shown, it is equally framed by growing diversity. The rapid and significant settlement of immigrants in suburban communities surrounding the city of Dallas represents not only what sociologists Mary Waters and Tomás Jiménez describe as the changing geography of immigrant settlement but also the changing landscape of suburban and exurban America.[38]

A few questions stand out as this process continues and matures. In the 2004 election Collin County, with the city of Plano at its heart, gave George W. Bush 71 percent of its vote. The story in Dallas County was quite different. There, Bush only garnered 50 percent of the vote, possibly the result of the changing demographics of the county and, in particular, the city of Dallas. In the midterm elections of November 2006, local Democratic candidates won handily in Dallas County. Many Republican judges were surprised at being voted out of office. As Mexican immigrants become citizens, and as the native-born second generation grows up and becomes politically empowered, the political landscape of both the city and the suburbs may change further. Certainly pundits in the Dallas-Fort Worth area are watching this closely. An African American reporter for the *Dallas Morning News* observed that an increased voter turnout by a Latino population (77,000 registered voters in Dallas) galvanized by the immigration debates during spring 2006 would "signal that the area's normally sleepy Hispanic electorate is truly energized."[39] Immediately following the announcement in summer 2006 by Dallas Mayor Laura Miller that she would not be a candidate in the 2007 mayoral race, a reporter pointed to three local Hispanics who could be potential candidates. None of them ran and in June 2007, an Anglo businessman, Tom Leppert, was elected in a runoff. Less than a week after his election, Leppert was lobbied by immigrants to open an Office of Immigrant Affairs that would focus on the integration of immigrants.[40] The failure of Congress to pass an immigration reform bill, they argued, made it urgent for cities themselves to act.

As the Asian populations mature, what roles will they assume in local government? The city of Addison, an inner ring "suburb," has already elected a mayor who was born in China, and increasingly North and South Asians are becoming involved in local school boards and on suburban city boards and commissions. Indeed they have more opportunities in these suburban places than they might have in the city of Dallas itself. During the May 2006 election for the mayor of Plano, the Muslim community organized itself to back the incumbent. One member of the community held a "meet and greet" open house and fundraiser at his home, and his group of friends were active in posting yard signs in their neighborhoods. It is these dynamics of suburban politics that we should watch as we move forward in the twenty-first century.

Notes

1. The term *metroplex* was coined in 1971 to describe the greater metropolitan area. In 2000 the Dallas Primary Metropolitan Statistical Area (PMSA) included Collin, Dallas, Denton, Ellis, Henderson, Hunt, Kaufmann, and Rockwall counties. The Fort Worth-Arlington PMSA included Hood, Johnson, Parker, and Tarrant Counties. These two PMSAs made up the Consolidated Metropolitan Statistical Area (CMSA). The metropolitan area definitions changed after the 2000 census, and Dallas and Fort Worth were combined into one metropolitan area. Two counties (Hood and Henderson) were dropped from the definition, while two other counties (Delta and Wise) were added.

2. Robert Prince, *A History of Dallas from a Different Perspective* (Dallas: Nortex Press, 1983).

3. For further discussion of the history and development of Dallas and the DFW metropolitan area more broadly, see Caroline B. Brettell, "Immigrants in a Sunbelt Metropolis: The Transformation of an Urban Place and the Construction of Community," in *Renegotiating the Immigrant City,* edited by Blair Ruble and Lisa Hanley (Washington: Woodrow Wilson Center for International Scholars, 2008). Also see Robert V. Kemper, "Dallas-Fort Worth," in *Encyclopedia of Urban Cultures,* vol. 2 (Danbury, Conn.: Grolier), pp. 94–107; and Darwin Payne, *Big D: Triumphs and Troubles of an American Supercity in the 20th Century* (Dallas: Three Forks Press, 2000).

4. Reynolds Farley, "Residential Segregation in Urbanized Areas of the United States in 1970: An Analysis of Social Class and Racial Differences," *Demography* 14 (1977): 497–518. Dallas in the early 1960s was characterized as race-baiting, strongly anticommunist, and Kennedy phobic. According to Jim Schutze in *The Accommodation: The Politics of Race in America* (Secaucus, N.J.: Citadel Press, 1971), this attitude was fed by the editorials of the *Dallas Morning News.* Following John F. Kennedy's assassination in Dallas in 1963, the Citizens Council that "ruled" the city began to negotiate quite deliberately with the African American population. Schutze writes that "race relations in Dallas were the object of intense and thoughtful management" (p. 146). An accommodation was reached that avoided the more violent civil rights events of other cities at this time.

5. Caroline B. Brettell, "Meet Me at the Chat/Chaat Corner: The Cultural Embeddedness of Immigrant Entrepreneurs," in *From Arrivals to Incorporation: Migrants to the U.S. in a Global Era,* Hasia Diner, Elliott Barkan, and Alan M. Kraut, eds. (New York University Press, 2007).

6. The author would like to thank Lyssa Jenkens, an economist with the Dallas Chamber of Commerce, for providing many of these data.

7. For further discussion, see Anne Fisher, "The Best Cities for Business," *Fortune Magazine,* December 20, 1999, pp. 214–23.

8. Joseph Wood, "Vietnamese American Place Making in Northern Virginia," *Geographical Review* 87 (1997): 158–72; and Elizabeth Chacko, "Ethiopian Ethos and the Making of Ethnic Places in the Washington Metropolitan Area," *Journal of Cultural Geography* 20 (2003): 21–42.

9. Terrance J. Reeves and Claudette E. Bennett, *We the People: Asians in the United States* (U.S. Census Bureau, Census 2000 Special Reports, December 2004).

10. Esther Wu, "Housing Push May Transform Little Asia," *Dallas Morning News,* Sunday, June 25, 2006, p. B1.

11. For further discussion, see Brettell, "Meet Me at the Chat/Chaat Corner."

12. For a study of Indian nurses, see Sheba Mariam George, *When Women Come First: Gender and Class in Transnational Migration* (University of California Press, 2005).

13. Wilbur Zelinksy and Barrett A. Lee, "Heterolocalism: An Alternative Model of the Sociospatial Behaviour of Immigrant Ethnic Communities," *International Journal of Population Geography* 4 (1998): 1–18. See also Wilbur Zelinsky, *The Enigma of Ethnicity: Another American Dilemma* (University of Iowa Press, 2001).

14. For further discussion, see Caroline B. Brettell, "The Spatial, Social, and Political Incorporation of Asian Indian Immigrants in Dallas," *Urban Anthropology* 34 (2005): 247–80; and Caroline B. Brettell, "Voluntary Organizations, Social Capital, and the Social Incorporation of Asian Indian Immigrants in the Dallas-Fort Worth Metroplex," *Anthropological Quarterly* 78 (2005): 821–51.

15. In the 2000 census, 433,534 foreign-born Mexicans, 36,522 foreign-born Vietnamese, 30,030 foreign-born Indians, and 26, 271 foreign-born Salvadorans were counted in the four-county metroplex. Foreign-born Chinese (14,379) and Koreans (14,001) made up the final two of the top six (in total number) immigrant populations. The number of foreign-born Nigerians enumerated in 2000 was 7,342.

16. The diversity lottery program makes 55,000 immigrant visas available to people who come from countries with low rates of immigration to the United States. See the website for U.S. citizenship and immigration services for further information (www.uscis.gov).

17. Plano attracted attention during the 1980s and 1990s because of drug problems (primarily heroin use) among teenagers, several of whom overdosed and died. The *Dallas Morning News* covered the hard-driving "price of prosperity" in this suburb in a three-part series during the late summer of 2005. Among other things, this article covered the excessive debt taken on by many young families in the area, simply to "keep up the lifestyle of their friends and neighbors." See Paula Lavigne, "The Price of Prosperity," *Dallas Morning News,* August 14, 2005 (www.dallasnews.com/sharedcontent/dws/news/longterm/stories/081505dnccowealth).

18. Richa Nagar and others, "Locating Globalization: Feminist (re)Readings of the Subjects and Spaces of Globalization," *Economic Geography* 78 (2002): 4.

19. Renato Rosaldo and William V. Flores, "Identity, Conflict, and Evolving Latino Communities: Cultural Citizenship in San Jose, California," in *Latino Cultural Citizenship: Claiming Identity, Space, and Rights,* edited by William Flores and Rina Benmayor (Boston: Beacon Press, 1997), p. 57.

20. Interview with author, November 8, 2005.

21. Michael Alexander, "Local Policies toward Migrants as an Expression of Host-Stranger Relations: A Proposed Typology," *Journal of Ethnic and Migration Studies* 29 (2003): 415.

22. Ibid., p. 419.

23. "Letters to the Editor," *Dallas Morning News,* August 24, 2006, p. A18.

24. The activities in Farmers Branch spilled over into neighboring Carrollton. An individual running for city council in that community whom pundits placed as a

distant second pulled off a win. His platform included implementing ordinances similar to those passed in Farmers Branch. See Stephanie Sandoval, "Immigration Issues Seep into Carrollton Contest," *Dallas Morning News,* January 5, 2007, p. B13; see also Stephanie Sandoval, "Did FB Issue Swing Neighboring Council Race?" *Dallas Morning News,* January 11, 2007, p. B16. As of mid-January 2007, the implementation of the ordinances was put on hold pending a referendum election scheduled for May 2007. At the same time, a story in the *Dallas Morning News* reported on a pilot bilingual education program in the Farmers Branch school district as an example of "diverging" local missions. Seventy-four percent of the population in the Farmers Branch school district is minority, largely Latino. See Katherine Leal Unmuth, "Diverging Missions in Farmers Branch?" *Dallas Morning News,* January 21, 2007, p. A1.

25. Stephanie Sandoval, "Farmers Branch: Victory May Prompt Similar Measures Elsewhere; Court Battle Likely," *Dallas Morning News,* May 12, 2007, p. A1. In the summer of 2007, Councilman Tim O'Hare was promoting the construction of a patriotic park in Farmers Branch where the city could "fly the world's biggest American flag" (Stephanie Sandoval, "FB Revitalization Leaders Thinking Red, White, Blue," *Dallas Morning News,* July 15, 2007, p. B13).

26. Sergio Chapa, "Dallas Bishop Takes Issue with FB Ordinance," *Dallas Morning News,* January 15, 2007, p. B3.

27. Macarena Hernández, "Immigration View from Another Suburb," *Dallas Morning News,* September 9, 2006, p. A25.

28. Isabel C. Morales and Brandon Formby, "Irving's Border War," *Dallas Morning News,* September 22, 2007, p. A19.

29. Brandon Formby, "Hundreds Protest Increase in Deportations," *Dallas Morning News,* September 27, 2007, p. B12.

30. The chief, Jimmy Fawcett, said that as long as he was chief, "We won't have any gooks working in Farmers Branch." See Esther Wu, "Chief's Slur Tarnishes Residents' Trust in Police," *Dallas Morning News,* January 12, 2006 (www.modelminority.com/article1066.html [December 18, 2006]). See also Sarah Dodd, "Police Chief Suspended for 'Gooks' Comment," *Model Minority,* January 13, 2006 (www.modelminority.com/article1066.html [December 18, 2006]).

31. Stephanie Sandoval, "Farmers Branch Prepares for Police Chief Hunt," *Dallas Morning News,* March 26, 2006 (www.waterconsulting.com/News/waternews/032606DMN-FBPoliceChief.pdf [December 18, 2006]).

32 Stephanie Sandoval, "Residents in a Paint Brawl in FB," *Dallas Morning News,* October 10, 2007, p. A1.

33. Chris Coats, "Helping Local Officials Think Globally," *Dallas Morning News,* September 23, 2007, p. B13.

34. Farmers Branch is part of the Carrollton-Farmers Branch School District. Creekview High School (which serves north Carrollton) feeder schools are 65 percent minority and 36 percent Hispanic, with 39 percent of the students from low-income families; Newman Smith High School (in central Carrollton) feeder schools are 77 percent minority (50 percent Hispanic), and 54 percent of the students are from low-income families; Ranchview High School (in West Carrollton and the more prosperous Las Colinas area) feeder schools are 77 percent minority (17 percent Hispanic), and 31 percent of the students are from low-income families. See

Katherine Leal Unmuth, "Schools' Racial Makeup Fuels Tension in FB," *Dallas Morning News,* May 5, 2007, p. A1.

35. Karen Brooks, "Illegal Immigration's Give-and-Take," *Dallas Morning News,* December 8, 2006 (www.dallasnews.com/sharedcontent/dws/dn/latestnews/sotires/120806dnteximmigr [December 18, 2006]).

36. Mark Ellis, "Unsettling Immigrant Geographies: U.S. Immigration and the Politics of Scale," *Tijdschrift voor Economische en Sociale Geografie* 97 (2006): 50.

37. Rick Lyman, "Far and Away: In Exurbs, Life Framed by Hours Spent in the Car," *New York Times,* December 18, 2005, p. 41.

38. Mary C. Waters and Tomás Jiménez, "Assessing Immigrant Assimilation: New Empirical and Theoretical Challenges," *Annual Review of Sociology* 31 (2005): 105–26.

39. Gromer Jeffers, "Bond Election Offers Hispanics a Chance to Flex Their Muscle," *Dallas Morning News,* July 5, 2005, p. B2.

40. Dianne Solis, "Leppert Supports Immigrant Office," *Dallas Morning News,* July 3, 2007, p. A1. Other cities that have opened such offices include New York, Boston, Chicago, and Houston.

4

Diverging Trajectories

Asian and Latino Immigration in Metropolitan Phoenix

ALEX OBERLE and WEI LI

With its proximity to Mexico and Latin America to the south and California and the Pacific Rim to the west, metropolitan Phoenix, as of 2006, the fifth largest U.S. city and one of the fastest-growing metropolitan areas in the nation, is an emerging immigrant gateway for both Latino and Asian immigrants. The trajectories of its two largest immigrant groups are quite different, however. In general, the metro area's Latino population is less skilled and more economically disadvantaged, while its Asian immigrants are more highly skilled, as the metro area asserts itself as a nascent knowledge economy with growing demand for Indian and other Asian talent. Among both Latinos and Asians, however, there is a strong trend toward suburbanization.[1]

Although other foreign-born populations live in metropolitan Phoenix, we focus on Latin Americans and Asians because Latin American immigrants are, by far, the largest foreign-born immigrant group in Phoenix and Asian immigrants are among the fastest growing.[2] We begin with a brief history of these two groups, followed by the contemporary picture of their presence in the metro areas. We document their residential patterns, with a particular focus on differences between the suburban and central city populations. We also document their divergent socioeconomic profiles and discuss how each group has responded to its new home, with a focus on immigrant entrepreneurship and cultural and political identities and networks.

We are indebted to Arizona State University's Asian Pacific American Studies Program for financial support and to Yun Zhou and Jianfeng Zhang for invaluable research assistance.

Latin Americans and Asians in Phoenix

Although Phoenix is a quintessentially western metropolis, its early history reflects only modest Hispanic and limited Asian influences. These influences were quickly overshadowed by the post–World War II Anglo population boom, which further diluted the city's comparatively small Spanish-Mexican and Asian populations and diminished the nascent heritage of those groups. In that regard, Phoenix stands in stark contrast to other cities in the region such as Albuquerque, El Paso, Tucson, and Los Angeles where Hispanic cultural influences are deeply rooted and evident in the cultural landscape and in the residents' collective identity. It is also distinct from California cities such as Los Angeles and San Francisco that have been uniquely shaped by a mosaic of Asian cultures.

Mexican Immigrant History

The area near the Salt River, today downtown Phoenix, was the core of the city's Hispanic population throughout much of the early and mid-1900s. The earliest barrios were generally isolated, impoverished, and lacking in basic services. The advent of World War II improved economic conditions for Hispanics, largely because of an influx of capital from the disproportionately large numbers of Hispanic servicemen who fought in the war.[3] A booming postwar Phoenix that provided ample employment in construction and other service-sector jobs also strongly influenced the barrio.

Despite these advances, segregation and racism remained. Latino schools were separate and unequal, and many pools, restaurants, and other establishments often barred Hispanics. Although Hispanics began to settle in other areas adjacent to the west and south of *Nuestro Barrio*—in a contiguous area commonly known as South Phoenix—redlining and discrimination limited the scope of Latino settlement.[4] In addition, as the African American population of South Phoenix increased, the area became more diverse and less dominated by Latinos. The expansion of Sky Harbor Airport into adjacent residential areas in the 1970s and 1980s resulted in the demise of the Golden Gate barrio, one of the first Latino neighborhoods in Phoenix.

The diminishing Hispanic dominance in South Phoenix was offset by a more widespread and sizable increase in the Latino population elsewhere. This Hispanic growth, although no longer confined to South Phoenix, still remained largely clustered and segregated. In 1980, 15 percent of Phoenix's neighborhoods contained more than half of the city's Hispanic population, while 32 percent of Phoenix neighborhoods had few or no Latino residents.[5]

Map 4-1. Rate of Change of Hispanic Population Compared with Total Population, 1990–2000

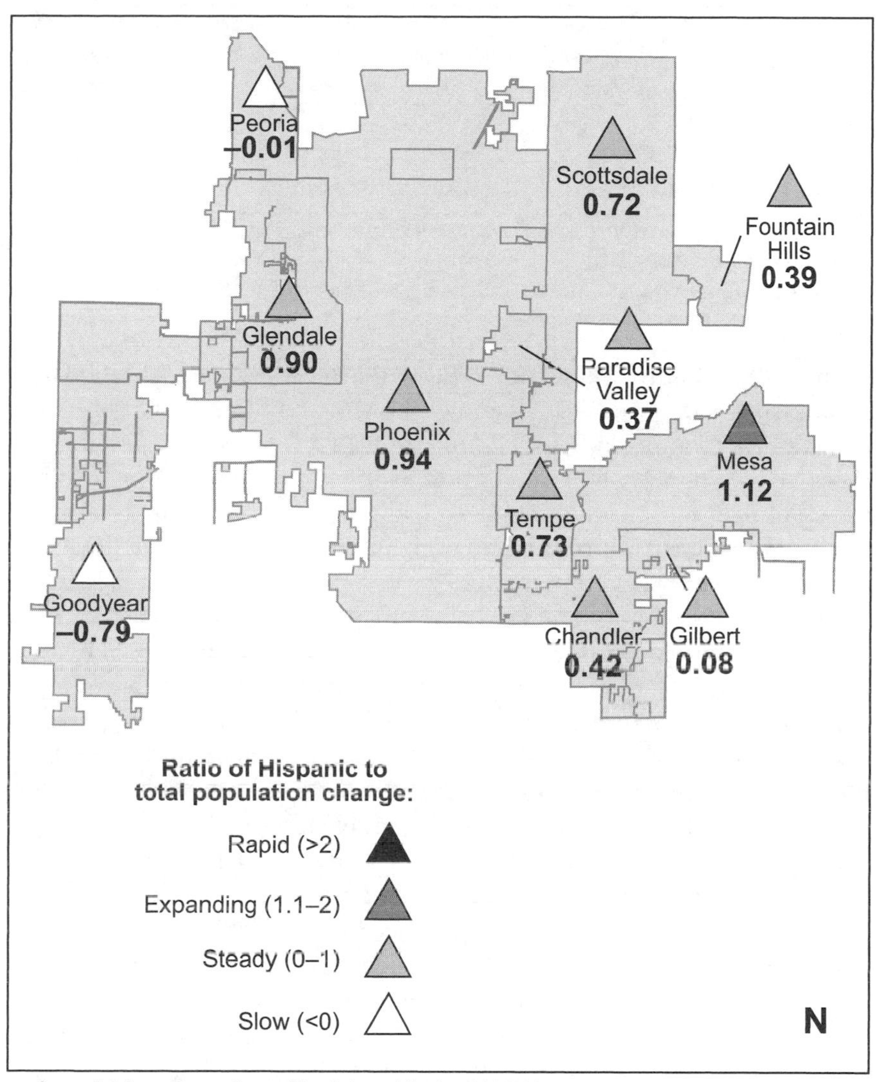

Source: U.S. Census Bureau, *Census of Population and Housing 1990, 2000.*

In the past twenty years, the metro area's Latino population has expanded rapidly, with Hispanics settling in more distant parts of the city (map 4-1). A recent study by Brookings classifies Phoenix as a "fast-growing Latino hub."[6] Of the eleven fast-growing hubs, only Dallas and Houston surpassed Phoenix in their rate of suburban Hispanic population growth

Table 4-1. Hispanic, Asian, and Foreign-Born Populations, 1990–2005
Percent

Year	*Hispanics in Phoenix MSA*[a]	*Hispanics in Phoenix central city*	*Asians in Phoenix MSA*[a]	*Asians in Phoenix central city*	*Foreign-born in Phoenix MSA*[a]	*Foreign-born in Phoenix central city*
1990	16	20	1.7	1.7	8	9
2000	25	34	2.0	2.2	14	19
2005 (est.)[b]	29	42	2.6	2.0	16	23

Source: U.S. Census Bureau, *Census of Population 1990, 2000;* U.S. Census Bureau, *American Community Survey 2005.*
a. MSA—Metropolitan Statistical Area.
b. The *American Community Survey* data do not include group quarters and may reflect an undercount.

from 1990 to 2000. This suburban growth is most evident in Mesa, Glendale, and to a lesser extent, Chandler. In Mesa and Glendale, the Latino growth rate is approximately double that of the general population in those cities (see map 4-1). According to the 2000 Census, about one in three Phoenix-area Latinos lives in the suburbs. As of 2000 approximately one in five residents in both Mesa and Chandler was Hispanic. In Glendale, one in four was Latino.[7]

However, the pull of the central city remains strong. From 1990 to 2000 the Latino population in the central city increased from approximately one-fifth Hispanic to more than one-third Hispanic, although not all of these Hispanics are foreign-born. This is the result of more non-Hispanics relocating in suburban Phoenix along with large numbers of foreign-born Hispanics moving into the city. During that same ten-year period, the foreign-born population in Phoenix proper doubled, from about one in ten to nearly one in five. Recent 2005 estimates show that the central city of Phoenix is 23 percent foreign-born and 42 percent Hispanic (table 4-1). No other southwestern city has experienced such a dramatic increase: not Albuquerque, El Paso, Las Vegas, Los Angeles, or Tucson. Remarkably, as of 2000, Phoenix's Latinos made up almost as large a share of the population (34 percent) as did Latinos in Tucson (36 percent), where Mexican influence has long been a hallmark of the city's heritage.[8] Phoenix, both the central city and larger metropolitan area, now stands as a top Hispanic immigrant destination and one of the largest Latino population clusters in the United States. Skop and Menjívar argue that Phoenix has now, in fact, become a gateway city that often serves as a temporary place of residence for immigrants who then disperse to other parts of the country.[9]

Among Hispanics, Mexican immigrants dominate, representing 83 percent of total Latino immigrants; the second largest group, Guatemalans,

Table 4-2. Distribution of Hispanics and Asians in Central City Phoenix and Suburban Phoenix, 2000

Group or subgroup	*Phoenix suburban (number)*	*Phoenix suburban (percent of total group/subgroup)*	*Phoenix central city (number)*	*Phoenix central city (percent of total group/subgroup)*
Total population	1,930,831	59	1,321,045	41
Hispanic (all)	367,040	45	449,972	55
Mexican	304,703	45	375,096	55
Central American	5,976	50	6,085	50
Cuban	1,600	45	1,952	55
Puerto Rican	6,892	36	5,089	74
South American	3,818	42	2,199	58
Other Hispanic	44,051	42	59,551	58
Asian (all)	41,082	61	26,449	39
Chinese	10,507	65	5,761	35
Japanese	3,204	65	1,728	35
Vietnamese	3,761	42	5,301	58
Filipino	7,448	61	4,757	39
Korean	4,229	69	1,877	31
Asian Indian	7,043	61	4,481	39
Other Asian	4,890	66	2,544	34

Source: U.S. Census Bureau, *Census of Population 2000.*

constitutes only about 1 percent. Puerto Rican and Cuban immigrants collectively accounted for less than 3 percent of the Hispanic population in 2000. Of the Hispanic subgroups, most have a slight predilection for the central city, except for Central Americans, who are evenly distributed between the central city and suburb, and Puerto Ricans, who have a strong tendency toward the central city (table 4-2).

Asian Immigrant History

Even with its proximity to California, Phoenix was never a major gateway for Asian immigrants relative to West Coast cities such as Los Angeles or San Francisco. Asian immigrants in early twentieth century Phoenix were largely Chinese and Japanese. The Asian population increased slowly in the first half of twentieth century largely from natural growth: U.S. immigration policies at the time barred Chinese immigration and restricted Japanese immigration, and later stopped all Asian immigration. Asian numbers began to increase only after immigration policy changed in 1965. During

World War II Arizona was the site of two internment camps for both immigrant and native-born Japanese; the camps were on land seized from Native American tribes in Gila River and Poston, respectively. As a result of the incarceration of Japanese, the populations of these two places reached roughly 13,000 and 18,000, respectively, making them the state's third and fourth biggest cities at the time and by far the largest concentrations of Asians in the state.[10]

Although the size and percentage of Asian Americans in the Phoenix metropolitan area are still small compared with Latinos, Asians are one of the fastest-growing groups in the state. In the 1990s alone their numbers grew by 95 percent. Many of these immigrants are bypassing the city. By 2000, for instance, suburbs in metro Phoenix had a larger Asian population than the central city, both in total number and by all major groups: Chinese, Filipino, Indian, Japanese, Korean, Vietnamese, and other Asians.

Early on, the Chinese typically lived in or next to their small businesses in towns and cities across Arizona, whereas many Japanese chose to live in Glendale in Phoenix's West Valley, especially after being released from the World War II internment camps. Immigrants in recent decades, many with better human capital, mainstream employment, or small businesses, settled directly in the suburbs to be close to their jobs. Asian Indian doctors arriving during the 1970s, for instance, often lived in the northern part of Phoenix, an area possessing a more suburban character, despite being classified as part of the central city.[11]

The small number of existing Asian populations continued to sponsor their family members' immigration through chain migration. Small business owners, mainly Chinese, Korean, and Vietnamese, tired of heated intra-ethnic competition in southern California and lured by better business opportunities, an affordable cost of living, and lower taxes in Arizona, chose to move to greater Phoenix. Higher overhead in Phoenix proper also prompted Asian businesses to suburbanize.[12] However, it was the high-tech employment boom in the 1990s that fueled the increase of highly skilled Asian immigrants, many of whom settled near their jobs at Honeywell, Intel, and Motorola in the East Valley suburbs (map 4-2).[13] The Asian population in Gilbert grew more than ten times faster than that of Phoenix proper from 1980 to 2000. Similarly, the percentage of Asians grew from 2 percent in 1990 to 4.3 percent in 2000 in suburban Chandler. This Asian population growth in Chandler is more than double the rate of the total population growth there. In Gilbert, it is more than four times the general rate of increase for the population at large (see map 4-2). Some argue that Phoenix may be at the brink of becoming a high-tech mecca like Silicon Valley, with multiracial neighborhoods where Asians play important roles.

Map 4-2. Rate of Change of Asian Population Compared with Total Population, 1990–2000

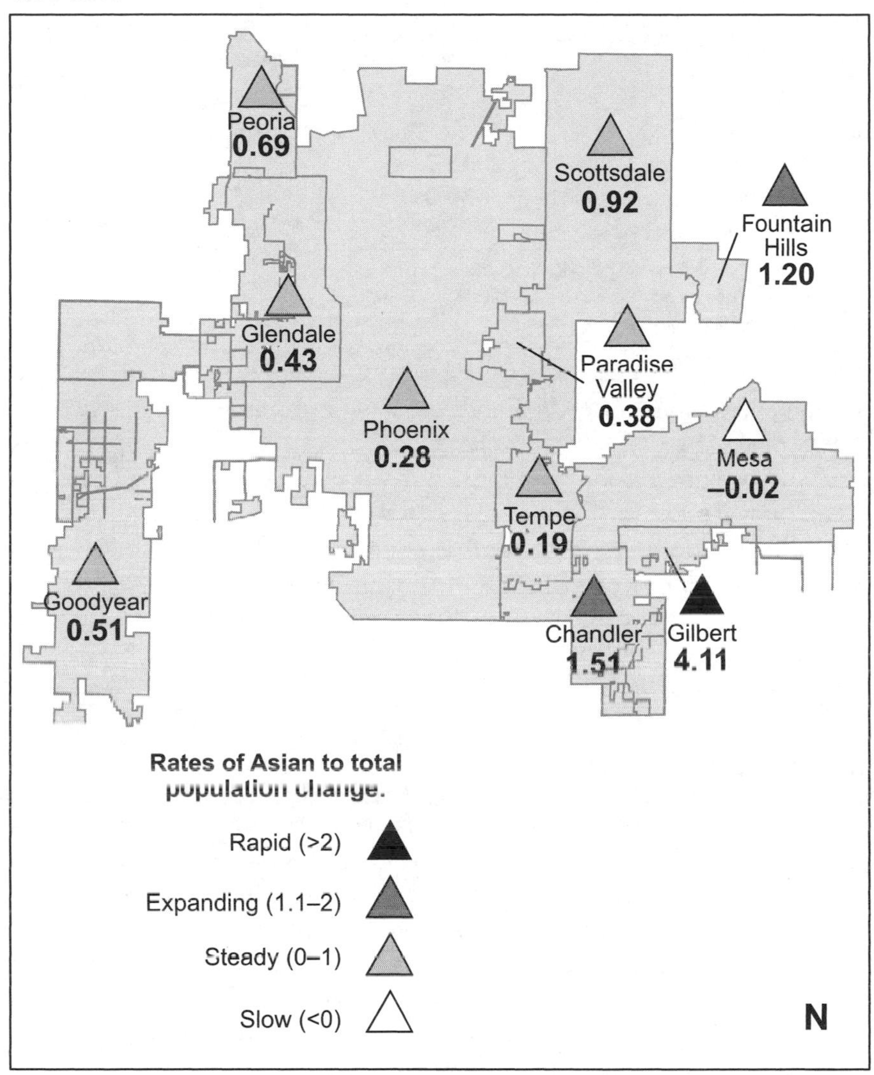

Source: U.S. Census Bureau, *Census of Population and Housing 1990, 2000.*

Yet even with this growth in the East Valley, the current number of ethnic Asians has yet to reach a critical mass to form an enclave or "ethnoburb" in any particular area.[14]

While Chinese and Japanese populations constituted major Asian groups historically, contemporary Asian populations in the valley have become increasingly diverse. The growth of the Indian, Filipino, and

Table 4-3. Comparison of Select Socioeconomic Variables among Hispanics, Asians, and Whites in the Phoenix Metropolitan Statistical Area[a]
Percent unless otherwise shown

Socioeconomic category	*Asian*	*Hispanic*	*White*
Foreign-born	68	39	9
Linguistic isolation	19	26	4
Bachelor's degree or higher	47	8	25
Homeownership	60	52	72
Median household income	$50,904	$33,915	$46,825

Source: U.S. Census Bureau, PUMS (2000).

a. Data are limited to respondents who self-identified as only one race or ethnicity and exclude those who self-identified as multiple races or ethnicities.

Korean populations since 1965 and Vietnamese and other Southeast Asian groups since 1975 account for a large portion of the total Asian increase. Japanese, by contrast, have diminished in size to become the smallest Asian group in metro Phoenix as of 2000. Latino and Asian immigrants are further differentiated by the proportion of their respective top five groups. Mexican immigrants make up four-fifths of Hispanics, with other groups accounting for around 1 percent each. In contrast, the proportions of Asian immigrant groups in metro Phoenix are more balanced across the top five groups.

Socioeconomic Profiles

Contemporary Latino and Asian immigrant populations in metro Phoenix present a complicated picture of increasing diversity in both their spatial distribution and their socioeconomics. Among Latinos, the Mexican or Mexican American influence is dominant, but there is also a gradual diversification of national-origin groups, low to moderate—but changing—socioeconomic profiles, and increasing suburban settlement. Some marked characteristics of Asian immigration include the diversifying national-origin groups, varying socioeconomic profiles, and increasing suburban settlement. In this section, we analyze these two groups' socioeconomic characteristics, with particular attention to subgroup differences.[15]

Divergence between Latino and Asian Immigrants

The overall socioeconomic characteristics of Latino and Asian immigrants are noticeably different (table 4-3). Asians have higher levels of education, occupational prestige, annual income, and homeownership. Forty-seven percent of Asian immigrants have at least a bachelor's degree,

Table 4-4. Comparison of Selected Occupations That Illustrate Notable Differences between Hispanics and Asians
Percent

Occupation	*Hispanic*	*Asian*
Other services[a]	31	16
Education, health, and social services	9	22
Professional services	3	31
Construction	21	4

Source: U.S. Census Bureau, *Census of Population 2000.*
a. Other services include retail sales and personal services.

while only about one-fourth have not graduated from high school. Among Latino immigrants, only 8 percent hold bachelor degrees, although the percentage is considerably higher in some subgroups. For example, 27 percent of Cubans have at least a bachelor's degree, whereas 78 percent of Mexicans have only a high school degree or less. Among Asians, Indians have the highest educational attainment level: 62 percent hold a bachelor's degree or higher, while Vietnamese have the lowest, with only 16 percent holding a bachelor's degree or higher.

Such varied education partially contributes to the different types of jobs Asians and Latinos take (table 4-4). Both groups have very low unemployment rates, and there is some overlap among the top occupations among these groups in areas such as manufacturing, lodging, and food services. However, three other top categories of employment reveal drastically different divisions. For example, 22 percent of Asians work in education, health, and social services, compared with only 9 percent of Hispanics. Nearly one in three Asians is employed in one of the professional services, compared with only 3 percent of Hispanics. Only 4 percent of Asians work in a construction trade, compared with more than one in five Hispanics.

With the exception of the Vietnamese, internal variations among Asian immigrant groups are small, although Indians have the highest percentage working in professional, science, and technology services (15 percent), management (9 percent), and professional and related occupations (52 percent). They also have the lowest proportion in services (5 percent). Chinese immigrants are more likely involved in lodging and food services (18 percent), but they are also well represented in business and financial sectors (7 percent). In contrast, Vietnamese immigrants are more likely to have production, transportation, and material-moving occupations (37 percent) and jobs in manufacturing (44 percent). These rankings are higher than among Latino immigrant groups. Asians are also more likely to be self-employed (7 percent) than Latinos (5 percent), with Vietnamese (9 percent) and Cubans (8 percent) the most likely to be self-employed. Filipinos (4 percent) and Puerto Ricans (less than 1 percent) have the lowest rates of self-employment. Given that Mexican immigrants dominate the Latino immigrant workforce, it is not surprising that internal variations among Latino groups are quite small.

As a result of their higher human capital and greater job prestige, Asian immigrants have a higher median household income, $50,904 in 1999, than do Latinos ($33,915; see table 4-3). Fifty-one percent of Latinos live below the poverty line, with Mexicans having a slightly higher percentage below the poverty line (54 percent) than other Latino groups. In contrast, even among Vietnamese, the poorest Asian immigrant group, only 32 percent live below the poverty threshold. Asian immigrants have higher homeownership rates as well, 60 percent compared with 52 percent for Latinos.

Suburbanization and Entrepreneurship

The rapid growth of the minority and immigrant population in prototypical white suburbs has yielded changing business and institutional landscapes. Both the changing patterns of Hispanic settlement in Phoenix proper as well as the suburbanization of Latinos in metropolitan Phoenix can be seen through the lens of emerging Hispanic-oriented businesses.[16] In particular, *carnicerías*—which translates literally into English as "meat markets," but which are better described as small grocery or general stores—serve as an early sentinel for rapid neighborhood change resulting from an influx of Latinos.[17] The other business types typically follow and signal further neighborhood evolution to majority Hispanic districts. In metropolitan Phoenix, *carnicerías* and other "pioneer" businesses continue to emerge in previously non-Hispanic neighborhoods, particularly in suburban cities. In several cases, these Hispanic-oriented businesses established a single store in a traditionally Latino neighborhood in Phoenix in the 1990s, followed by other satellite establishments in the suburbs as the Latino immigrant population began to disperse outside of the central city.

Unlike Latino businesses, Asian establishments—due to their smaller numbers—generally do not serve such a "signifier" function for Asian residential communities. However, the total number and locations of Asian-owned businesses have increased and changed dramatically in recent decades. Table 4-5 shows the distribution of Asian business in metro Phoenix in 1997. Although there are still more Asian-owned firms in the central city than in the suburbs, firms in the East Valley cities (with or without employees) have much higher total sales and receipts per firm, and

Table 4-5. Businesses Owned by Asians and Pacific Islanders in Metro Phoenix: Central City versus East Valley, 1997

Category	Phoenix	East Valley cities					Group total
		Chandler	*Gilbert*	*Mesa*	*Tempe*	*Scottsdale*	
Asian population, 2000	26,449	7,453	3,937	5,917	7,531	3,964	28,802
Native Hawaiian and other Pacific Islanders, 2000	1,766	251	134	932	455	167	1,939
Total API population, 2000[a]	28,215	7,704	4,071	6,849	7,986	4,131	30,741
Number of API firms	2,164	418	183	494	401	398	1,894
Sales and receipts ($1,000)	535,825	48,122	17,513	96,856	534,069	72,342	768,902
API firms per 1,000 API residents	77	54	45	72	50	96	62
Average sales per establishment ($1,000)	248	115	96	196	1,332	182	406
Number of firms with paid employees	855	132	19	157	194	106	608
Sales and receipts ($1,000)	478,723	44,703	9,880	71,111	528,370	59,132	713,196
Annual payroll ($1,000)	85,730	17,718	815	14,039	39,474	10,281	82,327
Employees	5,041	522	34	1,236	1,444	384	3,620
Number of establishments per 1,000 API residents	30	17	5	23	24	26	20
Annual sales per establishment ($1,000)	560	339	520	453	2,724	558	1,173
Average number of employees per establishment	6	4	2	8	7	4	6
Average payroll per establishment ($)	17,007	33,943	23,971	11,358	27,337	26,773	22,742

Source: U.S. Census Bureau, *U.S. Economic Census, Minority Owned Businesses 1997;* U.S. Census Bureau, *Census of Population 2000.*
a. API = Asian and Pacific Islander.

higher pay for their employees than those in the central city. This suggests a better situation for ethnic Asian firms in suburban areas. Higher shares of Indians and Chinese in particular own businesses than other Asian groups, particularly relative to their share of the total Asian population. These businesses are no longer all family owned and operated; many are firms with paid employees. Indian firms generate more total sales and receipts per firm (both with and without employees) than their Chinese counterparts. Such patterns again imply both locality and group differences.

Suburbanization and the Formation of Cultural and Political Identities

With the increasing settlement of recent Latino immigrants in suburban Phoenix and on the fringes of the central city, new Latino residents are often separated from the Hispanic core of the city, in some cases by as much as twenty or thirty miles. Although a degree of physical isolation and cultural estrangement occurs in these situations, several institutions—both formal and informal—have served to unite disconnected suburban Latinos with Phoenix's Hispanic core and with Mexico and elsewhere in Latin America. In the absence of formalized institutions, Hispanic-oriented businesses serve as a mechanism for maintaining cultural ties and ethnic identities.

Carnicerías, for example, often are a leading center for various social and cultural activities. Much as early American general stores were pioneer outposts on the wild frontier, *carnicerías* are Latino outposts in the Anglo suburban frontier. Locally, these shops provide a place to gather, sometimes as more of a serendipitous encounter while standing in line, at other times through more formal interactions such as at a sit-down lunch within the shop's small restaurant. Some *carnicerías* post flyers or advertisements that inform local Latino residents about events or services in other neighborhoods, often in distant parts of Phoenix or in far suburbs. *Carnicerías* further serve as transnational connectors where Latino immigrants can wire remittance money back home, purchase international phone cards, or find transportation into both border communities and the interior of Mexico. *Carnicerías* also cultivate a distinctive sense of place that counters the Anglo character of surrounding suburban neighborhoods. This is most evident in the use of hometown place names, bucolic symbols, nostalgic décor, and a well-stocked, intimate store layout.

Similarly, existing research indicates that Asians typically maintain their culture and identity through social networks.[18] Ethnic festivals, in particular, are one of the most prominent ways local Asians promote their ethnic culture and maintain their ethnic identity, especially in educating their American-born younger generations. Since 1981 Chinese communities have held an annual weekend-long Chinese lunar New Year celebration, cohosted by the Chinese Week Committee, Phoenix's Sister City Commission, and one of the two Chinese sister cities, rotating between Chengdu, China, and Taipei, Taiwan. Local and international dignitaries participate in the festival, cultural performances are held on a main stage, and merchants and community organizations operate several dozen booths. Since the late 1990s, this festival has moved to the Chinese Cultural Center, a newly built cultural landmark complete with a large tile roof, traditional Chinese-style buildings, and replicas of some of the most famous southern Chinese gardens. Participants and spectators cross racial and ethnic group boundaries, and the annual event draws as many as 200,000 spectators.[19]

Other Asian cultural festivals have also gained recognition and participation. Every March local Japanese-American communities host the Matsui Festival, and Hawaiian and Pacific Islander communities host an Aloha Festival. The spring Asian festivities often end with the Arizona Asian Festival in April, organized by the pan-Asian Arizona Asian American Association (AAAA). All three festivals are held downtown in popular public squares and encompass an entire weekend. Participants come from all over the state, and some merchants come from California and even as far as Hawaii. These Asian festivals have become deep-rooted in greater Phoenix's cultural scene. People of different backgrounds are brought together, including new immigrants as well as native-born Asian Americans, and people of different race-ethnicities, classes, and age groups. Equally important to the organizers, the festivals pull geographically scattered communities together to celebrate their cultures and sustain ethnic identities.

Formal institutions have also emerged to link widely dispersed Latino populations across the greater Phoenix area. The most evident of these are media outlets. *La Prensa Hispana* is the most widely read and broadly circulated of the local Spanish language newspapers. Although it is distributed across Arizona, it focuses on Latinos in the Phoenix area. The other major Spanish-language paper, *La Voz*, is published by the *Arizona Republic*, Phoenix's flagship daily English-language newspaper. Originally designed to translate English articles into Spanish, it has since evolved into a more traditional, autonomous newspaper. In a similar fashion, local radio stations have proliferated, as the Latino community in the Phoenix area has grown larger, more dispersed, and increasingly heterogeneous. These include two Spanish-language AM news stations and eight FM music stations that broadcast a wide range of Latino music. As with similar English-language stations, each of these Spanish-language stations sponsors various promotions and events that link together scattered Latino residents with social and cultural activities in Phoenix, throughout the region, and even across international borders.

In recent years several *clubes de oriundos* have blossomed in the metro area. These "hometown associations" connect immigrants with their home state, region, or community. Examples include a Guanajuato club, which represents Mexican immigrants from this particular Mexican state, and a club representing Ocampo, Durango, which connects newcomers to one particular community. These clubs serve multiple functions, including assisting immigrants in adjusting to Phoenix and the United States, providing important social and cultural connections, serving as a channel of communication between the home community or state and its former residents, and—in some cases—channeling remittance money back to home communities for use in public development projects.

Although Asians have no local radio or TV stations, nearly every group has its own newspaper. Moreover, Asians are no less organized than Latinos overall, as is evident in various formal institutions, whether professional, cultural, or political. For instance, several high-tech professional organizations have been formed, including the Arizona Chinese American High-Tech Association and the Association of Chinese Scientists and Engineers. Major companies in the area, such as Honeywell, Intel, and Motorola, host their own Asian American groups.

Because they lack an understanding of American politics or are not citizens, many new immigrants often steer clear of political activism. However, participating in a community organization may well be the first step to becoming involved in local politics. Three of the board members of AAAA were appointed as the governor's Asian-American Advisory Council. Business organizations, trade unions, and professional organizations can also serve political functions. The Chinese Chamber of Commerce, established in 1939, is very active in presenting their business interests to local politicians and the broader business community. In the 1980s the Asian Chamber of Commerce was established in response to the increasingly diverse Asian immigrant population. Today, the Asian Chamber of Commerce is quite active in local politics through its support of scholarships and its establishment of an Asian American high school leadership training program through the Asian LEAD Academy. This academy takes place every summer in cooperation with Arizona State University and is vocal about almost every major issue facing local Asian American communities. The Asian Chamber of Commerce also publishes a monthly English-language newspaper, *Asian SuNews,* which is one of the main media venues in which Asian Americans can voice their concerns.

An Asian political presence in Arizona dates back to World War II. The first Chinese American to be elected to a state office in the continental United States (in 1946) was Wing F. Ong, a Phoenix resident. He served six terms as a state legislator and was subsequently elected to the state senate. Today his daughter, Madeline Ong-Sakata, is the executive director of the Asian Chamber of Commerce, publisher of *Asian SuNews,* and a lifelong community activist and leader. Some forty years after Wing Ong's election, a third-generation Chinese American attorney, Barry Wong, was elected to the state legislature, representing a largely non-Hispanic white district in northern Phoenix until the early 2000s. Another Chinese American, Ed Tang, also served as mayor of the suburban city of Peoria.

However, relatively few Asian Americans have been active in politics in the Phoenix area. It will take time for first-generation adult Asian immigrants to acquire English proficiency, become accustomed to the American political system, and build up their political resumes to become politically active and serve as potential candidates. However, active participation in community organizations and volunteering in local events will likely serve as an initial step for further political integration and activism of Asian newcomers.

Conclusion

As Phoenix comes of age, several efforts are under way to dig deeper into its history, particularly its ethnic and immigrant roots. For example, the City of Phoenix has historians working to catalog the area's original African American, Latino, Asian, and Native American landmarks and neighborhoods. Through this and similar processes, residents are slowly becoming aware that the recent arrival of Latinos, Asians, and others has historical antecedents that were swept aside during the unprecedented urban growth in recent decades.

Yet these historical immigrant and ethnic populations were small, underrepresented, and intentionally excluded from the larger political and economic forces that shaped the city. This new and substantial influx of Latino and Asian immigrants is several hundred thousand strong and gaining both economic and political clout. Their presence results in both tremendous tensions and awkward contradictions, particularly in regard to Latinos, who are unequivocally front and center in the immigration debate. Although knee-jerk anti-immigration discourse has raged locally for years, the debate has moved to a national platform and is now even more prominent at the local and state level than in years past. The resulting local media coverage of Hispanic immigration is rather contradictory: at times sensationalistic and ideological, while at other times much more measured and pragmatic. The media highlight immigrant drop houses and "coyotes" (immigrant smugglers), and Central American gang infiltration; at times there is the overt suggestion that immigrants are somehow responsible for a general increase in crime in the Phoenix area. At the same time, the media also emphasize the emerging economic clout of Hispanic immigrants, their burgeoning entrepreneurship, and their future voting potential.

At both the national and local levels, Asian immigrants and native-born Asian Americans in general are perceived as a "model minority." Such perceptions often lead to myths that Asian Americans do not have problems, and as a result their concerns and issues are overlooked by elected officials, funding agencies, and mainstream nongovernmental organizations, according to a Chandler city official and Asian American community leaders. In reality, urgent issues among Asian immigrants in metro Phoenix include poverty (among certain segments) and health care disparities. In addition, issues of undocumented Asian immigrants are almost completely ignored in recent immigration debates. Moreover, tensions have increased in the post-9/11 era, mainly directed toward South Asians—Sikhs in particular—who have been the targets of hate crimes. Therefore, it is imperative to study and address the needs of Asian immigrants in emerging gateways such as metro Phoenix, despite their smaller numbers.

The greater Phoenix area is indeed an emerging immigrant gateway city and may be an indication of changing immigration patterns that will further shift foreign-born groups away from traditional destinations like New York, Los Angeles, and Miami. Concomitant with this emergence is a geographic and cultural remapping of metro areas themselves. As the chapters in this book detail, suburbanization of immigrant groups is occurring in cities across the nation, and Phoenix is no exception. Hispanics and Asians in Phoenix exhibit vastly different socioeconomics, which may be a harbinger of future changes; some immigrant groups may more readily achieve lasting economic success while others continue to struggle or suffer setbacks. Furthermore, as immigrant groups settle in more dispersed suburban locales, the business landscape may be one of the visible signs of ethnic change. Complex arrays of social, cultural, and political networks may also form to bring together scattered pockets of co-ethnics across large metropolitan areas. Phoenix and other such emerging gateway cities may eventually become the norm rather than the exception in urban immigrant settlement in the United States.

Notes

1. The unique urban environment of metropolitan Phoenix presents a challenge when the "central city" is compared with the "suburbs." Unlike many other American cities, the central city of Phoenix continues to grow and expand as it annexes desert land to the north. In addition, many parts of Phoenix are more "suburban" in character, with newer, low-density neighborhoods.

2. The authors use the term "Hispanic" and "Latino" interchangeably to refer to individuals of Latin American ancestry. Similarly, we use the term "Asian" to

describe all individuals with an ancestry traced back to one or more Asian countries. Because of some of the changes in the way the U.S. Census collects data, occasionally the term "Asian and Pacific Islander" will be used. This refers to Asians and individuals whose ancestry is linked to the Pacific Islands. We are keenly aware of, and in fact analyze, the internal diversity among both Latino and Asian immigrant groups but use these two umbrella terms to cover the larger groups.

3. Bradford Luckingham, *Minorities in Phoenix: A Profile of Mexican American, Chinese American, and African American Communities, 1860–1992* (University of Arizona Press, 1994).

4. Ibid. See also Roberto Suro and Audrey Singer, *Latino Growth in Metropolitan America: Changing Patterns, New Locations* (Brookings, 2002).

5. Suro and Singer, *Latino Growth in Metropolitan America.*

6. U.S. Census, *Census of Population, Summary File 1, 1990, 2000,* Washington.

7. Thomas Sheridan, *Los Tucsonenses: The Mexican Community in Tucson, Arizona 1854–1941* (University of Arizona Press, 1992).

8. Emily Skop and Cecilia Menjívar, "Phoenix: The Newest Latino Immigrant Gateway?" in *Yearbook, Association of Pacific Coast Geographers,* vol. 63 (University of Hawaii Press, 2001), pp. 63–76.

9. Amanda Ho, *The Asian American and Pacific Islander Community in Arizona and the Use of Panethnicity through Events, Organizations, and Publication* (honor thesis, Arizona State University, 2004); Thomas Nakayama, *Transforming Barbed Wire. The Incarceration of Japanese Americans in Arizona during World War II* (Phoenix: Arizona Humanities Council, 1997); Eric Waltz, "The Issei Community in Maricopa County: Development and Persistence in the Valley of the Sun, 1990–1940," *Journal of Arizona History* 38 (Spring 1979): 1–22.

10. Emily Skop, *The Saffron Suburbs: Asian Indian Community Formation in Phoenix* (unpublished dissertation, Arizona State University, 2002).

11. Jim Walsh, "Asian-Themed Shopping Site Set for Mesa's West Side: Demographics Look Good for Mekong Plaza," *Arizona Republic,* May 8, 2006, p. B5.

12. Skop, *The Saffron Suburbs.*

13. Wei Li, "Anatomy of a New Ethnic Settlement: The Chinese Ethnoburb in Los Angeles," *Urban Studies* 35 (1998): 479–501.

14. Because of data constraints (as noted in the text), some of the information presented here reflects the total Latino and Asian population instead of the Latino and Asian foreign-born population. Whenever 2000 PUMS (public use microdata samples) data are used to differentiate central city and suburb, super PUMAs (public use microdata area) 04302, 04304, and 04305 represent City of Phoenix, 04301 represents the western suburbs, and 04303 and 04306 represent the eastern suburbs, known locally as "East Valley." Unless otherwise noted, all numbers presented in this section are one-race data and from the U.S. Census 2000.

15. Alex Oberle, "Se Venden Aquí: The Latino Commercial Landscape in Phoenix, Arizona," in *Hispanic Spaces, Latino Places,* edited by Daniel Arreola (University of Texas Press, 2004), pp. 239–54.

16. Alex Oberle, "Latino Business Landscapes and the Ethnic Economy," in *Landscapes of the Ethnic Economy,* edited by David Kaplan and Wei Li (Lanham, Md.: Rowman and Littlefield, 2006), pp. 149–64.

17. See, for instance, Skop, *The Saffron Suburbs*; Emily Skop and Wei Li,

"Asians in America's Suburbs: Patterns and Consequences of Settlement," *Geographic Review* 95, no. 2 (2005): 167–88; Kathleen Wong (Lau), "The Asian American Community in the Southwest: Creating 'Place' in the Absence of Ethnic 'Space'," in *Asian Pacific Americans and the U.S. Southwest,* edited by T. K. Nakayama and C. F. Yoshioka (Arizona State University, 1997), pp. 79–90.

18. Wei Zeng and Wei Li, "Chinese Week: Building Chinese American Community through Festivity in Metropolitan Phoenix," in *Negotiating Space: New Asian American Communities,* edited by Huping Ling (University of Hawaii Press, forthcoming).

| 5

Unsettled in the Suburbs

Latino Immigration and Ethnic Diversity in Metro Atlanta

MARY E. ODEM

On April 10, 2006, Atlanta witnessed one of the largest marches and rallies for social justice since the civil rights era. Fifty thousand people, the vast majority Latino, walked a three-mile loop from the Plaza Fiesta shopping center down Dresden Avenue and then listened to speeches by local Latino, African American, and white politicians and activists. Marchers in Atlanta were part of nationwide demonstrations that brought millions of immigrants and their supporters to the streets to call on Congress to offer legal status and citizenship to millions of undocumented immigrants and to protest a proposed House bill that would speed up deportations, build a wall at the Mexican border, and criminalize illegal immigrants. Protesters in Atlanta had an additional goal, to challenge State Senate Bill 529, the Georgia Security and Immigration Compliance Act. Bill 529, which would eventually pass, was one of the most far-reaching state efforts to date to address undocumented immigration. Introduced by a Republican lawmaker from the predominantly white suburban county of Cherokee, the act would deny unauthorized immigrants in Georgia access to public benefits and employment and would enlist state and local police in the enforcement of federal immigration laws.

The state legislation and the immigrant rights march protesting it are signs of the dramatic demographic changes that have occurred in metropolitan

I wish to acknowledge the support of the Pew Charitable Trusts, the Emory Center for the Study of Law and Religion, and the research assistance of Joy Henderson of the Emory SIRE program.

Atlanta during the past twenty-five years. With a population of more than 4 million, metro Atlanta is the business and financial capital as well as the main transportation hub for the southeastern United States. For most of its history, Atlanta, like the rest of the South, was a biracial society, with African Americans and whites constituting the vast majority of inhabitants. The black-white racial divide profoundly shaped the politics, social structure, and physical layout of the region. The ethnic-racial landscape of metro Atlanta began to change in the 1980s as relief agencies resettled Southeast Asian refugees in the area, and a booming economy attracted large numbers of legal and illegal immigrants, principally from Mexico and Central and South American countries.[1] With the dramatic growth of its foreign-born population over the next two decades, Atlanta has become a "major new immigrant gateway" in the United States.[2]

Although a boon to the region's economy, mass immigration has posed challenges to local governments, public institutions, and residents. Immigrants initially settled in predominantly white suburban areas, just north of the central city, where they were drawn by affordable housing and access to job opportunities. The suburban destination of Atlanta's immigrants is part of an overall shift in immigrant settlement patterns away from the inner cities and into the suburbs, as Singer notes in the introduction.[3]

Immigrant settlement has unsettled many in the suburbs. While residents worry about the social transformation of their neighborhoods and schools, local governments struggle to address the increased demands on education, transportation, and housing resources. The heated immigration debates in Georgia in 2006 followed more than a decade of efforts on the part of suburban county and municipal governments to respond to the rapidly expanding immigrant populations in their jurisdictions. Local authorities have created a range of policies in education, law enforcement, housing, and transportation. While some measures focus on integrating immigrants, others aim to exclude and penalize them, with the latter measures directed primarily at undocumented Latino immigrants (see also chapters 3 and 6 in this volume). In the wake of federal inaction and growing anti-immigrant sentiment in recent years, state, county, and municipal authorities have pursued more aggressive measures, such as Georgia's Senate Bill 529, to control unauthorized immigration. The policies of local and state governments warrant closer study because of their importance in determining how this current generation of immigrants will be incorporated into American society.

I begin this chapter by examining Atlanta's emergence as a major new gateway for Latin American immigrants and by analyzing the patterns of immigrant settlement in specific suburban localities, as well as the reasons

Map 5-1. Foreign-Born Population in the Atlanta Metropolitan Area, 2000

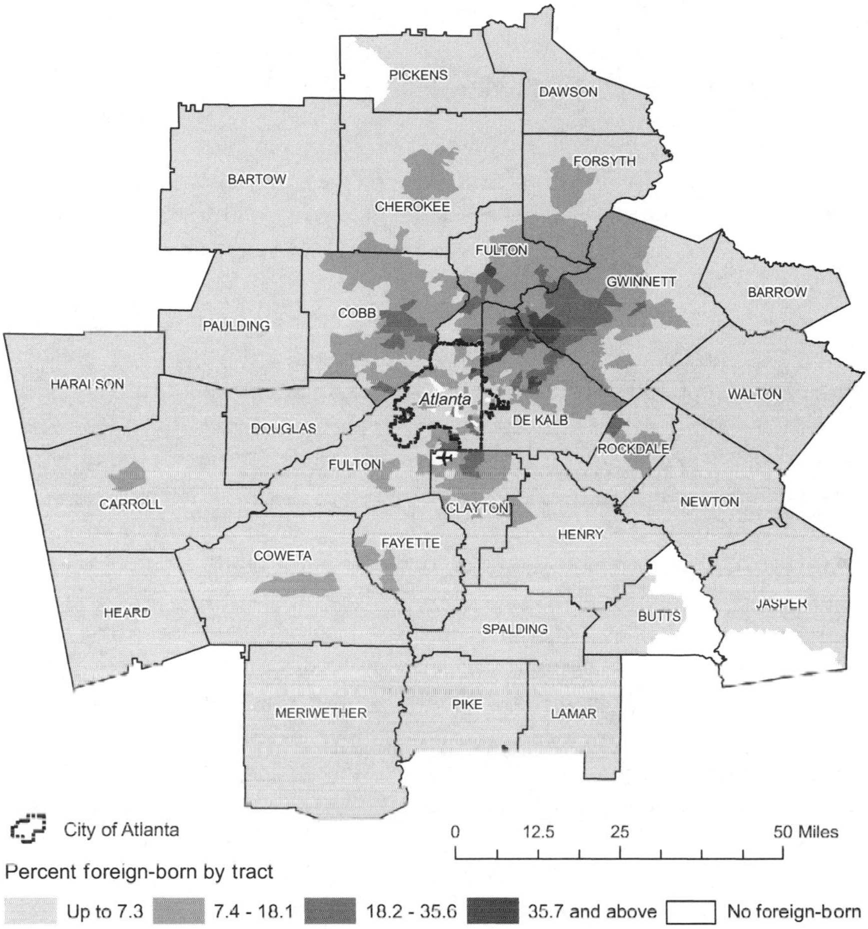

City of Atlanta

Percent foreign-born by tract

Up to 7.3 | 7.4 - 18.1 | 18.2 - 35.6 | 35.7 and above | No foreign-born

Source: U.S. Census Bureau, *Census of Population 2000, SF3.*

for such choices. I then analyze and compare local policy responses of suburban counties and municipalities to the expanding population of Latin American immigrants in the region. The chapter draws on both quantitative and qualitative data. The analysis of immigrant population growth and settlement uses U.S. decennial census data for 1980, 1990, and 2000 and data from the 2005 American Community Survey for the Atlanta metropolitan statistical area (as defined in 2003). Map 5-1 shows the residential distribution of metropolitan Atlanta's foreign-born. The qualitative data include interviews with public officials and immigrant leaders and advocates in Atlanta, and a content analysis of newspapers for the region (the *Atlanta Journal-Constitution* in English and *Mundo Hispánico* in Spanish), as well as county and municipal records and reports.

The Emergence of a Latino Immigrant Gateway

Historically the South has not attracted immigrants in large numbers (unlike the Northeast, Midwest, and Southwest) because of its slower pace of industrial development and the presence of a large number of poor blacks and whites who provided a steady pool of low-wage labor. In the last two decades economic transformation and growth, linked to larger patterns of change in the global economy, have attracted many foreign-born as well as domestic migrants to the region. The urban South, and Atlanta in particular, experienced a period of robust economic growth in the 1990s, driven by the service and financial industries, and by construction, transportation, and public utilities. Economic expansion created a diverse range of job opportunities in white-collar and high-tech employment as well as for skilled and unskilled labor. The Atlanta metro area added more jobs than any other U.S. metropolitan area, except Dallas, during the 1990s.[4] As native-born blacks and whites took advantage of white-collar jobs, Latin American immigrants increasingly filled positions as laborers. A Brookings Institution study in 2000 defined Atlanta as "one of the nation's great metropolitan success stories." According to the report, "population and job growth show no sign of slowing in the Atlanta area. . . . The region is a place of economic opportunities for both whites and African Americans, and it is a magnet for new immigrants from Latin America and Asia."[5]

The total population of the Atlanta metro area (as defined in 2003) grew rapidly, from 2.3 million in 1980 to 3 million in 1990 to 4.8 million in 2005. Non-Hispanic African Americans composed 30 percent and non-Hispanic whites 56 percent of the total population in 2005. Although native-born blacks and whites contributed significantly more to overall population growth, the foreign-born population grew at a rapid pace, from 2 percent of the metro area population in 1980 to almost 4 percent in 1990 to 10 percent in 2000 to almost 13 percent (12.7) in 2005. In numbers, the foreign-born population grew from 47,815 in 1980, to 117,253 in 1990, to 424,519 in 2000, and to 612,759 in 2005—a growth rate of 262 percent from 1990 to 2000 alone and an amazing 1182 percent from 1980 to 2005. The rapid growth reflects the fact that immigrant numbers started quite small, but it nevertheless represents a major demographic change, one that has profound consequences for the economy, social structure, culture, and politics of the Atlanta region.

Table 5-1. Birthplaces of the Foreign-Born in the Atlanta Metropolitan Area, 2005[a]

Birthplace	*Number*	*Percent*
Total population	4,828,838	100.0
Foreign-born population	612,759	12.7
Latin America	320,978	52.4
Asia	152,993	25.0
Europe	69,587	11.4
Africa	53,587	8.7
Northern America	12,549	2.0
Oceania	3,065	0.5

Source: U.S. Census Bureau, *American Community Survey 2005.*

a. The authors defined the Atlanta metropolitan area using the definition adopted by the Office of Management and Budget (OMB) in 2003. The data do not include populations in group quarters (such as dormitories, prisons, and other institutions).

Immigrants in Atlanta come from dozens of countries and all regions of the world.[6] In 2005 the largest regional group came from Latin America (52 percent), followed by 25 percent from Asia, 11 percent from Europe, and 9 percent from Africa (table 5-1). Mexicans constitute by far the largest national group of immigrants; more than one in every four immigrants in Atlanta is from Mexico. Central Americans make up another 6 percent, while South Americans form nearly 9 percent of this population (the largest sending countries are, in order, Colombia and Brazil). The countries of China, India, Korea, and Vietnam together contribute 17 percent of the immigrant population. Atlanta is also a favored destination of African immigrants; among all metropolitan areas, it has the fourth-largest African-born population.[7]

Atlanta's immigrants work in a diverse range of jobs. A small but significant number work in well-paid professional and technical fields. However, the vast majority of Mexican and other Latin American immigrants work as low-wage laborers in various industries. The construction and service industries in Atlanta have been the main employers of Latin American workers. More than 60 percent of Latino workers are employed in these industries, with 30 percent in construction and 34.6 percent in services, including work in hotels, restaurants, landscaping, and other services to buildings and dwellings. (These figures include both immigrant and native-born Latinos.) The participation of Latinos in construction work is especially notable; in 2000 they accounted for 45 percent of the construction workforce in DeKalb County, and 25 percent in Gwinnett and Fulton counties. Another 12 percent of Latino workers in Atlanta are employed in manufacturing, largely in carpet and poultry-processing factories. Contrary to national trends, Georgia added manufacturing jobs between 1990 and 2000.[8]

A substantial share of Latin American immigrants working in Atlanta is undocumented. A report published by the Urban Institute in 2004 estimated that between 40 percent and 49 percent of all immigrants in the state in 2000 were undocumented.[9] The majority of unauthorized immigrants in Atlanta are very likely from Latin America, mostly from Mexico. Jeffrey Passel's 2005 report, "Unauthorized Migrants," estimates that nationally Latin Americans compose 81 percent of the unauthorized immigrants (using March 2004 *Current Population Survey* data).[10]

Patterns of Latino Immigrant Settlement in Atlanta

Latino immigrants to Atlanta are settling directly in suburban areas, where most of metropolitan Atlanta lives. Nearly 96 percent of the foreign-born in metropolitan Atlanta lives in the suburbs. Immigrant settlement in Atlanta does not fit the traditional assimilation model, based on the experiences of European immigrants in the early twentieth century, where immigrants settle first in ethnic enclaves in the central city until their economic situation improves, after which they or their children move to higher-quality neighborhoods in the suburbs, where they are more integrated socially and geographically with the majority group (see chapters 1 and 2 for discussion of the spatial assimilation of immigrants).

Several alternative models have been proposed to account for the different patterns of residential settlement among contemporary immigrants.[11] In Atlanta, Latino immigrant settlement shows evidence of both dispersal and concentration. Latino immigrants reside in all twenty-two counties that make up the metro area, and most live in neighborhoods where they make up less than 20 percent of the population.[12] At the same time, they have formed several residential and commercial clusters in suburban areas outside of the city of Atlanta (map 5-2).

The main clusters of Latino immigrant settlement are located in inner-ring suburbs north of the city in DeKalb, Cobb, Gwinnett, and northern Fulton counties; all were predominantly white neighborhoods before the arrival of immigrants. The places with the highest concentration of Latin American immigrants (where they make up more than 20 percent of the population) include the area along Buford Highway and I-85, which run through northern DeKalb County and into southwestern Gwinnett County; the area around the city of Marietta just west of I-75 in Cobb County; and a

Map 5-2. Latin American Foreign-Born Population in the Atlanta Metropolitan Area, 2000

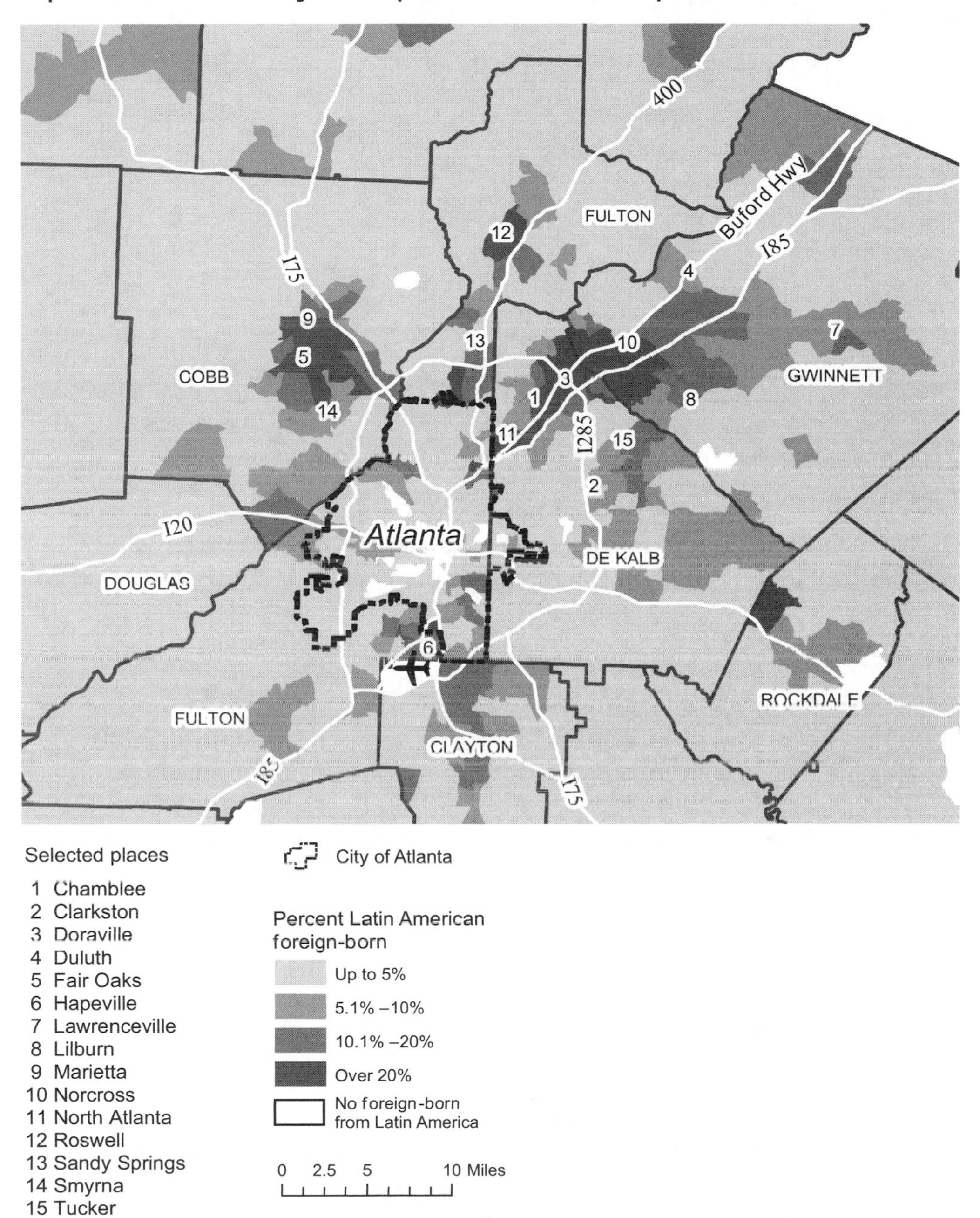

Source: U.S. Census Bureau, *Census of Population 2000, SF3*.

Table 5-2. Foreign-Born Population for Selected Counties and Cities in the Atlanta Metropolitan Area, 1990–2005[a]

	1980			1990			2000			2005[b]		
County and City/Place	*Total*	*Foreign-born*	*Percent*	*Total*	*Foreign-born*	*Percent*	*Total*	*Foreign-born*	*Percent*	*Total*	*Foreign-born*	*Percent*
Cobb	297,718	6,734	2.3	447,745	18,461	4.1	607,751	70,439	11.6	653,715	102,037	15.6
Fair Oaks CDP[c]	8,486	244	2.9	6,996	170	2.4	8,602	3,022	35.1	—	—	—
Marietta city	30,829	772	2.5	44,129	2,254	5.1	58,374	11,522	19.7	—	—	—
Smyrna city	20,312	696	3.4	30,981	1,834	5.9	40,780	7,159	17.6	—	—	—
DeKalb	483,024	17,256	3.6	545,837	36,492	6.7	665,865	101,320	15.2	662,973	105,197	15.9
Chamblee city	7,137	439	6.2	7,668	2,519	32.9	9,838	6,315	64.2	—	—	—
Clarkston city	4,539	149	3.3	5,385	484	9.0	6,826	2,301	33.7	—	—	—
Doraville city	7,414	270	3.6	7,626	1,093	14.3	10,135	4,725	46.6	—	—	—
North Atlanta CDP	30,521	2,864	9.4	27,812	4,116	14.8	38,403	13,400	34.9	—	—	—
Tucker CDP	25,399	577	2.3	25,781	1,729	6.7	26,616	4,410	16.6	—	—	—
Fulton	589,904	13,653	2.3	648,951	26,777	4.1	816,006	78,619	9.6	884,079	103,360	11.7
Hapeville city	6,166	173	2.8	5,483	586	10.7	6,180	1,386	22.4	—	—	—
Roswell city	23,337	516	2.2	47,923	3,036	6.3	79,844	12,562	15.7	—	—	—
Sandy Springs CDP	46,877	1,654	3.5	67,842	4,602	6.8	85,524	15,052	17.6	—	—	—
Gwinnett	166,903	2,760	1.7	352,910	17,803	5.0	588,448	99,518	16.9	719,398	171,477	23.8
Duluth city	2,956	33	1.1	8,937	431	4.8	22,388	4,531	20.2	—	—	—
Lawrenceville city	8,928	39	0.4	16,848	499	3.0	22,512	3,995	17.7	—	—	—
Lilburn city	3,765	39	1.0	9,301	503	5.4	11,350	2,432	21.4	—	—	—
Norcross city	3,317	23	0.7	5,947	607	10.2	8,358	3,486	41.7	—	—	—
Total Atlanta metro area	2,326,639	47,815	2.1	3,069,425	117,253	3.8	4,247,981	424,519	10.0	4,828,838	612,759	12.7

Source: U.S. Census Bureau, *Census of Population, Summary Files 1980, 1990, 2000;* U.S. Census Bureau, *American Community Survey 2005.*

a. Cities shown are those where at least 15 percent of the population was foreign-born in 2000; the metro-level data correspond to the twenty-two-county definition adopted by OMB in 2003.

b. The 2005 data do not include populations in group quarters (such as dormitories, prisons, and other institutions). Cells with — indicate data were unavailable because of the small sample size in the *American Community Survey.*

c. CDP = Census-designated place.

smaller area along Highway 400 in northern Fulton County (see map 5-2). Fulton, a long, narrow county, contains the city of Atlanta, but immigrants are concentrated in the northern suburbs outside the urban core.[13]

Certain localities within these counties have an especially high concentration of foreign-born residents. In the cities of Chamblee and Doraville in DeKalb County, 64 percent and 47 percent, respectively, of residents are foreign-born, while in Norcross in Gwinnett County, 42 percent are foreign-born. The Fair Oaks census designated place (CDP) in Cobb County and the North Atlanta CDP in DeKalb County each have a population that is 35 percent foreign-born (table 5-2).

When Asian and Latin American immigrants began to arrive in Atlanta in large numbers in the 1980s and early 1990s, they initially settled in Chamblee and Doraville in DeKalb County. The immigrant population in DeKalb jumped from 17,256 in 1980 to 101,320 in 2000. Estimates for 2005 show that the population has not grown much over the 100,000 mark in DeKalb. However, Cobb, Fulton, and Gwinnett have outpaced DeKalb's rate of immigrant growth since 2000 (even though the number of immigrants and their share of the population in Cobb and Fulton are smaller than in DeKalb) (see table 5-2).

By 2005 the most dramatic growth had occurred in Gwinnett County, which had more than 171,000 immigrants (and the largest number of both Latin American and Asian immigrants of any county in the metro area), according to the 2005 American Community Survey. Its population of immigrants grew by an estimated 72 percent between 2000 and 2005; 24 percent of the county's population is now foreign-born (see table 5-2).

In the remainder of the chapter I focus on the four counties with the highest concentrations of foreign-born residents: Cobb, DeKalb, Fulton, and Gwinnett. Together these counties include 83 percent of all immigrants and 82 percent of all Latin American immigrants in the twenty-two-county metropolitan area.

DeKalb County

Until 1960 DeKalb was mainly an agricultural county with a predominantly white population. Its population and economy expanded and diversified over the next decades as Atlanta grew from a small southern city to a major metropolis, home to top national and multinational corporations, a commercial transportation hub with a busy international airport, and a major hospitality and convention center. The construction of housing subdivisions, shopping plazas, and highways quickly took over what had once been farmland and dairy country. DeKalb contains many of the region's more mature suburbs, including a number of African American and blue-collar neighborhoods. The county has become one of the most racially and ethnically diverse in the state; in 2005 its population was 30 percent white, 55 percent black, 9 percent Latino, and 4 percent Asian (table 5-3). Many middle-class African Americans have made their home in DeKalb, settling mostly in the eastern suburbs. African Americans have attained significant influence in county government: the chief executive officer of the county in 2007, Vernon Jones, is African American; four of the seven county commissioners are African Americans, as are the district attorney, police chief, and the chair of the Board of Education. Along with the presence of a large

Table 5-3. Race-Ethnicity for Selected Counties and Cities in the Atlanta Metropolitan Area, 1990–2005[a]

Percent unless otherwise noted

	1990						2000						2005[b]					
County/city	*Total*	*White*	*Black*	*Hispanic*	*Asian*	*Other*	*Total*	*White*	*Black*	*Hispanic*	*Asian*	*Other*	*Total*	*White*	*Black*	*Hispanic*	*Asian*	*Other*
Cobb	447,745	86.3	9.8	2.0	1.7	0.3	607,751	68.8	18.4	7.7	3.0	2.1	653,715	61.7	21.5	10.5	4.1	2.3
Fair Oaks CDP[c]	6,996	82.4	13.3	3.0	0.1	1.2	8,602	36.7	21.3	39.4	0.2	2.4	—	—	—	—	—	—
Marietta city	44,129	74.2	20.2	3.2	1.8	0.5	58,374	48.4	29.3	17.0	2.3	3.1	—	—	—	—	—	—
Smyrna city	30,981	78.0	15.8	3.7	2.2	0.3	40,780	54.1	26.4	13.2	3.9	2.4	—	—	—	—	—	—
DeKalb	545,837	52.2	42.1	2.7	2.9	0.3	665,865	32.3	53.7	7.7	3.9	2.2	662,973	30.2	54.9	9.1	3.9	1.8
Chamblee city	7,668	45.6	18.5	23.7	12.0	0.2	9,838	23.8	4.6	54.2	14.5	2.9	—	—	—	—	—	—
Clarkston city	5,385	36.3	55.4	2.5	5.8	0.0	6,826	14.6	60.6	4.4	11.6	8.8	—	—	—	—	—	—
Doraville city	7,626	65.3	18.5	8.4	7.5	0.4	10,135	29.5	13.3	44.9	8.7	3.6	—	—	—	—	—	—
North Atlanta CDP[c]	27,812	65.3	20.7	7.8	5.7	0.6	38,403	49.2	16.7	27.1	4.3	2.7	—	—	—	—	—	—
Tucker CDP[c]	25,781	88.2	5.1	2.3	4.2	0.2	26,616	68.9	13.7	7.7	7.4	2.2	—	—	—	—	—	—
Fulton	648,951	46.8	49.7	2.1	1.2	0.2	816,006	45.3	44.1	5.8	2.9	1.8	884,079	44.8	41.9	7.5	4.1	1.7
Hapeville city	5,483	75.4	10.4	3.3	10.3	0.6	6,180	42.0	25.4	21.8	8.8	2.1	—	—	—	—	—	—
Roswell city	47,923	90.4	4.8	2.9	1.7	0.1	79,844	75.6	7.8	10.6	3.7	2.3	—	—	—	—	—	—
Sandy Springs CDP[c]	67,842	87.8	7.6	2.8	1.6	0.2	85,524	72.7	12.0	10.0	2.9	2.4	—	—	—	—	—	—
Gwinnett	352,910	89.6	5.1	2.3	2.8	0.3	588,448	67.1	13.0	10.8	6.9	2.1	719,398	54.4	18.5	16.2	9.3	1.6
Duluth city	8,937	89.0	6.0	2.5	2.0	0.5	22,388	64.3	11.6	9.1	12.2	2.8	—	—	—	—	—	—
Lawrenceville city	16,848	90.7	5.7	1.5	1.9	0.2	22,512	68.4	14.0	12.3	3.3	2.0	—	—	—	—	—	—
Lilburn city	9,301	92.4	2.2	2.5	2.7	0.2	11,350	61.8	11.9	11.6	12.9	1.8	—	—	—	—	—	—
Norcross city	5,947	71.7	19.3	3.8	5.1	0.2	8,358	31.5	21.0	38.8	7.1	1.6	—	—	—	—	—	—
Total metro Atlanta	3,069,425	71.2	25.1	1.8	1.6	0.3	4,247,981	60.4	28.3	6.3	3.1	1.8	4,828,838	55.6	30.1	8.7	3.9	1.7

Source: U.S. Census Bureau, *Census of Population, Summary Files 1990, 2000;* U.S. Census Bureau, *American Community Survey 2005.*

a. Cities shown are those where at least 15 percent of the population was foreign-born in 2000; the metro-level data correspond to the twenty-two-county definition adopted by OMB in 2003.

b. The 2005 data do not include populations in group quarters (such as dormitories, prisons, and other institutions). Cells with — indicate data were unavailable because of the small sample size in the *American Community Survey.*

c. CDP = Census-designated place.

black middle class, DeKalb has a sizable population of poor African Americans, who are concentrated in the south side of the county.[14]

In the 1980s and 1990s northern DeKalb became a magnet for immigrants from Asia and Latin America. Before 1970 Chamblee and Doraville, two cities in the county, were home to mostly white blue-collar workers who labored in the numerous factories nearby, including General Motors, Frito-Lay, Kodak, and General Electric. The economic slowdown of the 1970s resulted in factory closings, layoffs, and the departure of many white working-class residents from the area. The major thoroughfares, Peachtree Industrial Boulevard and Buford Highway, were lined with empty commercial and industrial properties and sparsely populated apartment buildings.

At about the same time, private relief agencies designated Atlanta as one of the favored locations for the resettlement of Southeast Asian refugees, and during the late 1970s and 1980s, approximately 10,000 Vietnamese, Laotians, and Hmong arrived in the city. As the number of housing and rental vacancies climbed in Chamblee-Doraville, apartment managers began marketing to recently arrived refugees, and eventually two-thirds of the refugees settled in the area. Immigrants from China, Korea, and Latin America were soon drawn to the area because of the availability of low-cost housing, especially the large stock of moderately priced rental units. The arrival of two Metropolitan Area Rapid Transit (MARTA) stops by the 1980s made the area even more attractive to low-income residents dependent on low-wage jobs spread throughout the metropolitan region.[15]

By 1990 the Chamblee-Doraville area had become the most ethnically diverse area in Georgia and one of the most ethnically diverse in the Southeast (excluding Florida). The ethnic transformation of the population was particularly pronounced in Chamblee. In 1980 non-Hispanic whites composed 89 percent of Chamblee's population; African Americans, Asians, and Latinos together composed 11 percent. In 2000 whites composed only 24 percent of the Chamblee population, while Latinos had become the majority group with 54 percent of the population; Asians made up another 14.5 percent, and African Americans, 5 percent (see table 5-3).

As one of the earliest areas of immigrant settlement, the Chamblee-Doraville area has also become a bustling center of ethnic-owned businesses and commercial activity. The busy six-lane Buford Highway that runs through Chamblee and Doraville is the commercial center of the area. Numerous aging strip malls that line the highway have been converted to large ethnic and multiethnic plazas, with names like Chinatown Square (1988), Asian Square Mall (1993), and Plaza Fiesta (2000). In many ways, immigrants have economically and socially revived an area that faced economic stagnation and population decline.[16] As Susan Walcott noted in her article on the area:

> The multiethnic shopping plazas contain an array of shops, restaurants, and offices run by immigrant entrepreneurs of diverse ethnic backgrounds, including Vietnamese, Mexican, Korean, Chinese, Colombian, and Salvadoran, among others. The businesses include restaurants, bakeries, book and music stores, and clothing shops as well as the offices of travel agencies, doctors, real estate brokers, and insurance agents. The five-mile stretch of highway running through Chamblee, Doraville, and Norcross constitutes the greatest concentration of ethnic-owned businesses in the southeastern U.S.[17]

The Latino presence is strong and growing in these shopping areas. Latino entrepreneurs, mostly Mexican, have established numerous restaurants, music and video stores, bakeries, butcher shops, and clothing stores to cater to the growing number of Mexican, Central American, and South American immigrants in the metro area. Rather than renting a single building space, many Mexicans and other Latinos have rented stalls and other less expensive retail outlets in the Buford Highway Flea Market and Plaza Fiesta. An important gathering place for immigrants, Plaza Fiesta also fosters social networks and establishes a Latino presence in Atlanta. Nearly every weekend Latino organizations and groups host events such as dance and music performances, beauty contests, and fundraisers in the open space in the plaza.

Cobb, Gwinnett, and Northern Fulton Counties

Predominantly white and politically conservative, this arc of northern suburbs grew rapidly in the 1970s and 1980s as a result of white flight from the city of Atlanta following the desegregation of its public schools, parks, and neighborhoods. White citizens and local governments in these suburbs successfully pursued policies (exclusionary zoning, real-estate steering, discriminatory lending policies) to resist meaningful racial integration and to separate themselves and their tax dollars from the inner city.[18]

This attitude was most clearly expressed in their forceful opposition to the extension of the region's public transit system, MARTA, to their neighborhoods in the early 1970s. Resistance to MARTA was particularly strong in Cobb and Gwinnett counties, where residents predicted that the system would promote racial integration, lower housing values, and encourage public housing in white suburbs. Cobb and Gwinnett have continued to reject the extension of MARTA rail and bus lines into their jurisdictions even in the face of major traffic congestion. (Commute times in this region are among the longest in the country.) To this day MARTA operates only in Fulton and DeKalb counties, a restriction that has limited the transit system's effectiveness in stemming transportation and pollution problems.[19]

These northern suburbs continued to grow as a result of mass migration from other parts of Georgia and the rest of the country. The Brookings Institution classified all three areas as major job-residential hubs for the region, with rapid job and population growth and high average household incomes.[20] Population expansion was especially pronounced in Gwinnett, which was one of the fastest-growing counties in the nation in the 1980s, and it led the metropolitan region in net population increase in the 1990s. As large suburban job centers, Cobb, Gwinnett, and northern Fulton have witnessed the rapid and extensive construction of low-density single-family housing, shopping malls, country clubs, car dealerships, office buildings, and industrial parks, all connected by a vast network of highways and freeways. Some of the major industries and employers in these northern suburbs are Primerica and CheckFree Corporation, Lucent Technologies, Lockheed Martin, WellStar Health System, American Express, and Federal Express.[21]

Economic and suburban expansion has been supported by the white, Republican-controlled county governments. Cobb and Gwinnett have similar local political systems. Each is governed by a five-member Board of Commissioners, which has both legislative and executive authority. Gwinnett County's government is virtually all white and Republican. Cobb's Republican-dominated government is predominantly white, with one African American commissioner and an African American county manager.

The explosive economic development of the 1990s also attracted a growing number of immigrants and ethnic minorities to the northern suburbs. Cobb and Gwinnett counties saw their Latino populations soar during this period. In 1990 Latinos (both immigrant and native-born) composed 2 percent of Cobb's population and 2.3 percent of Gwinnett's population. In 2005 those shares had jumped to 10.5 percent in Cobb and 16.2 percent in Gwinnett (see table 5-3). The Latino immigrant population in Cobb is clustered around the city of Marietta, just west of I-75. In Gwinnett it is concentrated in the southwestern part of the county in and around the city of Norcross. Immigrant settlement has expanded northeast from DeKalb County into Gwinnett along the Buford Highway and I-85 corridors, creating the largest concentration of Latino immigrant settlement in the metropolitan area (see map 5-2).

Similar to the Chamblee-Doraville area, these areas contain older apartment complexes built in the 1970s that have attracted immigrants because of the affordable rents. More significantly, immigrants have been drawn by the numerous moderately priced single-family homes in subdivisions built in the late 1960s and 1970s. A common path for Latin American immigrants, as well as for Vietnamese and Koreans, is to leave the apartment complexes in Chamblee and Doraville once their economic position improves and head north to better housing districts in Gwinnett, northern Fulton, and Cobb counties, where many have bought single-family homes. Many pool their resources by sharing homes with family members or acquaintances to cover the down payment and monthly mortgage payments for a suburban home. These formerly all-white subdivisions with one- and two-story ranch houses are now home to an increasingly diverse ethnic population.

New clusters of ethnic businesses are also emerging in Cobb and Gwinnett counties. The section of Jimmy Carter Boulevard in Gwinnett running east from Buford Highway past I-85 has become a bustling center of ethnic commerce. The busy four-lane boulevard contains a number of small and large shopping plazas, with numerous Latino and Asian businesses including restaurants, groceries, video stores, clinics, and real estate, accounting, and law offices. Many of the people who frequent these ethnic businesses live in apartment complexes and small suburban homes in the neighborhoods that border Jimmy Carter Boulevard.

The Legacy of Segregation

Immigrant settlement in Atlanta has been shaped by the region's history and politics of racial segregation and inequality. The city and metro region have long been divided between predominantly white neighborhoods in the north and predominantly African American neighborhoods in the south. This division deepened with the white exodus from the city of Atlanta to the northern suburbs following the desegregation of the city's neighborhoods and public institutions in the 1960s and 1970s.[22] Inequalities in economic opportunity and growth correspond to the geographic racial divide. The economic growth of the 1980s and 1990s occurred in the predominantly white suburban areas north of the urban core. According to a Brookings study on Atlanta in 2000, "Jobs, people, and prosperity have moved northward and outward, leaving a large arc of little or no population growth, economic decline, and an unusually high concentration of poverty on the south side of the City of Atlanta and its close-in southern suburbs," areas whose population is predominantly African American.[23] The division is not simply one between city and suburb, because parts of the city of Atlanta gained jobs and population in the 1990s, but the prosperity and growth are concentrated in the north and northeast sectors of the city, populated by upper-middle-class white residents. The growth of the African American middle class and of predominantly African American and racially mixed suburbs in the region has mitigated, but by no means erased, the sharp north-south divide between prosperity and poverty.[24]

As map 5-3 shows, immigrants are not moving into historically African American communities. There is very little foreign-born settlement in areas with the highest concentrations of African American residents, mainly in south Fulton County, including southwestern Atlanta, and southern DeKalb County, where African American communities compose more than three-fourths of the population. These are also areas with the highest rates of poverty and slow-to-stagnant economic growth. However, there are clusters of immigrants in northeastern Clayton County and central DeKalb County, where African Americans make up at least one-third of the population.

Furthermore, both the African American and immigrant populations are growing in Cobb and Gwinnett counties (see table 5-3). Since 1990 a steady stream of African Americans has ventured into suburban areas north of the city. In 2005 African Americans composed 18.5 percent of Gwinnett's population and 21.5 percent of Cobb's population. Non Hispanic whites, who in 1990 accounted for 90 percent and 86 percent of the populations of Gwinnett and Cobb, respectively, represented only 54 percent and 62 percent in 2005. With the increase of both African American and immigrant residents, Atlanta's inner-ring suburbs are becoming more racially and ethnically mixed.

Factors Explaining the Growth of Latin American Immigrant Clusters

Several factors explain the high concentration of Latin American immigrants in certain suburban locales in Atlanta. Foremost is affordable housing. Latin American immigrants have settled in suburban areas that have numerous apartment complexes with affordable rents and moderately priced single-family homes: Chamblee and Doraville in DeKalb County, Norcross in Gwinnett County, and the Fair Oaks CDP and Marietta in Cobb County. Inexpensive apartments are especially numerous in the Chamblee-Doraville area. This includes older apartment complexes that were built in the 1970s for single professionals and young families, as well as newer complexes built more recently in response to growing immigrant demand.

Map 5-3. Black Population and Foreign-Born Population in the Atlanta Metropolitan Area, 2000

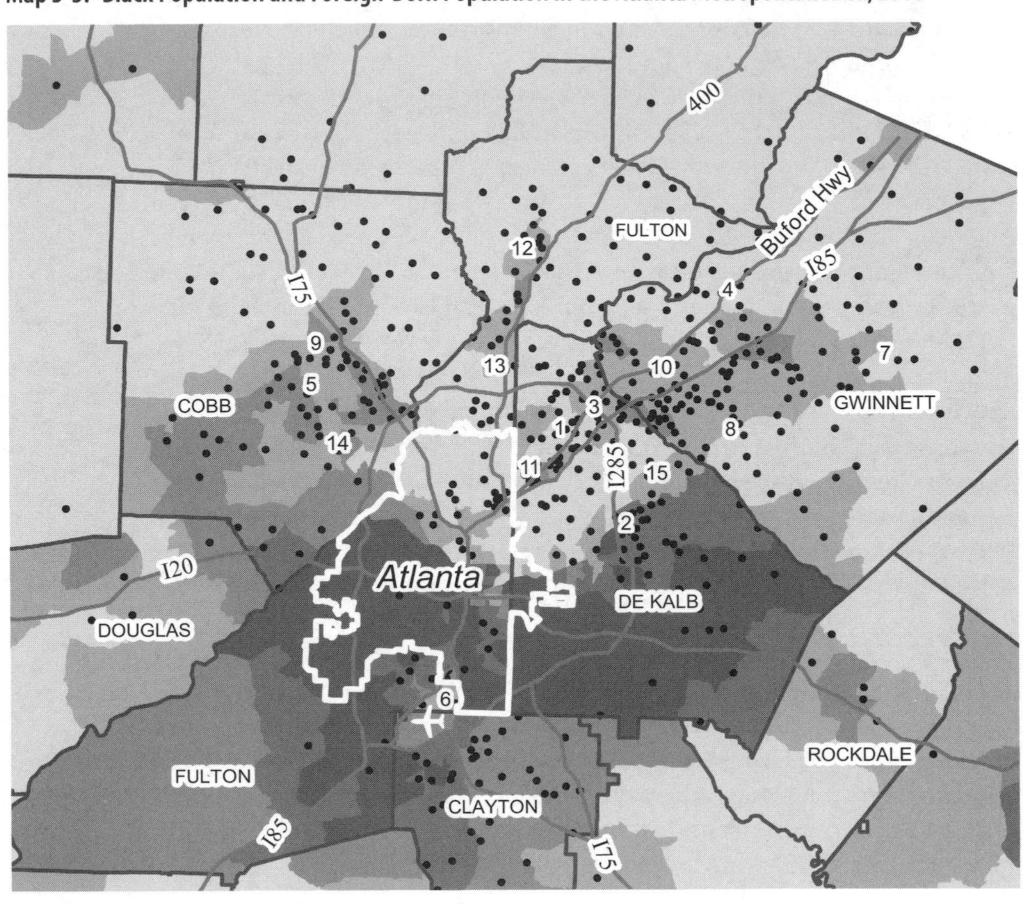

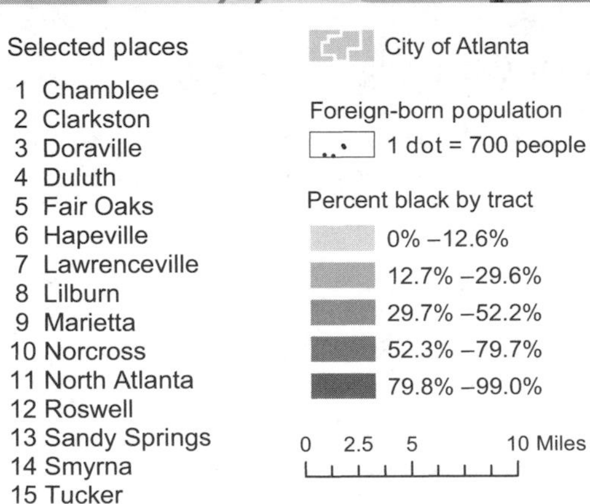

Source: U.S. Census Bureau, *Census of Population 2000, SF3.*

Two additional factors that explain Latin American immigrant settlement in inner-ring northern suburbs are the growth of jobs for skilled and unskilled laborers and access to major transportation routes. The most densely populated Latino immigrant neighborhoods are located along major transportation corridors: Buford Highway and I-85 in DeKalb and Gwinnett Counties, I-75 in Cobb County, and Highway 400 in northern Fulton County. Latino immigrants have also settled near public transportation routes: MARTA subway stops in Chamblee and Doraville and bus routes along Buford Highway and Jimmy Carter Boulevard. Given the limited reach of the public transportation system in Atlanta, however, immigrant workers rely heavily on driving, carpooling, and private taxis for transportation. For them proximity to the interstate and major highways is key.

A final factor helps explain settlement patterns: established immigrant neighborhoods tend to attract still more immigrants through social, cultural, and commercial networks. Family and other social ties influence immigrants' decisions about where to live. New arrivals from Mexico and Central America frequently move in with or near family members or acquaintances from their home towns. It is not unusual for people from a small town in Mexico or Guatemala to settle together in the same apartment complex. Cultural and religious institutions, such as churches, also serve to attract Latino immigrants to particular neighborhoods. Latin American immigrants are especially drawn to the concentration of ethnic businesses and shopping plazas in DeKalb, Cobb, and Gwinnett counties because they offer convenience, a familiar environment, and job possibilities.

Local and State Government Responses to Latin American Immigration

Unlike traditional immigrant destination areas, the state of Georgia and metropolitan Atlanta did not have programs and policies in place before the 1990s to deal with a large population of Mexican and other Latin American immigrants. Over the last two decades state and municipal governments in Georgia have struggled to come to terms with the large and expanding number of immigrants residing in the state. Their responsibilities have increased in the face of federal inaction on immigration reform, especially on the issue of unauthorized immigration. It falls on local governments to address the demands on the educational, health care, and law enforcement systems caused by immigration, as well as the increased needs for housing and transportation.

The multiple layers of governance at city, county, and state levels have led to a diverse array of measures that often differ from county to county and city to city. Policies range from those that seek to integrate immigrant newcomers to those that aim to discourage their settlement and participation in social and civic life. As others in this volume have documented, the exclusionary policies are directed almost exclusively against undocumented Latino immigrants.

In general, DeKalb County has responded to immigrants in a more welcoming manner than have many other counties, in part because of its longer history of immigration, the greater racial and ethnic diversity of the county, and the Democratic leadership in government. The official website for the county government describes DeKalb as "Georgia's most culturally diverse county, with over 64 spoken languages," and identifies this ethnic diversity as a benefit to the county: "The richness of life that these diverse groups of people bring to DeKalb transcends every facet of the county, from shopping and retail venues to a reflection of the community's very heart and soul."[25]

Of the suburban municipalities in metro Atlanta, Chamblee in northern DeKalb County has most actively encouraged the integration of its immigrant population. In contrast to other municipalities, the city acknowledges and even celebrates its ethnic diversity. The promotional material on its official Internet site identifies Chamblee as "a true international city in Georgia, with one of the most ethnically diverse populations of any municipality in the Southeast."[26] Chamblee views its ethnic diversity as a means to attract businesses, developers, and tourists to the area. The city council developed new zoning for the creation of an International Village, a mixed-use development district (one of the first in metro Atlanta) that features offices, retail shops, restaurants, a bank, hotel, international trade center, performing arts facilities, and pedestrian plazas. The plan for the International Village is meant to address the needs of its Asian, Latino, and other ethnic residents and entrepreneurs and also to attract visitors and tourists to the area.[27]

Other metro-area localities have been far less welcoming to immigrant newcomers. Cherokee County in northern Georgia has pursued some of the most restrictive measures in the South that target undocumented immigrants. Formerly a white rural area and now an outer-ring suburb of metro Atlanta, Cherokee County has drawn a growing number of Latino immigrants since the 1990s. In December 2006 the Republican-controlled County Board of Commissioners unanimously passed legislation that declares English the county's official language and penalizes landlords who rent housing to undocumented immigrants. Commissioner Karen Mahurin, who introduced the ordinance, said illegal immigrants strain local resources and have "the effect of lowering the quality of life locally."[28] When immigrant advocates filed a lawsuit in January 2007 challenging the landlord ordinance in U.S. District Court, Cherokee commissioners decided to delay enforcement and await the resolution of legal challenges to similar ordinances in Pennsylvania and Missouri.[29]

Public Schools

Even in localities that have been ambivalent or hostile to immigrants, certain public institutions, notably schools, could not ignore the rapidly growing population of foreign-born students. Public schools are mandated by federal law to provide equal educational opportunity to immigrant and language-minority students. Title VI of the 1964 Civil Rights Act prohibits discrimination on the basis of race, color, or national origin in federally funded programs, and in 1982 the Supreme Court ruled that the Fourteenth Amendment guarantees free public education to all immigrant children, regardless of their parents' legal status (*Plyler* v. *Doe*). When California voters attempted to bar undocumented immigrants from public schools with the passage of Proposition 187 in 1994, a U.S. District Court held that the denial of free education to undocumented children violated the Equal Protection Clause of the Fourteenth Amendment (the state eventually dropped its appeal of that ruling).

The Bush administration's No Child Left Behind Act, passed by Congress in 2001, has placed additional pressure on schools to integrate immigrant students. Schools are required to show improvement in the test scores of students who speak English as a second language. Public schools thus face considerable pressure to address the needs of immigrant students from Latin America and other regions of the world. Schools were among the first public institutions in Georgia and metropolitan Atlanta to develop programs and policies to incorporate immigrants.

In the 1980s the state of Georgia passed legislation to establish and fund a state educational program for K–12 students whose native language is not English. First established to serve the children of Southeast Asian refugees, this program greatly expanded in the 1990s to meet the needs of rapidly growing Latino and Asian immigrant student populations. Following trends in the rest of the country, Georgia legislators and education officials have rejected bilingual education and supported instead programs that place primary emphasis on learning English as quickly as possible. English for Speakers of Other Languages (ESOL) offers English language instruction combined with a schedule of content classes in math, sciences, social studies, and language arts for English-language learners, as they are called.[30]

In addition to ESOL programs, a number of school districts have established international welcome centers that provide orientation and language assessment and placement for newly arrived immigrant students. The DeKalb County school district established its international center in 1985; at the time there was one ESOL teacher who floated from school to school and taught fewer than 300 students, mostly of Asian background. Today the center has a staff of seventeen, with more than 400 ESOL teachers serving approximately 4,000 students from 170 countries. Cobb County's international welcome center opened in 1996 and now has a staff of sixteen. In 2005 the county's ESOL program served more than 5,000 students from 131 countries who spoke 81 different languages. The Gwinnett school district established an international newcomer center in Lawrenceville in 1991. Since then, the county's foreign-born student population has skyrocketed. Its ESOL program served more than 15,000 students in 2005, more than any other county in the state.

Translation services in multiple languages are available to varying degrees in the school systems for the translation of school correspondence and documents for immigrant parents and students. The DeKalb district has made its detailed, informative website available in Spanish. Spanish is by far the most common language of non-English-speaking students in the public schools in metro-area counties; other significant language groups are Brazilian Portuguese, Vietnamese, Korean, and Bosnian.

One of the most innovative integration efforts in public school education in metropolitan Atlanta has been the creation of the International Community School, a charter elementary school in the DeKalb County school district. Located in Clarkston, an area that is now home to thousands of refugees and immigrants, the school provides an "international education" in an "intentionally multiethnic environment" to refugee, immigrant, and native-born children. The school's curriculum is based on the International Baccalaureate, a highly recognized program operating in countries throughout the world that emphasizes inquiry-based learning, language acquisition, and "international-mindedness." In addition to the subjects required under the Georgia Core Curriculum—math, science, social studies, physical education, and art—all students in Atlanta's International Community School learn a second language. As immigrant and refugee children learn English, native-born students learn French or Spanish. The school now enrolls approximately 300 students who represent thirty-four countries and over forty different language groups. Approximately one-half are refugee and immigrant children, and the rest are native-born.

Even with these innovative programs, public schools in metro Atlanta have a long way to go to achieve the successful integration of immigrant students. Georgia has one of the highest dropout rates for Latino students in the country, owing, in part, to the high percentage of recent immigrants among Latino students. Nevertheless, public schools in the metropolitan area have made significant progress in addressing the tremendous challenge they face. With little prior experience, the Atlanta public schools have developed programs to accommodate the fastest-growing immigrant student population of any metropolitan area in the country.

Housing Ordinances

Although local education policies focus on accommodating and integrating immigrant students, policy responses in areas of housing, day labor, and transportation have been far more ambivalent toward immigrant newcomers. A number of suburban localities in Atlanta have used housing and zoning ordinances to discourage the settlement of Latino immigrants in their neighborhoods. Local governments typically have housing codes and zoning ordinances that define what kind of housing is legally permissible. In suburban Atlanta, as elsewhere in the country, these codes are intended to maintain low-density suburban neighborhoods characterized by detached single-family homes set on large lots and to discourage multifamily housing and dense population of neighborhoods.

The different household arrangements of Latino immigrants have disrupted this suburban ideal in northern Atlanta suburbs. Immigrants often share apartments or houses with relatives and acquaintances to save on housing costs. Sometimes groups of young men, frequently from the same home town, live together in rented apartments or houses to save money; many of them are supporting parents, siblings, wives, and children in their home countries. Some immigrant families (husband, wife, and children) who own or rent a home take in boarders, typically relatives or friends, to cover housing payments. These living strategies are very similar to those of European immigrants in the early twentieth century, except European immigrants lived in tenement houses in inner cities instead of apartments and single-family homes in suburban neighborhoods.

Large immigrant households have upset established residents and led to many complaints to local authorities about overcrowding. In response, local governments have pursued both stricter enforcement of existing housing codes and passage of new or revised ordinances to tighten regulation of immigrant households. Housing officials in Gwinnett County and its various municipalities stepped up enforcement of occupancy limits in response to an increasing number of complaints about overcrowding in suburban neighborhoods. A zoning inspector from the city of Duluth reported that about 98 percent of the complaints received are in reference to immigrants. Some housing codes are based on square-footage per bedroom, while others limit the number of unrelated people that can live together. Gwinnett County and the city of Lilburn limit occupancy to one person per seventy square feet of bedroom space, and fifty square feet per additional person, while the city of Norcross limits occupancy to one person per 150 square feet of total floor space, and the city of Duluth allows no more than three people who are not related by blood, marriage, or adoption to live together. "We're a nice, clean city, and we just want to stay that way," explained Lilburn's mayor at a city council meeting in 2001.[31]

Cobb County created a new housing policy to curb the increase in large immigrant households. Complaints about neighborhood homes turning into "boarding houses" occupied by immigrant workers, their families, and friends led Cobb County commissioners in January 2005 to change its existing housing ordinance, which set no limit on the number of people living in a house as long as they were related. The new ordinance requires fifty square feet of sleeping space per person, regardless of whether occupants are related. Penalties range from $100 to $1,000 and up to sixty days in jail. One of the first people cited under the new law was Jose Cruz Rodriquez, the owner of a three-bedroom home in southern Cobb County that he rented to Manuel Flores, a Mexican laborer who lived in the house with his wife, five children, two cousins, and another relative. Rodriquez eventually pleaded guilty and was fined $135 after agreeing to adjust living conditions in the home according to the new ordinance. A code enforcement officer in Cobb County indicated that "ninety-five percent of the complaints I get are white folks complaining about Hispanic folks."[32] Two years later Cobb passed an even stricter housing ordinance that requires at least 390 square feet of space for each adult resident and for each car parked overnight. The measure limits the people living in a home to one family or no more than two unrelated adults and their children and grandchildren, and it restricted the meaning of "family" to include only parents, children, brothers and sisters, grandparents, and grandchildren.[33]

The city of Roswell also amended its housing ordinance and redefined "family" in its effort to shut down "illegal boardinghouses in single-family neighborhoods." The city council approved a new housing law in July

2006 that allows no more than three unrelated people to reside in one single-family home; the law also altered the previous definition of "family" so that cousins no longer count as relatives.[34] A May 18, 2006, editorial in the *Atlanta Journal-Constitution* supported the efforts of Roswell residents and authorities to do something about the "devastating" impact of illegal immigration on suburban neighborhoods: "Two- and three-bedroom homes once occupied by families of five or six have become de facto boarding houses where a dozen or more adults and children—sometimes related, often not—live in basements and garages and where everyone shares the same bathroom."[35]

Regulation of Day Laborers

Local governments have sought further restrictions on Latin American immigrants through anticongregating ordinances directed at day laborers. A drive through metropolitan Atlanta on any weekday morning starting at 7 a.m. will reveal numerous street corners where groups of Latino immigrant men wait to be hired by local employers to perform a range of labor-intensive jobs: painting walls, building homes, clearing debris, moving furniture, weeding, and mowing lawns. Most of the men who wait for work are undocumented; workers with legal papers have access to steadier and more secure forms of employment. Many local employers in the lawn maintenance, construction, and restaurant industries depend on day laborers for their businesses to survive. Although they provide a crucial source of labor, these workers are often viewed with suspicion by local residents and merchants, who complain that day laborers scare off customers and threaten the peace and security of their neighborhoods.

As a result of such complaints, a number of city councils have passed ordinances forbidding laborers from gathering on street corners. The city of Chamblee passed an ordinance in 1996 that forbade people to "assemble on private property for the purpose of soliciting work as a day laborer without the permission of the property owner."[36] In 1998 the city of Roswell in northern Fulton County passed a similar law, followed in 1999 by the cities of Marietta in Cobb County and Duluth in Gwinnett County.[37] In March 1999 police in Roswell arrested five workers waiting at a day-labor pickup spot in front of an apartment complex after the managers of the complex complained to authorities. That same year U.S. Immigration and Naturalization Services agents conducted a raid at a day-labor site in Marietta and with the help of local police arrested sixty-four migrant workers. Undercover agents had posed as contractors looking for workers.[38]

In an attempt to address the ongoing tensions around day laborers, church groups have established several day-labor centers to provide a safe, legal space for workers to wait for employers. The centers match laborers with employers and keep a record of employers' names and addresses to help ensure the fair payment and treatment of workers. Local Methodist churches have funded a day-labor center in Duluth in Gwinnett County for several years. Directed by María García, the wife of a Latino Methodist minister, the center operated initially out of the basement of a local Methodist church. Another religious group, MUST (Ministries United for Service and Training), operates a day-labor center in Canton in Cherokee County. In January 2001 the city of Roswell opened Georgia's first publicly financed center for day laborers (the city devoted $40,000 to the project). The center also relied on funding and support from Latino businessman Jose Bernal, a member of the Roswell Intercultural Alliance, a nonprofit organization created to address immigrant labor issues. The center provided a waiting area for workers, matched contractors and employers with employees, and provided English classes and "seminars on state laws and other issues to help Hispanics assimilate."[39] Despite the promising opening, the center closed after only one year because of public opposition. The Georgia Coalition for Immigration Reform (one of several immigrant-restriction organizations established in Georgia during the last two decades) protested the opening of the center in letters to city leaders in Roswell, as well as to federal immigration officials in Atlanta. Coalition members complained about the use of public funding for a center that served "illegal" workers and called on immigration officials to uphold the law by arresting and deporting the workers who gathered there.[40] Public opposition persuaded the Roswell City Council to cut the funding and close the day-labor center, but it has not stopped workers from gathering on street corners or local employers from hiring them.

English-Language Ordinances

Several municipalities (Norcross, Doraville, Smyrna) have responded to the growing Latino presence in their communities by passing ordinances requiring that English be used in signs and billboards in front of local businesses, churches, and offices. Norcross passed an ordinance in 1995 that required the content of signs to be at least 75 percent English. When the Covarrubías family, the Mexican owners of El Super Mercado Jalisco, was fined under this ordinance in 1999 for hanging a sign in Spanish in front of the store, they successfully sued the city. In response the Norcross City Council annulled the existing ordinance, but a month later it passed another version of the law. Local authorities defended the ordinance as a public safety measure, arguing that police, firefighters, and ambulance drivers needed to be able to read signs and addresses to carry out their duties and respond to emergencies.[41]

To Latino community leaders and small business owners, the ordinance appeared to be a form of ethnic discrimination. As Maria Covarrubías stated, "Uno se siente como discriminado porque ese es el idoma de uno, ese es el negocio y si no nos podemos comunicar en nuestro idioma para nuestra gente, ¿Qué vamos a hacer." (You feel discriminated against because it's your language and your business. If we can't communicate in our language with our people, what are we going to do?)[42] Representatives of the Mexican American Legal Defense and Educational Fund, the American Civil Liberties Union (ACLU), and the Association of Hispanic Lawyers of Georgia filed suit in federal court in 2000 to compel the city to eliminate the ordinance. The suit was filed on behalf of Carlos Guevara, the pastor of a Hispanic church who had been issued citations for having Spanish language signs on the sidewalk in front of his church. Several months later, the U.S. District Court dismissed the case because Guevara no longer pastored the church. The ACLU filed an appeal with the Eleventh U.S. Circuit Court of Appeals, where the case was also dismissed; thus, there was never a final decision on the constitutionality of the law.[43]

Driver's Licenses

A public policy issue of great concern to immigrants and their advocates in metro Atlanta has been access to driver's licenses. Georgia, like most states in the United States, prohibits undocumented immigrants from obtaining driver's licenses, which is a significant hardship for those who live and work in a sprawling metropolitan area such as Atlanta. Given the limited public transportation system, immigrants depend on private automobile transportation to get to work, go shopping, visit health clinics, and attend school meetings. Workers frequently must travel long distances to get to job sites. Every month hundreds of immigrants in Georgia are arrested, fined, and sometimes jailed for traffic violations; the most common is driving without a Georgia license. The substantial fines of several hundred dollars provide a healthy source of revenue for suburban governments but present a real economic hardship to immigrant households.

Since 2000 Latino community leaders and immigrant advocacy groups in Atlanta have made access to driver's licenses a central political goal. State Representative Pedro Marin of Gwinnett County, one of the first Latino legislators in the state, coauthored a bill in the House in 2003

(House Bill 578) that would have enabled unauthorized immigrants to obtain a driver's license with certain restrictions. Under the proposed act, immigrant drivers would have to renew their license annually and could use it for transportation to work, school, church, and medical clinics only. Marin and his supporters contended that public safety for all Georgians would be served if immigrants had to pass driving exams and were licensed by the state. The measure provoked an outcry from opponents, who claimed that the bill would sanction "illegal" immigration.[44] The measure was defeated in the House, and two years later state legislators passed a bill (House Bill 501) that mandated that only legal residents of the state could obtain driver's licenses.[45] Federal legislation signed into law in 2005 reinforced Georgia's stance on the issue. Legislators in the U.S. House attached a provision (called the REAL-I.D. Act) to a military spending bill that prohibits states from offering driver's licenses to immigrants who cannot provide identification approved by the U.S. Department of Homeland Security, effectively barring unauthorized residents from obtaining driver's licenses.[46]

Georgia Security and Immigration Compliance Act (Senate Bill 529)

The state of Georgia took even more aggressive action to control unauthorized immigration in 2006 with the passage of the Georgia Security and Immigration Compliance Act (Senate Bill 529). The bill was introduced by Republican lawmaker Chip Rogers of Woodstock in Cherokee County, an outer-ring suburb of metro Atlanta that in recent years has drawn a growing number of Latino immigrants, attracted by jobs in poultry-processing plants and in the booming construction industry. The introduction of Senate Bill 529 in Georgia followed an aggressive effort on the part of Republican lawmakers in the U.S. House of Representatives, who proposed legislation (HR 4437) that would speed up deportations, criminalize undocumented immigrants, and authorize the construction of a wall at the Mexico-U.S. border.[47] Supporters of the Georgia bill claimed that illegal immigrants were stealing jobs from U.S. workers and costing taxpayers millions of dollars for social benefits they did not deserve. Opponents asserted that undocumented immigrants pay taxes and contribute significantly to the state's economy, yet they are mistreated and denied a legitimate place in social and civic life.[48] For the next few months, heated debate on the issue of unauthorized immigration took place in the newspapers, legislative halls, and even the streets as pro- and anti-immigrant forces organized rallies and marches in defense of their positions.

Although legislation stalled at the federal level, state Senate Bill 529 easily passed the Republican-controlled House and Senate and was signed into law by Republican governor Sonny Perdue on April 17, 2006. Recognized as the most sweeping immigration bill enacted by a state, Senate Bill 529 addresses a range of issues related to unauthorized immigration. The act

—requires contractors and subcontractors doing business with the state to ensure that all of their workers have legal authorization to work;

—denies tax-supported benefits, including health care, to adults (eighteen years of age and older) who cannot prove their legal residency;

—requires police to check the legal status of anyone who is arrested for a felony or driving under the influence (DUI) and to report any undocumented immigrants to immigration authorities;

—authorizes the state to work with the federal government to train Georgia law enforcement officers to enforce immigration laws;

—prohibits employers from claiming as a state tax deduction wages paid to undocumented workers.

The final form of the bill reflects a compromise between those seeking aggressive action to end illegal immigration to the state and business groups seeking to maintain an available pool of low wage immigrant labor. After consulting with business lobbyists, Rogers crafted the bill so that companies would not be held responsible if an employee used false documents or if a subcontractor hired illegal workers without the knowledge of the company. More aggressive measures were considered but ultimately not included in the act, such as denying undocumented children access to public education and charging undocumented immigrants a 5 percent tax on money transfers. Rogers and his supporters did not want to threaten the passage and viability of the bill by including constitutionally questionable provisions.[49]

Senate Bill 529 went into effect on July 1, 2007, except for the provisions that penalize employers for hiring undocumented immigrants, which will not take effect until 2008. While it is too soon to know the full social and economic impact of the law, it is clear that the measure has created a climate of uncertainty and fear among Latino immigrants in the state. Realtors, car dealers, and retailers in immigrant neighborhoods have reported a noticeable decline in Latino customers and attribute that decline to the sense of economic and social vulnerability that immigrants feel in light of the new law. Police involvement in the enforcement of immigration law, as authorized by SB 529, has made Latino immigrants even more fearful and less willing to notify law enforcement when they are victims of or witnesses to crime. Cobb County has gone even further than the new state law requires by training sheriffs to determine the legal status of all foreign-born people detained by the police, no matter how minor the charge, and to initiate deportation proceedings of those who are undocumented. Sheriffs in Cobb have not only investigated immigrants already held in the county jail but have also set up traffic checkpoints where they have arrested and jailed dozens of immigrants for minor traffic violations and held them for deportation.[50] The further impact of Senate Bill 529 in Georgia warrants close attention because the measure has already become a model for many legislators in other states who are developing their own immigration policies.

Conclusion

Despite the desire of some state and local officials, it is too late to turn back the clock on immigration in Georgia. The state and its major metropolis are multiethnic, multicultural places with diverse and still expanding immigrant populations. Latino immigrants, both documented and undocumented, form a substantial part of this population. The robust economic growth in Atlanta and Georgia in the last few decades has depended heavily on their labor, especially in the construction, service, agriculture, and poultry-processing industries. The question is not *whether* they will become a part of southern society, but rather *how* they will be incorporated into that society.

Although Latino immigrants have been well integrated into the economy of Atlanta and Georgia, their integration into the region's social and civic life has been more complex and contested. While public schools have made notable efforts to incorporate immigrant children, state and local governments have enacted policies related to housing, labor, and transportation that aim to exclude and penalize immigrants, especially undocumented Latino immigrants. Such measures at the state and local levels will not succeed in driving undocumented immigrants from the metro area or from the state—not when key industries and many residents' suburban lifestyles depend on their labor. The exclusionary policies will only contribute to the marginalization and exploitation of a significant part of the region's multiethnic society.

Notes

1. David Goldfield, "Unmelting the Ethnic South: Changing Boundaries of Race and Ethnicity in the Modern South," in *The American South in the Twentieth Century,* edited by Craig S. Pascoe, Karen Trahan Leathem, and Andy Ambrose (University of Georgia Press, 2005), pp. 19–38; Raymond A. Mohl, "Globalization, Latinization, and the Nuevo New South," *Journal of American Ethnic History* 22

(2003): 31–66; Arthur D. Murphy, Colleen Blanchard, and Jennifer A. Hill, *Latino Workers in the Contemporary South* (University of Georgia Press, 2001); Mary E. Odem, "Global Lives, Local Struggles: Latin American Immigration to Atlanta," *Southern Spaces: An Internet Journal and Scholarly Forum* (May 2005) (www.southernspaces.org/contents/2006/odem/1b.htm); Mary E. Odem and Elaine Lacy, eds., *Latin American Immigration to the Contemporary U.S. South* (University of Georgia Press, 2008, forthcoming); Susan M. Walcott and Arthur Murphy, "Latino Communities in Atlanta: Segmented Assimilation under Construction," in Heather Smith and Owen Furuseth, *Latinos in the New South: Transformations of Place* (Burlington, Vt.: Ashgate, 2006), pp. 153–66.

2. Audrey Singer, *The Rise of New Immigrant Gateways* (Brookings, 2004).

3. Richard Alba and others, "Immigrant Groups and Suburbs: A Reexamination of Suburbanization and Spatial Assimilation," *American Sociological Review* 64 (1999): 446–60; John R. Logan, Richard D. Alba, and Wenquan Zhang, "Immigrant Enclaves and Ethnic Communities in New York and Los Angeles," *American Sociological Review* 67 (2002): 299–322.

4. U.S. Department of Commerce, Bureau of Economic Affairs, "Total Employment by Industry, 1990–2005," Regional Economic Indicators System, table CA25.

5. Center on Urban and Metropolitan Policy, *Moving beyond Sprawl: The Challenge for Metropolitan Atlanta* (Brookings, 2000), p. 4.

6. The ten countries of origin that accounted for the most immigrants in 2005 were Mexico (29.7 percent), India (6.8 percent), Korea (4.1 percent), Jamaica (3.9 percent), Vietnam (3.5 percent), China (2.6 percent), Colombia (2.4 percent), Brazil (2.2 percent), El Salvador (2.1 percent), and United Kingdom (2 percent).

7. Jill H. Wilson, "African-Born Residents of the United States," *Migration Information Source* (Washington: Migration Policy Institute, 2003) (www.migrationinformation.org/USfocus/display.cfm?id=147 [July 3, 2007]).

8. Rakesh Kochhar, Roberto Suro, and Sonya Tafoya, "The New Latino South: The Context and Consequences of Rapid Population Growth" (Washington: Pew Hispanic Center, 2005).

9. Jeffrey S. Passel, Randolph Capps, and Michael E. Fix, "Undocumented Immigrants: Facts and Figures" (Washington: Urban Institute, 2004) (www.urban.org/url.cfm?ID=1000587).

10. Jeffrey S. Passel, "Unauthorized Migrants: Numbers and Characteristics" (Washington: Pew Hispanic Center, 2005) (http://pewhispanic.org/files/reports/46.pdf).

11. W. Zelinsky and B. A. Lee, "Heterolocalism: An Alternative Model of Sociospatial Behavior of Immigrant Ethnic Communities," *International Journal of Population Geography* 4, no. 4 (1998): 281–98; Wei Li, "Anatomy of a New Ethnic Settlement: The Chinese Ethnoburb in Los Angeles," *Urban Studies* 35 (1998): 479–501.

12. Roberto Suro and Sonya Tafoya, "Dispersal and Concentration: Patterns of Latino Residential Settlement" (Washington: Pew Hispanic Center, Dec. 27, 2004).

13. The reader will notice that a small area of Rockdale County, the Lakeview Estates CDP, also has a high concentration of Latin American immigrants. One of the largest mobile home parks in Georgia, Lakeview Estates, contains over 600 trailers and is home to at least half of the county's Latino immigrant population,

which explains the high concentration of Latin Americans in the community. Rockdale, however, is not yet a major destination county for Latino immigrants and therefore is not discussed in this chapter. See Brenden Sager, "A 'New Town' Making a Mark at Trailer Park," *Atlanta Journal-Constitution,* September 11, 2000, p. 1B; Duane D. Stanford, "Trailer Park Turnaround," *Atlanta Journal-Constitution,* Rockdale Extra, October 15, 1998, p. 4.

14. "DeKalb County," *New Georgia Encyclopedia* (www.georgiaencyclopedia.org/ [March 17, 2007]); Charles Rutheiser, *Imagineering Atlanta: The Politics of Place in the City of Dreams* (London: Verso, 1996), pp. 105–110.

15. Judith Waldrop, "The Newest Southerners," *American Demographics* 15 (1993): 38–43; Rutheiser, *Imagineering Atlanta,* pp. 88–93; Audrey Singer and Jill H. Wilson, "From There to Here: Refugee Resettlement in Metropolitan America" (Brookings, 2006).

16. Susan M. Walcott, "Overlapping Ethnicities and Negotiated Spaces: Atlanta's Buford Highway," *Journal of Cultural Geography* 20 (Fall/Winter 2002): 51–75; Waldrop, "The Newest Southerners."

17. Walcott, "Overlapping Ethnicities," p. 2.

18. Kevin Kruse, *White Flight: Atlanta and the Making of Modern Conservatism* (Princeton University Press, 2005); Matthew D. Lassiter, *The Silent Majority: Suburban Politics and the Sunbelt South* (Princeton University Press, 2006).

19. Kruse, *White Flight,* pp. 242–51; Lassiter, *The Silent Majority,* pp. 109–18; Larry Keating, *Atlanta: Race, Class, and Urban Expansion* (Temple University Press, 2001), pp. 113–41; Center on Urban and Metropolitan Policy, *Moving beyond Sprawl.*

20. Center on Urban and Metropolitan Policy, *Moving beyond Sprawl,* pp. 40–43.

21. "Cobb County" and "Gwinnett County," *New Georgia Encyclopedia* (www.georgiaencyclopedia.org/ [March 17, 2007]); Kruse, *White Flight,* pp. 243–66.

22. Ronald H. Bayor, *Race and the Shaping of Twentieth Century Atlanta* (University of North Carolina Press, 1996); Keating, *Atlanta*; Kruse, *White Flight.*

23. Center on Urban and Metropolitan Policy, *Moving beyond Sprawl,* pp. 4–5.

24. Andrew Wiese, *A Place of Their Own: African American Suburbanization in the Twentieth Century* (Chicago: University of Chicago Press, 2004).

25. DeKalb County Visitors Bureau, "DeKalb Facts" and "DeKalb History" (www.co.dekalb.ga.us/index.html [June 19, 2007]).

26. City of Chamblee, "About Chamblee" (www.chambleega.com/ [July 19, 2007]); see also *City of Chamblee Guidebook* (February 2000).

27. City of Chamblee, Community Development Department, "International Village Cultural and Community Center Master Plan Update," May 2001; Mary Swint, "Asian Plaza, Mediterranean Village to Rise in Chamblee's International Development," *The Atlanta Story* (online newspaper), April 7, 2005 (www.thestoryatlanta.com/).

28. Christopher Quinn, "Cherokee Targets Illegals' Landlords," *Atlanta Journal-Constitution,* November 15, 2006; Christopher Quinn, "Cherokee OKs Illegals Law," *Atlanta Journal-Constitution,* December 6, 2006, p.A1.

29. Mary Lou Pickel, "Illegal Immigrant Rental Law Put on Hold," *Atlanta Journal-Constitution,* January 6, 2007, p. B1.

30. Scott A. L. Beck and Martha Allexsaht-Snider, "Recent Language Minority Education Policy in Georgia: Appropriation, Assimilation, and Americanization,"

Education in the New Latino Diaspora, edited by Stanton Worthan, Enrique G. Murillo Jr., and Edmund T. Hamann (Westport, Ct.: Ablex, 2002), pp. 37–66.

31. Andrea Jones, "Occupancy Limits Growing as an Issue," *Atlanta Journal-Constitution,* July 22, 2001, Gwinnett Extra, p. 1. On similar efforts to deflect immigrants through housing regulation in Los Angeles, see Ivan Light, *Deflecting Immigration: Networks, Markets, and Regulation* (New York: Russell Sage Foundation, 2006), pp. 129–49.

32. Richard Whitt, "How Many People Live Here?" *Atlanta Journal-Constitution,* June 20, 2005, p. 1A; Richard Whitt, "Cobb Fines Owner over Full House," *Atlanta Journal-Constitution,* July 22, 2005, p. 1D.

33. Tom Opdyke, "Cobb Toughens Law on Occupants in One Home," *Atlanta Journal-Constitution,* July 2007, p. 5B.

34. Paul Kaplan, "Law Tackles Boarding Houses," *Atlanta Journal-Constitution,* July 13, 2006, p. 3JH.

35. Mike King, "Immigration: Crowding Concerns Hit Home," *Atlanta Journal-Constitution,* May 18, 2006, p. A15.

36. City of Chamblee, Georgia, *Code of Ordinances,* Sec. 58-13, Ord. No. 429, 11-19-96 (www.municode.com [June 20, 2007]).

37. *City Code of Marietta, Georgia,* Sec. 10-4-130 (www.municode [June 20, 2007]); City of Duluth, Georgia, *Code of Ordinances,* Sec. 10-13 (www.municode.com [June 20, 2007]).

38. Mark Bixler, "Day Laborers in Roswell Get a Place to Call Their Own," *Atlanta Journal-Constitution,* December 19, 1999, p. D1; Rick Badie, "Gwinnett Mulls Rules for Laborers," *Atlanta Journal-Constitution,* June 2, 2000, p. D1; Pilar Verdés, "Roswell pone manos a la obra," *Mundo Hispánico,* August 5, 1999; "Centro está por abrir sus puertas," *Mundo Hispánico,* December 28, 2000, p. 3.

39. Bixler, "Day Laborers in Roswell"; Mark Bixler, "Few Employers Know about Day-Laborers Center," *Atlanta Journal-Constitution,* July 9, 2001, p. B1; Martha Durango, "Centro está por abrir sus puertas," *Mundo Hispánico,* December 21, 2000, p. 4.

40. Bixler, "Few Employers Know about Day-Laborers Center."

41. Sophia Lezin, "Fines Anger Latino Merchants," *Atlanta Journal-Constitution,* March 7, 1999, p. E1; "Demandan a ciudad Norcross," *Mundo Hispánico,* December 28, 2000, p. 3.

42. Pilar Verdés, "Letreros en Norcross podrán estar en español," *Mundo Hispánico,* May 13, 1999, p. 3.

43. Rick Badie, "Court Upholds Translation Law," *Atlanta Journal-Constitution,* December 7, 2001, p. 6D; Rick Badie, "Sign Law of No Use to Cops," *Atlanta Journal-Constitution,* January 6, 2002, p. J1, "Demandan a ciudad Norcross," *Mundo Hispánico,* December 28, 2000, p. 3; Eileen Drennen, "Lost in Translation," *Atlanta Journal-Constitution,* October 1, 2007, Sec. Gwinnett News, J1.

44. Mark Bixler, "Illegal Immigrants' License Try Revs Up," *Atlanta Journal-Constitution,* August 27, 2001, p. B1; Stephanie A. Bohon, "Georgia's Response to New Immigration," *Immigration's New Frontiers: Experiences from the New Gateway States,* edited by Greg Anrig Jr. and Tova Andrea Wang (New York: Century Foundation Press, 2006), pp. 87–9.

45. Georgia House Bill 501, enacted May 2, 2005 (www.legis.ga.gov/legis/2005_06/fulltext/hb501.htm).

46. Eunice Moscoso, "Driver's Licenses for Illegals to End," *Atlanta Journal-Constitution,* May 5, 2005, p. A1.

47. Eunice Moscoso, "House OKs Stiff Immigration Bill," *Atlanta Journal-Constitution,* December, 17, 2005, p. A1.

48. Carlos Campos, "Bill on Illegals Gets First Test," *Atlanta Journal-Constitution,* February 28, 2005, p. B5; Jim Tharpe, "Center Stage in Illegals Debate," *Atlanta Journal-Constitution,* February 19, 2006, p. A5; Patricia Guthrie, "Doctors Demand Services for Illegals," *Atlanta Journal-Constitution,* February 14, 2006.

49. Carlos Campos, "Bills Plentiful, Unity Lacking on Immigrant Issue," *Atlanta Journal-Constitution,* January 30, 2006, p. A1; Jim Tharpe and Nancy Badertscher, "House Approves Wire Fee for Illegals," *Atlanta Journal-Constitution,* Feb. 15, 2006, p. B1; Jim Tharpe, Carlos Campos, and Mary Lou Pickel, "Senate Bill Reveals Rift on Illegals," *Atlanta Journal-Constitution,* February 26, 2006, p. A1.

50. Linda Carolina Pérez, "Aplican Leyes Perforadas," *Mundo Hispánico,* July 26, 2007, p. A6; Mary Lou Pickel, "Last Stop for Immigrants," *Atlanta Journal-Constitution,* July 30, 2007, p. A1; Linda Carolina Pérez, "Una prolongada Espera," *Mundo Hispánico,* October 25, 2007, p. A6.

6

Edge Gateways

Immigrants, Suburbs, and the Politics of Reception in Metropolitan Washington

MARIE PRICE and AUDREY SINGER

In the space of a generation, Fairfax [a county in metropolitan Washington] lost its rural character and its middle-class white identity. In exchange it has won jobs, businesses and bustling, hustling immigrants.

DAVID PLOTZ, "NOTES FROM TYSONS CORNER; A SUBURB ALL GROWN UP AND PAVED OVER," *NEW YORK TIMES*, JUNE 19, 2002

In just two decades, immigrants have ethnically and racially transformed the suburbs of metropolitan Washington, one of the latest top destinations in the country for newcomers. Immigrants are widely dispersed throughout the region, forming relatively few single-ethnic enclaves.[1] In the metropolitan area as a whole, the foreign-born are a mix of highly skilled and less-skilled workers, the majority report a good command of the English language, and they live primarily in moderate- to high-income neighborhoods, not the poorest ones.[2] Immigrants to this region come from nearly every country in the world, and some localities are home to people from more than one hundred countries.[3] Yet until the 1980s immigrants were not a significant demographic force in the city or its suburbs. Today immigrants settling in Washington suburbs are breaking with historical

We are grateful for the research assistance of David Park, Jill Wilson, and Sarah Ireland of the Brookings Institution. We thank Esha Clearfield for her assistance in organizing our interviews and field notes.

patterns of residential settlement seen in more established immigrant gateways. Borrowing loosely from Joel Garreau's concept of the edge city—the concentration of business, shopping, and entertainment outside the traditional urban core—we contend that many of Washington's immigrants have settled into *edge gateways*.[4] Edge gateways are localities that have recently attracted immigrants in great numbers, transforming those areas from native-born, white suburbs into identifiable places where a diverse mix of immigrant groups cluster. In many ways these edge gateways are performing the functions of traditional inner-city neighborhoods where immigrants still cluster, but because of their suburban setting, they may offer advantages—better schools, services, and housing, and less crime—not found in the inner city. At least in the Washington context, these edge gateways are multiethnic communities in which no single immigrant group dominates.

Edge gateways are a function of metropolitan growth and change, namely, the decentralization of jobs and housing away from the urban core to the suburbs. In many metropolitan areas, native-born and immigrant alike show a preference for living and working in the suburbs. Over time edge gateways have developed a local identity as places where immigrants can find housing, transportation, jobs, and goods and services that cater to them. It can be argued that many edge gateways are performing the same functions that early twentieth-century enclaves provided. Some of these gateways may evolve into a more familiar pattern of either distinct ethnic communities or ethnic enclaves. Yet it is also possible that a different pattern of immigrant settlement is being realized in suburban Washington, and possibly elsewhere, one in which clusters of immigrants are not easily organized into distinct ethnic communities but live in a more multiethnic context. This pattern may have important implications for the long-term process of integration in American society.

This chapter documents the breathtaking pace of change in the Washington area, using census data and interviews with local officials to identify the processes by which large numbers of immigrants first settle in the suburbs. We focus on three questions: How have residential settlement trends changed from 1980 to 2000 with respect to the foreign-born? Which suburban destinations are immigrants settling in and why? What are the local responses to this sudden influx of diverse newcomers? With more immigrants now residing in suburbs than in central cities, immigrants are a vital force shaping the suburban future.[5] Thus, suburbs should be the key location in which to understand how a multiethnic society will function in the twenty-first century.

Conceptualizing Urban and Suburban Immigrant Settlement

In the tradition of the Chicago School of urban sociology, the spatial assimilation model describes an earlier wave of immigrant settlement that assumes immigrants, upon arrival in the United States, cluster mainly with their own ethnic group in urban neighborhoods. Although these neighborhoods offer housing, jobs, and social and material resources within a familiar ethnic setting, they are often not of the highest quality.[6] Self-segregation in ethnic neighborhoods typically ends once immigrants improve their economic status and move to suburban areas with greater social and economic status.

In general, although support remains for the spatial assimilation model in long-standing, major immigrant gateways, other forms of immigrant settlement are emerging. In a study comparing metropolitan Los Angeles and New York, Logan and colleagues find that many groups are residing in what they term "ethnic communities" rather than "ethnic enclaves."[7] The main difference between the two settlement types relates to residential preferences and relative location within the metropolitan fabric. Immigrants living in ethnic enclaves are constrained to such locations, but those living in ethnic communities choose to live among immigrants even though they have the economic means to live elsewhere. Ethnic enclaves are typically found in the urban core, and ethnic communities tend to be in the suburbs. These communities have been termed "ethnoburbs" by geographer Wei Li.[8] Such communities are thriving socially and economically, as numerous studies attest.[9]

Despite these recent studies, more work is needed to improve our understanding of suburban immigrant residential patterns and how they vary across metropolitan areas. In particular, the spatial assimilation model fails to characterize the residential choices of newcomers in newer gateways.[10] Singer, and Waters and Jiménez make the case that newer destinations (such as those in the emerging gateways of Atlanta or Dallas) and pre-emerging gateways (such as Charlotte and Austin) differ from more established destinations because they lack the institutional networks that newcomers require.[11] This absence of immigration history in emerging gateways means that the "place of immigrants in the class, racial, and ethnic hierarchies is less crystallized and immigrants may thus have more freedom to define their position."[12] Because of Washington's recent emergence as an immigrant gateway, there are few historical ethnic neighborhoods or enclaves. Only a few neighborhoods in the District of Columbia, such as Mount Pleasant–Adams-Morgan and Chinatown, have a relatively long history of receiving and settling immigrants. The overall lack of such areas suggests that the majority of immigrants reside outside the urban core, mainly in the suburbs.

In metropolitan Washington, many cities, towns, or census designated places (CDPs)—entities that are readily identifiable by local residents but are not incorporated places—outside the urban core have foreign-born communities that total 30 percent or more of the population. We designate these as *edge gateways* here.

Study Design

We use census data from 1980, 1990, and 2000 to examine the residential patterns of the foreign-born. We use the Census 2000 definition of the Washington metropolitan area when discussing metropolitan trends. However, because our focus is suburban, most of our analysis targets three counties surrounding the urban core: Montgomery and Prince George's in Maryland and Fairfax in Virginia, where 55 percent of the total metropolitan area population resides, but 71 percent of the foreign-born population lives. In much of our analysis, the area considered the urban core (the District of Columbia, and the Virginia jurisdictions of Arlington County and the City of Alexandria) is not included, although we recognize that this area also receives immigrants.[13]

We assess settlement patterns of the foreign-born at the local level by examining demographic change in cities, towns, and CDPs. Using this methodology, we are able to capture a broad range of suburban localities. The majority of localities are CDPs, with a handful of towns and cities in both Maryland and Virginia. For the sake of simplicity, we refer to this mix of localities as "places," "localities," or "communities."

We mapped the distribution of the foreign-born in 1980, 1990, and 2000 for the three suburban counties and parts of Prince William County in Virginia. Given the tremendous growth of the metropolitan area during the last three decades, some areas designated as CDPs in 2000 were not CDPs in 1980. Thus, the maps reflect the CDP boundaries as they were defined in each census. However, in table 6-1, which shows changes in the foreign-born population between 1990 and 2000, it was necessary to make a statistical adjustment to bring the 1990 CDP boundaries in line with 2000 boundaries.[14]

Of twenty-three localities where the foreign-born population was 30 percent or higher in 2000, we selected five for an in-depth examination of where immigrants were settling and how the communities responded to

Table 6-1. Growth of the Foreign-Born in Cities, Towns, and Census-Designated Places (CDPs) in Suburban Washington, D.C., 1990–2000

Place	*County*	*Total population 2000*	*Percent foreign-born 1990*	*Percent foreign-born 2000*	*Percent change in foreign-born population, 1990–2000*
Centreville CDP	Fairfax, VA	48,661	8.8	20.3	323.5
West Gate CDP	Prince William, VA	7,286	6.8	22.2	260.7
Chantilly CDP	Fairfax, VA	41,041	11.3	22.2	175.2
Herndon Town	Fairfax, VA	21,655	18.2	36.5	168.9
Germantown CDP	Montgomery, MD	55,419	11.1	20.1	144.3
Burtonsville CDP	Montgomery, MD	7,309	12.9	24.9	141.2
Merrifield CDP	Fairfax, VA	11,080	24.2	41.8	127.8
Gaithersburg City	Montgomery, MD	52,613	20.3	34.4	124.8
Oakton CDP	Fairfax, VA	29,348	14.0	26.1	122.8
Lincolnia CDP	Fairfax, VA	15,788	26.6	47.7	116.6
Huntington CDP	Fairfax, VA	8,430	12.7	24.3	116.1
Reston CDP	Fairfax, VA	56,407	11.8	22.0	115.9
Dunn Loring CDP	Fairfax, VA	7,851	16.3	29.1	114.6
Tyson's Corner CDP	Fairfax, VA	18,540	23.1	34.5	111.3
Beltsville CDP	Prince George's, MD	15,725	14.7	27.7	104.5
Annandale CDP	Fairfax, VA	54,994	18.7	34.5	99.1
North Potomac CDP[a]	Montgomery, MD	22,945	18.7	29.2	99.0
Montgomery Village CDP	Montgomery, MD	38,051	16.7	28.1	98.1
Fairfax City	Fairfax, VA	21,498	14.8	25.4	88.0
Redland CDP	Montgomery, MD	16,998	18.8	33.4	87.8
Groveton CDP	Fairfax, VA	21,296	13.9	24.2	84.9
Hybla Valley CDP	Fairfax, VA	16,817	15.5	26.3	84.3
Fairland CDP	Montgomery, MD	21,738	16.7	27.8	83.0
East Riverdale CDP	Prince George's, MD	14,961	19.8	33.8	80.3
Greenbelt City	Prince George's, MD	21,456	15.3	27.1	79.8
Springfield CDP	Fairfax, VA	30,417	26.5	36.9	78.6
Silver Spring CDP[a]	Montgomery, MD	76,725	25.9	35.1	77.5
Mount Rainier City	Prince George's, MD	8,463	16.9	27.7	75.0
Aspen Hill CDP	Montgomery, MD	50,228	19.4	30.5	73.7
Chillum CDP	Prince George's, MD	34,252	24.0	38.0	73.3
Idylwood CDP	Fairfax, VA	16,005	24.0	37.6	70.7
White Oak CDP	Montgomery, MD	20,973	23.0	34.8	70.2
Wheaton-Glenmont CDP	Montgomery, MD	57,694	25.0	39.6	69.9
Bladensburg Town	Prince George's, MD	7,557	12.3	22.1	68.9
Burke CDP	Fairfax, VA	57,737	12.4	20.2	63.8
Colesville CDP	Montgomery, MD	19,863	15.4	23.7	62.3

(continued)

Table 6-1 ***(continued)***

Place	*County*	*Total population 2000*	*Percent foreign-born 1990*	*Percent foreign-born 2000*	*Percent change in foreign-born population, 1990–2000*
Mount Vernon CDP	Fairfax, VA	28,582	13.4	20.9	62.1
Jefferson CDP	Fairfax, VA	27,422	25.4	37.8	58.5
North Bethesda CDP[a]	Montgomery, MD	38,643	21.6	31.8	57.5
Seven Corners CDP	Fairfax, VA	8,701	47.6	61.2	53.8
Calverton CDP	Prince George's, MD	12,608	17.0	25.0	53.2
North Springfield CDP	Fairfax, VA	9,176	15.9	23.6	52.0
North Kensington CDP	Montgomery, MD	8,859	17.7	25.7	49.3
Rockville City	Montgomery, MD	47,388	22.0	30.9	48.7
Bailey's Crossroads CDP	Fairfax, VA	23,166	43.3	54.0	47.8
West Springfield CDP	Fairfax, VA	28,378	14.0	20.1	44.7
Takoma Park City	Montgomery, MD	17,299	21.3	28.4	38.5
Lake Barcroft CDP	Fairfax, VA	9,041	20.9	27.7	38.0
Pimmit Hills CDP	Fairfax, VA	6,113	18.8	25.5	37.4
Langley Park CDP/Adelphi CDP[b]	Prince George's, MD	31,212	44.9	53.2	34.0
Cloverly CDP	Montgomery, MD	8,000	17.2	21.2	24.7
Potomac CDP[a]	Montgomery, MD	44,821	21.3	24.7	23.2
McLean CDP	Fairfax, VA	38,929	19.7	21.4	10.7
Bethesda CDP[a]	Montgomery, MD	55,300	22.8	21.4	–8.5
Riverdale Park CDP	Prince George's, MD	6,563	—	38.4	—
Forest Glen CDP	Montgomery, MD	7,376	—	26.4	—
Kemp Mill CDP	Montgomery, MD	9,927	—	24.6	—
Travilah CDP	Montgomery, MD	7,549	—	21.3	—
Total (58):		1,471,459	19.6	29.6	76.1

Source: Authors' calculations from U.S. Census data.

a. CDPs adjusted to account for changes made to CDP boundary lines between 1990 and 2000 censuses.

b. Combination of CDPs Langley Park and Adelphi; Langley Park CDP adjusted to account for changes made to CDP boundary lines bewteen 1990 and 2000 censuses.

— CDP did not exist in 1990.

newcomers. Three are CDPs (Wheaton-Glenmont, Langley Park/Adelphi, and Annandale), one is a town (Herndon), and one is a city (Gaithersburg).[15] We selected these case studies on the basis of location within the metropolitan area (an illustrative sample from within each of the three suburban counties), population (at least 20,000 people), and popular identity as immigrant areas. We toured the five communities and interviewed public officials (usually county or city supervisors or planners) along with immigrant service providers (educators and directors of two day-labor sites). We also reviewed selected government planning documents and relevant town meeting notes. We consulted newspaper articles regarding some of the more controversial issues surrounding immigrants, especially the location of day-labor sites. The community interviews were essential in understanding how local jurisdictions cope with diversity.

Changing Metropolitan Immigrant Settlement

As the nation's capital, Washington has long been an international city, yet it only recently joined the ranks of major metropolitan immigrant destinations. In 1970 just 4.5 percent of greater Washington's population was born outside the United States. By 2000, 17 percent of the population was foreign-born. As with most metropolitan areas, much of this growth has occurred in the suburbs.

Immigrant preference for suburbs was clear as early as 1980, when 65 percent of the foreign-born (167,000) resided in three suburban counties (Fairfax, Montgomery, and Prince George's).[16] Map 6-1 shows areas of immigrant concentration in the northern and western suburbs, straddling the Capital Beltway. In 1980 the foreign-born accounted for 20 to 29 percent of the population in only three CDPs in the three counties (Langley Park, Seven Corners, and Bailey's Crossroads).[17] Nowhere did the foreign-born make up more than 30 percent. Relatively few immigrants resided in Prince George's county at this time, with the exception of Langley Park. Of the five selected communities, Langley Park/Adelphi had the highest percentage of immigrants in 1980. Gaithersburg and Herndon had the least (9 percent or less), and Annandale and Wheaton-Glenmont ranged between 10 and 19 percent.

By 1990 the immigrant population in these suburban counties had more than doubled to nearly 350,000 (map 6-2). During the 1990s immigrants began concentrating in Montgomery County, following the transportation lines (interstates and Metrorail) that link Silver Spring, Wheaton-Glenmont, Rockville, and Gaithersburg. All these suburban localities were more than 20 percent foreign-born by 1990 and many were more than 30 percent foreign-born. The pattern in Fairfax is more confined. The highest concentrations of immigrants were in the easternmost CDPs (along the border with Arlington County) and between the major transportation corridors (Interstates 395 and 95 and Route 50). Almost all of eastern Fairfax was at least 10 percent foreign-born during the 1990s, six places were between 20 and 29 percent foreign-born, and Seven Corners and Bailey's Crossroads were greater than 30 percent foreign-born. The northern half of Prince George's County by 1990 was home to significant numbers of foreign-born (including

Map 6-1. Foreign-Born Population, Selected Suburban Places, Washington Metropolitan Area, 1980

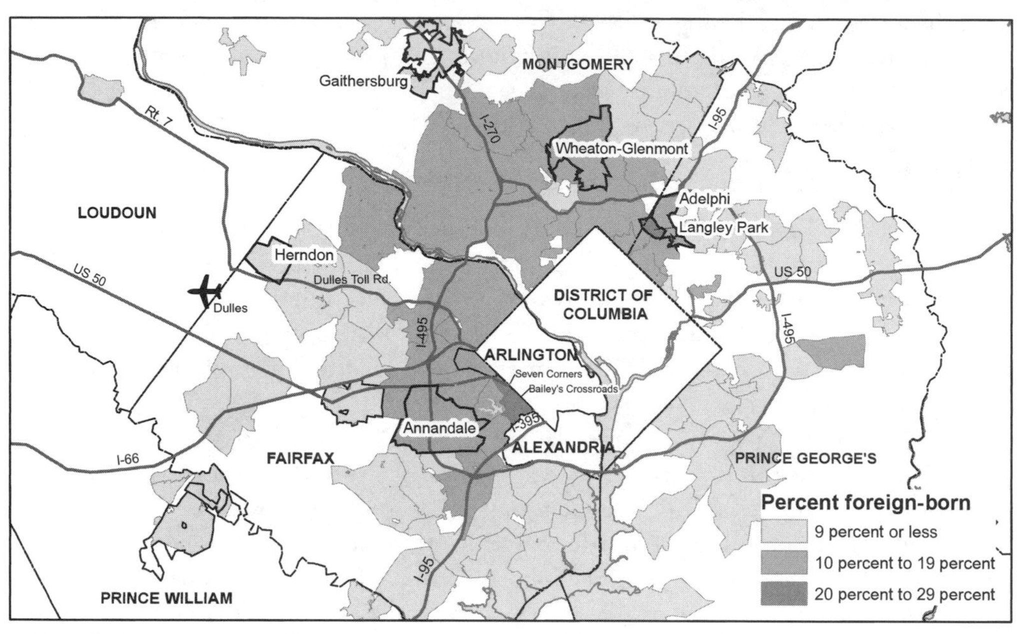

Source: U.S. Census Bureau, *Census of Population 1980.*

Langley Park, which was more than 30 percent foreign-born, and the adjacent Adelphi, which was 29 percent foreign-born). In addition, new immigrant settlement areas were evident in eastern and southern Prince George's County, many outside the beltway.[18]

As map 6-3 shows, the most significant change occurred in the 1990s. By 2000 the foreign-born were a significant portion of the overall population in these three counties, accounting for 588,000 people, or 22 percent of the total population. Throughout Montgomery and Fairfax counties, the majority of CDPs were 20 percent or more foreign-born. The most striking feature about map 6-3 is the spread of immigrant settlement: foreign-born make up 30 percent or more of the total population in two dozen places. Overall the map shows a deepening of immigrant settlement trends that were in place by 1990. Yet there were also sudden growth areas, most notably Herndon, which was 18 percent foreign-born in 1990 and 36.5 percent foreign-born by 2000. The foreign-born populations in Prince George's and Prince William counties continued to grow during this decade, but at a slower rate than the other two counties, with fewer areas logging more than 30 percent foreign-born (Prince George's had three

Map 6-2. Foreign-Born Population, Selected Suburban Places, Washington Metropolitan Area, 1990

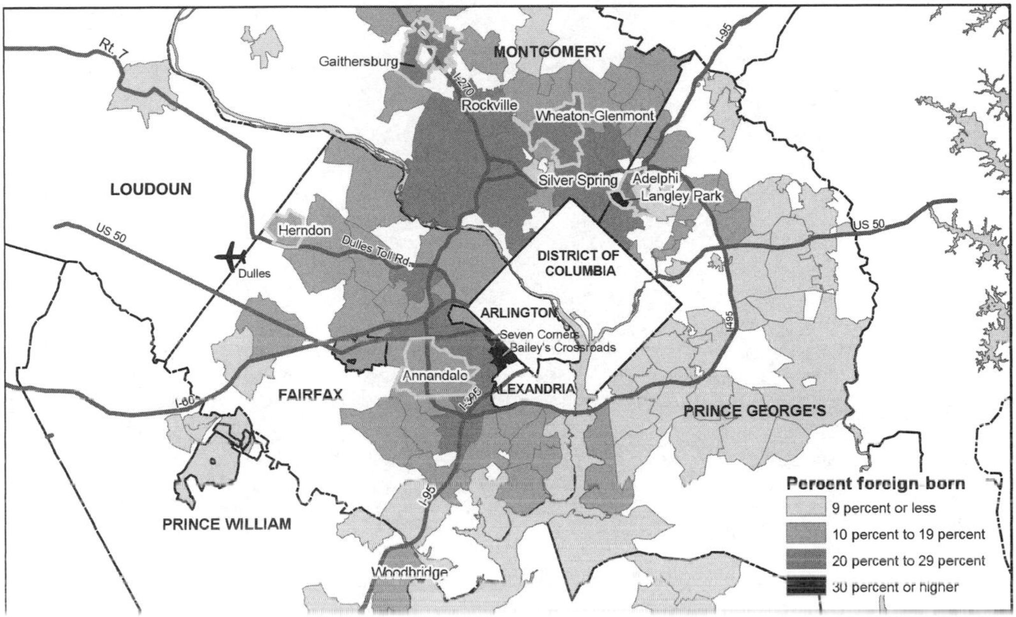

Source: U.S. Census Bureau, *Census of Population 1990.*

CDPs with more than 30 percent foreign-born, and Prince William had none). Map 6-3 also shows that more distant suburbs were gaining immigrant newcomers.

Combined, these three maps illustrate the dramatic growth of immigrants in the region and their dispersion throughout the suburbs. Thus, in answer to the first question posed in this chapter, immigrants in the Washington metropolitan area live overwhelmingly in the suburbs, with large numbers settling farther and farther from the urban core. There are also clear areas where the foreign-born are clustered, residing in communities where more than one in three people is foreign-born. The distribution of the foreign-born, however, is not even throughout the suburbs. There is a clear preference of immigrant clusters in Fairfax and Montgomery counties, usually near major transportation corridors.

Localities Experiencing Greatest Growth in Immigration

The fifty-eight places shown in table 6-1 are home to just over one-half of the entire immigrant population in the metropolitan area in 2000. Together, they grew by 76 percent during the 1990s; however, many of

Map 6-3. Foreign-Born Population, Selected Suburban Places, Washington Metropolitan Area, 2000

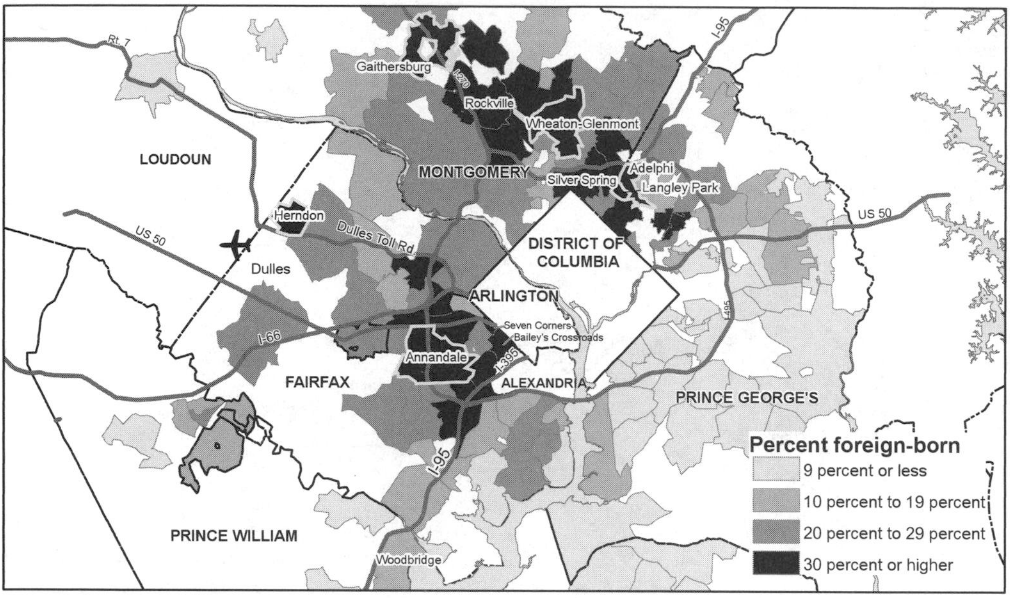

Source: U.S. Census Bureau, *Census of Population 2000.*

these places registered much higher growth of the foreign-born during the same period. Eighteen places doubled (or very nearly doubled) their immigrant population, including three edge gateways, Herndon, Gaithersburg, and Annandale. Herndon's immigrant population mushroomed during the decade, growing by 169 percent, ranking fourth in table 6-1. Gaithersburg's immigrant population rose by 125 percent, while Annandale's grew by 99 percent. In both Langley Park/Adelphi and Wheaton-Glenmont, where the foreign-born population was more established in 1990, the growth rates were slower, but Wheaton-Glenmont's immigrant population nevertheless grew by 70 percent. Notably, Centreville—a distant Fairfax County suburb—experienced the fastest growth rate between 1990 and 2000 among the foreign-born, at 324 percent. There the foreign-born more than tripled from approximately 9 percent of the population to 20 percent, or nearly 10,000 immigrant residents.

The five case study locales experienced growth at different points in time. Langley Park/Adelphi ranked third among all places with immigrants, with 53 percent of its residents foreign-born, up from 45 percent in 1990. The residents of Wheaton-Glenmont were 40 percent foreign-born in 2000, a rise from only 25 percent in 1990. Herndon's population was only 18 percent foreign-born in 1990, but registered 37 percent foreign-born ten years later. Annandale and Gaithersburg showed similar trends: they rose from 19 percent and 20 percent foreign-born, respectively, in 1990 to 35 percent and 34 percent, respectively, in 2000.

Not only are there many foreign-born in the suburbs, but nearly one in four are recent arrivals directly from abroad. For metropolitan Washington as a whole, 22.6 percent of the foreign-born population counted in 2000 had migrated from abroad within the last five years. In most of the edge gateways, the percentage of new arrivals in the last five years was comparable to the metropolitan average. However, only 19 percent of Wheaton-Glenmont's immigrants arrived during the last five years, while Herndon's new arrivals topped 31 percent. The relative newness of the foreign-born population in the metropolitan region and their suburban residence suggest a pattern that is not always observed in more established gateway destinations.

As figure 6-1 shows, these five localities also host different compositions of immigrants. Salvadorans are the largest group in four of the five case studies, a finding that is not surprising given that El Salvador sends the most immigrants of any country to the metropolitan area and accounted for 12.6 percent of all foreign-born residents in 2000. The other top countries of origin, in descending order, are Korea, India, Vietnam, Mexico, China, the Philippines, Peru, Guatemala, and Bolivia. Yet, by exploring immigration at the local scale of these five suburban places, additional country-of-origin groups become significant, such as Honduras, Jamaica, Pakistan, Iran, Nicaragua, Nigeria, Taiwan, and the Dominican Republic (figure 6-1). These pie charts illustrate the *hyperdiversity* of Washington's edge gateways, as characterized by the many origin groups within them and the distinct lack of concentration of a single group. This pattern may not be true for edge gateways in other metropolitan areas, but it is a significant feature in Washington.

Case Examples

Before presenting evidence about why these gateways formed where they did, we offer a brief description of each of these communities that focuses on their changing ethnic composition, relative location, and local structures of governance. Table 6-2 reflects the dramatic changes in the racial-ethnic composition of these areas, which in 1970 were predominantly white. By 2000 Adelphi, Gaithersburg, Wheaton, and Herndon had no majority racial-ethnic group. In Langley Park, Hispanics were the majority

Figure 6-1. Top Ten Countries of Birth for the Foreign-Born in Edge Gateways, 2000

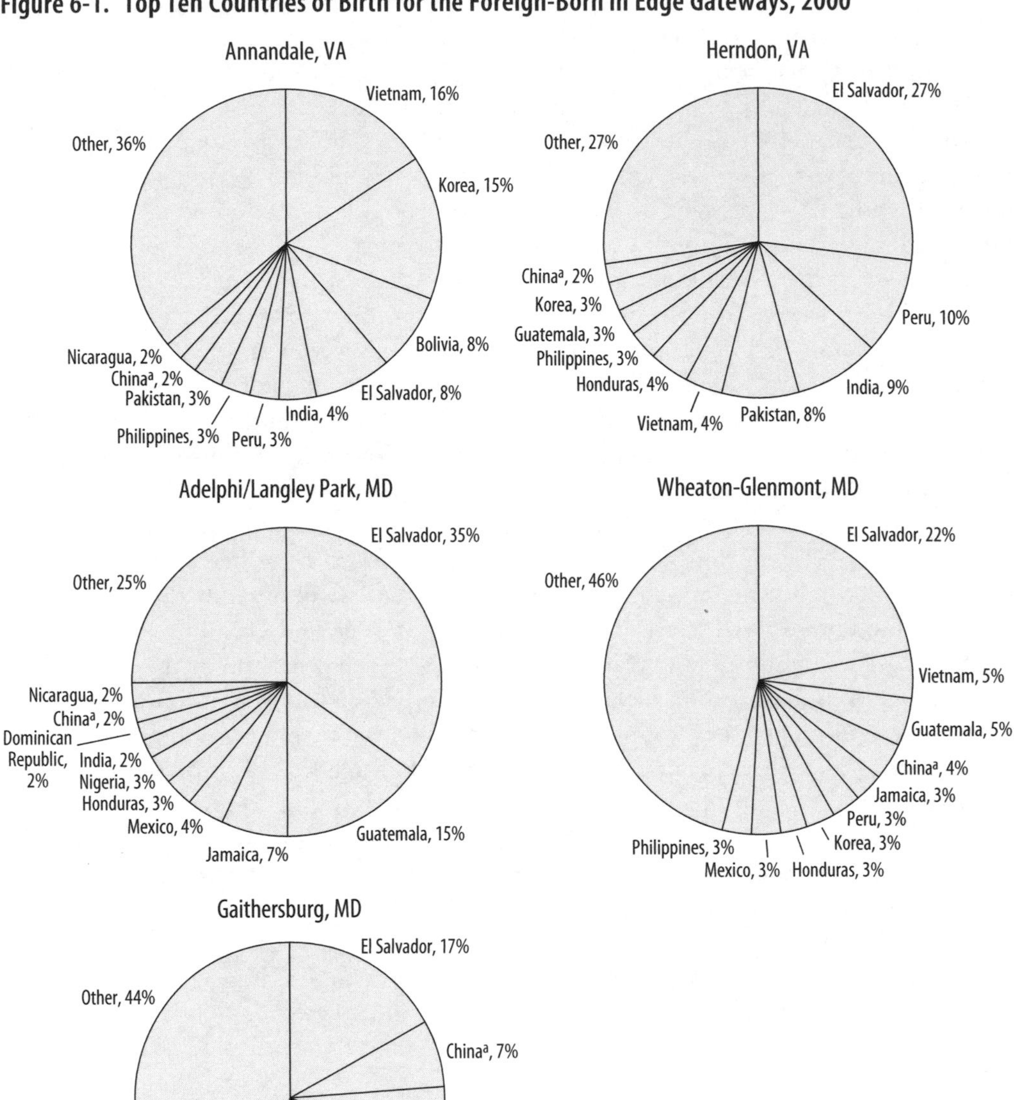

Source: U.S. Bureau of the Census, *Census of Population 2000,* SF3.
a. Excludes Hong Kong and Taiwan.

Table 6-2. Race and Ethnicity in Selected Edge Gateways, 1970 and 2000

		1970				
Place	*State*	*White*	*Black*	*Hispanic*	*Other*[a]	
Adelphi[b]	MD	—	—	—	—	
Langley Park	MD	93.0	3.5	6.8	0.7	
Gaithersburg	MD	96.3	0.7	0.8	0.7	
Wheaton-Glenmont	MD	94.8	2.5	2.9	1.3	
Annandale	VA	98.3	0.1	0.3	0.5	
Herndon	VA	96.1	2.5	2.2	0.2	
		2000				
Place	*State*	*White*	*Black*	*Hispanic*	*Asian*[c]	*Other*[d]
Adelphi[b]	MD	21.5	38.8	25.7	9.9	4.1
Langley Park	MD	5.4	25.1	63.5	3.4	2.6
Gaithersburg	MD	49.1	14.2	19.8	13.7	3.3
Wheaton-Glenmont	MD	40.0	18.3	25.9	12.1	3.6
Annandale	VA	57.2	5.7	14.5	19.3	3.3
Herndon	VA	47.0	9.2	26.0	13.8	4.0

Source: U.S. Census Bureau, *Census of Population 1970, 2000.*

a. In 1970, "other" refers to individuals who identified as any race other than black or white, which included American Indian, Eskimo or Aleut, Asian and Pacific Islander, and "other." In 2000, "other" refers to American Indian and Alaska Native, Native Hawaiian, and "other." In addition, because Census 2000 allowed individuals to identify as more than one race, these individuals are also included in the "other" category.

b. Adelphi was not yet a CDP in 1970.

c. There was no separate category for Asian in 1970; therefore Asian is presented for 2000 only.

(63.5 percent) in 2000, while in Annandale whites were still the majority (57.2 percent).

Langley Park/Adelphi: Highest Concentration of Foreign-Born

The first focus area is Langley Park/Adelphi, an unincorporated, inside-the-beltway suburb in Prince George's County near the northern boundary of the District of Columbia, giving it more of an urban than suburban feel. This locality has the longest history of immigrant settlement in the region (since the 1960s), perhaps originating with its proximity to the University of Maryland. It also has the highest concentration of foreign-born residents among the five case studies in 2000. Langley Park/Adelphi is a Latin American enclave, with Salvadorans accounting for 35 percent of the foreign-born, Guatemalans representing another 15 percent, and other Spanish-speaking immigrants composing another 12 percent. Here *pupusa* trucks and fruit vendors line the main streets and serve a steady stream of customers on foot and in cars. Locals refer to it as the Barrio de Langley Park, and many immigrants consider the area a cultural center for the Salvadoran community. Yet even this Latin American enclave has considerable diversity in its commercial establishments. A drive along the commercial corridor on University Boulevard reveals "Bollywood" (Indian) video stores and Caribbean, Vietnamese, Chinese, and Indian markets and restaurants.

This is an area that has seen waves of ethnic and racial change. In 1970 it was predominantly white, but by 2000 Adelphi was about one-quarter white and Langley Park was only 5 percent white. There is a relatively long history of Latino settlement in the area. In 1970 Langley Park was almost 7 percent Hispanic—very high for the region as a whole—and that rose to 63 percent in 2000.[19] It was one of three places in the area in 1980 that had an immigrant population of more than 20 percent. Currently Adelphi is more racially mixed, with approximately one-quarter of the population white, one-quarter Latino, and nearly 40 percent black. The succession of new arrivals is evident in the experience of Langley Park–McCormick Elementary School, which shifted from a predominantly white to a predominantly black school and then to a predominantly Hispanic school over a period of four decades. The public school is also a cultural center for the Salvadoran community; on Sundays the gym is used for Catholic religious services with several hundred people in attendance.

Under the jurisdiction of Prince George's County, the Langley Park/Adelphi area is governed by mostly African American leaders. However, the county council member who currently represents the Langley Park area is the first Latino elected official. Tensions have emerged between Hispanics and African Americans. These tensions are occasionally manifested by police enforcing anti-loitering ordinances and restricting informal food vendors. Newcomers express frustration over the lack of immigrant-related services and the need for a multicultural service center such as those found in neighboring Montgomery County.[20]

Wheaton-Glenmont: Multiethnic Beacon

About seven miles from Langley Park/Adelphi is Wheaton-Glenmont, at the end of a Metrorail line. Wheaton-Glenmont is a large suburb of more than 50,000 people in 2000, due north of the District of Columbia, just outside the Capital Beltway. Here one finds a major mall and a mix of housing: new expensive town homes, post–World War II apartments, and single-family houses. The human diversity is stunning—two out of every five residents are foreign-born, with El Salvador the top sending country (accounting for 22 percent of Wheaton's foreign-born residents). Salvadorans are the largest group by far, although they are by no means alone. Immigrants from Vietnam, Guatemala, China, Jamaica, Peru, Korea, Honduras, Philippines, and Mexico and more than 80 other countries make up Wheaton's foreign-born population.

Wheaton was more than 90 percent white in 1970, when it was a quintessential first-ring, post-WWII suburb. By 2000 it had transformed into a multiethnic place, where the population was 40 percent white, 18 percent black, 26 percent Hispanic, and 12 percent Asian. Although Wheaton-Glenmont is unincorporated, it is under the jurisdiction of Montgomery County, specifically the Mid-County region. The Mid-County Services Center in downtown Wheaton provides several important services for immigrants, such as *Proyecto Salud*, providing full-service and low-cost primary medical care through a public-private partnership. The Gilcrest Center is a multiethnic and multicultural community center with outreach programs offering English classes, legal advice, and computer training. The director of the Mid-County Services Center acknowledges that immigration to the area has brought challenges, but it is has also played a major role in the resurgence of downtown Wheaton. County officials contend that immigrants have contributed to the "branding" of Wheaton as an eclectic, multiethnic community filled with mom-and-pop restaurants and small grocery stores. This reputation was highlighted in a regionwide campaign highlighting the diversity of ethnic restaurants in Wheaton as "Deliciously Habit Forming."[21]

Gaithersburg: Affordable and Accessible

In the heart of Montgomery County, twenty-five miles northwest of downtown Washington, lies the city of Gaithersburg. Formerly a small agricultural town, it now punctuates an area that has developed into a high-technology corridor. Like most of the other edge gateways, Gaithersburg was almost exclusively white in 1970 and is now racially and ethnically mixed: 20 percent Latino, 14 percent black, and 14 percent Asian.

The city manager of Gaithersburg describes his community of more than 50,000 people as "an immigrant gateway," but quickly adds that this change "has not been an overwhelming challenge or burden" despite the city's recent struggle with where to place a formal day-labor site. Day workers had been congregating on a private site near a nonprofit facility that offered services to immigrants. After that facility moved, workers continued to congregate at a nearby church, drawing complaints from neighboring business owners. The city decided the best way to manage the day-labor issue was to open a formal center, working with the county and nonprofit organizations. City residents opposed all of the proposed city sites for a center, citing concerns that the city would be overrun by workers soliciting jobs. Eventually the city ceded the decision to the county government, which found a location and worked with a local nonprofit organization to run the center. Very soon after it opened, it was the target of a small fire, allegedly set by arsonists.

In 2000 Gaithersburg was 34 percent foreign-born (up from 3 percent in 1970) and the top sending countries were El Salvador, China, India, Mexico, Iran, Korea, Peru, Honduras, Taiwan, and Vietnam, which together accounted for 56 percent of the foreign-born (see table 6-2). Places like Gaithersburg are indicative of dramatic demographic change in local areas. Here the local governance structure, consisting of a mayor and city council, allows Gaithersburg to create laws or programs that respond to the needs of immigrants in ways that Langley Park/Adelphi and Wheaton cannot.

Gaithersburg has some of the most affordable housing in all of Montgomery County, especially its rental stock. The city manager observed that many newcomers have settled in the area, leaving more expensive closer-in locations such as Silver Spring or Wheaton. In addition to affordability, Gaithersburg is located near many high-tech and bio-tech firms that employ highly skilled foreign-born workers. Important government institutions, such as the National Institute for Standards and Technology, are also located in or near the city.

Annandale: Supporting Immigrant Entrepreneurs

Not far from the Arlington County border in Virginia, Annandale has been a distinct geographical entity since 1830. Located on the site of a former tobacco plantation, parcels of which were sold to farmers and small-scale manufacturers, it remained a small town on the periphery of Washington for much of its history. Yet since it is approximately ten miles from the core, and straddles the beltway, it was eventually folded into the sprawling suburbs. Annandale was almost exclusively white (98.3 percent) until the late 1970s, when immigrants (many of them refugees from Vietnam and Afghanistan) began to arrive. What was once a white, middle-class, bedroom community in 1970 is now a place where one in three people are foreign-born and whites make up only 57 percent of the total population. The top five immigrant groups (Vietnamese, Korean, Bolivian, Salvadoran, and Indian) account for one-half of the foreign-born population. Annandale is under the jurisdiction of Fairfax County and is part of the Mason District. The district supervisor summarized this area as "the most densely populated, the most diverse, and the most dynamic" place in Fairfax County.

Annandale is often referred to as "Koreatown" in the press. The district supervisor bristles at this popular nickname because Koreans are only one of many ethnic groups in the area. (Roughly 15 percent of Annandale's foreign-born residents are Vietnamese, which is slightly larger than the foreign-born Korean population.) However, the Korean commercial presence is very pronounced: there are twenty-eight Korean restaurants in an eight-block area. Many of the town's commercial and religious institutions cater to a Korean population that is scattered throughout northern Virginia.

Local officials say that Annandale's attractiveness to immigrants is its proximity to major transportation corridors (the beltway and Interstate 395), availability of public transport (bus routes to Metrorail lines), and a large stock of relatively affordable apartment complexes. Annandale also has a large number of older business properties on smaller lots (less than 1,500 square feet) that are ideal spaces for small family-run businesses. Immigrant entrepreneurs (most notably Korean immigrants) began renting and purchasing commercial properties in Annandale beginning in the mid-1980s. At one point in the 1990s, Korean business owners lobbied for official designation of a Koreatown in Annandale, but they eventually backed off in the face of resistance from non-Korean business owners and residents.

With Annandale's rising real estate values, the downtown is poised for major development, which will likely "change the face of Annandale," according to an Annandale Planning Committee report. Interestingly, two Korean American investors are involved in developing the Annandale Community Business Center, a twelve-story, mixed-use residential and commercial center that will increase density and add properties of higher value. Much like Wheaton, the ethnic mix of Annandale makes it an attractive location for many people. Yet the older commercial properties and rental units that made the community attractive to new immigrants twenty years ago are likely to be phased out in the future.

Herndon: Rapid Change and Resistance

The town of Herndon has more than 21,000 residents and is located about twenty-three miles west of the District of Columbia. The settlement was established in the mid-nineteenth century on a railroad line that linked Herndon to Loudoun County and Alexandria. In the 1970s Herndon was still a small, majority-white outpost in the expanding metropolitan area of Washington. Located near Dulles International Airport, the town has many older and cheaper apartments in its center, which became attractive to low-income immigrants who were finding jobs plentiful in adjacent Loudoun County. During the late 1980s high-tech telecommunications firms, including AOL and Nextel, began expanding in the area, creating both high- and low-skilled jobs. Herndon is also a site of expensive single-family homes and townhouses. Moreover, the political structure of Herndon as a town gives it some independence when responding to new immigrant populations. More than one-third of the population in Herndon was foreign-born in 2000, with those from El Salvador, Peru, India, Pakistan, and Honduras accounting for nearly two-thirds of all foreign-born.

In July 2005 Herndon drew national attention when town residents divided sharply over using public dollars to create a formal day-labor site. This measure drew the attention of the Minutemen, the national anti-immigrant group, as well as other anti-immigrant groups. The debate over the day-labor site became a lightning rod issue for many residents in Herndon, reacting to the speed with which their community had changed. Herndon's foreign-born population increased 169 percent from 1990 to 2000. In 2000 Herndon was 26 percent Latino and 14 percent Asian. The growing numbers of day laborers suggested to many residents that their community was overrun with immigrants of questionable legal status and, if not controlled, even more would come. This is not a community accustomed to thinking of itself as an immigrant gateway, and unlike the other communities in this study, it has experienced serious tensions surrounding the issue of day laborers, which we discuss later in this chapter.

The Making of Washington's Edge Gateways

In large part because of the stability that the federal government and associated industries bring to the region, metropolitan Washington has maintained one of the lowest unemployment rates and steadiest rates of job growth among U.S. metropolitan areas.[22] Although the District maintains a large and still-growing sector of jobs, the suburbs account for 75 percent of jobs in the metropolitan region.[23] During the 1990s and into the mid-2000s, job growth in information, professional, and business services, as well as in government, construction, education, and health services, was strong, particularly in suburban jurisdictions.

Immigrants come to the region because of employment opportunities, and their presence has fed the region's overall economic growth. Although communities have absorbed highly skilled immigrants with relative ease, the poorer and less-skilled immigrants—who are often the backbone of the service economy—have met more resistance. Yet overall, immigrants buttress the region's economy and contribute their share to the tax base. A recent study found that a majority of the region's immigrants are citizens or legal permanent residents and that they paid taxes at nearly the same rate as the native-born.[24]

There are several reasons why immigrants are settling in the suburbs and in edge gateways in particular. One important reason is housing affordability. Among foreign-born householders in metropolitan Washington, 51 percent own their homes, compared with 67 percent of those born in the United States. In three of our five suburbs, the rates are higher than the average for immigrant households: Annandale (52 percent), Herndon (53 percent), and Wheaton-Glenmont (62 percent). Mapping census tracts by median housing value in 2000 shows that tracts with higher concentrations of immigrants (greater than 30 percent foreign-born) have lower median housing values than the regional average ($173,000). Likewise, the rental market shows a similar pattern of housing affordability. In the edge gateways, many of the census tracts have median gross rents near or above the monthly median of $811.

Interviews with local officials underscored the relationship between affordable housing and edge gateways. When asked why immigrants were settling in their communities, all mentioned housing costs. Moreover, each local official could point to areas of older apartment complexes or smaller homes with high concentrations of foreign-born residents. The director of neighborhood resources in Herndon noted that the older apartment complexes built in the late 1960s and 1970s, once occupied by a then mostly white and middle-income population, were now nearly all occupied by immigrants, primarily from Latin America. The community has no publicly funded housing, but some renters receive Section 8 housing vouchers (that is, rents are federally subsidized).

Access to major transportation corridors and public transportation is another significant feature of the edge gateways. Although only one community (Wheaton) had its own Metrorail stop, all of these suburban communities are near major interstates or are well served by buses, and in the case of Gaithersburg, a commuter rail line. Of the five case study areas, one is inside the beltway (Langley Park/Adelphi), one straddles the beltway (Annandale), and three are beyond it (Wheaton-Glenmont, Gaithersburg, and Herndon). The closer-in areas were the first to experience significant immigrant settlement. Yet county officials noted that the proximity to major transportation arteries (and thus jobs) was an important factor in the overall growth of their communities (including their attractiveness to foreign-born residents).

Another reason why immigrants tend to cluster in these edge gateways may be because of their residential preferences, or more specifically, their avoidance of black neighborhoods. Relatively few immigrants reside in the census tracts where gross rents are well below the median value, such as in the eastern half of the District and in bordering Prince George's County (inside the beltway). Most of these areas, which are majority black, receive few immigrants, with the exception of Langley Park/Adelphi. Asians, as a group, tend to avoid living in areas with sizable shares of blacks.[25] Hispanics are generally more likely to live in mixed-race areas, but results from focus groups conducted by political scientist Lorrie Frasure suggest that race-ethnicity factors influenced the location decisions of Latinos in suburban Washington.[26] One Latino described her decision to live in Montgomery County rather than Prince George's in these terms:

> [W]hen we were figuring out where we wanted to live, because the schools and the kind of people who live in Montgomery County are very different from those in PG [Prince George's], that was one of the reasons we chose Silver Spring [in Montgomery County], and the fact that there are stores and restaurants. It seems to me that there [are] a lot more—from Hyattsville and over—there [are] a lot more black people, and you don't see that many in Montgomery County. My little girl was in a PG County school, and we had a lot of problems with them [blacks]. We didn't have the same communication with them; it's much better here. It was racism more than anything from them [blacks].

In previous research on Washington, sociologist Samantha Friedman and colleagues documented a racial hierarchy in residential decisions of recent immigrants.[27] African newcomers were more likely than other immigrant groups to reside in zip codes where the share of the black population was above the mean for the region. At the same time, African-born blacks are commonly found in areas where other immigrants cluster, regardless of race.[28] Recent European immigrants, in contrast, showed the most pronounced avoidance of predominantly black neighborhoods, followed by Asian and Latin American immigrants.

A final reason why immigrants are settling in these edge gateways stems from their social networks. Previous research has clearly shown the importance of immigrant ties in determining residential location.[29] Many immigrants rely on their co-ethnics to determine where they will live. One

Fairfax County official, himself an immigrant from Jordan, labeled it the "cousin syndrome," saying, "one ends up living in a place like Annandale because you have a cousin or relative that lives here."

Social networks feed into what can be broadly termed the receptivity of a place. As a locality in the suburbs becomes known for affordable housing and good transportation, a complex web of immigrant social networks draws in still more immigrants. As more immigrants arrive, the networks of institutional services (places of worship, clinics, and immigrant-run associations) grow. At the same time, it is possible that large numbers of diverse immigrants settling in a place may make it less attractive for native-born residents, who relocate and thus allow room for more immigrants to settle.

The rate and intensity of immigrant settlement in the suburbs has an impact on their reception. The contention in Herndon is, in part, a response to the sudden and rapid growth of immigrants in the community. Nearly one-third of the foreign-born population arrived from abroad within the preceding five years. In the other edge gateways, this proportion is lower; newcomers directly from abroad compose between one-fifth and one-fourth of the immigrant residents. Overall, community reactions in the suburbs have been both inclusive and restrictive toward immigrants.

The Politics of Place: Community Reactions in Edge Gateways

Localities and their residents respond generally in two ways to the opportunities and problems resulting from recent immigration: they either accommodate diversity or deflect immigrants (especially poor ones).[30] Local immigration responses often compensate for or conflict with national policies. Urban geographer Mark Ellis suggests that the "downloading" of responsibility for immigrant social welfare and integration by the federal government to localities produces resentment and frustration. In particular, he writes, "This downloading generates conflict between localities responsible for hosting immigrants and the federal government which has ultimate control over entry."[31] In the politics of scale, localities have little say over who enters the country, but the local reception of these immigrants shapes the prospects for their integration.

Community planners and various nongovernmental associations often accommodate immigrant newcomers by responding to needs for housing, transportation, health care, and education. As several of the chapters in this book reveal, city officials can also make public space available for festivals and other events that display the cultural diversity of new residents or provide formal sites where day laborers can await employers. Local governments can also take direct measures designed to intimidate or regulate undocumented immigrants. Recently several cities around the country (such as Farmers Branch in the Dallas metropolitan area and Hazleton, Pennsylvania) have debated or passed laws designed to restrict employment or rentals only to those who can show proof of legal U.S. residence. Although many of these debates are unlikely to result in new laws, they stir up local tensions and create a chilling effect on the behavior of local immigrants, even those in the United States legally.

A more common approach is to use existing laws in response to specific immigrant groups. As have other metropolitan areas, several local jurisdictions in metropolitan Washington have used residential zoning and housing ordinances—not originally aimed at immigrants—to curb the growth of unwanted and usually poorer immigrants. The reaction of localities also depends on the structure of local government. In the five case studies, Gaithersburg and Herndon have elected officials who can craft explicit responses to immigration in the areas of language accommodation, housing, health care and, particularly, day-labor sites. Any animosity can also be directed toward those local officials if they are perceived as out of step with public opinion, as happened in Herndon, where incumbents who supported an immigrant day-labor site were ousted in a recent election. In contrast, the responses of Wheaton-Glenmont, Langley Park/Adelphi, and Annandale are more clearly directed by countywide policies, which may limit the influence of local actors. For example, in Prince George's County (where Langley Park/Adelphi is located), immigration issues receive less attention because there are fewer immigrants countywide and the county's largely black constituency has other concerns.

These scales of governance do matter, even though the politics of immigration is currently centered on the national debate. Regardless of the government structure (county-level or local control), it is local jurisdictions that shape the response to these newcomers.

Accommodating Immigrants

One of the basic ways that local governments reach new immigrants is by publishing materials in languages other than English. Each of the edge gateways publishes materials in multiple languages, tailored to their immigrant communities. For example, the *Fairfax County Guide to Emergency Preparedness* (where Annandale and Herndon are located) is available in six languages (English, Arabic, Farsi, Korean, Spanish, and Vietnamese). Reflecting a slightly different mix of newcomers, Prince George's County public school information is in five languages (English, Chinese, French, Spanish, and Vietnamese). Montgomery County public schools publish information in those five languages as well as Korean. Local emergency service providers, especially police and fire departments, seek staff with different language skills that reflect the makeup of their jurisdictions. Both Montgomery and Fairfax counties take advantage of over-the-phone translation services for lesser-known languages.

Public schools are places where linguistic diversity cannot be ignored. All three of the counties studied have significant outreach programs for public school students with limited English skills (both native- and foreign-born). Integrating students into core curricula has become a more pressing problem given the demands of the federal No Child Left Behind program, which assesses school performance on the basis of test results; students with limited English proficiency (LEP) can pull down test scores. Yet in a context of growing immigration, resources are usually inadequate to respond to the greater demand. In Prince George's County in 2000, ESOL (English for Speakers of Other Languages) programs operated in thirty-three schools; six years later ESOL programs were in place in sixty seven of the county's two hundred schools. In response to growing numbers of LEP students, a regional network of school administrators formed in 1992 to share experiences and best practices. Meeting several times a year, the group exchanges assessment tools, training ideas, and other resources. Recently administrators from the outer counties of Howard, Prince William, and Loudoun joined the network.

Public schools are also important outreach centers for immigrant parents with school-age children. For example, the Boar Parent Resource Center, located at a Gaithersburg elementary school, provides information to parents about community resources, including a clinic. In addition to schools, public libraries, places of worship, various nonprofit groups, and local governments provide diverse services for immigrants and offer settings where people of different backgrounds can interact. For example, the Gilcrest Center in Wheaton is funded by Montgomery County. In addition to English and citizenship classes, the center provides information on housing and health services. Reflective of its accommodation strategy toward diversity, the Montgomery County government has an Office of Community Outreach with separate liaisons for the African American community, African immigrants, Asian and Pacific Americans, and Latinos.[32] Annandale offers a Day Labor Education Program with seed money from Fairfax County, various nonprofits, and many volunteers (including immigrants themselves). The program offers classes in English and skills training.

County officials provide public space for the courses, believing that skill and language training for community members is a tangible benefit for relatively little cost. The Herndon Neighborhood Resource Center opened in 1999 and was developed by the town and Fairfax County. Located in a shopping center, the resource center is open to everyone, but it predominantly serves Latinos.

Communities can also marshal their resources to foster better dialogue between natives and immigrants. In 1998 the district supervisor for Annandale began a monthly dialogue on diversity, called the Kaleidoscope Group, in an attempt to mitigate negative issues and to bring people from diverse communities together. The district supervisor believed it was important to create such an organization because the tone of public and private discourse was troubling, leading to ugly comments about "those" people, who were actually neighbors. In 2002 the Herndon Dulles Chamber of Commerce held two multicultural summits to address the need for greater cultural sensitivity and to assist immigrants in being good citizens. Participants discussed cultural assimilation, health, housing, business, and legal issues.

Localities can also take stands on issues that may be in opposition to federal policy. For example, Montgomery County passed a law in 2003 that allowed immigrants to use identification cards issued by foreign consulates. In fact, more than 400 cities and jurisdictions consider the cards proper identification. The consular cards (issued by Mexico and Guatemala) say nothing about a person's legal status, but immigrants can use them to open bank accounts, to enroll children in schools, and in some states to obtain driver's licenses. The federal view is that the consular ID cards are too easily forged and they can be interpreted as a de facto legality because they are usually held by undocumented or illegal immigrants. In passing the law, the executive director of Montgomery County argued that it was an important step to provide access to basic amenities to everyone who is living in the county.[33]

The most striking aspect conveyed to us by local administrators is that diversity is now considered the norm. By branding immigrants and their ethnic businesses as a desirable form of diversity, immigration is viewed as an asset rather than drawback. A county official in Wheaton noted that the area was both "accommodating and capitalizing on the immigration trend" by promoting Wheaton's "funky, ethnic mix that makes it feel like a true urban environment without the urban problems." As noted above, the city manager for Gaithersburg refers to his community as an "immigrant gateway." Likewise, the district supervisor for Annandale champions her community's diversity as part of its dynamic character.

Deflecting Immigrants

The most direct official actions aimed at immigrants in the edge gateways tend to focus on poor or undocumented immigrants. Thus the anti-immigrant discourse in suburban Washington is rarely aimed at *all* immigrants but usually only at those who are perceived to cost local communities more resources than is deemed fair. In the Washington region, the two main deflection strategies that we studied are zoning against excessive occupancy and the regulation of day-labor sites. Yet in the fall of 2007 two outer jurisdictions (Prince William and Loudoun counties in Virginia) introduced policies that required county residents to prove their legal status in order to obtain certain county services. This particular deflection strategy was aimed at the population of undocumented immigrants. The impact of these new local ordinances is still unclear, but many Latinos fear their community is being disproportionately targeted.

All of the case study communities have zoning ordinances that restrict excessive occupancy. In response to complaints about overcrowding, Herndon in 2004 amended its zoning ordinance to strengthen occupancy limitations and to amend the definition of "family."[34] In the amended ordinance, the number of "unrelated people" who could share a residence was limited to four persons. The director of the Neighborhood Resources Center in Herndon said her office receives about 200 complaints a year and at any given time 200–300 units are not in compliance. Most of the noncompliance issues in Herndon involve Latino immigrants who crowd into apartments and single-family homes in an effort to save money. Always couched in terms of maintaining public safety, the aggressive enforcement of such measures may make it difficult for some immigrants to stay in a locality. Moreover, immigrants themselves complain that they are more often targets of complaints than native-born residents.

Immigrants also run into compliance problems when they modify their dwellings without proper permitting. In Wheaton permitting information is available in multiple languages, and the government uses the ethnic presses to relay the need for permits when residences are modified as well as information about occupancy limits. Here, too, overcrowding is an issue, especially when it results in too many cars or excessive trash and noise. As one Montgomery County official observed, the county has strict zoning and housing regulations, but a "lack of knowledge" about these codes can cause "true problems" for immigrants and the country officials who must see that they comply.

Most metropolitan areas have formal or informal day-labor sites where groups of mostly Latino men gather in front of shops or at busy intersections to await work. These sites are often seen as problematic by local communities—even while residents of these same communities often use the services of these laborers. All five focus areas have formal or informal day-labor sites. Currently two formal sites are found near Langley Park/Adelphi and in Wheaton. A formal site has been proposed but is actively being contested in Gaithersburg. And in September 2007, the formal day-labor site in Herndon was closed.

Communities can attempt to eliminate an informal day-labor site by aggressively enforcing anti-loitering laws. Although this curtails the formation of a large site, communities have difficulty keeping informal sites of a half-dozen workers from popping up in areas where immigrants reside. The impetus for communities to turn an informal day-labor site into a formal center arises when an informal location is viewed as problematic—when large numbers of young men hang out on street corners for several hours each day with no facilities or services available to them. Day-labor centers thus solve the problem of loitering and provide outreach to community members in need. The facilities are typically funded by local governments, but religious and secular groups are often involved as volunteers and support staff. Yet because day-labor centers cater to a largely undocumented population of poor immigrants, they are also contested spaces at the local and national level.

One illustration of how the politics of scale can conflate over the issue of day laborers is the battle over Herndon's day-labor center. Since the early 1990s, Latino men gathered to await work at the intersection of Elden and Alabama streets in downtown Herndon. This location is on a busy street in an area central to a number of apartment complexes where many immigrants live. In 2000 a task force was created of local officials, religious groups, and contractors to deal with the growing number of day laborers. In 2003 an amendment was made to the local zoning ordinance that allowed for a day-labor site in a residential portion of Herndon. In the summer of 2005 the Herndon town council, led by Mayor Michael O'Reilly, voted to create a formal day-labor center using Fairfax county funds and staff from a local nonprofit, Reston Interfaith.

Those opposed to the day-labor site objected to the idea that public monies were used to support *illegal* immigrant laborers; others expressed concerns that the presence of the site would attract still more undocumented workers to Herndon. Resolving Herndon's day-laborer problem took on national significance during the 2005 Virginia gubernatorial campaign. Both candidates used immigration as a major campaign issue and the day-labor center in Herndon was drawn into the debate. The Minutemen (an anti-immigrant vigilante group) opened a Herndon chapter, and Judicial Watch (a conservative nonprofit group that promotes government transparency) filed a lawsuit against the town and the center for aiding and abetting illegal immigrants using public money. At the same time a pro-immigrant group also formed in Herndon called HEART (Herndon Embraces All with Respect and Tolerance) in an attempt to support immigrant workers and their families. In December 2005 the Herndon day-labor center opened in a former police station with two years of funding from Fairfax County (not the town of Herndon directly).

In May 2006, when national attention turned to pro-immigration marches in cities across the country, Herndon voters quietly took their revenge. Mayor O'Reilly and several council members who supported the day-labor center were ousted. The new mayor, Stephen J. DeBenedittis, and several new council members rode into office in opposition to Herndon's day-labor site. DeBenedittis believes that his mandate goes beyond shutting down a day-labor site that serves illegal immigrants, and he supported the council decision to apply for a federal program that would train local police officers in enforcing immigration laws. In October 2006 the Herndon council sought a change in the labor center's staff, seeking to replace Reston Interfaith with an organization that would insist all day laborers show proof of legal residency before they could register through the center. A Reston Interfaith spokesperson responded that they "are not employing people" but focus on running a safe site.[35] The council also directed the town manager to ensure that no town contractors or subcontractors used illegal immigrants. Finally, in September 2007 the council decided not to renew the permit for the day labor site, nor was an alternative site selected; the action thus permanently closed the center. With the day-labor center closed in Herndon, small informal sites have begun to pop up again in different town locations.

Throughout metropolitan Washington local jurisdictions have responded to the perceived failure of the federal government to resolve the largest immigration question—the fate of undocumented immigrants. A series of legislative actions in 2007 illustrate the political urgency of this issue for suburban jurisdictions. The county boards of Prince William and Loudoun counties in Virginia introduced policies aimed at restricting access to public services by illegal immigrants. They also authorized local police to check the legal status of people arrested for crimes, with the aim of deporting undocumented individuals. Such aggressive deflection policies have had a chilling effect on the growing Latino population in these jurisdictions, with some Latinos opting to leave these counties. Yet not all jurisdictions have followed this trend. In Howard County, an outer Maryland jurisdiction, the county board voted down a proposal to restrict services to the undocumented. And, in an act of solidarity with immigrants, the Arlington County Board passed a resolution in September 2007 calling for elected officials in Northern Virginia to "promote the integration of immigrants" instead of enacting laws that would be divisive.[36]

Conclusion

In a relatively short period, immigration has made the Washington suburbs some of the most ethnically and racially diverse places in the country. Local jurisdictions vary in their responses to the challenges brought on by such rapid change, taking actions that both accommodate and deflect immigrants. In detailing how and where immigrants have changed suburban Washington, we advance a model of immigrant settlement that bypasses the inner city and goes straight to the suburbs.

In the Washington case, edge gateways form in those suburbs that offer both access and affordability. Located within some of the wealthiest counties in the United States, the five focus areas offer affordable housing, are located along major transportation arteries, are largely perceived as safe areas with good schools, and have grown as immigrant destinations through social networks. Consequently, these communities find themselves on the front line of the immigration debate. Such a pattern diverges significantly from the assumptions about immigrant residential settlement patterns put forth in the spatial assimilation model that assumes initial settlement in the urban core and residential clustering among co-ethnics.[37]

The distinction of ethnic community versus ethnic enclave developed by Logan and colleagues—where immigrants in enclaves are constrained to such locations, but those living in ethnic neighborhoods choose to live among immigrants even though they have the economic means to live elsewhere—has some relevance to the findings in our five case studies.[38] Of the five, Langley Park/Adelphi functions more like an ethnic enclave, where Salvadoran immigrants of limited means are the dominant group and the relative level of services available to them is low. In contrast, Annandale has developed the look and feel of an ethnic community in which the commercial and economic presence of Koreans is unmistakable even though their residential numbers are far from dominant.

The other three communities—Gaithersburg, Herndon, and Wheaton-Glenmont—can be considered neither ethnic enclaves nor ethnic communities. These places attract large numbers of immigrants from an extremely diverse range of countries. Moreover, these areas are still quite mixed with regard to nativity. These cases are the most compelling examples of multiethnic immigrant concentrations that are producing a new sociocultural, hyperdiverse landscape. Whether these new spaces are stable creations or zones in transition on their way to becoming more like ethnic enclaves or communities remains to be seen. Also, we suspect that large numbers of immigrants settling in a place may make it less attractive for native-born residents, who over time may leave the area and thus allow room for more immigrants to settle. The demographic dynamic between native-born and foreign-born in edge gateways needs further study. Given the high cost of housing in the region, along with the pace of new housing construction, it is also likely that new edge gateways will form farther from the urban core.

In the absence of federal policy on immigrant integration, local governments are left to develop strategies that tend to both accommodate and deflect immigrants. This research illustrates how local communities create de facto immigration policy when a void is left at the national level and in response to rising concerns about undocumented immigrants. Many of the local policies discussed in this chapter are sound, but others are born out of frustration with the federal government's inability to control immigration. Thus, local concerns are often stoked by the national debate. Washington's local leaders, like those in other communities across the country, set the tone for whether immigrants are embraced or shunned in their communities.

Notes

1. Marie Price and others, "The World Settles In: Washington, DC, as an Immigrant Gateway," *Urban Geography,* 26, no. 1 (2005): 61–83.

2. Audrey Singer, *At Home in the Nation's Capital: Immigrant Trends in Metropolitan Washington* (Brookings, 2003).

3. Audrey Singer and others, *The World in a Zip Code* (Brookings, 2001).

4. These are not necessarily the same edge cities that Garreau identified in his work, *Edge City: Life on the New Frontier* (Random House, 1991), such as Tyson's Corner. Furthermore, the definition of an edge city includes a certain threshold of office space and retail space; a population that increases on workdays; local perception as a destination for jobs, shopping, and entertainment; and fast change in the function of the area, from residential or rural in character to urban.

5. Joel Kotkin, *The New Suburbanism: A Realist's Guide to the American Future* (Costa Mesa: The Planning Center, November 2005); Audrey Singer, *The Rise of New Immigrant Gateways* (Brookings, 2004); Sarah Mahler, *American Dreaming: Immigrant Life on the Margins* (Princeton University Press, 1995); Glenda Laws, "Globalization, Immigration, and Changing Social Relations in U.S. Cities," *Annals of the American Academy of Political and Social Science* 551 (May 1997): 89–104; Peter Muller, "The Suburban Transformation of the Globalizing American City," *Annals of the American Academy of Political and Social Science* 551 (May 1997): 44–58.

6. John R. Logan, Richard D. Alba, and Wenquan Zhang, "Immigrant Enclaves and Ethnic Communities in New York and Los Angeles," *American Sociological Review* 67, no. 2 (2002): 299–322.

7. Ibid.

8. Wei Li, "Anatomy of a New Ethnic Settlement: The Chinese Ethnoburb in Los Angeles," *Urban Studies* 35, no. 3 (1998): 479–501.

9. Elizabeth Chacko, "Ethiopian Ethos and the Making of Ethnic Places in the Washington Metropolitan Area," *Journal of Cultural Geography* 20, no. 2 (2003): 21–42; Joseph Wood, "Vietnamese American Place Making in Northern Virginia," *Geographical Review* 87, no. 1 (1997): 58–72; Peter Marcuse, "The Enclave, the Citadel and the Ghetto: What Has Changed in the Post-Fordist U.S. City?" *Urban Affairs Review* 33 (1997): 228–64; Emily Skop and Wei Li, "Asians in America's Suburbs: Patterns and Consequences of Settlement," *Geographical Review* 95, no. 2 (2005): 167–88; Susan Hardwick, "Nodal Heterolocalism and Transnationalism at the United States-Canadian Border," *Geographical Review* 96, no. 2 (2006): 212–28.

10. Price and others, "The World Settles In."

11. Singer, *The Rise of New Immigrant Gateways*; Mary C. Waters and Tomas R. Jimenez, "Assessing Immigrant Assimilation: New Empirical and Theoretical Challenges," *Annual Review of Sociology* 31 (2005): 105–26.

12. Waters and Jimenez, "Assessing Immigrant Assimilation," p. 117.

13. For a fuller description of metropolitan-wide trends, including the inner core, see Singer, *At Home in the Nation's Capital*, and Singer and others, *The World in a Zip Code*.

14. Using ArcGIS software, CDP boundaries were layered on top of each other to identify which CDPs had changed boundaries. Approximately one-third of the CDPs in the study showed boundary changes. Of those whose boundaries changed, CDPs were adjusted if 5 percent or more of their total population fell outside the 2000 boundary in 1990. In most cases, the boundary changes did not affect the population significantly as they typically occurred around parks, rivers, cemeteries, golf courses, highways, and industrial buildings. However, the boundary changes did affect more than 5 percent of the CDP population in six cases: Bethesda, North Bethesda, Langley Park, North Potomac, Potomac, and Silver Spring. These CDPs were adjusted by normalizing the 1990 boundaries to the 2000 boundaries. Five lost population between 1990 and 2000 (Bethesda, Langley Park, North Potomac, Potomac, Silver Spring), while one gained (North Bethesda).

15. We combined the CDPs of Langley Park and Adelphi because these two adjacent areas are often identified together. Combined, they have a total population more comparable with the other case studies.

16. This pattern holds for the U.S.-born population as well. The city (District of Columbia) has steadily lost population since 1950; only since 2000 has it started to gain again.

17. Adelphi was not yet a CDP in 1980.

18. In 1990 Woodbridge became the first locality in Prince William County to report that more than 10 percent of its population was foreign-born; like other immigrant destinations, Woodbridge is along a major commuter route, Interstate 95.

19. Adelphi was not yet a CDP in 1970; therefore, there are no comparable statistics for that period.

20. Parker Rodriquez, Inc., "Needs Assessment for a Multi-Cultural Center in Langley Park, Maryland," prepared for the Maryland National Capital Park and Planning Commission, Prince George's County Planning Department, March 2002.

21. See Walter Nicholls, "Eclectic Wheaton," *Washington Post,* October 25, 2006, p. F1.

22. U.S. Bureau of Economic Affairs, Regional Economic Information System, various years.

23. Stephen Fuller, "Perspectives on Regional Growth," paper presented to the Board of Trade Regional Development Task Force, 2003 (www.cra-gmu.org/forecastreports/regionalgrowthperspectives.ppt#258 [July 30, 2007]).

24. Randy Capps and others, *Civic Contributions: Taxes Paid by Immigrants in the Washington, DC, Metropolitan Area* (Washington: Community Foundation for the National Capital Region, May 2006).

25. Camille Zubrinsky Charles, "Neighborhood Racial-Composition Preferences: Evidence from a Multiethnic Metropolis," *Social Problems* 47 (2000): 379–407; Camille Zubrinsky Charles, "Processes of Residential Segregation," in *Urban Inequality: Evidence from Four Cities*, edited by Alice O'Connor, Charles Tilly, and Lawrence Bobo (New York: Russell Sage Foundation, 2001), 217–71.

26. Lorrie A. Frasure, "Beyond the Urban Core: Immigrants, Migrants and the New American Suburb." Unpublished manuscript, Cornell University, 2006, p. 32.

27. Samantha A. Friedman and others, "Race, Immigrants, and Residence: A New Racial Geography of Washington, D.C.," *Geographical Review* 95, no. 2 (2000): 210–30.

28. Ibid., p. 226.

29. James Allen and Eugene Turner, "Spatial Patterns of Immigrant Assimilation," *The Professional Geographer* 48, no. 2 (1996): 140–55; Terry Repak, *Waiting on Washington: Central American Workers in the Nation's Capital* (Temple University Press, 1995).

30. See Ivan Light, *Deflecting Immigration: Networks, Markets, and Regulation* (New York: Russell Sage Foundation, 2006).

31. Mark Ellis, "Unsettling Immigrant Geographies: U.S. Immigration and the Politics of Scale," *Tijdschrift voor Economische en Sociale Geografie* 97, no. 1 (2006): p. 50.

32. Cameron Barr, "Counties' Diversity Leads Officials into Foreign Territory," *Washington Post,* July 17, 2005, C01.

33. Patrick Badgley, "Montgomery to Allow Use of Consular IDs," *Washington Times,* September 17, 2003, B01.

34. Town of Herndon, Virginia, "Ordinance, August 10, 2004." Amending the

Zoning Ordinance to Clarify and Strengthen Occupancy Limitations of Residential Units and to Amend the Definition of Family, Among Others; ZOTA 03-05; 04-O-24.

35. Bill Turque, "Change in Center's Oversight Is Sought," *Washington Post,* October 31, 2006, B1.

36. Kirstin Downey, "Arlington Condemns Region's Immigrant Crackdown," *Washington Post,* September 19, 2007, B4.

37. Douglas Massey and Nancy Denton, "Spatial Assimilation as a Socioeconomic Outcome," *American Sociological Review* 50 (1985): 94–105.

38. Logan, Alba, and Zhang, "Immigrant Enclaves."

PART III

Re-Emerging Gateways: Attracting Immigrants Again

7

Immigrant Space and Place in Suburban Sacramento

ROBIN DATEL and DENNIS DINGEMANS

Over the past quarter century, metropolitan areas of all sizes have welcomed newcomers to America in numbers never before seen. New arrivals in both established and emerging immigrant gateways are settling increasingly in the suburbs and often in dispersed neighborhoods. This new pattern of immigrant settlement is rooted in a number of widespread trends: the overall suburbanization of homes and jobs in America; the wider availability of affordable housing outside the central city; the increasing number of middle- and upper-income immigrants; and the availability of technologies that enable "community without propinquity" locally and internationally.[1]

Sacramento is no exception to these trends. In 2005 Sacramento's suburbs had about 250,000 foreign-born, the city of Sacramento about 100,000. Moreover, the suburbs were home to a higher share of recent immigrants (80 percent of those who entered in 2000 or later) than of earlier immigrants (71 percent of those who entered before 2000).[2] This chapter details Sacramento's suburban immigrant settlement patterns and helps provide an understanding of the local forces that have shaped them, including Sacramento's history of immigrant and racial settlement, the region's role as a refugee magnet, the availability of inexpensive suburban housing aided by the closure of all three of its military installations in the late twentieth century, and demand for migrants with both brain (high-tech) and brawn (agriculture and construction). The chapter also describes how immigrants are shaping the Sacramento suburbs by rejuvenating commercial strips, creating a new religious geography, diversifying suburban schools, and using virtual and temporary spaces to stay connected across the region's rapidly expanding area. In doing so, they have enriched the cultural geography of the suburbs, while essentially leaving intact its socioeconomic cleavages.

In this work, we use a line of convenience, the boundary around the incorporated city of Sacramento, to separate central city from suburbs. At the same time, we recognize that areas on either side of this boundary are not necessarily very different from one another in age, physical appearance, or socioeconomic character. The city of Sacramento is not entirely built out and contains new subdivisions, while some of the region's fifty-one suburban places include hundred-year-old neighborhoods.[3]

Census data are central to our discussion; we also employ other published statistics, popular and scholarly publications, interviews, and field data to paint our portrait of immigrants in the Sacramento suburbs. The region covered in this chapter is currently known to the federal government as the Sacramento-Arden-Arcade-Roseville metropolitan area (map 7-1). It consists of four counties: El Dorado, Placer, Sacramento, and Yolo, which in 2005 had a combined population of 2 million people. In that year, two-thirds of these people lived in Sacramento County and 22 percent in Sacramento proper. Physically, the area covers 5,361 square miles, ranging from mostly flat Sacramento Valley in the case of Yolo and Sacramento counties, to Sierra Nevada foothill and mountain territory stretching to Lake Tahoe and the Nevada border in El Dorado and Placer counties. As of 2005 the foreign-born constituted 17.6 percent of the region's population of slightly more than 2 million. Nationally, it ranked eighteenth among all metropolitan areas in absolute number of foreign-born (353,592). It ranked twenty-seventh in total population. It was tenth among all American metros in absolute number of refugees resettled between 1983 and 2004 (37,436).[4]

Residential Patterns

Through the first half of the history of the four-county region (1870–1940), the share of its population that was foreign-born was nearly the same inside and outside the city of Sacramento (table 7-1). This changed after 1940 with suburbanization, which disproportionately involved native-born residents, and by 1970 the share of immigrants in the city's population was more than double that outside. After 1970 this trend was reversed, and currently the proportion of the suburban population that is foreign-born (16 percent) is about three-fourths as large as that of the city (22 percent).

Map 7-1. Foreign-Born, by Place in the Sacramento Metropolitan Area, 2000

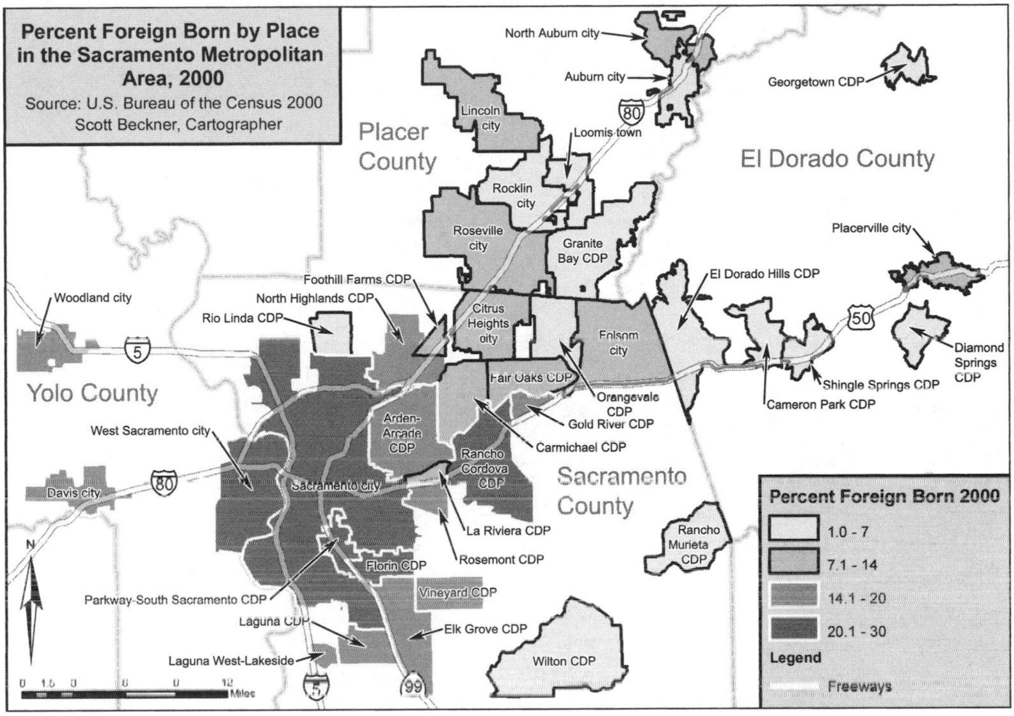

Source: U.S. Census Bureau, *Census of Population 2000.*

Because of Sacramento's West Coast location and particular history and economy, its immigrants came even in early decades not just from Europe but also from Asia and Latin America.[5] Some of the earlier residential choices made by these immigrant groups—shaped by the constraints they faced from the dominant Euro-American society—have influenced more recent patterns. Many Latino immigrants, who come overwhelmingly from Mexico, continue to be attracted to agricultural service centers and to neighborhoods near rail yards and adjacent industries, just as were their co-ethnics decades ago. Early twentieth-century Japanese immigrants created a vibrant Japantown in the urban core, but they also established a series of small farming communities south of the city in the direction of the Delta, planting the seed of today's large Asian southern sector. The current substantial Slavic refugee population has its roots in a small Russian immigrant community that bought lots in then-rural Bryte (now part of the city of West Sacramento) when it was first subdivided in 1911 and advertised in San Francisco's Russian-language press.[6] Virtually all the immigrant

Table 7-1. Foreign-Born in Sacramento City and Four-County Metropolitan Area, 1860–2005

	Population total and percent foreign-born						*U.S. percent*
Year	*City of Sacramento*		*Suburban/rural*		*Metro four-county total*		*foreign-born*
1860 to 1930: Sacramento was much above the nation in percent foreign-born.							
1860	n.a.		n.a.		62,690	41.5	13.2
1870	16,283	38.1	42,112	37.4	58,395	37.6	14.4
1880	21,420	32.9	49,607	33.6	64,029	33.9	13.3
1890	26,386	29.1	50,970	29.4	77,356	29.3	14.8
1900	29,282	23.0	55,023	25.5	84,305	24.6	13.6
1910	44,694	24.7	62,767	25.9	107,461	25.4	14.7
1920	65,908	19.7	67,236	24.3	133,144	22.0	13.2
1930	93,750	18.4	104,686	17.5	198,436	17.9	11.6
1940 to 1970: Sacramento was approaching the nation in percent foreign-born.							
1940	105,958	12.9	132,955	12.5	238,913	12.7	8.8
1950	137,572	10.3	238,064	8.3	375,636	9.0	6.9
1960	191,667	8.7	463,226	5.0	654,893	6.1	5.4
1970	254,417	10.0	590,008	4.2	844,425	5.0	4.7
1980 to 2005: Sacramento was increasingly above the nation in percent foreign-born.							
1980	275,741	10.0	824,073	6.3	1,099,814	7.3	6.2
1990	369,365	13.7	1,111,737	8.1	1,481,102	9.5	7.9
2000	407,075	20.3	1,389,782	12.8	1,796,857	14.5	11.1
2005	445,287	22.3	1,559,189	16.3	2,004,476	17.6	12.4

Sources: Tabulated from printed and online census sources by the authors, with estimates for 1910, 1920, 1930, and 1950 (except for national figures) due to incomplete data. In those years, we used California's rates of foreign-born for various "nonwhite" groups, and weighted them according to their shares of Sacramento's population. The source for national figures is Campbell J. Gibson and Emily Lennon, "Historical Census Statistics on the Foreign-Born Population of the United States: 1850–1990," Population Division Working Paper No. 29 (U. S. Bureau of the Census, 1999) (www.census.gov/population/www/documentation/twps0029/twps0029.html [June 2007]).

n.a. = Not applicable.

groups who settled in the area before World War II had their largest cluster in the old West End along the Sacramento River waterfront. Starting in the 1950s they were given a boost out if not up by the twin federal bulldozers of urban renewal and freeway construction.

As of 2000 the foreign-born composed 8 percent or more of the total population in thirty-one of the region's fifty-one suburban places (table 7-2).[7] Most of these places fall into three categories, defined by a combination of location (see map 7-1), income, and source of immigrants. First, there is a group of eleven inner-to-middle-ring suburbs. These have low-to-moderate median household incomes and housing costs, and their immigrants have come in significant proportions from diverse regions of the

Table 7-2. Places in the Sacramento Metropolitan Area with 8 Percent or More Foreign-Born, 2000

Place	*County*	*Total population 2000*	*Percent foreign-born 1990*	*Percent foreign-born 2000*	*1990–2000 percent change in foreign-born population*	*Median household income, 1999*[a]	*Group*[b]
King's Beach CDP	El Dorado	3,886	21.6	36.3	133.7	$35,507	C
Walnut Grove CDP	Sacramento	646	—	33.9	—	$40,179	C
Parkway-South Sacto. CDP	Sacramento	36,490	16.6	27.4	88.2	$31,194	A
Esparto CDP	Yolo	1,842	13.9	26.5	136.2	$41,389	C
West Sacramento city	Yolo	31,604	16.5	25.1	66.3	$31,718	C
Winters city	Yolo	6,113	18.9	24.2	68.3	$48,678	C
South Lake Tahoe city	El Dorado	23,720	18.8	22.4	31.1	$34,707	C
Florin CDP	Sacramento	27,577	12.5	21.8	97.2	$33,793	A
Rancho Cordova CDP	Sacramento	54,586	9.1	20.7	155.7	$40,095	A
Sacramento city	**Sacramento**	**407,075**	**13.7**	**20.3**	**63.4**	**$37,049**	**n.a.**
Isleton CDP	Sacramento	803	16.1	20.3	21.6	$33,958	C
Woodland city	Yolo	49,132	10.6	19.4	125.8	$44,449	C
North Highlands CDP	Sacramento	44,079	8.4	17.8	122.2	$32,278	A
Davis city	Yolo	46,209	13.9	17.2	61.1	$42,454	n.a.
Galt city	Sacramento	19,525	12.5	17.0	197.8	$45,052	C
Elk Grove CDP[c]	Sacramento	60,255	9.8	16.3	156.3	$60,661	B
Rosemont CDP	Sacramento	22,830	10.0	16.3	61.9	$45,044	A
Gold River CDP	Sacramento	8,360	—	16.2	—	$92,028	B
Laguna CDP	Sacramento	34,404	—	15.7	—	$67,447	B
Laguna West-Lakeside CDP	Sacramento	8,518	—	15.6	—	$76,404	B
Vineyard CDP	Sacramento	10,007	—	14.5	—	$65,192	B
Arden-Arcade CDP	Sacramento	96,004	7.9	14.3	88.0	$40,335	A
La Riviera CDP	Sacramento	10,273	12.1	13.0	0.2	$49,110	A
Foothill Farms CDP	Sacramento	17,393	6.4	12.3	93.8	$38,049	A
Lincoln city	Placer	10,939	8.0	12.2	128.5	$45,547	C
Tahoe Vista CDP	Placer	1,819	3.5	11.1	402.5	$51,958	C
Fair Oaks CDP	Sacramento	28,008	5.8	10.0	79.9	$63,252	B
Citrus Heights city[c]	Sacramento	85,230	5.3	9.2	76.3	$43,859	A
Placerville city	El Dorado	9,580	5.7	9.1	80.6	$36,454	C
Carmichael CDP	Sacramento	49,742	5.0	9.0	82.8	$47,041	A
Roseville city	Placer	80,092	6.5	9.0	148.8	$57,367	n.a.
Folsom city	Sacramento	51,912	7.8	8.8	98.3	$73,175	n.a.

Source: U.S. Census Bureau, *Census of the Population 1990, 2000.*

a. The 1999 median household income for the entire metropolitan area was $46,106.

b. Group A places are inner-to-middle-ring suburbs characterized by low-to-moderate median incomes and housing costs and immigrants from diverse regions of the world. Group B places are outer suburbs with high- income populations of which between 59 and 72 percent are Asian foreign-born. Group C places are free-standing settlements that provide low-wage jobs to mostly Mexican immigrants.

c. Elk Grove CDP and Citrus Heights city (Citrus Heights CDP in 1990) had major boundary changes between the 1990 and 2000 censuses. Figures were estimated for 1990 using the 2000 boundaries.

— = No CDP in 1990.

n.a. = Not applicable.

world (group A in table 7-2). In only two of these eleven places did a majority of immigrants come from just one world region. Second is a group of six outer suburbs (group B in table 7-2). These places have high incomes, and between 59 and 72 percent of their foreign-born came from Asia. Third is a group of eleven free-standing places located beyond the Census Bureau's boundary for the Sacramento Urbanized Area (group C in table 7-2). Most of these places are old agricultural service centers that retain that function. Also in this group are three places around Lake Tahoe (located beyond the area shown on the map) that house low-wage workers in the tourism economy. In nine out of eleven cases, median household income was below that of the metropolitan area ($46,106) in 2000, and the source region for the majority (usually the vast majority) of immigrants was Latin America. Not fitting well into these three categories is the university town of Davis (free-standing, high social status—but moderate income, due to students—with Asian-dominant immigration), together with Fair Oaks and Roseville (both outer suburbs, high income, with diverse sources of immigrants).

In the following sections, we examine in more detail the residential patterns of immigrants from the three major world regions that together account for 85 percent of the metropolitan area's current foreign-born: Asia (41 percent), Latin America (33 percent), and Eastern Europe (11 percent). To do so, we identified those places in which each group was "overrepresented" among the foreign-born by at least 50 percent (thus, Asians had to make up more than 61 percent, Latin Americans more than 50 percent, and Eastern Europeans more than 17 percent of the foreign-born to meet this criterion). Underlying the observed patterns are other patterns of housing cost and availability, job opportunities, provision of services, and earlier settlement by co-ethnics.

Patterns of the Foreign-Born from Asia

Ever since the Gold Rush and subsequent agricultural booms in the Sacramento Valley, the region has had immigrant Asian populations, most significantly from China, Japan, and the Philippines. These streams were truncated by anti-Asian federal and state legislation and the general decline of immigration in the decades leading up to the 1965 federal immigration reform. After that, the picture for Asian immigration changed. Between 1975 and 1990 (as measured in federal fiscal years), Sacramento received 14,240 primary refugees, mostly from Vietnam and Laos, after the fall of Saigon.[8] Although federal policy hoped for a widely dispersed pattern of Southeast Asian refugee resettlement, a highly clustered pattern had emerged by the mid-1980s, owing to family reunifications and the lure of places with the best government benefits and services.[9] Sacramento became an important place for Vietnamese (many of whom were of Chinese heritage), Hmong, Mien, and other Southeast Asian refugee groups. Nonrefugee flows from China, India, the Philippines, and other Asian countries have also been significant in recent decades, reflecting family ties and job opportunities. Table 7-3 shows the population change by immigrant group between 2000 and 2005, and the percentage of each group that is living in the suburbs.

Asians (immigrant and nonimmigrant—the latter are 43 percent of the total) are overrepresented in a sector on the south side of the metropolitan area, both within and beyond the city of Sacramento. This pattern has roots in the agriculturally oriented settlements of the Chinese, Japanese, and Filipinos, dating back one hundred years and more. Also, when urban renewal destroyed downtown's Chinatown and Japantown, displaced businesses, institutions, and residents faced fewest barriers in the south. By the time the influx of Southeast Asian refugees began, the south side also had ample inexpensive housing and commercial property. These latter resources were tied to earlier overbuilding, a broad "minority" presence that included Latinos and African Americans (Sacramento's first subdivision marketed as "interracial" was in this sector), and arterials with bargain rents resulting from freeway-induced circulation blight. Refugee sponsorship by south side churches, notably Bethany Presbyterian at 24th Street and Fruitridge Road, also played a role. Refugee services, such as Sacramento Lao Family Community, Inc., and the Hmong Women's Heritage Association, sprang up on the south side, tending to reinforce the attractiveness of the area to additional refugees. They settled in the city and adjacent unincorporated Sacramento County, in both cases occupying suburban-style landscapes of postwar single-family homes and garden apartments.

As of 2000 all five places in which people from Asia are overrepresented among the foreign-born by at least 50 percent were on the south side: Vineyard, Laguna, Laguna West-Lakeside, Elk Grove, and Rosemont. The first four of these places are outer suburbs, with median household incomes well above those of the metropolitan area. Their Asian immigrant populations are highly diverse, with sizable numbers of Chinese, Filipinos, Indians, Koreans, and Vietnamese. Other places with high shares of immigrants from Asia include additional high-income outer suburbs, such as college town Davis, and Folsom and Gold River, which house many professional and technical workers. Rosemont is a moderate-income inner suburb particularly favored by Koreans and Armenians, but also with high Asian diversity.

Table 7-3. Share of Suburban Population for Selected Native- and Foreign-Born Groups, Sacramento Metro Area, 2000 and 2005[a]

Group	*Population 2000*	*Percent suburban*	*Population 2005*	*Percent suburban*	*Median household income, native- and foreign-born, 1999*
Total	1,796,857	77.4	2,004,476	77.8	$46,106
Native-born	1,536,746	78.9	1,650,884	79.0	
White alone	1,161,747	84.8	1,205,746	85.2	$49,090
Hispanic or Latino	193,083	68.7	237,762	69.4	$37,332
Asian alone	68,608	56.0	97,503	61.6	$43,640
Black alone	121,863	49.8	137,302	49.1	$33,499
Foreign-born[b]	260,111	68.2	353,592	72.0	
Armenia	1,650	98.1	4,855	n.a.	$46,438
Korea	5,007	88.3	4,855	n.a.	$39,631
Canada (9, —)	6,642	87.4	6,216	n.a.	$47,887
Germany	5,408	86.8	5,885	n.a.	$53,010
Ukraine (6, 5)	12,123	82.4	20,911	n.a.	$29,231
United Kingdom (—, 10)	5,748	82.3	6,286	n.a.	$57,340
Russia (8, 7)	7,296	82.0	12,978	n.a.	$42,944
South America	3,754	80.5	5,021	n.a.	$53,417
India (7, 4)	9,215	77.4	21,106	n.a.	$52,262
Africa	4,397	76.1	6,457	n.a.	$34,127
Japan	3,960	75.1	5,288	n.a.	$56,105
Philippines (2, 2)	18,530	70.2	28,857	n.a.	$50,206
Mexico (1, 1)	74,634	67.1	99,307	n.a.	$37,086
Vietnam (3, 3)	17,478	60.8	22,122	n.a.	$28,464
China (4, 6)	16,363	48.2	20,809	n.a.	$43,608
Melanesia	6,280	45.2	n.a.	n.a.	$32,390
Thailand (10, 9)	5,799	38.9	6,352	n.a.	$40,769
Laos (5, 8)	13,170	35.9	10,412	n.a.	$28,924

Source: U.S. Census Bureau, 2000 Census, and *American Community Survey 2005* (http://factfinder.census.gov).

a. The figures for 2000 are for the four-county Sacramento region known as a Consolidated Metropolitan Statistical Area (CMSA). By 2005 the nomenclature had changed and the region was called a Metropolitan Area (MA).

b. Numbers in parentheses indicate the ranks of the top-ten origin countries by size in 2000 and 2005. A — indicates a lower ranking for that year.

n.a. = Not available.

The Hmong and Mien (who come from Laos and Thailand), on average, have lower incomes than other Asian immigrant groups in Sacramento, and therefore they tend to occupy less expensive housing and cluster much more in the city of Sacramento and in older, inner suburbs (see table 7-3).

The greater degree of clustering in general among immigrants from Laos and Thailand is evident in four census tracts in 2000 that each housed at least 5 percent of the region's immigrants from Laos, and in three that housed at least 5 percent of immigrants from Thailand. In contrast, no tracts met that threshold for foreign-born Chinese, Filipinos, Indians, or Vietnamese. The Hmong and Mien arrived in the United States with very few economic resources, very low levels of education, traumatic refugee experiences, and a huge culture gap with America.[10]

The foreign-born Chinese, Filipinos, Indians, and Vietnamese are less concentrated than the Hmong and Mien. Vietnamese immigrants have formed loose clusters (ten census tracts each with between 2 and 5 percent of the region's foreign-born Vietnamese) along Stockton Boulevard running south-southeast from central Sacramento, and encompassing a mix of the city and unincorporated territory. The largest Chinese immigrant clusters are within the city, as are those of nonimmigrant Chinese. Immigrant Filipinos have only three tracts that contain between 2 percent and 5 percent of their Sacramento population, two of which are in the southern suburbs and may be tied to much earlier patterns established when Filipinos were field workers and had links to an ethnic enclave in Stockton. Today, the south side hospitals are also a draw for many Filipinos.[11] The four tracts with 2 to 5 percent of the region's Asian Indian immigrants are in four scattered middle-to-high-income suburbs. Clearly, there are markedly different degrees of suburbanization among different immigrant Asian groups in Sacramento, but overall they are about as suburban as native-born Asians and also share with native-born Asians a strong southside orientation.

Patterns of the Foreign-Born from Latin America

Immigrants from Latin America constitute more than 50 percent of the foreign-born in seven places in the Sacramento suburbs: King's Beach (98 percent), Winters (93 percent), Woodland (81 percent), Galt (80 percent), Lincoln (73 percent), South Lake Tahoe (72 percent), and Placerville (64 percent). Three of these places—Woodland, South Lake Tahoe, and Galt—are also among the top-ranked places in terms of absolute numbers of Latin American immigrants to the Sacramento region outside the central city. Every one of these places is still a freestanding settlement. All provide unskilled or semi-skilled jobs in agriculture, forestry, and related industries or in tourism services. Median household incomes are near or below that of the metro area as a whole. Many migrants from Latin America, 85 percent of whom are from Mexico, have limited job skills and little English-language knowledge on arrival, which limits their upward mobility.

Parkway-South Sacramento's 4,690 foreign-born Latinos make up 47 percent of its total foreign-born. This place is more genuinely suburban than the towns described above. It is the inner suburban extension of Barrio Franklin, the spine of which, Franklin Boulevard, begins in the city of Sacramento. This area has had a Latino presence for many decades, in part because of the nearby rail-oriented industrial district, including a large Campbell's Soup plant that opened in 1947. In ten other suburban places in the region, the share of foreign-born from Latin America tops 25 percent. These places are diverse in location and range in income from low (North Highlands, for example) to upper-middle (Roseville). These suburbs are also home to many of the native-born Latinos in the area, who compose 70 percent of the region's total Latino population. Foreign-born Mexican immigrants are as suburbanized as native-born Latinos in Sacramento, while the comparatively limited numbers who come from South America are even more so (see table 7-3).

Patterns of the Foreign-Born from Eastern Europe

The flow of refugees to Sacramento from Ukraine, Russia, and other former Soviet states was encouraged by the passage of the Lautenberg Amendment in 1989. Jews, evangelical Christians, and some members of the Ukrainian Catholic and Orthodox churches—groups with histories of persecution under the Soviet and successor regimes—were given a "reduced evidentiary burden" when applying for refugee status. Nearly half a million people have entered the United States under this provision, representing more than one-third of all refugees admitted since 1989.[12] Tens of thousands have come to Sacramento. According to the California Department of Social Services, Refugee Arrivals Data, between 1995 and 2005 Sacramento County received more than 19,000 primary refugees from the former Soviet Union, nearly three times as many as Los Angeles County and five times as many as San Francisco County. Most of these have been evangelical Christians, who learned about the Sacramento area through *Word to Russia,* an evangelical Christian shortwave-radio program that reached behind the Iron Curtain beginning in the early 1970s. From 1980 the program was headed up by Michael Lokteff, a resident of the old Bryte Russian enclave in Yolo County, and it painted an attractive portrait of "the wonders of life in America, particularly Sacramento."[13] Also in the 1970s the Russian Church of Evangelic Christian Baptists in Bryte (founded in 1928) was publishing "the only Russian Christian newspaper in the Western Hemisphere," and mailing it to more than 2,000 people worldwide.[14]

Through these media, information spread about Sacramento as a place that would welcome evangelical Christians.

As of 2000 ten places in the suburbs had high shares (above 17 percent) of their foreign-born from Eastern Europe. These were Arden-Arcade (22 percent), Carmichael (25 percent), Citrus Heights (28 percent), Fair Oaks (33 percent), Foothill Farms (21 percent), North Highlands (38 percent), Orangevale (19 percent), Rancho Cordova (32 percent), Rio Linda (26 percent), and West Sacramento (26 percent). All but one of these places—West Sacramento in Yolo County—are Sacramento County suburbs located in a wide wedge northeast of the downtown. Those with the largest absolute numbers of Eastern European immigrants—Arden-Arcade, Carmichael, Citrus Heights, North Highlands, and Rancho Cordova—have median household incomes around or below that of the metro area ($46,106 in 1999). In a personal interview in June 2006, Laura Leonelli, the executive director of the Southeast Asian Assistance Center, said the "whiteness" of this group suggests they have likely had an easier time settling in this predominantly white sector of Sacramento than immigrants of other races would have had.

The attraction to West Sacramento is clearly a continuation of the historic settlement patterns, offering newcomers already established churches (Baptist, but also Orthodox for the minority of arrivals who practice that faith rather than Protestantism), and Russian immigrants of an earlier generation. As for the rest of the pattern, the presence of many low-cost residential units, both apartments and houses, near Sacramento's three major military facilities—all in the process of shrinking and closing during the 1990s—made nearby places such as Rancho Cordova, North Highlands, and Foothill Farms especially affordable just as post-Soviet refugees were arriving, and they were coming for the same reason—the end of the cold war.[15] According to Victor Tikhomirov, case manager supervisor at the International Rescue Committee, many Slavic refugees have gone to work in automotive businesses located in the Elkhorn–North Highlands industrial district and along Sunrise Boulevard in Rancho Cordova. It has also been suggested that Slavic immigrants may seek out this location to avoid public schools perceived as dangerous and tainted by a loose morality not in keeping with their conservative Christian values. The places with the largest numbers of Slavic immigrants are growing more ethnically diverse, but with just a short move they can be in the "whitest" contiguous suburbs in the Sacramento metro, in Placer and El Dorado counties. Already, more than 600 Eastern European foreign-born live in Roseville, and some of the student leaders of recent Slavic protest movements against gay rights in the Sacramento area attended high school there. Research has shown that Sacramentans are sorting themselves politically as they make residential choices, and if Slavic evangelicals want to be near their fellow conservatives, then heading out toward Placer and El Dorado counties is the logical choice.[16]

Rancho Cordova has been especially attractive to Eastern European immigrants, and in 2000 it was home to approximately 15 percent of the region's foreign-born Ukrainians. Rancho Cordova provides a good example of a large apartment complex, Cordova Meadows, occupied entirely by a single immigrant group (a phenomenon not restricted to Slavic immigrants). It experienced a complete turnover in tenants to those from the Ukraine, because, as Larry Ladd, a Rancho Cordova activist told us in a July 6, 2006, interview, they were quiet, did not engage in drug dealing on the premises, and always paid their rent on time. Similar favoritism shown to Southeast Asian refugees has caused tensions with African Americans; according to Leonelli of the Southeast Asian Assistance Center, the two groups compete for the lowest-priced housing and neighborhoods in the region. It should be noted, however, that African American suburbanites do not appear to have been displaced by immigrants between 1990 and 2000. Low-to-moderate income, high-immigration places in the Sacramento suburbs (group A in table 7-2)—as well as in the city itself—generally gained African Americans, while losing non–Hispanic whites.

Although the settlement patterns of groups from different source regions are distinctive, there is also considerable sharing of residential space among groups at the place and census tract scales. This is particularly characteristic of the older, inner, low-to-moderate-income suburbs, which display "a kaleidoscope of colors and languages and customs" like that in Sacramento's West End before urban renewal.[17] Culturally similar groups have the greatest residential proximity, but there are also examples of sizable numbers of Ukrainians and Indians, for example, or Mexicans and Laotians, living in the same census tract. In 2000, fewer than ten tracts out of the region's more than four hundred contained as much as 5 percent of any one of Sacramento's major foreign-born groups.[18]

Commercial Patterns

Not only have the foreign-born in Sacramento become increasingly suburban in their residential patterns over the past several decades, but they have become increasingly suburban in their patterns of commerce, worship, school, and play. Immigrant business districts, because of their size and visibility, are potent symbols of the new suburban diversity. By far the most important of these is "Little Saigon" along Stockton Boulevard, with 350 Asian businesses—similar in concentration to other high-profile suburban Chinatowns in the larger immigrant gateways of Atlanta; California's Orange County, San Gabriel Valley, and Santa Clara Valley; and Toronto.[19] The Stockton Boulevard Little Saigon contrasts with Sacramento's old Chinatown and Japantown—now gone—in several ways: suburban versus downtown location, automobile-oriented strip versus densely packed pedestrian district, and a dispersed and pan-Asian customer base versus a clustered and mostly co-ethnic clientele.[20]

Emergence of a Nationally Significant Little Saigon

Between 1975, when Saigon fell, and 1980, nearly 3,000 Vietnamese streamed into Sacramento. The emergence of a section of Stockton Boulevard as an Asian commercial district quickly followed. In 1978 the *Sacramento City Directory* and the *Sacramento Suburban Directory* listed no Vietnamese residents or businesses on Stockton Boulevard south of 21st Avenue. A few professionals with Chinese and Japanese names were the only Asian presence on the street. Its rapid rise began in the early 1980s, when Vietnamese first appeared as tenants of the Stocktonian apartments (renamed the Cara Bay in 2006) on the boulevard. This residential complex became an incubator for Vietnamese entrepreneurs. As Al Pham, onetime manager of the Stocktonian, said, "You stay for awhile, you save your money, and then you get your own home or business. Nearly every successful Asian merchant on Stockton Boulevard began life in Sacramento in the Stocktonian."[21]

In the 1981 directory, two Asian markets appeared on Stockton Boulevard. The following year brought a third market as well as the Sacramento Chinese of Indo-China Friendship Association. By 1990 *The Haines Sacramento City and Suburban Directory* listed fifty-one businesses with Asian names along Stockton. Although the majority of businesses were Vietnamese or Chinese, other Asian ethnicities were evident, including Hmong, Indian, Japanese, and Korean.

The 2000 Census revealed the deepening significance of Sacramento's southern sector for its 161,000 Asians in general, and of the Stockton Boulevard corridor for 18,000 Vietnamese in particular. The emergence of a large and prominent Asian business district, especially one with a Vietnamese visage, in this particular location reflected these settlement patterns. Affordability also played a role. The Stockton Boulevard corridor

The Stocktonian Apartments, sixty-nine low-rent units and the epicenter of what became the Little Saigon residential and commercial area, experienced chronic high vacancies before 1980. After this it filled with Vietnamese residents, including many who became the earliest Vietnamese business owners on Stockton Boulevard. Stockton Boulevard's provision of both inexpensive housing and cheap commercial property made it an ideal immigrant business incubator.

was once the highway to Stockton but was bypassed in 1963 by the construction of a parallel freeway, U.S. 99. With the bypass, rents declined. In addition, the north end of Stockton Boulevard ran alongside Oak Park, a neighborhood that had become largely low-income and African American in the 1960s. Expectations of further racial change down the boulevard contributed to blighted conditions. By the 1970s vacancies were common and rents depressed, thus providing opportunities for fledgling immigrant businesses. Still, the street remained a major arterial linking city and suburbs, providing good visibility and bus service.

In May 2006, of the 708 visible businesses along the four miles between 21st Avenue and Massie Street, we identified 354, or 50 percent of the total, as Asian enterprises.[22] The boulevard displays a typical suburban mix of free-standing buildings housing single businesses, small strip malls with

With twenty-nine Asian enterprises, Pacific Rim Plaza is among the newest and largest of the eleven ethnic-themed centers in Sacramento's Little Saigon on Stockton Boulevard. Today, professional services are more common than food businesses, some twenty-five years after entrepreneurs opened the first Asian grocery stores and restaurants.

a few enterprises, and larger shopping centers. Five of these nineteen shopping centers, including four of the largest, have Asian names: China Town Plaza, Asian Plaza, Little Vietnam Plaza, Pacific Rim Plaza, and Pacific Plaza. The Asian presence is intensified in the shopping centers, amounting to two-thirds of the businesses, suggesting that Asian capital is a big investor on the boulevard. New centers under construction include Little Saigon Plaza, which will offer business condominium ownership, a form of tenure imported from Hong Kong.[23] The scale and business mix of this district are on par with that of older, centrally located Chinatowns in Los Angeles, Oakland, and San Francisco, as well as of suburban Little Saigons elsewhere in California (table 7-4).

While Stockton Boulevard's revival was begun by local Asian entrepreneurs (albeit initially with capital they brought with them), more recently it

Table 7-4. Sacramento's Little Saigon Compared with Other Central City and Suburban Asian Business Clusters
Percent

Enterprise type	*Four Chinatowns in California and New York City*	*Sacramento's Stockton Boulevard Little Saigon*	*Orange County's Bolsa Avenue Little Saigon*	*San Jose's Little Saigon*	*Eleven of Bay Area's Asian-theme neighbor-hood centers*
1. Gifts, clothes, furniture	20.3	7.6	9.4	10.9	5.9
2. Professionals	19.8	20.6	24.0	22.5	14.6
3. Eating establishments	14.4	15.5	10.1	21.8	35.4
4. Food sales, markets	10.5	9.3	6.2	8.3	13.4
5. Jewelry	8.1	5.6	10.6	6.0	3.8
6. Beauty, barber	4.9	12.7	6.9	9.8	8.8
7. Travel agents	3.8	2.3	2.2	1.6	1.5
8. DVDs, music, video	1.9	2.5	3.7	4.2	2.3
9. Bank, financial	2.5	7.1	4.6	3.4	5.0
10. Other	12.3	16.7	22.5	11.6	9.4
Total enterprises (number)	3,183	354	1,002	386	342

Source: The authors did field surveys enumerating shops and entities with visible Asian name or signage characteristics. Category 2 (professionals) includes medical, dental, legal, optical, acupuncture, brokers, CPAs, real estate, tax advice, and insurance. Category 1 (gift, clothing, furniture) also includes shoes, art objects, variety stores, fabrics, and home furnishings. Category 9 (bank, financial) includes all banks within the dominantly ethnic areas as well as ethnic-character offices offering loans and mortgages. The Bolsa Avenue Little Saigon is a four-mile-long stretch through Orange County's city of Westminster. The San Jose Little Saigon is an eight-mile-long zig-zag connecting Senter, Tully, and Mclaughlin streets. The eleven Bay Area neighborhood shopping centers are those with an Asian supermarket anchor (nine are "99 Ranch Market," the nation's largest such chain); they are in San Jose (2), Cupertino, Milpitas, Fremont (2), Newark, Richmond, San Pablo, Foster City, and Daly City. The four central city Chinatowns are those in San Francisco (1,150 enterprises), Los Angeles (472), Oakland (455), and New York City (1,106). These are the four communities in the United States with the largest number of enterprises within a contiguous, dominantly Chinese business area historically known as a Chinatown. (The New York Chinatown counts are from online business directories; the California Chinatown counts are from field observations by the authors in August 2006.)

has attracted out-of-town investors. Pacific Plaza, the strip's largest shopping center, was developed by five men who came to the Bay Area as refugees from Vietnam in the 1980s. They all created successful food businesses there and chose Stockton Boulevard—100 miles away—as the new locus for their investment because of its growing nearby Asian population and relatively cheap land. The increased scale of development made possible by this infusion of Bay Area capital now attracts customers from well beyond Sacramento.[24] Additional Bay Area capital, fleeing from the dot.com bust and realizing that Sacramento was no longer "*khi ho co gay,* literally, where monkeys cough and herons crow," has helped to create a shopping destination that can compete with classic suburban magnets such as regional malls and big-box centers.[25]

Other Ethnic Commercial Places

Although Little Saigon is by far the largest and most impressive ethnic commercial landscape in Sacramento, there are others. An inventory of the two most Latino strips in the metropolitan area—six miles of Franklin Boulevard (located to the west and roughly parallel to Stockton Boulevard and like it, partly in the city and partly in the county) and four miles of Main Street and nearby streets in Woodland—counted 111 and 87 identifiably Latino businesses, respectively. Along the Franklin strip, Latino enterprises composed one-quarter of the total. A wide diversity of business types was evident, including professional offices and those enterprises Oberle found to be indicative of older, core Latino neighborhoods.[26] Latino businesses dominated two of Franklin Boulevard's six shopping centers. Other ethnic shopping areas include clusters of Korean businesses along Folsom Boulevard, which runs eastward from downtown Sacramento, through the city, the unincorporated county, and the City of Rancho Cordova. Russian, Ukrainian, and other Slavic businesses can be found in small clusters in the northeastern sector and elsewhere, although no single street is a flagship commercial space for them.

Variations among Sacramento's immigrant groups with respect to a visible commercial presence are tied to a variety of factors, including size of group, residential patterns, time of arrival, resources available to them, kinds of businesses they favor, and varying inclination to display ethnic markers. While the details of each group's presence differ, in general, it is safe to say that seeing immigrant businesses along the Sacramento metropolitan area's older suburban and small town commercial districts has become the norm.

Other Places and Patterns

Residential neighborhoods and commercial districts are not the only spaces in Sacramento shaped by increasingly suburban immigrant communities. Suburban places of worship, schools, sports and entertainment venues, community centers, social service providers, parks and plazas, and virtual media spaces increasingly reveal immigrant imprints. On a more somber note, some well-publicized crimes by immigrants have had suburban settings, such as two dozen marijuana houses in Elk Grove subdivisions that were tied to a drug ring in San Francisco's Chinatown; Hmong gangs in the

Stockton Boulevard corridor; and sturgeon poaching and illegal caviar sales by Slavic immigrants in North Highlands, Orangevale, and Citrus Heights.[27]

Places of Worship

Sacramento has many examples of immigrant-founded places of worship that have remained in the central city, as well as of institutions that have relocated with their members to the suburbs. The newest contributions to Sacramento's geography of religion are the many immigrant churches, temples, and mosques that have been started in the suburbs. These include Buddhist, Tao, Hindu, and Sikh temples, and Asian Christian churches. The region's Korean and Vietnamese Catholic churches are in the suburbs. Muslim mosques in Davis and Folsom, both elite suburbs with initially modest facilities, have begun building much expanded ones—with only minor controversy. Protestant *iglesias* and *templos* are found in both urban and suburban neighborhoods of Latino immigrants, while Catholic churches offering services in Spanish are widespread in the suburbs. The central city's Our Lady of Guadalupe sanctuary, the region's most important Latino Catholic space, has grown too small, and plans are being made to build a larger one on Franklin Boulevard near the city-suburb boundary.[28]

By far the biggest story involving immigrant religion and Sacramento is that of the refugees from Ukraine, Russia, and adjacent countries, whose very presence in the area is tied to their religious persecution by anti-Protestant Soviet and post-Soviet authorities. Using the Russian "Yellow Pages" (www.rypweb.com) and web searches (www.slavicbaptist.org), we identified fifty-eight churches in the region associated with the ex-Soviet immigrant community. Of these, only eight are located in the city of Sacramento. A cluster exists in the city of West Sacramento, which encompasses the old Russian settlement at Bryte. Most of the others are located in the northeast suburbs of Arden-Arcade, Carmichael, Citrus Heights, Fair Oaks, Foothill Farms, North Highlands, Orangevale, and Roseville. Although their spatial distribution is similar to that of Slavic immigrant residences, these are not necessarily neighborhood churches. Bethany Slavic, said to be the largest Slavic Pentecostal congregation in the United States, pulls people from across the metropolitan area.[29]

The varying sizes and resources of refugee Slavic congregations mean that the buildings they occupy are quite diverse. Several churches have chosen large, barn-like former commercial structures on busy suburban arterials, giving them high visibility. In conversion to church use, new

One of Sacramento's largest Protestant churches, the Second Slavic Baptist Church, has a congregation composed chiefly of refugees from the former Soviet Union. On a busy commercial street adjacent to Sacramento's largest decommissioned air base, this once was a big-box commercial building. The prominent barrier fencing is characteristic of Slavic immigrant churches in the city.

architectural details are added, such as stained-glass or Gothic-arched windows, wood trim, and Christian crosses. The most notable new feature is almost inevitably a high fence surrounding the property and lockable gates, which often remain closed when services or other church events are not being held. This feature is not particularly welcoming for a church and indeed conveys a sense of exclusion. It may represent a legacy of wariness about state or other intrusion into church property and affairs.[30]

Sacramento's Slavic refugee churches have been in the spotlight recently because of their encouragement of antigay protest. Slavic Christians, mostly Baptists and Pentecostals, have packed board meetings in three Sacramento area school districts to object to local high school participation in a national "Day of Silence," recognizing the history of abuse of homosexuals. Thirteen Slavic students, many of them members of the Third Slavic Evangelical Baptist Church in Citrus Heights, wore T-shirts declaring

Uzbekistan Food, featuring Turkish-inspired cuisine from Central Asia, shares space in a small strip mall with two Asian food shops. At this stage there are few businesses obviously operated by residents of the former Soviet republics along Sacramento's commercial streets, in contrast to churches, although the most common are food markets. A decade from now, entrepreneurs from the former USSR will be offering a greater diversity of products and services.

"Homosexuality is a sin" to Oakmont High School in Roseville in 2006, and similar incidents occurred at two other suburban high schools the same year. The Slavic Christian community fielded three candidates for suburban school boards in the fall 2006 elections, a sign of advancing civic engagement.[31] This story suggests that the typically highly fragmented nature of local governments of all types—not just school districts—in the suburbs may provide suburbanizing immigrants with many opportunities for political mobilization.

Schools

Schools are key sites for the integration of foreign-born children and youth into American society.[32] We focus here on the distribution of English learners (ELs), as only one of many factors that can influence processes of integration.[33] Although most Sacramento schools' EL student composition is a reflection of attendance area demographics, some schools have English language immersion programs that attract nonneighborhood children.[34]

About one in six of the metro area's public school students is an EL (table 7-5). Spanish is the dominant language, but fifty-two others—from Albanian to Vietnamese—are spoken by at least two students each in Sacramento County alone. There are few EL-majority schools (38 out of 650), although another 70 schools are one-third to one-half EL. Concerns are not with concentrations of ELs per se, but with the fact that high-EL schools also tend to concentrate minority students, poverty, and low student achievement.

Overall, El Dorado and Placer counties have low percentages of EL students, but two districts in these counties (both serving Lake Tahoe) and a few individual schools have more significant numbers. Spanish dominates in outlying areas; some Russian and Ukrainian are found in western Placer County, the outer edge of the northeastern sector they favor; diverse Asian languages in part reflect well-educated parents working at Intel, Hewlett-Packard, and other high-tech firms in the foothills.

In Yolo County one of five pupils is an EL, and most are Spanish-speakers (see table 7-5). Outlying agricultural towns Winters and Woodland, in addition to inner suburb West Sacramento, have multiple schools in which at least one-third of their pupils are ELs. Russian and Ukrainian follow Spanish in importance in West Sacramento, while college town Davis has fewer ELs, and of those, a higher share speak Asian languages.

In the suburban part of Sacramento County (see table 7-5 for definition in the school context), one of seven students is an EL. Spanish still rules, but not as powerfully as in the outer counties because of the greater presence of Asian languages; Russian and Ukrainian are also significant. About 10 percent of schools in the suburban districts of Sacramento County have more than one-third of their pupils in the EL category.

In the urban part of Sacramento County, two in seven students are ELs. Spanish is as important here as in the rest of the county, but of most significance is the greater importance of Hmong, as well as of Mien. Speakers of these languages are among the poorest immigrant (and refugee) groups in Sacramento. Schools that concentrate Spanish and Hmong or Mien often also have high populations of low-income African Americans. For immigrant children in these schools, learning to speak English is only one of many challenges.

To address some of these challenges, innovative programs have been designed for and with Sacramento immigrant communities. For example,

Table 7-5. English Learners (ELs) in Sacramento Metropolitan Region Public Schools, 2005–06

County	*Total enrollment*	*Percent minority*	*Percent EL*	*Top five native languages of ELs*	*Percent of ELs speaking top five languages*	*Number of EL-majority schools by language situation*
El Dorado	29,332	23.1	5.0	Spanish	89.7	1 Spanish supermajority[a]
(70 schools)				Filipino	3.1	0 Spanish majority
				Russian	0.8	0 Spanish plurality
				Punjabi	0.6	0 Other majority/plurality
				Korean	0.5	
Placer	63,742	26.1	6.5	Spanish	63.2	2 Spanish supermajority
(109 schools)				Russian	9.9	0 Spanish majority
				Ukrainian	7.7	0 Spanish plurality
				Punjabi	4.3	0 Other majority/plurality
				Vietnamese	2.4	
Yolo	29,460	54.6	21.2	Spanish	81.2	2 Spanish supermajority
(61 schools)				Russian	4.9	2 Spanish majority
				Ukrainian	2.3	0 Spanish plurality
				Punjabi	1.8	0 Other majority/plurality
				Hindi	1.1	
Sacramento	155,454	50.6	14.5	Spanish	50.2	4 Spanish supermajority
suburban[b]				Russian	9.0	1 Spanish majority
(266 schools)				Hmong	7.6	1 Spanish plurality
				Vietnamese	5.9	0 Other majority/plurality
				Ukrainian	5.9	
Sacramento	83,572	76.2	28.3	Spanish	50.2	1 Spanish supermajority
Urban[b]				Hmong	20.8	14 Spanish majority
(144 schools)				Russian	6.1	5 Spanish plurality
				Cantonese	3.6	5 Other majority/plurality
				Mien (Yao)	2.8	
Total	361,560	50.3	16.1	Spanish	55.8	10 Spanish supermajority
(650 schools)				Hmong	11.5	17 Spanish majority
				Russian	7.3	6 Spanish plurality
				Ukrainian	3.9	5 Other majority/plurality
				Vietnamese	3.5	

Source: California Department of Education (www.cde.ca.gov/ds/).

a. Supermajority = 90 percent or more of ELs speak this language; majority = 50.1–89.9 percent of ELs speak this language.

b. Urban Sacramento = Sacramento City Unified, Del Paso Heights Elementary, Grant Joint Union High, Natomas Unified, North Sacramento Elementary, and Robla Unified school districts, which together encompass a territory similar to that of the City of Sacramento. Suburban Sacramento = the remaining districts in Sacramento County.

the importance of gardens to some immigrant groups, most notably the Hmong and Mien, led to garden projects with heavy immigrant community involvement at various schools, particularly those in West Sacramento. The Folsom-Cordova district developed the Refugee Educators' Network and the Southeast Asia Community Resource Center, with a nationally recognized collection of materials related to Southeast Asian refugees and their education. That district also aided several immigrant communities in developing Saturday Schools to help their children retain and improve knowledge of their native languages. Another district, Grant, set up five charter schools that serve almost exclusively Slavic immigrant children. This last example is controversial because the schools are almost entirely white, while the Grant district is only 37 percent white, and because of the covert, if not overt, Christian messages delivered in these schools. Three of the schools are on church grounds. Other objections to these schools are based on concern that children attending them ultimately will face extra difficulty integrating into American life.[35] And that, of course, remains the challenge for all schools with many English learners, particularly those from impoverished households.

Virtual and Temporary Immigrant Spaces

Shopping areas, churches, and schools are not the only ways of bringing together Sacramento's dispersed immigrants. Radio, television, Internet, and print media—international to local—are available to Sacramentans in a variety of languages. As of 2005 Comcast, the major cable company in the region, offered viewers twelve channels with foreign broadcasts in Arabic, French, Filipino, Italian, Mandarin, Punjabi, Russian, and Vietnamese. Multiple Spanish-language channels are also available. At the other end of the spectrum, locals produce programs that play on two Sacramento public access channels in diverse languages, including Farsi, Romanian, Samoan, and Vietnamese. "Bollywood Tunes," music videos from South Asia played by a local math teacher, is one of the 25 percent of programs on these channels that are in languages other than English. Many Spanish-language radio stations are available to listeners in Sacramento; one of them, Magia (KLMG), has been credited with bringing out 60 to 70 percent of 5,000 people who protested against proposed immigration legislation in March 2006. Several Sacramento radio stations sell blocks of time to "ethnic" broadcasters. Programs in Arabic, German, Hindi, Hmong, Korean, Lao, Romanian Russian, Ukrainian, and Vietnamese are carried on KJAY, KLIB, and KSSG. Local newspapers are available in many languages, including

Chinese, Filipino, Lao, Russian, Spanish, Ukrainian, and Vietnamese.[36] These developments echo the extensive foreign language media of earlier waves of American immigrants.

A second way that immigrants in Sacramento come together, this time in real space, is through sports matches and cultural festivals. The top amateur soccer league in the region is the California Central Soccer League. According to James Faria, whom we interviewed in May 2006, "the majority are Latino teams, mainly Mexican" and "even the Portuguese teams have Mexicans playing on their teams" as do the "mainly white" teams from Davis. On July 30, 2006, the Copa Tecate, which according to its website is "the largest adult amateur sports league in the nation reaching Hispanics," played its western regional final games in Sacramento. After the fact, the *Sacramento Bee,* which had given the event virtually no publicity, expressed surprise that a 14,000-seat stadium in West Sacramento was packed. A Spanish-language radio network took credit for the crowd. Less exalted soccer matches, organized and pickup, are played in all kinds of venues around the metropolitan area, but major tournaments are most often held in the suburbs, where land has been available to develop multifield complexes. While soccer is undoubtedly the sport with the most widespread immigrant participation, ethnic teams and leagues exist also for basketball, baseball, and cricket. As one might expect, cricket matches are played regularly in Davis, Folsom, and Roseville, prosperous suburbs housing and employing growing numbers of South Asians. Roseville recently developed a dedicated cricket field in order "to say thank you [to its South Asian residents] for being here, and that we're glad you're here, and that we want more talented people to come here."[37]

Ethnic festivals have become a staple of organized entertainment and cultural outreach in the Sacramento region. Large ones take place in Old Sacramento, the Sacramento Convention Center, and Cal Expo (the state fair grounds). Others are held in parks, community centers, schools, and parking lots, often in the suburbs. Some of these are specific to one ancestry group, such as the Bengali Festival of Joy or Hmong New Year, while others embrace a bigger slice of the pie, such as the Festival de la Familia or the Pacific Rim Festival. Others are in transition toward greater multiculturalism, like the Tet festivities held along Stockton Boulevard.[38] Also making use of public space are protest marches, which to date have involved mostly Latino groups, who have a long history of this type of demonstration in California. It is noteworthy that the region's shared public spaces are available to all these groups who wish to gather and celebrate their cultures, whether with sport, food, music, or protest. They represent opportunities for integration, even as what sets groups apart is celebrated. Of particular weight symbolically is the use of Old Sacramento, a state park and commercial area celebrating the Gold Rush and railroading history of the region. This area of "establishment" history is now incorporating and being incorporated into the histories and cultures of new Sacramentans, some of whose co-ethnics were part of those earlier storied events.

Conclusion

Why are the patterns of the foreign-born in Sacramento so different today than they were in the past? Why are there higher rates of suburbanization and dispersal, which in previous eras came only in the second or subsequent generations after immigration?

First, the suburbs are different from those of the past. Suburbs are in fact no longer *sub-urban*. They include nearly the full range of urban goods and services, jobs, and types of housing found in the central city. This is the result of their accessibility, expansion, and maturation. Today, there is tremendous variability in the physical and socioeconomic character of Sacramento suburbs, including many offering housing that is comparatively cheap.

Second, the immigrants are different from those of the past. Sacramento's foreign-born are much less uniformly poor, uneducated, and non-English-speaking. Global forces have brought to the region streams of immigrants with abundant financial and educational capital, as well as groups that command few resources, and all types in between. Even within the ranks of refugees, some had assets that helped open up the suburbs to them. For example, the earliest wave of Vietnamese included people with college degrees and financial savings. The Russian and Ukrainian refugees often had suburban church sponsorship, and their skin color also likely worked to their advantage.

Third, the cultural context is different from that of the past. Schools and colleges, government agencies, local media, and many other voices praise the diverse national traditions of immigrants and California's resulting cultural hybridity. The dominant print medium locally is the *Sacramento Bee*, often a progressive Democratic voice, which has intentionally made its own staff more reflective of the region's growing diversity. Its reporters have won numerous awards for stories, such as a 2005 series on the abuse of Mexican and Central American forestry workers across America, which helped to change national policy.[39] Finally, technological and institutional ways of staying in touch across and beyond the metro area, in addition to a somewhat friendlier host society, mean that spatial clustering is less important than in the past.

In the Sacramento area, some stretches of inner suburb are in fact the new inner city. Here are concentrated many low-to-moderate-income immigrants, living in loose country-of-origin clusters but sharing considerable space with numerous other ethnic and ancestry groups (both native and foreign-born). Together these suburbs form an attenuated version of the old West End. Here, issues of poor schools and crime exist for immigrants, as they do for everyone else, but with additional cultural barriers to their resolution. Meanwhile, many native-born whites have decamped to the outer suburbs, where they still find that some of their neighbors are immigrants. These immigrants can afford expensive new housing and may work alongside them in the high-tech sector or provide them with medical and dental care. Their resources and lifestyles contrast with those of the Mexican immigrants, who live beyond the edge of the urbanized area in exurban towns with agroindustrial roots.

Sacramento's suburban immigrants have created a major Asian commercial landscape along Stockton Boulevard as well as more modest strips and clusters of Latino and Slavic enterprises. Distinctive religious edifices have been erected, and some Slavic Pentecostals and Baptists have left the security of their fences to criticize government and become politically active. Lots of soccer and a dab of cricket, a full calendar of ethnic celebrations, and a multiplicity of languages on the airwaves now characterize the Sacramento suburbs. Immigrants have made an impact on their new homes in diverse ways.

A key question for the future is the extent to which the Sacramento suburbs' political and administrative fragmentation presents immigrants with real opportunities for participation in civic life. When will the first Vietnamese American be elected to the Elk Grove City Council? How many Slavic Americans will be on suburban school boards ten years from now? Will newly incorporated Rancho Cordova, home of Aerojet rocket motors that took Americans to the moon, use its Fourth-of-July patriotism to nurture naturalization among its foreign-born residents? What role will recent immigrants and their children play in creating additional independent cities out of Sacramento's vast unincorporated but already urbanized territory? Can the suburbs, with all their diversity, be genuine incubators for new leaders and new programs to further enhance the life chances of immigrants to America?

Notes

1. Melvin M. Webber, "Order in Diversity: Community without Propinquity," in *Cities and Space: The Future Use of Urban Land,* edited by L. Wingo Jr. (Johns Hopkins University Press, 1964). For the application of this idea to recent immigrant residential choice, see Wilbur Zelinsky and Barrett A. Lee, "Heterolocalism: An Alternative Model of the Sociospatial Behaviour of Immigrant Ethnic Communities," *International Journal of Population Geography* 4 (4): 281–98.

2. U. S. Census Bureau, *American Community Survey 2005* (factfinder.census.gov). All 2005 census figures in this chapter are from this source. All 1990 and 2000 census figures are from Summary Tape Files 1, 3, and 4 for those years, also at the American Factfinder website.

3. A place is "a concentration of population either legally bounded as an incorporated place, or identified as a census designated place (CDP). CDPs are delineated cooperatively by state and local officials and the Census Bureau." More details are at: (factfinder.census.gov/home/en/epss/glossary_p.html).

4. Audrey Singer and Jill H. Wilson, *From "There" to "Here": Refugee Resettlement in Metropolitan America* (Brookings, 2006), p. 23.

5. J. S. Holliday, *The World Rushed In: The California Gold Rush Experience* (New York: Simon & Schuster, 1981).

6. Shipley Walters, *West Sacramento: The Roots of a New City* (Woodland, Calif.: Yolo County Historical Society, 1987).

7. Eight percent is an arbitrary cutoff. It allowed inclusion in the table of seventeen of nineteen places in the Sacramento suburbs having 20,000 or more people, while excluding mostly small places with relatively few foreign-born.

8. California Department of Social Services, Refugee Programs Bureau, California Refugee Arrivals Data (www.dss.cahwnet.gov/refugeeprogram/ReportCent_48.htm [July 7, 2006]).

9. Jacqueline Desbarats, "Indochinese Resettlement in the United States," *Annals of the Association of American Geographers* 75 (December 1985): 522–38.

10. Jan Louise Corlett, "Landscapes and Lifescapes: Three Generations of Hmong Women and Their Gardens," Ph.D. dissertation, Department of Geography, University of California, Davis, 1999.

11. Ronnie I. Caluza, "Exploring the Presence of Filipinos in South Sacramento," Paper presented at the Association of Pacific Coast Geographers annual meeting, 2004; abstract published in the *APCG Yearbook* 67 (2005): 138.

12. U. S. Department of State, *Proposed Refugee Admissions for FY 2005–Report to Congress* (www.state.gov/g/prm/asst/rl/rpts/36116.htm [July 18, 2006]).

13. Laura Locke, "Ripping at the Tongues: A Bloody Rampage in Northern California Terrifies a Community of Religious Refugees from Ukraine," *Time,* September 3, 2001. For a history of *Word to Russia,* see (www.wordtorussia.org [June 27, 2007]).

14. Susan W. Hardwick, "A Geographical Interpretation of Ethnic Settlement in an Urban Landscape: Russians in Sacramento," unpublished manuscript (December 8, 1978); see also Susan Hardwick, "Russian Acculturation in Sacramento," in *Geographical Identities of Ethnic America: Race, Space, and Place,* edited by Kate A. Berry and Martha L. Henderson (University of Nevada Press, 2002), pp. 255–78.

15. Loretta Kalb, "McClellan Poses Big Question for Market," *Sacramento Bee,* June 25, 1995; and "Report: Area's Housing Slump Hard to Shake," *Sacramento Bee,* December 2, 1995 (www.sacbee.com [July 18, 2006]).

16. Michael Kolber, "Grant Charter Schools Caught in Cultural Bind," *Sacramento Bee,* May 22, 2005; Jim Sanders, "Voting against GOP Tide in Granite Bay," *Sacramento Bee,* October 4, 2004 (www.sacbee.com [July 19, 2006]).

17. Ernesto Galarza, *Barrio Boy* (University of Notre Dame Press, 1971), pp. 198–99.

18. For more on Sacramento's ethnic mixing, see Dennis Dingemans and Robin Datel, "Urban Multiethnicity," *Geographical Review* 85 (October 1995): 459–77. For comparison, see James P. Allen and Eugene Turner, "Ethnic Residential Concentrations in United States Metropolitan Areas," *Geographical Review* 95 (April 2005): 267–85.

19. Wei Li, editor, *From Urban Enclave to Ethnic Suburb* (University of Hawai'i Press, 2006); Shuguang Wang, "Chinese Commercial Activity in the Toronto CMA: New Development Patterns and Impacts," *Canadian Geographer* 43 (1999): 19–35; David H. Kaplan, ed., "Special Issue: Geographical Aspects of Ethnic Economies," *Urban Geography* 19, no. 6 (1998).

20. Steven M. Avella, *Sacramento, Indomitable City* (Charleston, S.C.: Arcadia, 2003); Wayne Maeda, *Changing Dreams and Treasured Memories: A Story of Japanese Americans in the Sacramento Region* (Sacramento: Sacramento Japanese American Citizens League, 2000).

21. Stephen Magagnini, "In the Garden, Hope Blooms, Immigrants Cultivate Diversity," *Sacramento Bee,* December 17, 1995.

22. Using signs and other largely visual clues, we decided whether each business was Asian, and we categorized it by type. We are aware that presentation as Asian does not guarantee that ownership is Asian, and we also recognize that a significant number of additional enterprises in this area are likely to have Asian owners. We also appreciate that many Asians (43 percent) in the Sacramento region are not immigrants and that some businesses along Stockton Boulevard belong to nonimmigrant Chinese Americans, Filipino Americans, and so forth.

23. Wang, "Chinese Commercial Activity in the Toronto CMA," p. 30.

24. Cathleen Ferraro, "Asian Dreams: Developers Hoping New Center Turns into Regional Powerhouse," *Sacramento Bee,* September 5, 1999.

25. Thuy-Doan Le, "For Many Vietnamese, Capital's a Gain," *Sacramento Bee,* January 6, 2004.

26. Alex Oberle, "Se Venden Aqui: Latino Commercial Landscapes in Phoenix, Arizona," in *Hispanic Spaces, Latino Places,* edited by Daniel D. Arreola (University of Texas Press, 2004).

27. Ryan Lillis, Dan Nguyen, and Dorothy Korber, "Trying to Solve Pot-Den Puzzle," *Sacramento Bee,* October 12, 2006; Mareve Brown and Elizabeth Hume, "Full-Blown War by Hmong Gangs Alarms Police," *Sacramento Bee,* February 28, 2005; M. S. Enkoji, "Alleged Sturgeon Ring Landed," *Sacramento Bee,* May 6, 2005; Matt Weiser, "Poaching Probe Nets a Big Haul," *Sacramento Bee,* June 30, 2006.

28. Jennifer Garza, "Kavanagh to End 58-Year Career as Priest at St. Rose," *Sacramento Bee,* October 28, 2006.

29. Stephen Magagnini, "Religious Rebels Test Limits of Free Speech," *Sacramento Bee,* January 18, 2004.

30. Hardwick, *Geographical Identities of Ethnic America,* reported that all Russian houses in the original settlement area of West Sacramento had front yard fences and locked gates (p. 261).

31. Dorothy Korber and Deepa Ranganathan, "Clash of Convictions," *Sacramento Bee,* August 6, 2006; Deepa Ranganathan, Kim Minugh, and Laurel Rosenhall, "Day of Silence Spurs Protests, Suspensions," *Sacramento Bee,* April 27, 2006; Rone Tempest, "For Gays, a Loud New Foe; Sacramento's Large Enclave of Immigrant Slavic Evangelicals Is Becoming a Force on Social Issues," *Los Angeles Times,* October 13, 2006, p. A.1.

32. All figures in this section come from the California Department of Education Educational Demographics Unit (data1.cde.ca.gov [January 16, 2007]).

33. The California Department of Education defines ELs as "those students for whom there is a report of a primary language other than English . . . and who . . . have been determined to lack the clearly defined English language skills of listening comprehension, speaking, reading, and writing necessary to succeed in the school's regular instructional programs." See California Department of Education, online glossary, at (data1.cde.ca.gov/dataquest/gls_learners.asp [January 17, 2007]). We recognize that not all ELs are immigrants nor are all immigrants ELs.

34. San Juan Unified School District English Language Learner Program (sanjuan.edu/programs/ell/ [Oct. 7, 2006).

35. Lorie A. Hammond, "Building Houses, Building Lives," Unpublished manuscript, Department of Education, California State University, Sacramento, no date; Refugee Educators' Network (reninc.org [July 17, 2006]); Kolber, "Grant Charter Schools," 2006.

36. Mark Larson, "Comcast Expands Lineup for Non-English Speakers," *Sacramento Business Journal,* July 1, 2005; Sam McManis, "Protest in the Air," *Sacramento Bee,* April 4, 2006; David Forster, "International Flair on the Air," *Sacramento Business Journal,* May 14, 2004; Stephen Magagnini, "Confluence of Cultures," *Sacramento Bee,* January 30, 1994.

37. Bobby Caina Calvan, cited in "Bowling Them Over in Roseville," *Sacramento Bee,* June 21, 2007; Marcos Breton, "Latino Media Lure Fans for a Fiesta of Soccer," *Sacramento Bee,* July 31, 2006; Jamie Francisco, "Cricket Remains a Key Part of Players' Heritage," *Sacramento Bee,* May 10, 2004. For the importance of soccer to Latino immigrants in Washington, D.C., see Marie Price and Courtney Whitworth, "Soccer and Latino Cultural Space: Metropolitan Washington *Futbol* Leagues," in *Hispanic Spaces, Latino Places,* edited by Arreola, pp. 167–186.

38. John DeFao, "Tet Starts with a Bang," *Sacramento Bee,* February 12, 1996; Jon Ortiz, "Hallmark Holiday: Lunar New Year Is Poised for a Cultural Crossover," *Sacramento Bee,* February 6, 2005.

39. Tom Knudson and Hector Amezcua, "Special Report: The Pineros—Men of the Pines," *Sacramento Bee,* November 13–15, 2005.

8

Impediments to the Integration of Immigrants

A Case Study in the Twin Cities

KATHERINE FENNELLY and MYRON ORFIELD

Minnesota is a place of contradictions. On the one hand, the state can boast of some of the most affluent, politically engaged, and highly educated residents in the nation. Among the twenty-five largest metropolitan areas in the United States, the Twin Cities region of Minneapolis and St. Paul is the second whitest and the fourth most affluent.[1] It ranks first in percentage of citizens who vote and among the highest in rates of volunteerism.[2] At the same time, Minnesota is home to severely impoverished African American, Native American, and Latino residents who have been highly concentrated in the central cities. In 2000 the ratio of city-to-suburban poverty in the Twin Cities metro area was 4.5, almost twice the national rate of 2.7 and second only to Milwaukee.[3]

As with other growing economic regions in the United States, the Twin Cities are attracting international immigrants, even though the cities are within a low immigration state. In 2005 only 7 percent of the state's residents were immigrants, and more than two-thirds of them arrived between 1990 and 2005. During that same period, however, the foreign-born population of Minneapolis-St. Paul increased by over 200 percent. This influx raised the share of the metropolitan area population that was foreign-born from less than 4 percent to nearly 9 percent.

One distinctive feature of the immigrant population in Minneapolis-St. Paul is its diversity, a result of the large number of refugees present. Between 1983 and 2004, the Twin Cities ranked eighth in the number of refugees resettled; the metropolitan area has traditionally had a larger percentage of immigrants who are refugees than most other metropolitan areas in the United States.[4]

Refugees and other foreign-born residents have historically settled in cities themselves, but recently in Minneapolis-St. Paul they have begun moving to the suburbs, mimicking a national trend. In 2005 more than 172,000 foreign-born residents in the Twin Cities metro area lived in the suburbs—nearly double the total living in the central cities of Minneapolis and St. Paul (see appendix B, under re-emerging communities, in chapter 1). In fact, in the suburban core, immigration increased at a time when it was leveling off in the cities and also when domestic migration was declining.[5] Some foreign-born suburban residents have relocated from the Twin Cities, but others settle directly in the suburbs. Among the refugee population, 34 percent percent of the 6,715 refugees who arrived in Minnesota between January 2005 and May of 2006 settled in the seven-county metro area suburbs of Minneapolis-St. Paul.[6] The largest groupings were Liberian refugees in Brooklyn Park, Hmong in Brooklyn Center, and Somalis in Eden Prairie. Immigrants in the suburbs are also highly diverse in terms of socioeconomic status. Some, particularly South Asians, are highly educated and highly skilled, while others have low levels of education and may not even be literate in their native languages.

A move to the suburbs does not necessarily represent upward mobility, especially for immigrants of color.[7] As in the cities, many suburbs are becoming increasingly segregated. As Margaret Pugh O'Mara has pointed out, the settlement of nonwhites in the suburbs is hardly new, although their presence on the periphery of American cities for more than a hundred years has not eradicated the cliché of suburbs as wealthy, lily-white residential enclaves.[8]

In this chapter, we employ demographic and survey data to study the characteristics and experiences of immigrants in the suburbs, as well as impediments to their economic prosperity and social integration. Specifically, we examine the experience of blacks, Latinos, and Asians in Twin Cities' suburbs and contrast it with the experience of the broader population of color in terms of segregation in low-paying jobs, impoverished neighborhoods and schools, and exposure to xenophobia. The changes in the composition of suburban populations are reflected in census data, school enrollment statistics, and the increases in children with limited English proficiency.

Data and Methodology

This paper focuses on immigrants and refugees in fourteen suburban places in the metropolitan area, although we draw on a broader set of trends

Map 8-1. Fourteen Cities in the Twin Cities Study Area

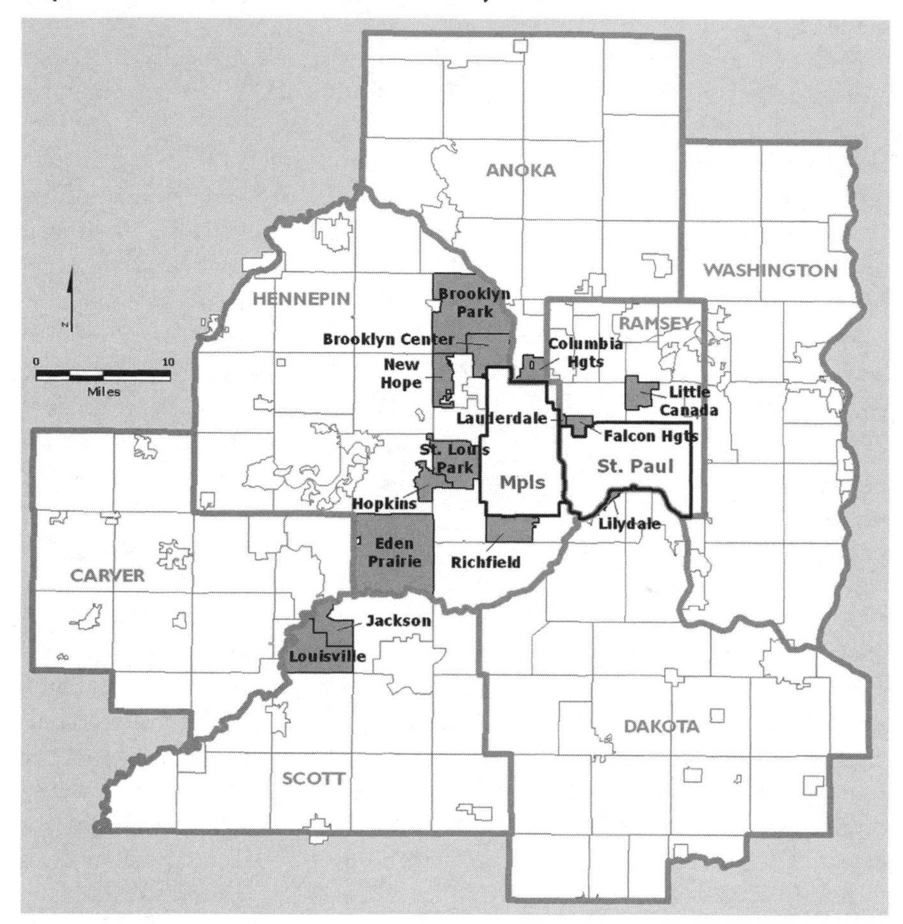

Source: Boundary files from U.S. Census Bureau.

within the state to provide context (map 8-1). In 2000, 81 percent of the foreign-born in the state of Minnesota lived in the Minneapolis-St. Paul metropolitan area. The fourteen communities were chosen because they had the highest percentage of foreign-born for all places in the suburbs of the Twin Cities in 2000; all were at least 8 percent foreign-born, higher than the metropolitan average of 7 percent. Brooklyn Park has both the largest number (9,000) and highest percentage (24 percent) of foreign-born. We use *Census 2000* to provide background on the communities of interest.

We are largely interested in how these local areas, including schools, are changing. We track this dynamic by examining changes in the composition of households, including their youngest members, using Minnesota

Department of Education Statistics and census data. In school data, national origin, immigrant status, and membership in a U.S. "minority" group become inextricably linked because the children of African-, Asian-, and Latin American–born adults are categorized as "black," "Asian," and "Latino," respectively, in school statistics, with no information on place of birth or citizenship status.

Because the majority of the children of immigrants are U.S.-born, we use race and ethnic categories instead of birthplace, which captures both first generation (who are foreign-born) and second generation (who are U.S.-born). Among the total population in the fourteen suburbs, 48 percent of Hispanics, 69 percent of Asians, 20 percent of blacks, and 3 percent of whites were foreign-born in 2000.

We examine school district data on language spoken at home to estimate the *location* of particular national origin groups and their children. This does not, however, produce an estimate of the *total number* of that group in each city.

An important question in writing about immigrants in the United States is whether the U.S-born children of Asian, African, and Latino immigrants are forever considered immigrants, foreigners, or newcomers because of the color of their skin. The media visibility of second-generation African immigrants and the invisibility of first-generation Canadian immigrants are obvious cases in point. Hmong Minnesotans provide another cogent example. The largest wave of Hmong refugees arrived in Minnesota in the 1970s, and few have been admitted in recent years (with the exception of a sizable group of refugees who arrived in 2004, after the last Thai refugee camp closed). Because the largest influx of Hmong to Minnesota arrived more than thirty years ago, the vast majority of Hmong school-age children and young adults were born in the United States and are thereby U.S. citizens. Despite this, contemporary media stories about immigrants in Minnesota invariably mention the Hmong.

Finally, to understand more about the context of reception in Minnesota, we turn to the Minnesota Community Study.[9] The study is a statewide survey of 700 likely voters in Minnesota, an additional 509 likely voters in six exurban counties—the fastest-growing in the state—and six focus groups (three all-male groups and three female) with suburban residents ages forty-five to sixty in three counties (Anoka, Hennepin, and Scott).[10] Respondents in each of the surveys had similar background characteristics, although those in the exurban communities were slightly more likely to be Republicans (37 percent versus 32 percent) and slightly more likely to define their views as conservative (40 percent versus 32 percent)

Table 8-1. Characteristics of Twin Cities Suburban Communities with More than 8 Percent of Population Foreign-Born, 2000

Community	*Population 2000*	*Number of foreign-born 2000*	*Foreign-born as percent of total 2000*	*Percent change foreign-born 1990–2000*	*Percent poverty rate 1999*	*Percent of affordable housing 1999*[a]	*Community type*[b]	*Property tax capacity per household 2004*[c]	*County*
Brooklyn Center	39,061	3,284	8.4	366	7.1	34.7	Stressed	$1,853	Hennepin
Brooklyn Park	37,388	8,951	23.9	344	4.9	24.0	Stressed	$2,094	Hennepin
Columbia Heights	18,512	1,547	8.4	111	6.2	42.1	Stressed	$1,319	Anoka
Eden Prairie	54,901	4,866	8.9	378	3.4	4.7	Developed job center	$3,709	Hennepin
Falcon Heights	5,505	1,062	19.3	−1	9.2	33.8	Stressed	$1,581	Ramsey
Hopkins	17,061	2,395	14.0	249	9.0	35.3	Stressed	$1,827	Hennepin
Jackson	1,428	281	19.7	1,177	11.5	53.8	Stressed	$1,837	Scott
Lauderdale	2,364	445	18.8	17	9.0	47.9	Stressed	$1,463	Ramsey
Lilydale	627	103	16.4	296	2.8	2.2	Developing job center	$3,532	Dakota
Little Canada	9,771	837	8.6	187	5.3	39.6	Stressed	$1,912	Ramsey
Louisville	1,246	105	8.4	1,400	4.1	10.3	Bedroom development	$3,126	Scott
New Hope	20,852	1,653	7.9	114	6.3	24.8	Stressed	$1,930	Hennepin
Richfield	34,441	3,917	11.4	179	6.1	25.1	Stressed	$1,852	Hennepin
St. Louis Park	44,120	3,842	8.7	35	5.0	23.3	Stressed	$2,281	Hennepin
Twin Cities metro	2,968,806	210,344	7.1	141	6.7	26.1	n.a.	$2,429	

Sources: U.S. Census Bureau, *Census of Population 2000.* Minnesota State Auditor (tax capacity). Community types are from Ameregis, Inc., *Growth Pressures on Sensitive Natural Areas in DNR's Central Region* (Minneapolis: 2006).

a. Percentage of housing (rental and owner occupied) affordable to households at 50 percent of regional median household income in 1999.

b. The community types are the result of grouping municipalities based on several local characteristics, including tax capacity per household, poverty rate, household growth, household density, age of the housing stock, and jobs per household.

c. Different types of property (residential, commercial, and so forth) are taxed at different rates in Minnesota. State law determines how tax rates vary across property types. A municipality's mix of property types therefore affects how much revenue it can generate per dollar of tax base. The "tax capacity" measure controls for this, showing how much revenue a municipality would generate at a given overall level of effort.

n.a. = Not applicable.

than others in the groups. A majority of the focus group participants were college educated. Some participants made spontaneous, unprompted comments on immigration, but most were responding to particular questions. Moderators also employed "word association" exercises, asking individuals to describe what comes to mind when they think about immigrants.

Are Immigrants Settling in Poor or Affluent Suburbs?

Table 8-1 shows various characteristics of the municipalities in our sample, including poverty rates, housing affordability, tax capacity, and community types. The most striking feature of the fourteen communities in this analysis is that they are far from affluent; in fact, the local governments and school districts in nearly all of these communities face significant fiscal stress.

Eleven of the fourteen municipalities were recently classified as fiscally stressed on the basis of tax capacity per household, jobs per household, poverty, growth, population density, and housing age.[11] "Stressed" places have a combination of characteristics that cause lower-than-average tax capacities and growth, as well as higher-than-average poverty and higher costs of providing public services, such as police and fire protection, parks, and schools. Most of the municipalities in the region with the largest shares of foreign-born populations are also places with the least ability to provide the special services that may be needed to help immigrants gain full access to the economic opportunities provided by the regional economy.

Three communities are exceptions to this pattern. Lilydale, Louisville, and Eden Prairie are characterized by greater-than-average local tax capacities, high growth, and lower-than-average poverty. Lilydale and Eden Prairie also have greater than average jobs per resident household and robust job growth. However, only 15 percent of the foreign-born population in the fourteen municipalities in our sample lives in these places, likely because of the high cost of housing.

Characteristics of Immigrants in the Suburbs

Table 8-2 shows the regions of origin of suburban immigrants in the cities highlighted in our analyses. The suburban communities vary greatly in the makeup of their populations. Some, such as Jackson and Louisville, have primarily Latino immigrants. Others, such as Hopkins and St. Louis Park, have a mix of Asian, African, Latino, and former Soviet-state immigrants (designated "other"). About one-third of the immigrants in two adjacent cities, Brooklyn Park and Brooklyn Center, are of African origin.

The reasons for these national-origin concentrations are poorly understood but may stem from immigrant networks that grew out of refugee resettlement, job opportunities in industries that have employed other co-ethnics, or the availability of affordable housing, coupled with "steering" of African or Latino immigrants to particular neighborhoods. These factors are discussed in detail in subsequent sections.

Race, Ethnicity, and Place of Birth

We examine a number of important economic and social indicators for race and ethnic groups that include both foreign- and native-born residents. In

Table 8-2. Region of Origin of Foreign-Born, Minneapolis-St. Paul Suburban Communities, 2000
Percent unless specified

Community	*Total foreign-born (number)*	*Asian*	*African*	*Latin American*	*Other*
Brooklyn Center	3,284	39.2	35.5	11.4	13.9
Brooklyn Park	8,951	47.0	32.3	12.3	8.4
Columbia Heights	1,547	31.2	20.9	19.6	28.3
Eden Prairie	4,866	49.8	8.6	9.1	32.4
Falcon Heights	1,062	71.4	11.7	9.3	7.5
Hopkins	2,395	40.1	13.8	28.9	17.2
Jackson Township	281	4.6	0.7	92.5	2.1
Lauderdale	445	56.9	12.6	16.4	14.2
Lilydale	103	69.9	0.0	10.7	19.4
Little Canada	837	55.8	20.3	4.2	19.7
Richfield	3,917	36.1	11.9	35.5	16.5
Louisville Township	105	3.8	0	79.0	17.1
New Hope	1,653	29.5	20.8	24.3	25.4
St. Louis Park	3,842	31.2	14.3	18.6	35.9

Source: U.S. Census Bureau, *Census of Population 2000.*

the suburban communities that we studied, nearly one-half of Hispanics, one-fifth of blacks, and two-thirds of Asians were foreign-born. In addition, large numbers of native-born black, Hispanic, and Asian children live in households with foreign-born parents

Asians

Asians make up a larger percentage of the suburban foreign-born than other national origin groups, and among Asians in Minnesota, Hmong are the largest group, followed by Vietnamese, Indians, Chinese, and Koreans.[12] Although the majority of Hmong refugees settled in St. Paul, many of their children and grandchildren have moved to other areas, such as Brooklyn Center, seeking jobs and opportunities for homeownership. At the other end of the economic spectrum are Asians who have been attracted or recruited to the metropolitan area to work in high-tech industries.

The backgrounds and socioeconomic status of the various groups are quite disparate. Indian and other South Asian professionals, for example, have high incomes and levels of education, while Hmong and some other, smaller groups of Southeast Asians have low levels of completed schooling and modest or low incomes. Likewise, poverty rates range widely. Very high percentages of Laotians (52 percent) and Hmong (33 percent) have incomes below the poverty line, compared with 4 percent of Filipinos. Despite the low incomes of some Asians, as a group they are the least disadvantaged of the race-ethnic communities in Minnesota. Statewide the median household income for Asians ($50,954) is closer to that of non-Hispanic whites ($58,641) and considerably higher than Hispanics or blacks.[13] Slightly more than one-half of Asians (52 percent) own their own homes. Although their average household size is considerably larger than that of non-Hispanic whites (3.62 individuals compared with 2.47), high rates of overcrowding (more than one occupant per room) "may reflect larger and extended families, the necessity for multiple family members to work and contribute to housing costs, or the inability of individual family members to afford to establish their own households."[14] Because of their disparate origins, Asians also are found at both the high and low ends of the educational spectrum. Just under one-third of Asians in Minnesota (29 percent) have less than a high school diploma (compared with 11 percent of whites), but Asians also surpass whites in postsecondary degrees (42 percent versus 36 percent).[15]

With the exception of the two cities in Scott County, Asians compose one-third or more of the foreign-born populations of the cities in our sample. In some communities, they constitute a much larger percentage. In Falcon Heights, for example, 71 percent of immigrants are Asians. Falcon Heights is home to a significant number of international graduate students and young international faculty from the University of Minnesota, and it ranks as the "70th best educated community in the United States."[16]

Latinos

The category "Hispanic" or "Latino" incorporates individuals of mixed visa status. Hispanics facing the greatest disadvantage are undocumented individuals, although many live in households with children who are U.S. citizens, or families in which one spouse is documented and the other is not. Mexicans represent more than two-thirds of the Latinos in Minnesota, with the majority residing in the Twin Cities. However, 37 percent of Latinos lived in metro area suburbs in 2000, up from 32 percent in 1990.[17] The suburban communities with the largest concentrations of Latinos are Jackson and Louisville Townships, although both of these are small communities. Of the suburbs with over 1,500 residents, the largest percentages of Latinos are in Richfield (6.3 percent) and Hopkins (5.6 percent).

Latinos in the United States (including both native- and foreign-born) have much lower incomes and education levels than non-Hispanic whites, and their experiences with housing and school segregation appear to parallel those of many African Americans. Two-thirds of poor Latinos live in high-poverty census tracts and, as a result, they are more than twice as likely as poor white students to attend schools of concentrated poverty, cut off from meaningful exposure to middle-class networks.[18]

In Minnesota the labor force participation of Latinos and non-Latinos is similar. However, the median Latino household income ($36,000 in 1999) was approximately $17,000 less than the white median household income. Although Hispanics represent only 4 percent of the population of Minnesota, they composed 9 percent of emergency food shelf clients in the state in 2005.[19] Some of the income disparities described here are attributable to Hispanics' lower educational levels; in 2000 nearly 42 percent of Hispanics over age 25 lacked a high school diploma. This is about four times the comparable percentage for non-Hispanic whites.[20] That said, the percentage of Hispanic individuals living in poverty declined during the 1990s, from 26 percent in 1990 to 20 percent in 2000.[21]

Africans

Only two of the communities in our sample, Brooklyn Park and Brooklyn Center, had significant numbers of African residents, primarily Liberians. We do not present data on black residents in the suburbs because less than one-third are foreign-born. However, it is worth noting that the percentage of blacks who are immigrants is much higher in the suburbs than in the central cities of Minneapolis and St. Paul.

Many Africans first came to Minnesota as refugees, and others (particularly Liberians) received Temporary Protective Status. The Minneapolis-based Center for Victims of Torture estimates that 8,500 refugees who are torture survivors have settled in the Brooklyn Park-Brooklyn Center area.[22] In the cities and in other parts of the state, Somalis are the largest African group, and a number of them have settled recently in the suburban community of Eden Prairie.

Motives for Relocation to the Suburbs: Job Growth and Commuting Patterns

There are no systematic and reliable data on what motivates foreign-born residents to settle in the suburbs. However, one driving force is clearly the movement of jobs outside the central cities. In Brooklyn Park, for example, a Liberian community outreach worker commented that suburban employers of West Africans include nursing homes and group homes, Medtronic, Boston Scientific, Wells Fargo, US Bank, Target, and Wal-Mart.

Jobs in the Twin Cities metropolitan area continued to decentralize and become less clustered during the 1990s. Job centers, which have greater than average numbers of jobs per square mile, are scattered across the region, but are overrepresented in the western and southwestern suburbs.[23] These centers ranged in size from 1,100 to 140,000 jobs in 2000. Most new jobs, particularly in the service sector, are growing in the second- and third-ring suburbs, where affordable housing and racial diversity are less common.[24] In 2000, 80 percent of the Twin Cities metropolitan area jobs were located more than five miles from the Minneapolis-St. Paul business districts, although the high-skilled jobs remained in the core.[25] Another motive for immigrants to move to the suburbs may be a decrease in the availability of affordable housing in the central cities. Between 1990 and 2000, the number of low-cost apartments declined in the Twin Cities, while remaining flat in the suburbs.[26]

We plotted the percentages of students of color (map 8-2) and students in homes where English is not the primary language (map 8-3) as a means of comparing the location of combined immigrant and nonimmigrant minority students and immigrant families in the Twin Cities suburbs. In both cases, the highest percentages of both groups live and work nearer slower-growing job centers in the core of the region, rather than in the faster-growing job centers in middle- and outer-ring suburbs (see map 8-2). As map 8-3 shows, students in non-English-speaking homes overlap with students of color in the central cities and in Lauderdale and parts of Brooklyn Park, but immigrants are also concentrated beyond these centers in suburbs to the south of the Twin Cities (Lilydale, Richfield, Jackson, and Louisville), and in Brooklyn Center and New Hope to the northwest.

The farther the job center from the core of the region, the less accessible the center is to affordable housing. Affordable housing is more common nearest the Minneapolis central business district and other job centers in the core. Map 8-4 shows the percentage of housing units that are affordable to households earning 50 percent of the regional median income. The clustering of affordable housing within census block groups closely parallels the concentrations of students living in non-English-speaking households shown in map 8-3.

Anecdotal data and special reports point to other possible reasons for the location of immigrants in the suburbs. As mentioned earlier, the Twin Cities area has a higher percentage of immigrants who are refugees than

Map 8-2. Student Populations of Color by Elementary School Zones in the Minneapolis-St. Paul Area, 2002

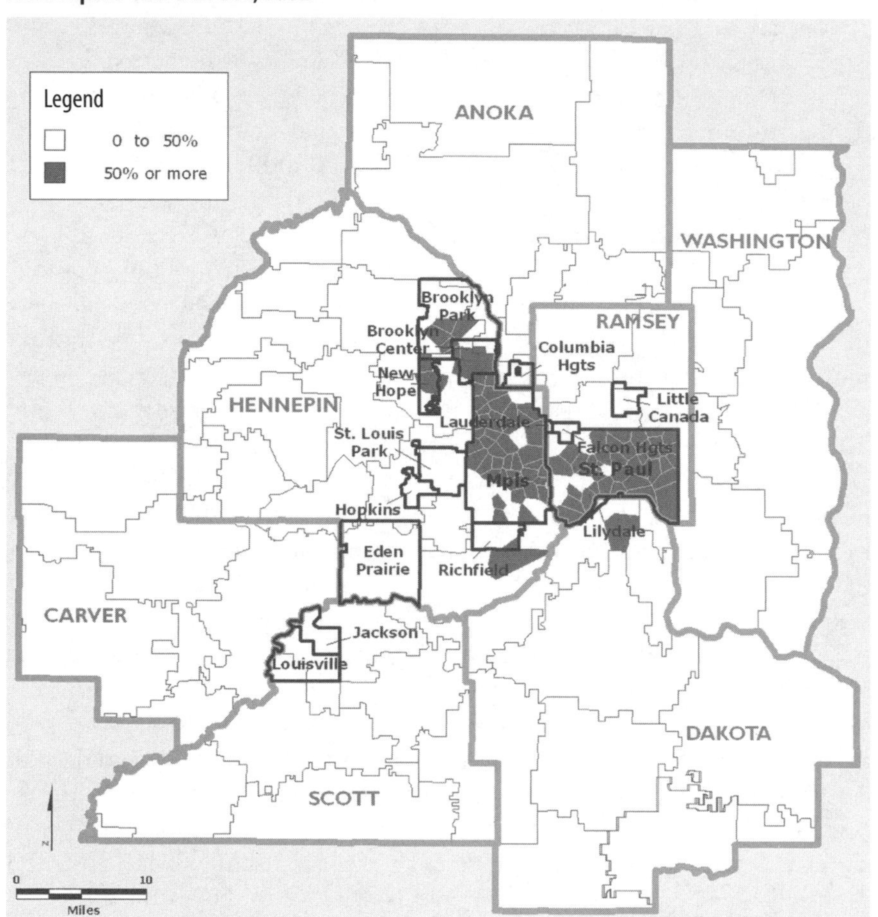

Source: Minnesota Department of Education.

most other states. Some of these refugees may have been resettled directly into suburban neighborhoods, where they receive some temporary assistance in securing jobs, housing, and ancillary services. This modest assistance has fueled the misperception that all immigrants receive government benefits. Also contributing to misperceptions is the visibility of African or Asian refugees in communities with little racial or ethnic diversity, which can lead to exaggerated estimates of the size of the refugee population.

Service-sector jobs and opportunities to open small businesses have attracted many Latinos to the suburbs. In an article in the May 14, 2006,

Map 8-3. Students in Homes Where English Is Not the Primary Language, by School District in the Minneapolis-St. Paul Area, 2006–07

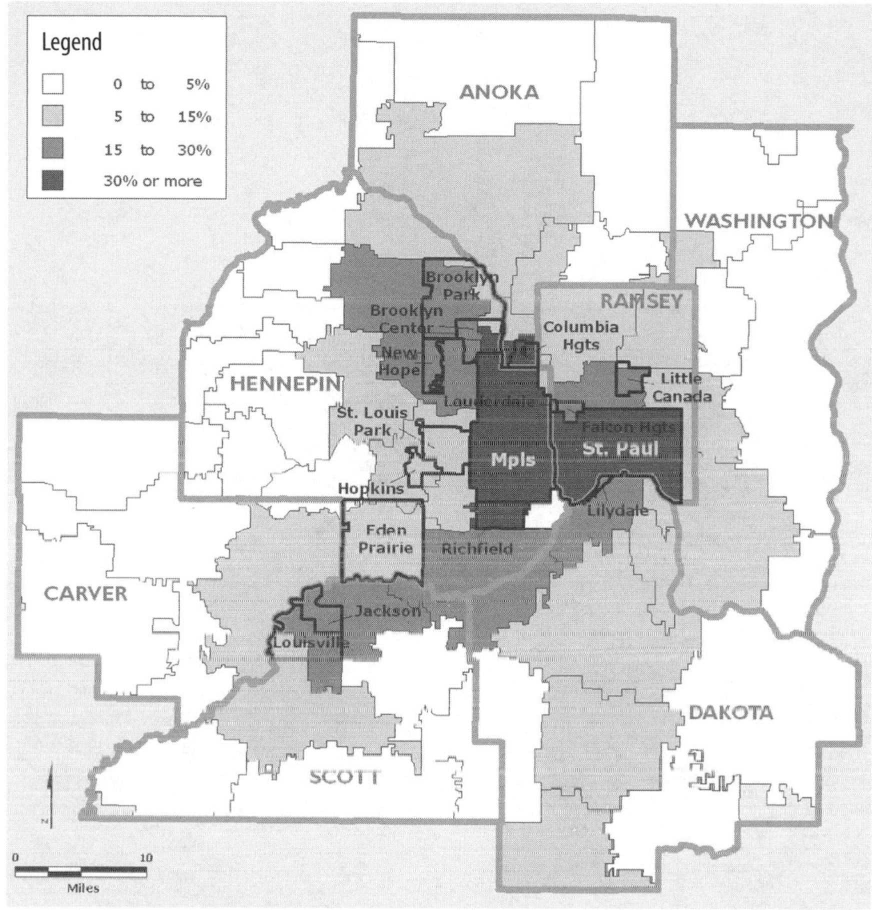

Source: Minnesota Department of Education.

edition of *La Prensa de Minnesota,* Rafael Leon, executive director of the Latino Economic Development Center, is quoted as saying that Hispanic small business owners face less competition in the suburbs than in the city, and that there is a growing ethnic market. A Hispanic business owner with two stores in the busy Lake Street area of Minneapolis agreed with this assessment, and added that new apartment complexes in the suburbs have created opportunities for an expanded market for Latino goods.

The desire to escape crime, crowding, and noise in cities is another reason for immigrants' move to the suburbs. An Ecuadorian resident whom

Map 8-4. Minneapolis-St. Paul Area Housing Units Affordable to Households at 50 Percent of the Regional Median Income, by Census Block Group, 2000

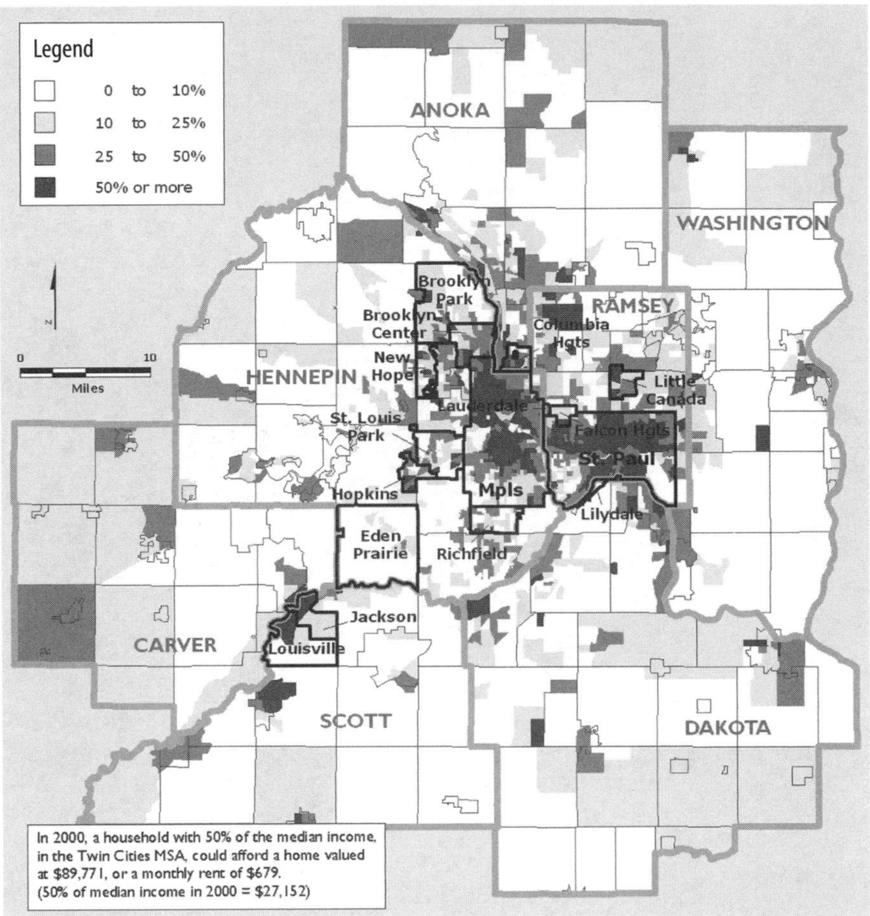

Source: U.S. Census Bureau.

we interviewed said, "Those who can afford to move do. . . . At first, new immigrants are drawn to the city where other immigrants are. Now some are moving outward, seeking quiet, away from the city chaos." A car and affordability were determining factors in moving, she said. An Asian realtor in north Minneapolis added that many Hmong families are moving to "affordable" inner-ring suburbs, such as Brooklyn Park, seeking bigger houses for their large families. Further, many non-Hmong Asians in the

Twin Cities metropolitan area earn high incomes working for major corporations and can afford to live in wealthy suburbs.

Impediments to Integration: Suburban Residents' Attitudes toward Immigrants

Turning to attitudes of native-born residents toward immigrants, we analyze data from the Minnesota Community Study of likely voters. These data provide insights into the receiving community's viewpoint and allow us to see more specifically where conflict lies. They also bring to light more positive points of view.

Among all respondents, the views and attitudes of suburban residents toward immigrants, and toward immigration more generally, fell between the more liberal views of urban respondents and the more restrictive views of rural respondents. Slightly more than one-third of urban respondents agreed with the statement "Immigrants are hurting our quality of life in Minnesota because they are putting big demands on our public schools and are draining resources from the whole community," while 44 percent of suburban, 51 percent of rural, and 52 percent of exurban likely voters agreed with the statement. The survey interviewers also asked open-ended questions about "What makes you proud to be a Minnesotan?" and "What makes you most discouraged about living in Minnesota?" In response to the latter, 13 percent of the respondents in the statewide survey and 20 percent of those in the exurban survey spontaneously mentioned "the influx of immigrants." Higher percentages of suburban residents than urban or rural Minnesotans chose negative items in a list of options that best described their feelings about immigrants in Minnesota, including "they take jobs nobody else wants; they are a drain on public schools; they do not assimilate, or they get too many government handouts." In focus groups the majority of the immigration-related comments were negative (58 percent), 22 percent were coded positive, and 21 percent were mixed.

The largest percentage of negative comments in the focus groups centered on the challenges associated with some immigrants' limited proficiency in English. A female participant from Hennepin County said: "I think that with so many people coming in here from other countries that don't speak English, I think it means a lot of trouble for a lot of people. I've had this happen at work."

Some participants commented on the importance of learning English to function successfully in society; many also perceived that immigrants do not want to learn to speak English, as did this man from Scott County, who said, "I think everyone should have an opportunity to come here, but I agree . . . that everyone should have to learn to speak English so that there is some sense of the ability to talk back and forth and communicate."

Others discussed the challenges faced by schools in accommodating the language needs of immigrant children, and the fear that coping with the language challenge detracts from the education of native-born children. A man from Anoka County attributed the demise of order in classrooms to multiple languages being spoken: "Moderate. I like the word 'moderate.' We don't have it anymore. . . . When you've got twenty different languages at one school, the word 'chaos' comes to mind. And that's what's going on in school today."

Another male respondent from Anoka County said, "They have to learn English, and they can't be mainstreamed into the schools with our kids and slow our kids down. Not that they're dumb. If they don't understand English, it's harder for them to get the whole grasp."

Several individuals expressed concern over the cost of accommodating immigrant children's language needs. A woman from Anoka County said: "The thing that . . . concerns me is the education. I have three kids and two of them have already graduated, but throughout the years I see them [immigrant children] taking more and more money away from our school systems."

The perception that immigrants are not assimilating into American culture was also prevalent, as demonstrated by the comment of this Hennepin County man: "There's no assimilation; like our forefathers—they came here to be Americans." A female Hennepin County resident believed that immigrants should "mold more into *America.* We don't need to make the Somalia neighborhood, the Hmong neighborhood, you come to America. . . ."

Some participants were frustrated over their perceptions that Americans were expected to adapt to accommodate the needs of immigrants. A man in the Scott County group said:

> I think that there's a difference between if you're coming over here with the intent to live the American dream . . . but if you're coming over here to hang you country's flag in your front yard and if you're coming over here trying to make me change, or I've got to stand up or apologize for who I am because you don't speak my language, or I don't understand your religion, and we've got to have all these laws and rules and regulations for you so that you can live here. I think that's crap. I think this is America. If you want to live here you abide by the rules and regulations that we have.

The perception that immigration takes an economic toll on the country or that immigrants are getting "a free ride" also provokes anger, as this Scott County man conveyed: "I need to ask myself why they all have health insurance and cars and are going to school . . . and no one can take care of my mom. So she can't get insurance and it pisses me off."

A woman from Anoka County was equally frustrated:

> The [inaudible] groups are getting very large, and it seems when they come over here they are getting all the tax breaks. They get all this help. They get this, they get that, they get this, they get that, and those of us who have fought for this country, who have paid our taxes, who raise our children, and who live in this country and in this state are the ones that are paying for all those people to get all those breaks, and our children and our lifestyles are not increasing, they are staying stagnant.

Not all of the focus group comments about immigrants were negative. Seventeen comments painted immigrants in a positive light. The most frequent theme (more than one-third of the comments) was an expression of sympathy for immigrants. On the difficulties of integration, this Anoka County woman said, "Virtually anybody that comes here, they have to be gutsy. Things had to have been pretty awful to leave everything you have. . . . [It takes] a lot of courage to go someplace new."

Several participants commented that immigrants have a good work ethic and are integral to the United States economy, taking jobs that native-born Americans refuse, as this Anoka County man says: "I work with a couple of immigrants, and . . . I gotta say they're the couple of hardest working guys in our entire plant. I mean they come in and they kick butt."

A few people described what they perceived to be positive aspects of diversity associated with immigration, saying, "I think it makes our country more interesting," or "It gives you some options for restaurants and stuff too. I don't really care for any type of that food, but. . . ." Another focus group participant noted the positive family values of Hmong immigrants: "I see the [Hmong] as being very family oriented. The whole family pitches in."

While exurban Minnesotans clearly have strong, dominantly negative attitudes toward immigrants, many also express some ambivalence. About 20 percent of all immigrant-related comments contained both positive and negative statements regarding the characteristics or impact of immigrants. In the most common mixed comment, focus group members raised concerns about the lack of assimilation and its potential impact, but they coupled their statements with expressions of sympathy regarding the challenges of adjusting to a new life. Individuals also discussed immigration as a "mixed bag," expressing concern over increasing costs resulting from immigration, but also noting that immigrants have strong work ethics that are valuable, as this Hennepin County man attests: "[There's a] lot of them where I work and quite frankly, we can't find people to do that work than these type of people. And they are hard workers. But, some of them are not paying their taxes, I know. So, it's a little bit of a mixed bag for me."

Housing, Poverty, and School Segregation among Immigrant Households

During the 1980s and 1990s the Twin Cities' share of nonwhite residents increased from 5 percent to 15 percent, and the region lacked school and housing policies to inspire development in ways that fully integrated these families of color. As we have shown, the location of immigrants in suburban Minnesota communities is very similar to that of people of color in general. As a result, many immigrants in the Twin Cities metro area attend schools with very high proportions of U.S.-born minority and poor children.

Housing discrimination and steering account for some of the residential segregation. In April 2006 the National Fair Housing Alliance (NFHA) completed a three-year, twelve-city housing discrimination study.[27] This and some local studies completed in the late 1990s suggest that housing discrimination against minority renters and homeowners is prevalent in the city of Minneapolis and its suburbs, including outright denial of service to blacks and Latinos, significant financial incentives offered only to whites, and steering of potential purchasers on the basis of race or national origin.[28] Some public affordable-housing programs also contribute to segregated housing, particularly the Low Income Housing Tax Credit, in which the state Housing Finance Agency disproportionately allocates tax credits to finance affordable housing development to projects in the central cities, instead of the suburbs. As a result, only 23 percent of housing near middle and inner suburbs in the Twin Cities metro area is affordable, compared with one-half of the units in the central business district.[29]

Some of the concentration of immigrants and U.S. race-ethnic minorities in the suburbs may be the result of white flight from the city and inner-ring suburbs, as has been evident in the past decade. Eventually, many nonwhite residents, usually middle-class families with reasonable resources, join more affluent residents in slightly integrated suburbs.[30] When the numbers of minority residents reach a tipping point, middle-class white families move farther out, purportedly in search of better schools. This trend has been exacerbated by real estate agents who steer white residents away from integrated neighborhoods, claiming that "the schools are bad," while simultaneously recommending the same neighborhoods to residents of color and promoting the schools as "integrated."[31] This steering increases school and residential segregation. In the northwestern suburbs shown in map 8-2, for example, 25 percent of the 373 elementary schools now have enrollments that are greater than 50 percent nonwhite.

A useful index of segregation is one that measures exposure to individuals of different racial and ethnic groups.[32] In 2005 Twin Cities schools had a Hispanic-white exposure index of 49, meaning that the average Hispanic student in the seven-county metro area attended a school that was 49 percent white (down from 64 percent in 1995). On average, Hispanic students are attending schools that are less white than they were ten years ago, and they are increasingly clustered in segregated schools.[33]

Without affordable housing in the affluent suburbs where jobs and opportunity are expanding, and with continued steering and white flight, the Twin Cities area risks a resegregation of concentrated poverty in the suburbs. Several inner suburban school districts now have eligibility rates for free and reduced cost lunch exceeding 30 percent (the proportion of students receiving free or reduced cost lunch indicates the level of poverty within a particular school) (map 8-5). Economic segregation is especially severe in the southern and northwest suburbs, where economic segregation is already mirroring racial segregation. In some schools in this part of the region, more than two-thirds of the students are eligible for free or reduced cost lunch Two of the northwestern school districts in our sample currently have enrollments of more than 50 percent poor students (Columbia Heights, 59 percent, and Brooklyn Center, 64 percent) and Richfield, in the south, has a rate of 49 percent. Between 2001 and 2006 the share of poor students increased by 19 percentage points in Columbia Heights, by 11 points in Brooklyn Center and by 20 points in Richfield. At the same time, white student shares dropped by 23 percentage points in these three districts combined.[34]

Decisions regarding land use and taxation are responsible for much of the social and economic inequity in regions in the United States today.[35] When cities zone out affordable housing, they are also zoning out low-income immigrants. At the same time, there are some promising signs. The City of Eden Prairie, home to many new immigrants and jobs, has been active in attempting to build affordable housing and has also drawn its school boundaries to encourage, rather than retard, racial and, hence, immigrant integration.

Map 8-5. Students in Twin Cities Area Receiving Free or Reduced Lunch, by School District, 2006–07

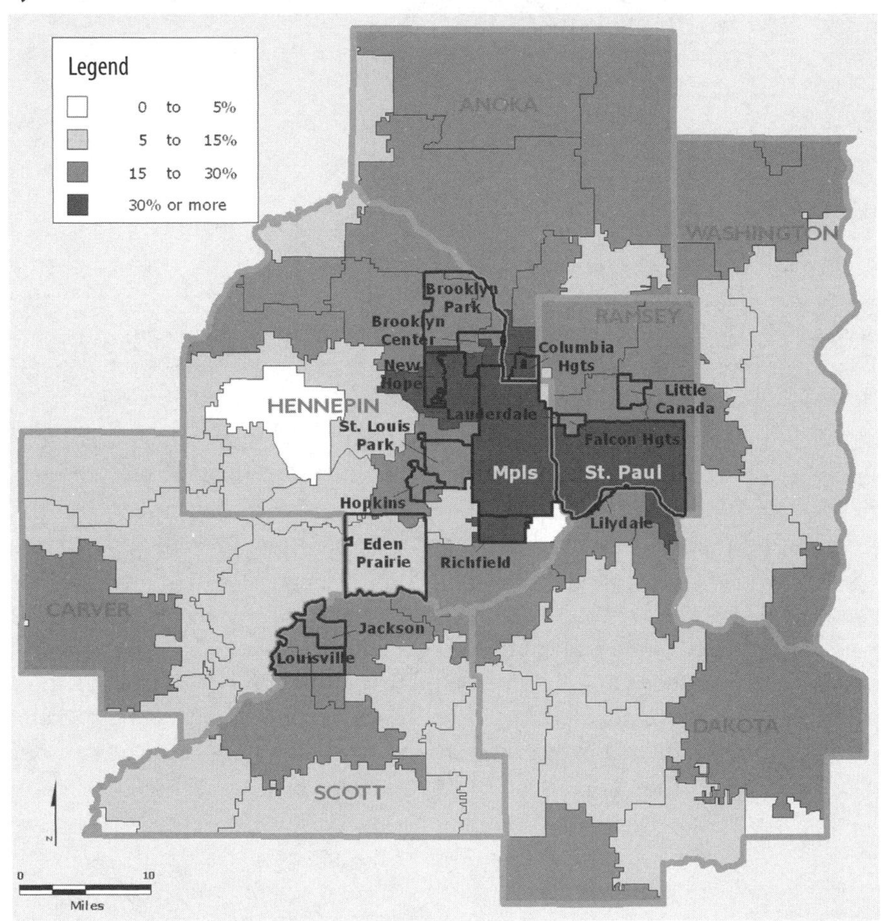

Source: Minnesota Department of Education.

Summary and Forecast for Minnesota

Immigrants are extremely heterogeneous, and there is as much diversity within any one national origin group as there is between U.S and foreign-born individuals overall. This is especially true in the Twin Cities because of the broad mix of immigrants and refugees. Foreign-born suburban residents in the Twin Cities metropolitan area include refugees and immigrants who differ greatly in their reasons for coming to the United States, in their ages upon entry, and on dimensions of language, education, job skills, religion, and cultural upbringing. Immigrants also vary greatly in their reasons for moving to the suburbs. Some are attracted by the availability of jobs, and some by larger or more affordable housing or quieter neighborhoods and better schools. The moves represent static, or even downward, socioeconomic mobility for some and upward mobility for others. Regardless of their socioeconomic status, more immigrants appear to be moving to the suburbs of the Twin Cities than ever before

Despite their diversity, once in the United States, very disparate groups of individuals may find themselves categorized as an undifferentiated group of "immigrants," or as individuals assumed to be different from native-born Americans. This category may include second- or even third-generation Americans who are assumed to be foreigners because of their physical appearance. Some of the broad stereotypes ascribed to immigrants are apparent in the examples from surveys of white suburban residents cited in this chapter. Furthermore, when immigrants are distinguishable by virtue of their skin color or accents, they are much more likely to be victims of school and residential segregation.

There may still be the time and the means to intercept these patterns in suburban districts. Although suburban school districts such as Columbia Heights, Richfield, and Brooklyn Center have very high concentrations of poverty, others are racially integrated and provide educational opportunities to many disadvantaged students. Elected officials should find ways to maintain stable integration in these places and to guard against the possibility of resegregation in communities such as St. Louis Park. Furthermore, most suburban districts could provide educational opportunity to many more disadvantaged students. Cities could learn from the example of Eden Prairie, which has been accepting students from poor backgrounds and working to ensure that they attend racially and socially integrated schools.

There is a sad irony in that the segregation of the foreign-born into failing schools and neighborhoods results in further distancing from the experiences of white, middle-class residents; that distance, in turn, is used as a justification for further prejudice. Examples include the lack of affordable housing that leads to overcrowded residences and may reduce the marketability or property values of neighborhoods, or the high dropout rates from poor schools that perpetuate stereotypes that black and Hispanic children cannot succeed academically. Evidence of the ways in which these and other forces converge to exclude, rather than to integrate, children can be seen in the increase in adolescent risk behaviors with each successive generation of immigrants in the United States.[36]

As jobs in the central cities continue to decentralize, the numbers of immigrants (and U.S.-born blacks and Latinos) seeking jobs in the suburbs is likely to increase. We have highlighted several impediments to their integration into suburban communities, but there are also positive signs. Nationally, Waldinger and Reichl, for example, find important gains between first- and second-generation Mexicans in the United States.[37]

Increasing diversity is itself a positive trend. Immigrant enclaves can rejuvenate sections of some suburban cities by stimulating new businesses and job creation. Furthermore, social contact among children of different ethnic and cultural backgrounds may reduce prejudice and xenophobia in the next generation. As the children of immigrants reach voting age, and move into the middle class, their political clout is likely to increase. Finally, in the 1990s litigation against the state and the city of Minneapolis led to a promising interdistrict school choice model. "Choice Is Yours" permits some students in segregated Minneapolis schools to attend integrated schools in the western suburbs. The results of a pilot evaluation at the end of the first four years found higher academic achievement for students participating in "Choice Is Yours" than for eligible students who chose to remain in Minneapolis schools. This model could be expanded to include more school districts as part of a comprehensive approach to provide quality, integrated schools for all of the children in the region. Because integrated schools are strongly linked to integrated housing markets, innovative school choice programs could also help to reduce housing segregation.[38]

Minnesota has also adopted a seven-county affordable housing law that gives authority to the Metropolitan Council to negotiate affordable housing goals with communities in the Minneapolis-St. Paul metropolitan area. The result has been the development of some new suburban family affordable housing. However the scope of the program is too small to alter existing patterns of residential segregation.

The numbers of foreign-born residents in most Twin Cities suburbs are small but rapidly increasing, and they and their children are subject to patterns of residential and school segregation that have served as barriers to U.S.-born Latinos and African Americans for years.[39] For the foreign-born, these trends are often exacerbated by native-born xenophobia that increases support for laws and policies that limit immigrants' protections from job discrimination and access to English-language programs, social services, and credit.[40] The Twin Cities would do well to consider the consequences of ignoring the barriers that limit the full economic and social integration of such a vital and growing segment of its population.

Notes

1. Myron Orfield and Thomas Luce, "Governing American Metropolitan Areas: Spatial Policy and Regional Governance," in *Metropolitan Areas, Megaregions, and Spatial Planning,* edited by Catherine Ross and Cheryl Contant (MIT Press, forthcoming 2008).

2. For voting data see, U.S. Census Bureau, "U.S. Voter Turnout Up in 2004," May 26, 2005 (www.census.gov/Press-Release/www/releases/). For volunteerism, see Corporation for National and Community Service, Office of Research and Policy Development, *Volunteering in America: 2007 State Trends and Rankings in Civic Life* (Washington: 2007), pp. 8–9.

3. Rebecca Sohmer, *Mind the Gap: Disparities and Competitiveness in the Twin Cities* (Brookings: 2005).

4. Audrey Singer and Jill H. Wilson, *From "There" to "Here": Refugee Resettlement in Metropolitan America* (Brookings, 2006). A refugee is any person who is unable or unwilling to return to his or her country of nationality and is unable or unwilling to avail him- or herself of the protection of that country because of persecution or a well founded fear of persecution on account of race, religion, nationality, membership in a particular social group, or political opinion. Katherine Fennelly, "Latinos, Asians, and Africans in the Northstar State: New Immigrant Communities in Minnesota," in *Beyond the Gateway: Immigrants in a Changing America,* edited by Elzbieta M. Gozdziak and Susan F. Martin (Lanham, Md.: Lexington Books, Migration and Refugee Studies series, 2006).

5. Kenneth Johnson, "The Impact of Immigration on Midwestern Cities," Presentation at the Chicago Council on Global Affairs, April 18, 2007.

6. Personal communication with Blain Mamo, epidemiologist, Refugee Health Program, Minnesota Department of Health, June 18, 2006.

7. See Katherine Fennelly, "Latinos, Asians, and Africans in the Northstar State."

8. Margaret Pugh O'Mara, *Cities of Knowledge: Cold War Science and the Search for the Next Silicon Valley* (Princeton University Press, 2005).

9. Stan Greenberg, Anna Greenberg, and Julie Hootkin, "The Changing Shape of Minnesota" (Minnesota Community Project, Minneapolis, December 14, 2004).

10. Ibid. We coded each discrete focus group statement on immigration as positive, negative, or mixed, and entered the response into the QS-4 software database for analysis. Immigration was only one of many topics broached in the groups; in total there were 7,610 comments (separate responses) made in the six groups, and only 78 of these were related to immigration.

11. The methodology used to derive the community types is described in *Growth Pressures on Sensitive Natural Areas* (Minnesota Department of Natural Resources, Central Region, and Ameregis, Inc., St. Paul, 2006), pp. 32–38 (www.ameregis.com). It is also applied in Myron Orfield and Thomas Luce, *Region: Law, Policy and Politics in Metropolitan America,* unpublished manuscript.

12. Asian Pacific American Community Development Data Center, "Minnesota: A Profile of the Asian American and Native Hawaiian/Pacific Islander Population" (Washington, May 2004).

13. Ibid., p. 2.

14. Ibid., p. 3.
15. Ibid.
16. Lilydale also has a very high percentage of immigrants of Asian origin, but it is an extremely small suburb (population 627) adjacent to the city of Mendota.
17. Chicano Latino Affairs Council, "The Hispanic/Latino Population in Minnesota: 2000" (St Paul: January 2003).
18. Richard Kahlenberg, *All Together Now: Creating Middle-Class Schools through Public School Choice* (Brookings, 2001); and Russell W. Rumberger and Gregory J. Palardy, "Does Resegregation Matter? The Impact of Social Composition on Academic Achievement in Southern High Schools," in *School Resegregation: Must the South Turn Back?* edited by John Charles Boger and Gary Orfield (University of North Carolina Press, 2005). In addition to the racially disproportionate burden on nonwhite children of attending poor schools, the rate of individual poverty is 2.5 times higher among nonwhite children.
19. Richard Chase and Laura Schauben, "The State of Hunger in Minnesota: Survey of Food Shelf and On-Site Meal Program Recipients in 2005" (Hunger Solutions Minnesota, in association with Wilder Research, Minneapolis, February 2006).
20. Chicano Latino Affairs Council, "The Hispanic/Latino Population in Minnesota: 2000," p. 2.
21. Ibid.
22. Center for Victims of Torture, *New Neighbors, Hidden Scars* 15, no. 4 (2005).
23. Thomas Luce, Myron Orfield, and Jill Mazullo, "Access to Growing Job Centers in the Twin Cities Metropolitan Area," *CURA* [Center for Urban and Regional Affairs] *Reporter* 36, no. 1 (2006). Job centers are contiguous "traffic analysis zones" with greater than average numbers of jobs per square mile. Large job agglomerations such as those in the centers of Minneapolis and St. Paul were divided into components on the basis of job densities. Job centers were grouped into four categories, based on 1990–2000 growth rates: declining centers (job losses during the decade); slow-growth centers (growth between 0 and 20 percent); moderate-growth centers (growth between 20 and 40 percent); and high-growth centers (growth more than 40 percent). In 2000 black workers were far more likely to work in declining or slow-growth centers than other workers: 49 percent of black workers compared with 31 percent of whites and 39 percent of Hispanics. Similarly, just 41 percent of blacks worked in high-growth job clusters or nonclustered jobs (the fastest growing category of jobs), compared with 56 percent of whites and 50 percent of Hispanics.
24. Ibid., p. 10.
25. Sohmer, *Mind the Gap*.
26. Curt Brown, "Ethnicity Fades by the Pool," *Minneapolis Star Tribune,* June 2, 2007.
27. National Fair Housing Alliance, *Unequal Opportunity: Perpetuating Housing Discrimination in America: 2006 Fair Trends Housing Report* (Washington: 2006). The NFHA tested seventy-three sales offices in twelve metropolitan areas: Atlanta, Austin, Birmingham, Chicago, Dayton, Detroit, Mobile, New York (including New York City, Long Island and Westchester County), Philadelphia, Pittsburgh, San Antonio, and metropolitan Washington (including northern Virginia, suburban Maryland, and Baltimore).

28. Ibid.; Myron Orfield, "Choice, Equal Protection and Metropolitan Integration: The Hope of the Minneapolis Desegregation Settlement," *Law and Inequality: A Journal of Theory and Practice* 24, no. 2 (2006); and John Yinger, *Closed Doors, Opportunities Lost: The Continuing Costs of Housing Discrimination* (New York: Russell Sage Foundation, 1995). For information on steering, see National Fair Housing Alliance, *Unequal Opportunity.* The NFHA tests revealed steering at a rate of 87 percent among testers who were given an opportunity to see homes. Testers were generally steered to neighborhoods based on their race or national origin, as well as religion and family status. The NFHA also reports that schools are used as a proxy for racial or ethnic composition of neighborhoods and communities. Rather than telling white testers to avoid certain neighborhoods because of racial or ethnic composition, many real estate agents would tell the tester to avoid certain schools that were racially identifiable.

29. Luce, Orfield, and Mazullo, "Access to Growing Job Centers," p. 11.

30. Many residents of color move to the suburbs for a variety of reasons. Some want to live in neighborhoods that match their socioeconomic status. Others move so they can send their children to better schools. Yet others simply want to escape the racially segregated urban neighborhoods of poverty.

31. National Fair Housing Alliance, *Unequal Opportunity.*

32. Douglas S. Massey and Nancy A. Denton, *American Apartheid: Segregation and the Making of the Underclass* (Harvard University Press, 1993), pp. 12–14; Gary Orfield and others, "Deepening Segregation in American Public Schools: A Special Report from the Harvard Project on School Desegregation," *Equity and Excellence in Education* 20, no. 2 (1997): 5–24; Gary Orfield and others, *The Growth of Segregation in American Schools: Changing Patterns of Separation and Poverty since 1968* (Alexandria, Va.: National School Boards Association, 1993).

33. Charter schools have attracted black and Latino students in both the central cities and suburban communities. In 2005 three charter schools in the seven-county metro area had 80 percent to 99 percent Hispanic enrollment; see Institute on Race and Poverty, *The Choice Is Ours: Expanding Educational Opportunity for All Twin Cities Children* (Minneapolis: May 2006).

34. Minnesota Department of Education, school years 2001–02 and 2006–07 (http://cfl.state.mn.us/MDE/Data/Data_Downloads/Student/Enrollment/District/index.html).

35. Myron Orfield, *American Metropolitics: The New Suburban Reality* (Brookings, 2002). Counties also make land use decisions over unincorporated areas.

36. Katherine Fennelly, "The Healthy Migrant Phenomenon," in *Immigrant Medicine: A Comprehensive Reference for the Care of Refugees and Immigrants,* edited by Patricia Walker and Elizabeth Barnett (New York: Elsevier, 2007).

37. Roger Waldinger and Renee Reichl, "Second-Generation Mexicans: Getting Ahead or Falling Behind?" *Migration Information Source* (March 1, 2006), (www.migrationinformation.org/Feature/display.cfm?id=382).

38. Myron Orfield, "Racial Integration and Community Revitalization: Applying the Fair Housing Act to the Low Income Housing Tax Credit," *Vanderbilt Law Review* 58, no. 6 (2005); Myron Orfield, "Choice, Equal Protection and Metropolitan Integration: The Hope of the Minneapolis Desegregation Settlement," *Law and Inequality: A Journal of Theory and Practice* 24, no. 2 (2006); Myron Orfield and

Thomas Luce, *Minority Suburbanization and Racial Change: Stable Integration, Neighborhood Transition and the Need for Regional Approaches* (Minneapolis: Institute on Race and Poverty, March 2006).

39. Some groups of Asian-Americans—particularly the Hmong—have also been adversely affected by these trends but to a lesser extent than other immigrants and U.S. race-ethnic groups. Research shows that Asians experience lower overall levels of segregation than blacks or Hispanics. See, for example, John R. Logan, Brian J. Stults, and Reynolds Farley, "Segregation of Minorities in the Metropolis: Two Decades of Change," *Demography* 41, no. 1 (2004): 1–22, especially table 1.

40. For a thorough discussion of these limitations statewide, see Katherine Fennelly, "State and Local Policy Response to Immigration in Minnesota," Case study for the Century Foundation Project on New Immigrant States, New York, 2006.

9

"Placing" the Refugee Diaspora in Suburban Portland, Oregon

SUSAN W. HARDWICK and JAMES E. MEACHAM

Walking in Beaverton reveals variety and surprise along the boulevards. The polyglot population is evident in the faces you see as well as [in] the thicket of languages on painted signs, [in the] specialty businesses sell[ing] prayer flags, halal meats and Middle Eastern spices, or [in the] heaps of obsolete computer parts.

—MATTHEW STADLER, *THE OREGONIAN*, 2006

The Portland suburban community of Beaverton defies common perceptions about life and landscape in the "burbs." One-fourth of the residents speaks a language other than English at home, and one-fifth of the population is foreign-born. In today's Portland metropolitan area, one in five new immigrants is settling in the suburbs. As a recent newspaper article reported, on a short jaunt through Beaverton's streets you are likely to see or hear: "South Indian *idli* and *vada,* Dutch *nagelkaas,* Korean *jim-jil bang saunas,* all-night reggae music at La Fogata, the festival of *Diwali*—and the city's schools, libraries, and huge farmer's market (one of the largest in the Northwest)."[1]

This chapter explores the political, economic, social, and cultural processes that are driving the suburban migration and settlement of foreign-

The support of NSF grant BCS-0214467, along with the invaluable research assistance of Ginger Mansfield and Susan E. Hume, and the cartographic design expertise of Demian Hommel, Anika Juhn, and the University of Oregon's InfoGraphics Laboratory, were deeply appreciated during the data collection and data analysis phase of this project.

born migrants in Portland. We rely on a case study of refugee migration, settlement, and suburban impacts in the Portland metropolitan area, which Audrey Singer has identified as a "re-emerging immigrant gateway."[2] In the decades following the Vietnam War, Portland's demographics changed dramatically as relatively large numbers of refugees from the war-torn countries of Vietnam, Cambodia, and Laos arrived in the Pacific Northwest. These groups were joined in the 1980s and 1990s by other migrants from the former Soviet Union, Romania, Southeast Asia, the Middle East, and Africa. The increasing population diversity, (especially in a region long dominated by majority white residents from other parts of the United States and Europe), makes Portland an ideal case study to reconceptualize larger sociospatial questions related to refugee diasporas in other U.S. cities.

Our analysis uses data gathered as a part of a long-term project focused on refugee migration, settlement, and adaptation in Oregon. The data include information from archival records, census data, survey questionnaires, and sixty-two structured interviews with refugees and resettlement agency and social service providers. In addition, an intensive spatial-cartographic analysis of the residential, religious, and economic patterns of the city's largest groups of refugees established that a layered network of processes is shaping the new and ever more spatially dispersed and densely populated Portland metropolitan area.

The thorough spatial analysis shown on the maps in this chapter was made possible by our close and ongoing collaboration with the Immigrant and Refugee Community Organization (IRCO), the largest resettlement agency in Oregon. Data from IRCO files provided detailed information on the total population, the anonymous home addresses, and places of origin of all documented refugees who arrived in the Portland metropolitan area. This rich data set, along with census reports detailing the location patterns of documented immigrants in the years 1990 and 2000, made possible a comprehensive cartographic analysis of the residential patterns of all immigrant and refugee groups in the Portland area. Subsequently, using data gathered and analyzed via structured and unstructured interviews with immigrants and refugees and with resettlement agency staff and other social service providers, as well as survey questionnaires, we were able to deepen our understanding of the overlapping political, socioeconomic, and cultural processes and networks that helped shape these mapped patterns.

Map 9-1, showing the Portland metropolitan area, provides a guide to the four focus counties and suburban places discussed in this chapter. Those counties are Multnomah, Washington, and Clackamas in Oregon, and Clark in Washington state. The population growth between 2000 and

Map 9-1. The Portland, Oregon, Metro Area, 2006

Source: U.S. Census Bureau, *Census of the Population 2000.*

2005 of each of the major cities and suburbs in this urban region is shown in table 9-1. The three largest cities in the metro area are Portland and Beaverton in Oregon and Vancouver, Washington (located north of the Columbia River and connected to Portland to the south by two well-traveled bridges spanning the Columbia River). These cities are surrounded by a host of suburbs and smaller incorporated and unincorporated communities such as Gresham, Hillsboro, and Milwaukie.

The foreign-born in the Portland metropolitan area more than doubled between 1990 and 2000, standing at 208,075 in 2000 and accounting for 12 percent of the total population in the metropolitan area. More than half of the foreign-born arrived after 1990. Latin Americans make up the largest immigrant group in the Portland metropolitan area (34.6 percent), with Mexican-born residents accounting for at least 28.8 percent of all foreign-born. Asians also constitute a large share of the foreign-born population in the urban region (33.5 percent with the majority born in Vietnam, China, Korea, India, and the Philippines). Map 9-2 documents the dramatic

Table 9-1. Recent Population Change in the Portland Metropolitan Area, 2000–05

City	*2000*	*2005*	*Change*	*Percent change*
Portland	514,129	513,627	−502	−0.1
Beaverton	75,212	83,447	8,235	10.9
Gresham	89,077	95,334	6,257	7.0
Hillsboro	69,236	82,732	13,496	19.5
Vancouver, Wash.	141,478	155,488	14,010	9.9

Source: U.S. Census Bureau, *Census of Population 2000;* U.S. Census Bureau, *American Community Survey 2005.*

increase of foreign-born residents between 1990 and 2000, and table 9-2 provides a summary of ethnic and racial change in the Portland metro area between 2000 and 2003.

Along with the arrival of these new groups of immigrants and refugees in recent years is the ongoing arrival of mostly white migrants from other U.S. states such as California and Colorado. United Van Lines reported in 2007 that Oregon ranked second in the nation (after North Carolina) in the total number of moves made to a particular state. Ongoing gentrification downtown and in older, inner suburbs, densification in the central business district and in outlying residential and commercial areas, and subsequent increases in land values in the urban core have resulted in the outer suburbs' becoming relatively more affordable than residential neighborhoods located in and adjacent to downtown districts. These social and economic changes, along with the decisionmaking of refugee and immigrant resettlement and social service agencies, have contributed to the *placing* of refugees and other immigrant groups in suburban neighborhoods, especially during the past two decades.

This era of rapid morphological and demographic change in the Portland metropolitan area has occurred against the backdrop of an urban area recognized as the "capital of good planning." Building on 1970s-era decisions related to concerns about environmental protection and a strong belief in civic engagement and in transportation's all-important role in shaping urban landscapes, the Portland metropolitan area today is a model of urban design and planning that "embodies the most hopeful and progressive trends in American city life."[3]

A key reason for Portland's high ranking among urban planners and urban economists is its diversified economy and broadly balanced base of manufacturing, wholesale, and retail trade and services sectors. The urban area is also a hub for high-technology industries, with more than 1,700 high-tech firms accounting for 36 percent of all factory jobs in the urban

Map 9-2. Foreign-Born Population, Portland Metro Area, 1990 and 2000

Source: U.S. Census Bureau, *Census of the Population 1990;* U.S. Census 2000, SF3; and TIGER/Line 1990 and 2000.

Table 9-2. Racial and Ethnic Change in the Portland Metropolitan Area, 2000–03

	Clackamas, Ore.			*Multnomah, Ore.*			*Washington, Ore.*			*Clark, Wash.*		
	2000	*2003*	*Percent change*	*2000*	*2003*	*Percent change*	*2000*	*2003*	*Percent change*	*2000*	*2003*	*Percent change*
Hispanic	16,744	20,231	20.8	49,607	60,423	21.8	49,735	62,190	25.0	16,248	20,759	27.8
White	302,737	314,409	3.9	510,115	509,459	−0.1	348,042	358,441	3.0	300,702	325,937	8.4
Black	2,378	2,877	21.0	38,897	40,667	4.6	5,488	6,748	23.0	6,049	7,660	26.6
Native American	2,556	2,733	6.9	7,263	7,378	1.6	3,250	3,629	11.7	3,052	3,257	6.7
Asian American/ Pacific Islander	9,115	11,365	24.7	41,036	45,401	10.6	31,868	39,822	25.0	12,707	14,036	10.5
Multiracial	6,262	7,441	18.8	18,725	20,593	10.0	9,797	12,285	25.4	8,066	9,811	21.6
Total population	338,391	357,435	5.6	660,486	677,813	2.6	445,342	479,496	7.7	345,238	379,577	9.9

Sources: U.S. Census Bureau, *Census of Population 2000,* and population estimates, 2003.

area. The largest of these is Intel, producer of Pentium microprocessors. Despite these important economic strengths in the local economy, however, there remains in the urban region a significant and challenging polarization between workers in high-skilled and low-skilled sectors. This situation makes it difficult for many of the city's newly arriving foreign-born migrants to find employment that pays them enough to survive. Yet, as our findings for this chapter demonstrate, immigrants and refugees have been drawn into the area since the early 1990s, with the total foreign-born population growing by 136 percent between 1990 and 2000. This large increase ranks Portland among the U.S. cities with foreign-born growth rates that are more than double the national rate, according to 2005 census reports.

Several policies, beginning with Goal 10 passed in the 1970s, have paved the way for the growing foreign-born suburban population, including several land use policies that protect the city's surrounding open land and natural resources. Goal 10 is a fair-share housing policy requiring every jurisdiction within the urban area to provide appropriate types and quantities of developed land to meet the needs of households of all income levels. This decision resulted in the prohibition of exclusionary zoning in Portland's suburbs (which paved the way for apartment construction) and thereafter helped level the socioeconomic playing field in the outer parts of the urban area.[4] Its implementation set the stage for the increasing diversity now visible in places such as Beaverton and other suburban communities located far from the city's central business district.

Although this policy helped remove economic barriers to residential choices, the physical geography of the Portland area, in this case the Columbia and Willamette Rivers, can create them naturally. The Columbia

River divides Portland to the south from Vancouver, Washington, to the north, and the Willamette River divides the urbanized area located south of the Columbia River into lower-cost east and higher-cost west sides (see map 9-1).[5] Most of the high-impact growth in Portland after World War II occurred east of the Willamette River on the most affordable and available land. This growth compounded the socioeconomic divide between higher-income residents who lived in the forested hills to the west and south and lower-income (and more often foreign-born and African American) residents who lived in the flats to the north and east.

Adding to these trends, most of the city's public housing projects constructed in the 1950s and the tract homes built after the 1960s were located east of the Willamette River. This divide remains an important indicator of immigrant and refugee settlement in the Portland metropolitan area, as well as a defining characteristic of its urban, economic, and social geography. The northeast and southeast sides of the city are now home to large numbers of African Americans, Eastern European, and Asian working-class families, while higher-income groups such as Indians and Pakistanis and second generation Vietnamese more often choose suburbs such as Beaverton in the West Hills. Also residing in West Hills suburbs are "brain drain" immigrants from places such as India, Pakistan, and Korea who work at high-tech firms that abound in Aloha, Beaverton, and Hillsboro. An anomaly is the densely clustered population of Latin Americans, mostly from Mexico, who live in Westside Hillsboro. This suburban community is close to the rural agricultural land where their immigrant forebears once worked in these fields Here, well-paid software developers and engineers who work at nearby Intel and other high-tech Hillsboro firms share suburban amenities, school classrooms, and grocery store aisles with formerly rural, Spanish-speaking residents.

The First Century of Immigrant Settlement in Portland

Kaplan's 1998 characterization in the *Atlantic Monthly* of the Pacific Northwest as "the last Caucasian Bastion in the United States" speaks to the lingering impact of Portland's early history, when streams of Germans, Scandinavians, Anglo Canadians, and residents from the British Isles moved to the area in the late nineteenth and early twentieth centuries.[6] (Interestingly, and perhaps not coincidentally, the largest refugee groups residing in the area today also are white, Protestant European groups, but they were born in Russia and Ukraine.) With a few exceptions, early immigrants settled in inner-city neighborhoods not far from the downtown business district in the least expensive housing, and each group had its own well-defined neighborhood as did most other North American cities during this time period. Jews and Italians were dominant in South Portland; Germans in Goose Hollow; Slavs and Scandinavians in Northwest Portland; and German-Russians, Central Europeans, and Scandinavians in the Albina district in North Portland.[7]

Also at the heart of the city was Chinatown, a place of refuge for Chinese migrants escaping the anti-Asian violence and protests in Seattle and Tacoma to the north. By 1900, the city's Chinese population had grown to 7,800 with almost all living in Chinatown at the city's center on First and Second Streets. As in other parts of the American West in the nineteenth century, the Chinese community in Portland was made up almost entirely of single men. Today's old Chinatown remains as a tourist landscape embedded within the city's history, a shrine to early diversity.

Japanese immigrants to the Portland area likewise found their choices of housing limited by local attitudes, socioeconomic constraints, and racism. As in other parts of the West, local insurance agents often cancelled the insurance coverage of building owners who rented to Japanese. Other exclusionary housing policies in Portland made it difficult for Japanese immigrants to find housing outside the North End red-light district downtown. Most were later displaced permanently from downtown Portland by federal legislation in 1942 that removed Japanese families to wartime relocation camps in California and Idaho. With the majority of Japanese residents in the city absent from census counts at the end of World War II, Portland's residential geography shifted to a distinctive black-white divide.

Post-1970s Immigrants and Refugees in the Suburbs

Changes in immigration laws in the 1960s made it possible for immigrants and refugees to enter the United States from Latin America, Africa, and Southeast Asia, and subsequently tens of thousands of new arrivals settled in cities in unexpected places in the Pacific Northwest and other parts of the country. This legislation, coupled with Portland's well-organized activist network of refugee and immigrant resettlement and social service agencies, and its promising economic situation through the late 1990s, provided the impetus for ever-increasing numbers of new arrivals. Table 9-3 shows the growth and shifting patterns of immigration for the Portland county of Multnomah.

As shown in figure 9-1, immigrants from Latin America have become the largest group of foreign-born residents in Oregon. Examination of the

Table 9-3. Foreign-Born Population of Multnomah County's Largest Immigrant Groups, 1870, 1900, 2005

Group	*1870*	*Group*	*1900*	*Group*	*2005*
Total population	11,510		103,167		672,906
Ireland	823	China	7,115	Mexico	25,682
Germany	639	Germany	5,040	Eastern European	11,165
China	506	Canada	2,257	Vietnam	10,597
England and Wales	400	England	2,187	China	5,479
British Americas	300	Sweden	1,948	Russia	2,761
Scotland	300	Ireland	1,896	United Kingdom	2,761
France	80	Japan	1,327	Canada	2,652
Sweden and Norway	42	Russia	1,031	Korea	2,264
Switzerland	23	Norway	956	East Africa	1,489
Denmark	21	Switzerland	878	Iran	1,398

Source: U.S. Census Bureau, *Census of Population 1870, 1900; American Community Survey, 2005.*

Portland metropolitan area as a whole between 1980 and 2000 shows that the total foreign-born population grew to 65,646 by 1980; to 88,072 by 1990; and to 208,075 by 2000, more than double the average immigrant growth rate nationally according to the 2000 census. In some of the city's suburban communities, such as Hillsboro, the total population growth for Latinos alone increased as much as 80 percent between 1990 and 2005. In the state of Oregon, Latinos, at approximately 130,000, were estimated to make up at least 10 percent of the population in 2005, according to the *American Community Survey.*

In Hillsboro Latino food stores, retail stores, and other businesses now compete with other longer-term commercial establishments near the city's trendy shopping centers at upscale Orenco Station. Along Tenth Avenue in downtown Hillsboro, Latino shopkeepers sell *quinceanera* dresses and snakeskin cowboy boots, and provide money-wiring services to Latin America. Similarly, in suburban Cornelius a 35,000-square-foot Latino supermarket opened in 2006 when a seventy-one-year-old grocery store reinvented itself for the large Spanish-speaking market. Latinos make up more than one-half the population of this small community. In smaller suburban areas such as Rockwood, residents born in Mexico account for at least 20 percent of this community's total population of 28,836, with nearly three-fourths having arrived between 1990 and 2000. More than one-half of all businesses located in Rockwood in 2006 catered to Spanish-speaking residents.[8]

Figure 9-1. Regions of Origin of Immigrant Groups in Oregon, 1870–2000

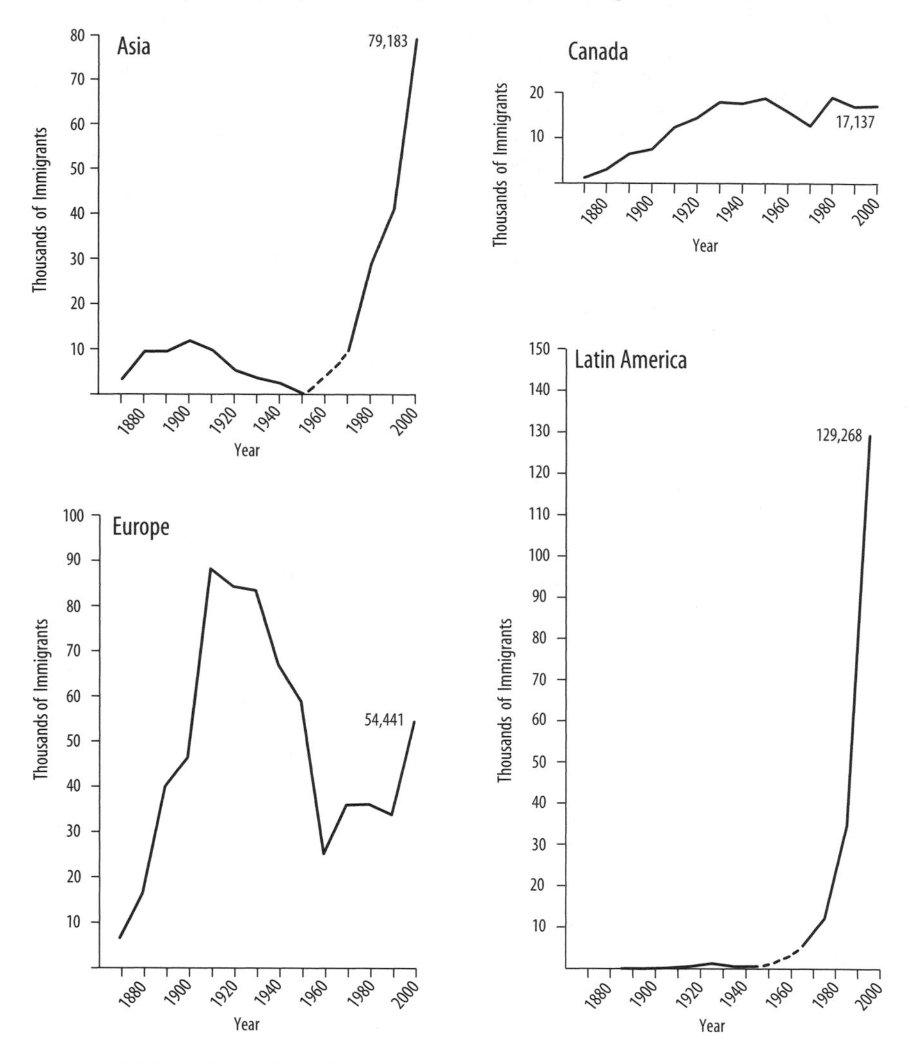

Source: U.S. Census Bureau, *Atlas of Oregon, 2001.*

Increasing numbers of Asian immigrants have also arrived in the Portland urban area since the 1970s. They too have changed the suburban landscape as new Asian businesses, ethnic newspapers and other media offices, and Asian religious establishments have appeared along suburban streets in eastside Portland and in the West Hills. Asians make up about 4 percent (79,183) of Oregon's population and 4.5 percent (12.8 million) nationally. In three of the Portland metropolitan area counties, Washington, Multnomah, and Clackamas, Asians and Pacific Islanders increased 91 percent between 1990 and 2000. Nearly 20 percent identified themselves on census forms as "Other Asian," the category that includes refugee groups from Southeast Asia such as Hmong, Mien, Cambodians, and Laotians. Many of these newcomers arrive directly from their homeland (or refugee camps in Thailand), while others are secondary migrants who relocate to the Portland area from California and other parts of the United States seeking employment opportunities, a more supportive resettlement system, clean air and lower crime rates, or family reunification. Within a short time after their arrival in Portland, many relocate to the city's surrounding suburbs to be closer to their jobs and to seek better educational opportunities for their children. According to the director of the Asian Family Center, Lee Po-Cha, the residential patterns of Asians in Portland are the most spatially scattered of any Asian population in any city in the United States.[9]

As discussed earlier, the Chinese are Portland's oldest Asian group. Dating back to the mid-1800s, this immigrant community began life in Oregon in downtown neighborhoods (an area still referred to as "Chinatown" by many of the city's older residents). Most came to work on railroad construction or opened their own shops and laundries to serve the needs of the city's increasing population. In contrast to these earliest arrivals from southern China, most of today's more recent mainland Chinese and Taiwanese come to work in high-tech industries in the suburbs.

The majority of Vietnamese and Korean immigrants in the metropolitan area have settled in suburban Portland. Many are small business owners in places like Sunnyside, Beaverton, and Lake Oswego. As the Korean population reached a critical mass in Beaverton, for example, demand for ethnic-specific businesses grew. An example of this is the concentration of Korean restaurants and shops along the Beaverton-Hillsboro Highway just east of the city of Beaverton. Word of mouth drew new Korean immigrants to Portland suburbs from Korea and point-of-entry states such as California and Texas.

Outpacing the Chinese, Vietnamese, Korean, and other Asians, Indians are now the most rapidly growing Asian group in Oregon. Their population has grown fivefold in the past twenty years, from 1,900 in 1980, to 3,500 in 1990, to nearly 10,000 in 2000. The immigration of Indians to the Portland metropolitan area parallels patterns in other parts of the country, although their arrival in the Pacific Northwest happened later than in cities such as Phoenix and Dallas, as outlined by Alex Oberle and

Wei Li and by Caroline Brettell in their chapters in this volume. Many came on work visas during the 1980s and 1990s to contribute to the region's growing high-tech industries. The majority of these migrants from India are young, well-educated men who ultimately return to India to marry and bring new wives back to Oregon. Because of their upward mobility, knowledge of English upon arrival in the United States, high-end employment skills, and relative invisibility in a rapidly changing multicultural city, migrants from India are the most residentially dispersed group in the Portland metropolitan area (as is largely true of Indians in the other cities documented in this volume). Most reside in upscale or middle-class neighborhoods in suburbs that ring the downtown, with concentrations in Beaverton, Hillsboro, and other West Hills "silicon suburbs." Today, the suburban expansion of Chinese, Korean, Vietnamese, South Asians, and other smaller Asian groups into suburbs located both east and west of the city's downtown continues unabated as employment opportunities, better schools, family networks, and affordable housing draw Asians and other immigrants away from downtown neighborhoods in ever larger numbers.

The Refugee Diaspora to the Suburbs

An important part of the larger foreign-born population in the Portland metropolitan area's suburbs are refugees from Eastern Europe, Africa, and Southeast Asia. According to the U.S. Office of Refugee Resettlement, the Portland urban area ranked twelfth of the top metropolitan areas of refugee resettlement between 1983 and 2004, with a least 34,292 refugees arriving during that time period. Of the recently arrived foreign-born population in the Portland-Vancouver metropolitan area, 18.9 percent resettled with refugee status in the year 2000.[10]

Refugees are admitted to the United States under very different rules and regulations than immigrants. Each potential refugee must meet a rigorous set of criteria, defined by the U.S. Refugee Act of 1980 and enforced by the Department of Homeland Security; refugees are approved for admission to the United States only after successfully completing this screening process. Refugee policies grew out of definitions first determined by the U.N. High Commission on Refugees at the Geneva Convention in 1951, which specified that refugees are those who are unwilling or unlikely to return home because of a well-founded fear of persecution owing to their race, religion, nationality, membership in a particular social group, or political opinion. Figure 9-2 shows the shift in places of origin of the city's largest refugee groups between 1975 and 2004.

Figure 9-2. Refugee Arrivals in Oregon, 1975–2004

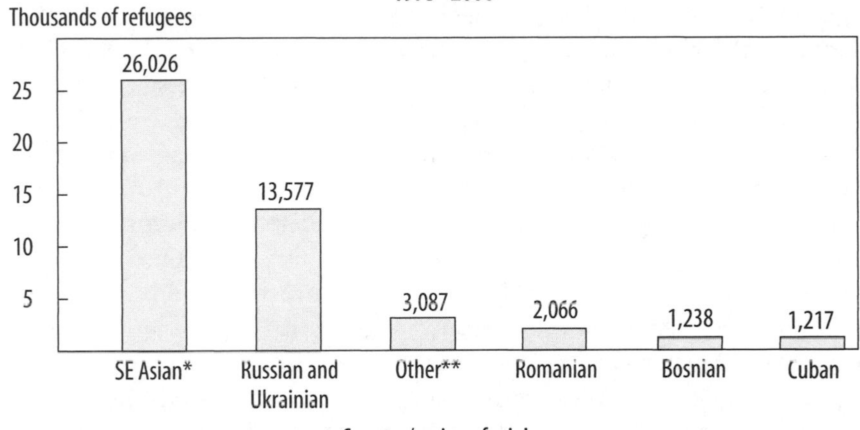

Source: Immigration and Refugee Community Organization Files, 1975–2000, Portland, Ore.
* SE Asian includes Vietnamese (16,793), Cambodian (3,474), and Lao (5,759).
** Other includes Hungarian, Sudanese, Czech, Kosovar, Haitian, Iraqi, Iranian, Polish, Somalian, Afghan, and Ethiopian.

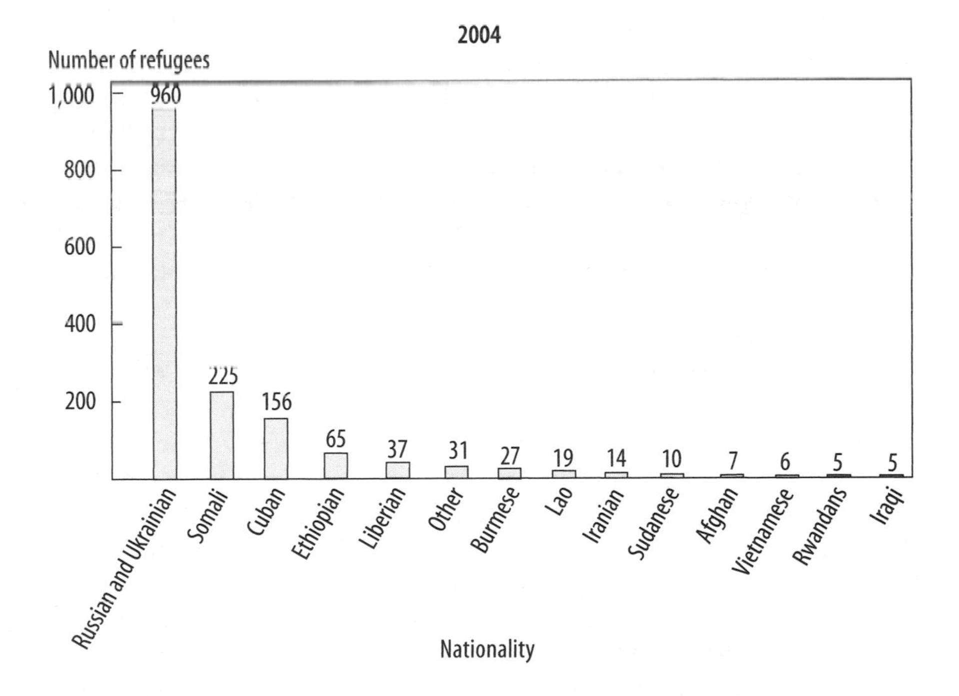

Source: Oregon State Refugee Program, 2004.

Along with these federal refugee policies, state and local resettlement agencies are critical in determining where refugees settle and how their adjustment process unfolds once they arrive. In Portland, as in many other places in the United States, a spate of voluntary agencies, or volags, such as Lutheran Social Services and Sponsors Organized to Assist Refugees (SOAR), work closely with the Oregon state refugee coordinator and other state-based social service programs and nonprofit mutual assistance programs, along with other networks of support that operate at the local level.

The largest and most successful of these resettlement nonprofits in Oregon is the Immigrant and Refugee Community Organization, with headquarters in a refugee-rich neighborhood in northeast Portland. In a model much like Jane Addams's historic Chicago Hull House, this visionary resettlement agency employs more than 150 multilingual social workers, counselors, linguistic assistants, and educational and employment training experts to help provide support for newcomers struggling to adjust to their new lives in Oregon. IRCO and other social and economic support organizations are required by federal policy to help resettle new refugees within one hundred miles of their volag (for those who are being reunified with family or friends) or fifty miles for refugees who arrive with no established network of contacts in the United States.[11] The ultimate goal of these overlapping networks of support is to help refugees increase their language and employment skills and adjust to their new environment. In Oregon refugees receive cash and medical support during their first eight months of support so long as they regularly attend English language classes and work skills sessions at IRCO or another social or educational refugee support agency.

The advantages of these early financial, employment, and sociocultural supports make the refugee experience, especially during the first year of settlement in Oregon, quite different from that of immigrants. Immigrants arrive with only the financial backing of money they bring with them or the help of family and friends, while refugees have sponsors in place prior to arrival and ongoing support for language and employment training. They also qualify for monthly financial support dispersed through IRCO by state agencies (who receive funding, provided by the U.S. Office of Refugee Resettlement, for each person who arrives in the United States with refugee status).

Findings from our interview data, however, indicate that this initial boost is often counterbalanced by the challenges of dealing with the label *refugee* and the trauma of the extreme conditions of their past lives. Some groups, such as Somalis, Bantus, and Ethiopians, escaped from their war-ravaged homeland with their lives. Others such as Vietnamese, Cambodians, and Laotians of the post–Vietnam War era, may have lived in refugee camps in Thailand for many years before finally gaining approval for relocation to the United States. The challenges brought on by the often desperate departure of these refugees from their homes may offset the best intentions and hard work of refugee providers in Portland as elsewhere in the nation. These factors, along with the economic, social, and cultural conditions of where they settle in the United States, may all affect the adjustment and incorporation of refugee newcomers on a day-to-day basis as well as over the long term.

To provide a more detailed analysis of the refugee experience in the Portland metropolitan area, we focus here on the experiences of the largest groups: refugees from Eastern Europe and the former Soviet Union, from Southeast Asia, and from sub-Saharan Africa.[12] We chose these particular groups because of their relatively large size and because of the different races, places of origin, and dates of arrival in the Portland area. The comparative patterns and related social, economic, and political processes of other groups of refugees in the area are also briefly analyzed to provide a more comprehensive picture of the refugee diaspora to the Portland-Vancouver metropolitan area during the past three and a half decades.

Russian, Ukrainian, and Romanian Refugees

Slavic refugees from the former Soviet Union and Eastern European countries dramatically increased their presence in the Pacific Northwest in the 1990s (table 9-4). Oregon and Washington added more new migrants born in Russia and Ukraine than did any other part of the country between 1990 and 2005. Although census data used to create the maps in this chapter reflect undercounts (caused by language barriers, fear of authority, and failure to include migrants who arrived without legal refugee status), it is estimated by refugee service providers and a tally of church membership lists that more than 80,000 refugees from the former Soviet Union now call the Portland urban area home. Attracted by sponsors affiliated with Christian fundamentalist church congregations; a network of well-organized social service and refugee resettlement agencies; and a physical environment that resembles their homeland, Russian, Ukrainian, and Romanian Baptists, Pentecostals, and Seventh Day Adventists combined are now the largest refugee group in the Portland-Vancouver metro area. Together, these groups of religious refugees have made Russian the fifth most important language spoken in the state, despite the much longer history in Oregon of foreign-born migrants from other parts of the world (table 9-5).

Table 9-4. Eastern Europeans in Oregon, 1990–2000

Ancestry[a]	*1990*	*2000*	*Change*
Russian	18,776	31,025	12,249
Ukrainian	4,616	8,469	3,853
Lithuanian	2,955	4,991	2,036
Latvian	931	1,624	693
Estonian	495	271	−224
Polish	30,940	36,439	5,499
Hungarian	6,861	9,773	2,912
Romanian	3,353	5,487	2,134
Bulgarian	617	622	5
Czech or Slovak	19,453	17,204	−2,249
Other eastern European[b]	1,326	2,341	1,015

Source: U.S. Census Bureau, *Census of Population 1990, 2000.*

a. Note that theses figures exclude people who listed their secondary ancestry as one or more of these eastern European countries.

b. Others listed their ancestry as Slavic or eastern European rather than one of the other categories listed in this table.

The exodus from Russia and Ukraine to the United States began in 1987 when then-president Mikhail Gorbachev made the unexpected announcement that religious minority groups could leave the Soviet Union for the first time since the Russian Revolution ended in 1922.[13] The U.S. Congress responded to this decision by easing restrictions on immigrants from Communist countries, especially religious refugees. Religious groups able to prove to the U.S. government that they were "refugees" under this legislation included Jews and evangelical Christian migrants who were persecuted for their religious beliefs under the Soviet system. The American evangelical lobby and the advocates for the religious right in the United States were influential factors in securing and holding onto the selective refugee status for these Protestant groups (even though their persecution virtually disappeared with the collapse of the Communist regime in 1991). In addition to large numbers of well-established congregations arranging for sponsors for newcomers, those who were already resettled in other states heard about the West Coast "mecca" and migrated to cities and small towns in Northern California, Oregon, and Washington.

The resettlement of these groups in Oregon is also the result of a historical migration stream from Russia that dates back to the 1960s-era migration of Russian Old Believers to Woodburn, just south of Portland.[14] In the 1970s a smaller group of Russian and Ukrainian Pentecostals who had migrated to the United States in the 1930s relocated to the city of Woodburn, with a

Table 9-5. Top Ten Languages Spoken at Home in Oregon, 2000

Language spoken at home	*Total number*	*Percent*
English only	2,810,654	87.9
Spanish	217,614	6.8
German	18,400	0.6
Vietnamese	17,805	0.6
Russian	16,344	0.5
Chinese	15,504	0.5
French	11,837	0.4
Japanese	9,377	0.3
Korean	9,185	0.3
Tagalog	6,181	0.2

Source: U.S. Census Bureau, *Census of Population 2000.*

mission to proselytize their Slavic brethren. It was this church that was first approached by the U.S. Department of State and asked to sponsor the earliest group of refugees from the Soviet Union in 1988. Overwhelmed by the chain migration that followed, Woodburn appealed to the larger city of Portland for help because of its already well-developed network of refugee support that had first been organized to assist with the resettlement of Southeast Asian refugees during the Vietnam War years.[15]

Chain migration intensified with the arrival of the parents, children, and other family members of these post-Soviet-era refugees in the Pacific Northwest.[16] According to Victoria Libov, a Russian social worker from Beaverton and program administrator at IRCO, "In a short time, you've almost moved an entire village to Portland."[17] An estimated 90 percent of these Slavic refugees remain in the area after their initial settlement in the Portland metropolitan area because of the support provided by refugee resettlement agencies, church networks, and resettled family and friends from home. According to one interviewee who prefers to remain anonymous, a thirty-four-year-old married woman from Kiev, Ukraine, who relocated to suburban Portland in 1997: "My sister gave me the idea really. She said we should go to Oregon to be with the others who already left our city. Then the minister here sent us a letter urging us all to come to his church. He assured us that my mother and father could come too."

Other Slavic refugees have joined these Russian and Ukrainian migrants in the Portland area. The Romanian Pentecostal Church in southeast Portland currently has more than 3,000 members, all of whom are refugees or children of refugees. Indeed, the Portland area is now home to one of the largest Romanian communities in the United States. A host of other

Romanian religious gatherings are held in suburban neighborhoods in southeast Portland, Gresham, and Vancouver. In addition, the Portland area Romanian community publishes the *Romanian Times* newspaper in suburban Gresham, which has served the community for the past six years.

Russian and Ukrainian refugees and their children have opened more than 400 businesses in the Portland metropolitan area that cater to their community, based on counts from the *Portland Slavic Yellow Pages.* Many of these are centered in the building industry, real estate, and banking. One of the characteristics of Russian, Ukrainian, and Romanian residents of the Portland metro area, in fact, is their strong desire for homeownership, a desire that was spawned in a homeland that eschewed private property and homeownership. Data from interviews and survey questionnaires indicate that the majority of Russian and Ukrainian families move from being renters to homeowners within the first three years of arrival in the Portland area. This consumer niche in the regional economy has resulted in Russian-speaking families' owning the majority of homes in some new suburban subdivisions such as Wood Village in eastern Multnomah County. Here the price of houses ranges from $220,000 to $315,000. Families such as the Paskalovs, who arrived in Oregon in 1997 from an industrial city in Ukraine with $600, their suitcases, and a new baby in tow, now reside in Wood Village and other new subdivisions. Like many other families, the Paskalovs were able to purchase their first home in an affordable neighborhood in southeast Portland within their first year of settlement with the help of family members and their dual incomes as a cabinetmaker and housecleaner. According to Mariya Paskalov: "Here it's a good investment when you buy a house. Maybe we don't understand it the first time we buy a house. But when we sell it, we understand."[18]

Refugee communities are beginning to play a role in Portland area politics as well. The Slavic Coalition, for example, provides a voice for the Slavic community to ensure maximum opportunities for gaining county and city funding and political power in the urban region. Their efforts have most recently resulted in being added as a voting member of the "Community of Color Coalition" in Multnomah County, an umbrella organization composed of Africans, African Americans, Asians and Pacific Islanders, and Latin Americans. Despite the whiteness of all of the members of the Slavic Coalition, Russians and Ukrainians now sit on funding decisionmaking bodies and serve on advisory committees as important players in the county-based Community of Color Coalition. Two leaders of the Slavic Coalition also were recently appointed to serve on the Portland mayor's new advisory board in support of immigrant and refugee issues in the metropolitan area.

A second example of the Slavic Coalition's increasing visibility and political power in the area was its active role in Portland's 2006 city council election. Not only did the first-ever Russian candidate run for an elected position on the city council, but one of the founders of the Slavic Coalition served as campaign manager for this candidate. This involvement in local politics and decisionmaking provides one of many examples of instances where well-organized and newly empowered groups are engaged in changing the political landscape of the city of Portland and its suburban communities. The growing significance of the largest groups of refugees in the Portland area, Russians, Ukrainians, and Vietnamese (discussed in the following section), in school classrooms, shopping districts, and health care facilities makes them increasingly visible in Portland's urban and suburban landscapes.

The expansion of home buyers from the former Soviet Union and Romania; dissemination of ethnic and church-based religious networks and newspapers in the Russian, Ukrainian, and Romanian language; and ever increasing numbers of businesses that cater to the Russian and Eastern European market are changing the residential and commercial landscape of suburban Portland. Along with this refugee-enhanced diversity at the city's edge is the expanding role of Slavic commercial nodes in the local and regional economy. These changes are helping broaden the economic, ethnic, and sociocultural networks already in place to support the arrival of refugees from Russia, Ukraine, Romania, and other parts of the world in the Portland urban area.

Southeast Asian Refugees

Since the earliest arrival of the first 1,600 Vietnamese in Portland in 1975 in the aftermath of the Vietnam War, the number of Southeast Asian refugees and their families in the Portland urban area has increased to approximately 40,000 people today. About 80 percent live in suburban communities in Multnomah, Washington, and Clackamas counties. Southeast Asians, like other immigrants in the region, have been affected by the increasing housing costs in the gentrified city core and are moving ever father out to the edges of suburban communities in the city's West Hills or to inner-ring suburbs on the east side.[19]

In recent years, significant spatial concentrations of Vietnamese have emerged such as Aloha in the West Hills and Happy Valley on the east side.

Drawn initially by affordable housing and employment opportunities at nearby Intel, Hewlett-Packard, and Nike headquarters, as well as opportunities in the service sector, these suburban nodes today boast Vietnamese newspapers, radio stations and recording studios, and numerous shops and restaurants that cater to the area's burgeoning Southeast Asian population.[20] Another draw to the area is the highly ranked schools. Even many of the business owners of the older and better established Vietnamese jewelry stores, restaurants, and clubs that line the streets of Sandy Boulevard closer to Portland's downtown business district now live in the suburbs and commute to work downtown on the city's light rail system, bus lines, or in private vehicles.

The dramatic increase in the Asian population in Aloha and Beaverton, in particular, has changed the ethnic and immigrant landscape of Portland's West Hills suburbs. The Asian enclaves in this part of the metropolitan area emerged recently and rapidly, and they have become ever more visible to insiders and outsiders alike because of their many businesses and increasing contributions to the local cultural and economic scene. According to Beaverton Mayor Rob Drake, the city was quite homogeneous until the early 1980s.[21] Census records show that in 1960, less than 0.3 percent of Beaverton's population was nonwhite, but by 2000, nonwhite minority groups made up one-fifth of the population. Both Aloha and Beaverton have significantly larger populations of Asians than the city of Portland, where Asians make up only 6.3 percent of the total population. In fact, Aloha currently has the most rapidly growing and largest Vietnamese population of any community in Oregon.

Refugees from Laos are also a part of the ethnic fabric of suburban landscapes in the Portland metropolitan area. Some came shortly after the arrival of the earliest Vietnamese in the mid-1970s, victims of their war-torn homeland in Southeast Asia. Others migrated to the Pacific Northwest a few years later, following the takeover of Laos by Communist forces at the end of the Vietnam War. Like their Vietnam neighbors, most Laotian residents of Beaverton, Aloha, Hillsboro, and Gresham remained in refugee camps in Thailand while they waited for approval of their refugee status to come to the United States. Others moved first to California and later made their way north to the Portland area to join family and friends from home.

Many of the refugee migrants from Laos are Hmong, part of a wide-ranging minority group whose homeland was in the mountains of Laos, China, Vietnam, Thailand, and Myanmar (Burma). The majority of the Hmong living in the Portland area came directly from refugee camps in Thailand. Thousands of Hmong had been recruited by the United States to be a part of a secret war against the Pathet Lao Communists, rescuing downed U.S. pilots, and fighting North Vietnamese soldiers. Because of their pro-American leanings, they were forced to escape from Laos by walking hundreds of miles to safety in Thai refugee camps or into the Laotian jungles to hide. Today approximately 250,000 Hmong live in the United States (with the majority in California's Central Valley and the Minneapolis-St. Paul area); about 3,000 Hmong reside in Oregon.[22]

The most recent group of Hmong was allowed to enter the United States in mid-2004 after more than three decades in refugee camps. After the United Nations closed its refugee processing center in Laos in the mid-1990s, the United States announced that it had no more plans to resettle additional Hmong. The stranded refugees were then left to try to survive by making handicrafts and working in rock quarries in Thailand. In December 2003, however, the U.S. ambassador in Thailand helped gain support for legislation that ultimately resulted in a major Hmong airlift operation, with more than 15,000 refugees relocating to the United States. About 200 of these refugees settled in the Portland metropolitan area, with most choosing affordable apartments in the city's diverse northeast Gateway district and other eastside neighborhoods.

Portland area refugees from Laos were joined by Cambodians who followed similar migration pathways from their homeland to refugee camps to eventual resettlement in the United States. From 1975 to 1979, more than two million Cambodians died, victims of the ruling Khmer Rouge terror. Many of those who survived walked for months to camps in Thailand or fled to other neighboring countries to find safety and security. Many continue to reside in northeast Portland after initial resettlement there by agencies such as IRCO. Typical of the employment experiences of Cambodian refugees in Portland is the work history of a fifty-one-year-old Cambodian woman, who arrived in Portland in 1979 with her husband and young children. Her first job was as a seamstress for a downtown company. She also picked strawberries and cucumbers on Saturdays to supplement the family income. She then worked for Tyco for ten years as an assembly worker and then for Pacific West as a maintenance worker. This hard-working refugee recalls: "When Pol Pot was coming, me and my family stay in Cambodia. Two of my brothers-in-law were sent to study and we don't see them come back again. They put the rest of us to the country. . . . You cleared the forest to make rice fields. We had to grind the rice from the shells . . . if you don't make it, you don't eat."

Although a smaller community in the Portland area than other Southeast Asian groups, Cambodians have a strong presence at cultural events, with second- and third-generation Cambodians organizing special cultural events in the region to increase awareness of their presence in the Portland area. The head of Oregon's largest refugee resettlement center, Sokhom Tauch, was the first Cambodian to arrive in Portland.[23] After gaining sponsorship to relocate to the United States with the help of Catholic Charities in Portland, he migrated to Portland in 1976 after a brief stay in a refugee resettlement center in central Pennsylvania. Before coming to the United States, Sokhom had spent his entire life in a refugee camp in northern Thailand. Today Sokhom is working with a group of other Portland Cambodians active in the Buddhist temple in suburban Aloha to create a Cambodian cultural center and several ethnically based organizations. His story, and the migration and settlement pathways and experiences of this Cambodian community leader and others like him, capture the impacts of various groups of Southeast Asian refugees on Portland's political, religious, economic, and cultural landscape.

Sub-Saharan African Refugees

African refugees fleeing war and persecution in their home countries have migrated to the Portland area since the early 1980s. The earliest to arrive came from Ethiopia and present-day Eritrea and were followed by others from Sudan, Somalia, Liberia, Democratic Republic of the Congo, Chad, Sierra Leone, and Togo. Unlike other immigrant groups in the metropolitan area, the majority of the most recent migrants from Africa reside in the city's inner north and northeast neighborhoods. A small but growing community also exists in suburban Beaverton in the heart of a diverse Muslim community. Here black Muslim neighbors gather for services and religious and cultural celebrations from a variety of African countries such as Eritrea, Ethiopia, Liberia, Senegal, and Somalia. They are joined by other immigrants of their same faith from the Middle East and Afghanistan.

After two decades in the United States, many Eritreans have purchased their own homes and dispersed throughout northeast and southeast Portland as well as across the Columbia River into Vancouver. In contrast, Somalis have relocated to southwest Portland and neighboring Beaverton to be closer to mosques. Many Congolese have also moved to Beaverton, while Sudanese have moved to Gresham on the east side. Other ethnic and national groups, such as Bantus from Somalia, have remained concentrated in northeast and north Portland, where housing costs are less expensive. Map 9-3 shows the residential patterns of all sub-Saharan Africans in the Portland urban area between 1990 and 2000.

Map 9-3. Sub-Saharan Africans in the Portland Metro Area, 1990 and 2000

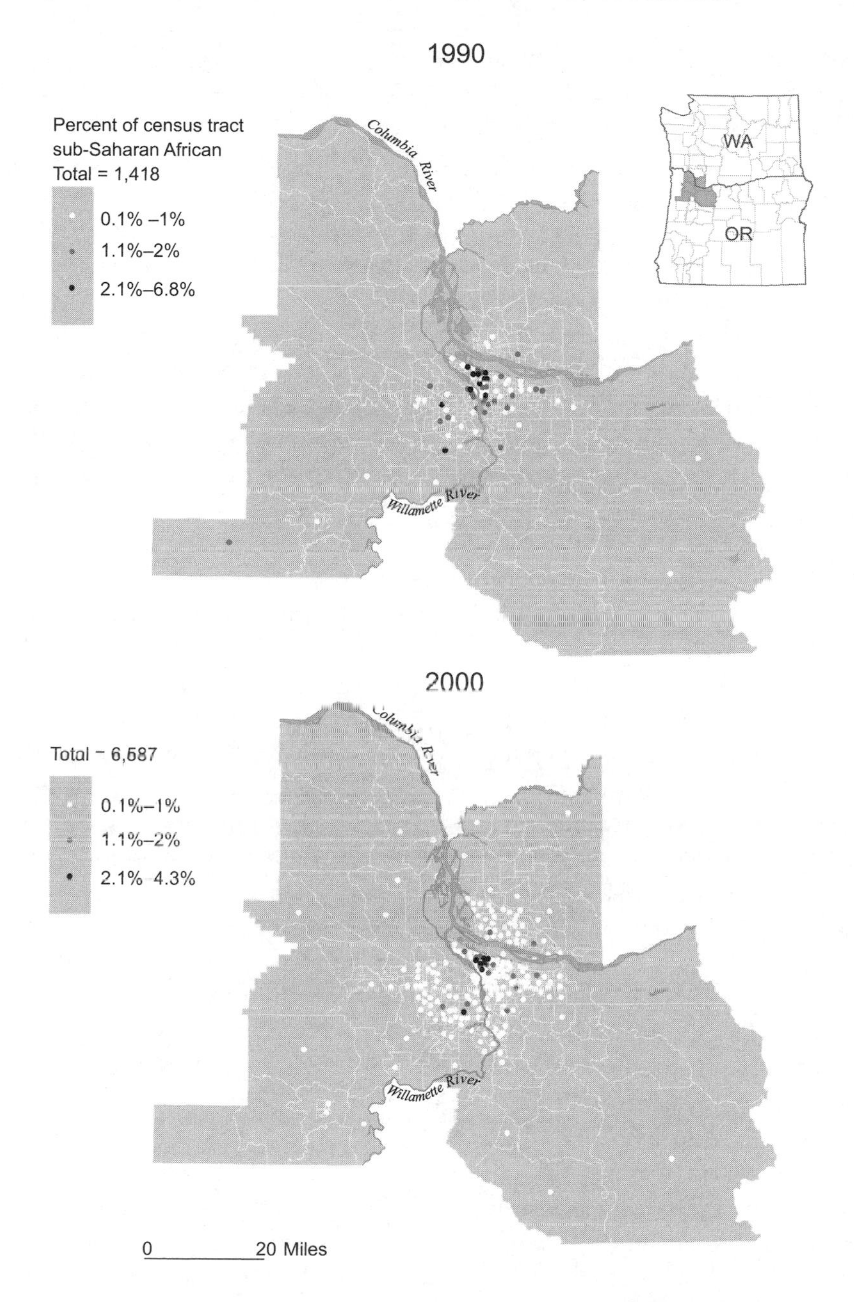

Source: U.S. Census Bureau, *Census of the Population 1990;* U.S. Census 2000, SF3; and TIGER/Line 1990 and 2000.

The Somalian Bantus are the most recent sub-Saharan refugees to arrive in the area. After years spent in refugee camps in east Africa, these former slaves of the Somali people have had a difficult time adjusting to life in the United States. "Since they have a tremendous need for personal space, are preliterate, and are only minimally connected to the Muslim faith, they can't connect to other African refugees here," says Michael Handley, volunteer program coordinator at IRCO in a personal interview with us in late 2005. These challenges, along with an inability to speak English and a lack of employment skills, have made it extremely difficult for most Bantu newcomers to adapt to Portland life.

This situation was exacerbated by a resettlement agency decision about where to house Bantu refugees. Because of limited affordable housing, and the perceived benefits of living near Somali neighbors, the agency, in collaboration with Somali community leaders, decided to house them in high-density apartments in suburban Beaverton. Not only did this mean that Bantus were a half hour or more away on public transportation from IRCO and other refugee support services, but it also placed them within the Somali community who had enslaved them in their homeland. Following this poor choice of residential location, Bantus were relocated to the Gateway District in east Portland, which is near social service, educational, and medical support (and far from most of the city's Somalian population).

African refugee groups who have larger populations and have resided in Portland the longest have begun to develop social and economic support networks. A decade after the first Somali refugees began to arrive, they founded the Somali Community Service Coalition of Oregon, with a community center in a shopping center on the edge of downtown Portland. The center helps refugees with questions about immigration, health care, education, jobs, and social services. Portland's Eritreans have opened two community centers, one of which is located in a converted house located in the heart of the city's largest African American neighborhood in northeast Portland. These community centers give Eritreans places to meet socially, discuss networking opportunities, offer cultural programs for their children, and vent frustrations in a safe and supportive atmosphere.

Hume and Hardwick found that two sets of social dynamics are at play for many African migrants in the Portland urban area: relationships between refugees from various African countries; and relationships between Africans and African Americans.[24] A well-organized group of African American Muslims in Portland is trying to foster ties between the city's African American community and new African refugees, according to Dapo Sobomehin, the African community development coordinator for

IRCO. In many other communities, it has been more common for Africans and African Americans to avoid living near each other or working together. An ongoing effort sponsored by Muslim groups, IRCO, and several neighborhood associations, however, is encouraging dialog between and among the two communities. Their goal is to provide a forum for discussion of commonalities and understandings of race, place, religion, and culture. In an ongoing effort to build solidarity between all of the African groups in the region, Sobomehin now heads the mainstream Sunni Muslim community in Portland, where more than half of the members were born in Africa and half are African American residents of the metropolitan area.

During the past year, with the support of local, state, and federal grants and donations, IRCO and the African community in Portland have successfully remodeled a historic house in southeast Portland to serve as a pan-African gathering place. This new "Africa House" is organizing a series of programs for youth and the elderly as well as celebrations of groups with widely differing backgrounds in Africa. The overarching goal of opening this facility is to foster a sense of solidarity among diverse African peoples now living in the Portland area.

Map 9-4 displays the residential patterns in 1990 and 2000 of the three largest refugee groups in the Portland area—Russians, Ukrainians, and Vietnamese. A comparison of this map with map 9-3 (showing sub-Saharan African refugee residential patterns during the same time period) provides summary evidence that refugees from Vietnam, Russia, Ukraine, and Africa are continuing to choose to settle in Portland's suburbs rather than in the downtown area. As we have seen, one of the reasons for this pattern is the relatively low cost of housing in the city's suburbs, compared with its gentrifying downtown. Ethnic social, political, and economic networks also continue to draw people from the same country of origin to suburban settlement nodes. The population growth and ongoing suburbanization of refugee groups focused upon in this chapter, as well as immigrants from Latin America and other parts of the world, are reshaping metropolitan Portland in ways few in the 1980s would have imagined.

Looking Back, Looking Ahead: Immigrant and Refugee Trajectories in the Portland Urban Area

This chapter has examined immigrant and refugee migration, settlement patterns, and landscape change in the Portland metropolitan area, with an emphasis on the area's ongoing refugee diaspora. As we have documented here, immigrants born in Mexico are currently the largest group of foreign-

Map 9-4. Russian, Ukranian, and Vietnamese Residential Patterns in the Portland Metro Area, 1990 and 2000

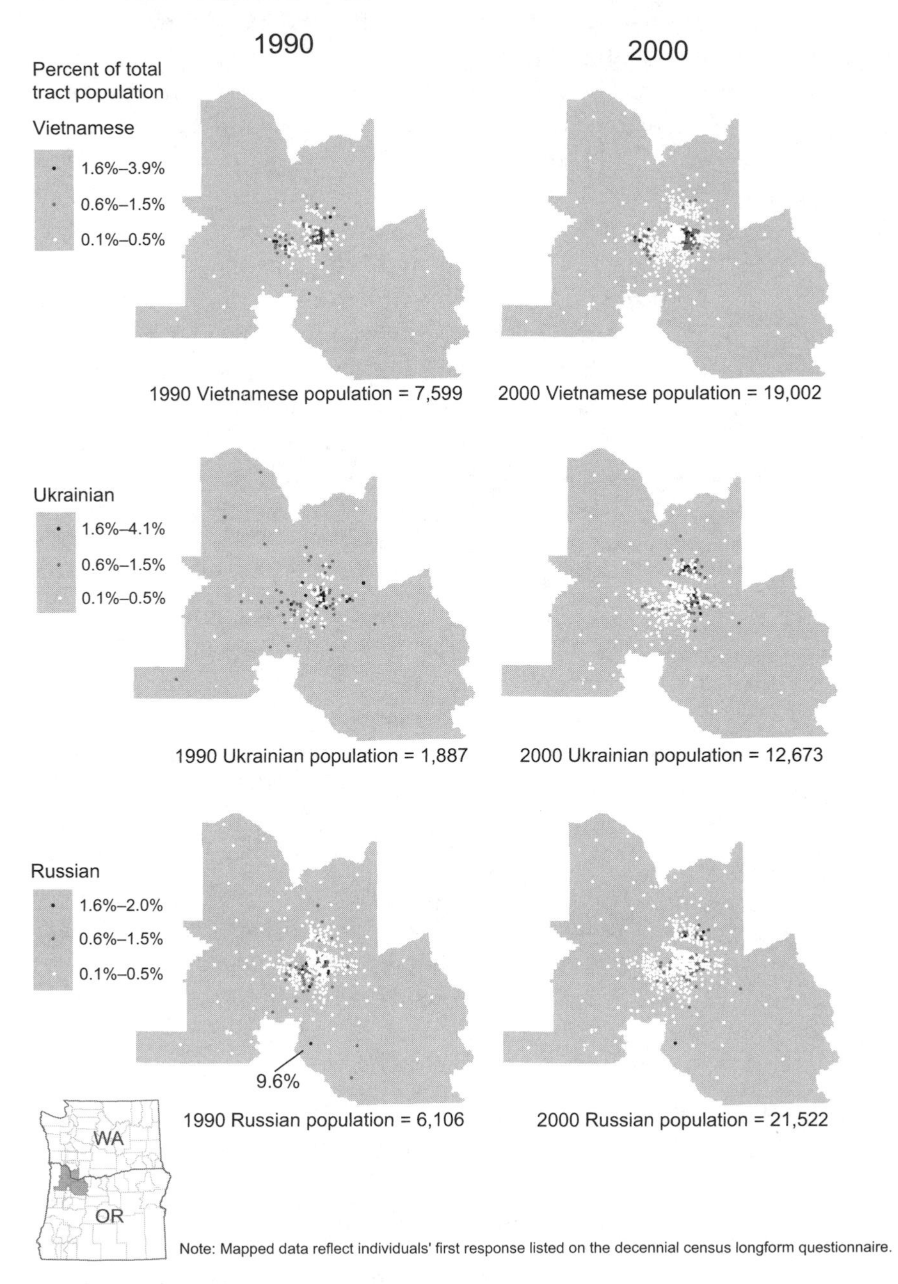

Source: U.S. Census Bureau, *Census of the Population 1990;* U.S. Census 2000, SF3; and TIGER/Line 1990 and 2000.

born residents in the city and its environs, with Russians, Ukrainians, and Vietnamese the largest groups of refugees.

What do these patterns and related processes say about larger questions of place and space, and the dynamics of changing urban landscapes in the Portland metropolitan area and other newly diversifying suburban gateway cities in the United States? And how might the findings of this chapter be theorized so they can be applied to the processes shaping Portland area suburbs and suburban landscapes in other metropolitan areas during the past two decades? To broaden the usefulness of the findings in this chapter, we build on discussions of one of the current sociospatial theories under discussion in the immigration literature—heterolocalism—in this concluding section of the chapter. As discussed in several other chapters of this book, heterolocalism, according to geographer Wilbur Zelinsky, refers to immigrant settlement patterns that are spatially dispersed across the urban landscape where residences, workplaces, and shopping districts are also widely separated.[25] Despite this lack of spatial propinquity common to certain immigrant communities in postmodern cities, he argues, immigrant groups are able to maintain strong community ties and their ethnic identities with cell phones, text messaging, e-mail, and other technological and transportation advances of the late twentieth century.

In an earlier publication, we argued that Zelinsky and Lee's heterolocal theory held rich possibilities for understanding the relationship between immigrant settlement and ethnic identity in many of the rapidly changing metropolitan areas in the United States.[26] Data compiled and analyzed for this chapter build on findings from this earlier study. Here, however, we focus more specifically on the overlapping processes shaping the patterns of new refugees and immigrants in suburban settlement nodes in the Portland area.

Map 9-4 reveals a surprising array of suburban settlement nodes for all three of these refugee groups (the three largest in the city) and provide evidence of a new form of heterolocalism emerging in the Portland urban area among the city's largest refugee groups. The 2000 census data established both a dramatic increase in the total numbers of refugees and an increase in each group's suburban dispersal. Both the dispersed spatial patterns and the refugee networks in Portland and its suburbs, therefore, are quite heterolocal (that is, widely dispersed across the urban landscape), but they also are centered on selected suburban nodes. As discussed earlier, this ongoing nodal heterolocalism is occurring in many eastside suburban Portland communities, including Gresham, Rockwood, and Happy Valley; westside communities such as Beaverton, Hillsboro, and Aloha; and north of the city's downtown in Vancouver, Washington.

This finding begs the final question in this chapter: What political, socioeconomic, and cultural processes are causing most Portland-area foreign-born migrants to congregate in heterolocal suburban nodes far from the city's downtown? At a political and economic level, the answer might seem obvious. Housing is more affordable and available in these particular suburbs than in Portland's downtown neighborhoods. And there can be no doubt that this economic factor has played a major role in shaping the residential decisions of refugee and immigrant resettlement agencies in Oregon, who continue to target certain areas for the resettlement of certain groups (such as Slavs in Clackamas County to the east; Africans in Beaverton to the west). Along with this economic situation, immigrant and refugee resettlement agencies also "do all we can to try to keep families and friends from home together in the same apartment building or the same neighborhood."[27]

Layered onto these interrelated economic and political processes have been the choices and personal preferences of families and individuals to remain close to one another in heterolocal suburban nodes. In the case of refugees from the former Soviet Union, common religious beliefs and values, spiritual and social networks, and church locations bind groups tightly together in religiously defined nodes. Vietnamese suburban clusters likewise depend on the power of ethnic networks along with the opportunity to open their own ethnic businesses in places such as Aloha, where Vietnamese stores, newspaper publishing headquarters, radio stations, and Buddhist temples are increasingly visible in the suburban landscape. Similarly some of the larger African refugee communities, such as Somalis, have changed the nature and membership patterns of mosques and religious and social gathering places in suburban communities such as Beaverton.

Other examples of the pull of suburbia for certain refugee and immigrant groups abound. Bosnian refugees with the economic clout to do so are choosing to live in all-Bosnian cul-de-sacs on the outer edge of Portland's eastside suburbs as well as north of the Columbia River in Vancouver; Mexicans are drawn to places like Rockwood and Gresham to the east and Hillsboro in the west in search of ethnic community ties, Latino shopping opportunities, and affordable housing. In Hillsboro, a Latino homebuying initiative has helped the area's mostly Mexican-born population become more involved in local politics. African groups such as the recently arrived Bantus from Somalia live near refugee social service agencies to be close to the support they need during their initial years in the Pacific Northwest. In sum, different processes shape the residential patterns of different groups in the Portland metroplex, but with one common result: the vast majority reside in the suburbs.

Rather than being a "re-emerging gateway city," Portland appears to have morphed into a "re-emerging suburban gateway city" since the 1990s. Another difference in the Portland story past and present is the relatively large number of refugees in the area's suburban population. Since newcomers who arrive with refugee status come under the wing of a well-organized system of resettlement decisionmakers at the local, regional, state, and national levels, heterolocal clustering may be more pronounced than in other cities and suburbs, where immigrants make up the bulk of the foreign-born populations.

As the ongoing cultural, social, economic, and political processes of change continue to reshape place and space in America's new suburban gateway cities, only one thing is clear: the evolution of these newly diverse suburban landscapes is certain to remain a rich terrain of fluidity and possibility for many years to come.

Notes

1. Matthew Stadler, "Dump Your Tired Suburban Notions," *Oregonian*, April 6, 2006, p. C4.
2. Audrey Singer, *The Rise of New Immigrant Gateways* (Brookings, 2004), pp. 1–35.
3. James Kuntsler, *The Geography of Nowhere. The Rise and Decline of America's Manmade Landscape* (New York: Touchstone, 1993).
4. Carl Abbott, *Greater Portland: Urban Life and Landscape in the Pacific Northwest* (University of Pennsylvania Press, 2001), p. 263.
5. Carl Abbott, "The Everyday City: Portland's Changing Neighborhoods," in *Portland's Changing Landscape,* edited by Larry W. Price (Portland State University, Department of Geography, 1985).
6. David Kaplan, "Travels into America's Future: Southern California and the Pacific Northwest," *Atlantic Monthly* 282 (1998): 37–61.
7. Abbott, *Greater Portland,* p. 100.
8. Jacob Blair, "Latino Settlement and Commercial Development in Rockwood," University of Oregon, Department of Geography, 2006.
9. Personal interview with Lee Po-Cha, director, Asian Family Center, Portland, October 16, 2004.
10. Audrey Singer and Jill H. Wilson, *From "There" to "Here": Refugee Resettlement in Metropolitan America* (Brookings, 2006).
11. Personal interview with Nehru Kanal, state refugee coordinator, Oregon Department of Human Resources, Salem, March 18, 2004.

12. For more comprehensive coverage of the migration experiences and networks of these refugee groups in the Pacific Northwest, see Susan W. Hardwick, "The Geography of Whiteness: Russian and Ukrainian 'Coalitions of Color' in the Pacific Northwest," in *Race, Ethnicity, and Place in a Changing America,* edited by John W. Frazier and Eugene I. Tettey-Fio (Binghamton, N.Y.: Global Academic Publishing, 2006); Susan W. Hardwick and James E. Meacham, "Heterolocalism, Networks of Ethnicity, and Refugee Communities in the Pacific Northwest: The Portland Story," *Professional Geographer* 57 (2005): 539–57; and Susan E. Hume and Susan W. Hardwick, "African, Russian, and Ukrainian Refugee Resettlement in Portland, Oregon," *Geographical Review* 95 (2005): 189–209.

13. Susan W. Hardwick, *Russian Refuge: Religion, Migration, and Settlement on the North American Pacific Rim* (University of Chicago Press, 1993).

14. Richard A. Morris, "Three Russian Groups in Oregon: A Comparison of Group Boundaries in a Pluralistic Environment," Ph.D. dissertation, Department of Anthropology, University of Oregon, 1981.

15. Mary Neuburger, "Exodus to Oregon: Russo-Ukrainian Pentecostals in the "Promised Land," Unpublished manuscript, Seattle, 1994.

16. Steve Suo and Angie Chuang, "Russians, Ukrainians Call Northwest Home," *Oregonian,* August 6, 2001, p. A1.

17. Personal interview with Victoria Libov, Immigrant and Refugee Community Organization, Portland, December 16, 2001.

18. Gosia Wozniacka, "Rooted in Real Estate," *Oregonian,* September 21, 2006, p. B1.

19. Personal interview with Lee-Po Cha, October 16, 2004.

20. Statistics gathered from the 5 percent sample of population of Census 2000 and recorded in the Integrated Public Use Microdata Series (IPUMS) population database showed that 35.8 percent of Aloha and Beaverton's Vietnamese residents worked in computer and peripheral equipment manufacturing; communications, audio, and video equipment manufacturing; or electronic component and product manufacturing. These industries employ significantly more Vietnamese that any other industry in these West Hills suburbs.

21. Kyle Walker, "Oregon's Ethnoburb: The Vietnamese in Beaverton," Honors College, University of Oregon, 2004, p. 42.

22. Personal interview with Lee Po-Cha, May 14, 2006.

23. Personal interview with Sokhum Tauch, executive director, Immigrant and Refugee Community Organization, Portland, August 19, 2005.

24. Hume and Hardwick, "African, Russian, and Ukrainian Refugee Resettlement in Portland, Oregon."

25. Wilbur Zelinsky, *The Enigma of Ethnicity* (University of Iowa Press, 2001); Wilbur Zelinsky and B. A. Lee, "Heterolocalism: An Alternative Model of the Sociospatial Behaviour of Immigrant Ethnic Communities," *International Journal of Population Geography* 4 (1998): 281–98.

26. Hardwick and Meacham. "Heterolocalism, Networks of Ethnicity, and Refugee Communities in the Pacific Northwest."

27. Personal interview with Victoria Libov, July 18, 2005.

PART IV

Pre-Emerging Gateways: Unexpected Change

10

Austin

Immigration and Transformation Deep in the Heart of Texas

EMILY SKOP and TARA BUENTELLO

In the past twenty years, Austin has become internationally known for its fast-growing technology based economy. The metropolis has consistently outperformed national growth levels and has been listed as a top city for local entrepreneurship and transnational business.[1] Austin has also repeatedly ranked high as a "creative center"—a place that promotes talent, technology, and tolerance.[2] Indeed, as both a university town and the capital of the state, Austin is often considered the one liberal bastion in Texas. These characteristics combine to make Austin stand out among other metropolises: it is known as the Live Music Capital, as the home of the South by Southwest (SxSW) music and film festival, as the headquarters of PBS's *Austin City Limits,* as one of the "most livable" cities in the United States, and as a place that likes to "keep things weird."

Although Austin is an economically booming "idea city" and home to young, restless, and tolerant members of the creative class, it is also a rapidly changing metropolitan area, largely the result of dramatic domestic and international migration. Indeed, the foreign-born population grew from 6.9 percent in 1990, to 13 percent in 2000, and to 14.2 percent by 2005. This chapter describes the changes from 1990 to 2005 in Austin's population, focusing particularly on the role of international migration in

The authors would like to sincerely thank Audrey Singer and Jill Wilson at the Brookings Institution for their dedication and determination to help make this chapter happen. Jill, especially, spent many hours working with us to ensure the accuracy of the IPUMS data and analysis.

transforming the character of the metropolitan area. Austin's immigrant population is diverse in education, income, and housing choice. Yet rapid change has led to the rise of some intense conflicts and the emergence of discriminatory local public policies that may ultimately impede the futures of recently arrived, poorer, nonwhite migrants.

Data and Methods

The data for this chapter come from the 1990 and 2000 U.S. Census Integrated Public Use Microdata Sample (IPUMS) 5 percent sample files, as well as from the 2005 U.S. Census *American Community Survey* 1 percent sample files.[3] The IPUMS is a particularly useful resource as it provides detailed information about sample households and their individuals, data that other secondary sources do not incorporate. These data include a housing unit record, which provides details on a variety of housing characteristics, and a person record, which specifies social, economic, and demographic attributes.

Despite the many benefits of the IPUMS, the data do have limitations. Confidentiality regulations prohibit the coding of counties after 1920 in the IPUMS. Census microdata, then, are based on Public Use Microdata Areas (PUMAs) rather than counties. Even though the U.S. Census Bureau defines Bastrop, Caldwell, Hays, Travis, and Williamson counties as composing the Austin metropolitan statistical area (MSA), our analysis is limited to three core counties: Hays, Travis, and Williamson, as this is how the Austin PUMAs are defined in IPUMS. These three counties capture 92.8 percent of the metropolitan total population and 95.9 percent of the metropolitan immigrant population. In addition to PUMS data, we extracted supplemental county-level data from the Census 2000 *American FactFinder* "County Fact Sheets" by racial-ethnic group (for native-born groups) and Census 2000 Sample File 3 (for immigrant groups).

Throughout this chapter, the terms "immigrant" and "foreign-born" are used interchangeably to refer to those individuals born outside the United States (or its territories) whose parents were not U.S. citizens. We obtained country-of-birth data for these individuals, and we used the top five countries of origin—Mexico, Vietnam, India, China, and Canada, according to 2000 IPUMS data for the Austin metropolitan area—for further analysis.

We also compare outcomes for native-born racial-ethnic groups. We obtained these data using the RACESING variable from IPUMS, which assigns one race to each individual. This is important for comparing race data across years because 2000 was the first year in which individuals could choose more than one race when filling out their census form. The

RACESING variable assigns multirace individuals from 2000 and 2005 to the single racial category "deemed most likely, depending on the individual's age, sex, Hispanic origin, region and urbanization level of residence, and the racial diversity of their local area."[4] This variable allows for more accurate comparisons with the 1990 data.

The native-born ethnic group categories are exclusive, in that all race categories (white, black, Asian, and other) are for non-Hispanics, and the Hispanic category represents all individuals, regardless of race, who identified as being of Hispanic or Latino origin. The Asian category includes Pacific Islanders, and the "other" category includes American Indians, Alaskan Natives, and any other race not delineated in the above categories.

We excluded persons living in group quarters from analysis because the procedures for enumerating these residents and for processing the information collected from them have not been well controlled or carefully executed.[5] These persons include residents of dormitories, prisons, and other institutions. In 2000 fewer than 3 percent of the population of the three-county area lived in group quarters. Of these, 4.5 percent were foreign-born, representing 1 percent of the metropolitan immigrant population.

All household-level variables in our analysis (median household income, household size, crowding, mortgage status, and homeownership) are based on the age and racial-ethnic classification of the householder. At the same time, all homeownership analysis is limited to persons age twenty-five and older. We excluded persons under age sixteen, in addition to those in military occupations and persons who had not worked in the previous five years, from classification by occupational status. Other data caveats are noted in the accompanying tables.

Composition of the Local Population

The population of Austin is growing quickly. Net domestic migration into the area has increased the total population by nearly 2 percent a year over the past two decades, which marks Austin as one of the top ten domestic migrant magnets in the country, according to William Frey, a demographer at the Brookings Institution. The vast majority of the growth occurred between 1995 and 2000, expanding more than 9 percent, as largely young, college-educated, white Americans arrived in Austin to take advantage of strong job markets and diverse employment opportunities.[6]

International migration to Austin is noteworthy as well. Although fewer than 49,000 foreign-born lived in the metropolitan area in 1990, by 2005 Austin was home to more than 186,000 foreign-born, a 270 percent increase. The area averaged a net increase of nearly 10,000 foreign-born

Table 10-1. Composition of the Austin Metropolitan Area Population, 1990, 2000, and 2005[a]

	1990		2000		2005	
Group	*Number*	*Percent*	*Number*	*Percent*	*Number*	*Percent*
Native-born white	464,589	66.9	681,521	60.1	745,454	56.9
Native-born Hispanic	111,335	16.0	208,390	18.4	267,092	20.4
Native-born black	64,980	9.4	80,556	7.1	84,040	6.4
Native-born Asian	3,259	0.5	11,879	1.1	17,284	1.3
Native-born other race	2,795	0.4	3,998	0.4	10,869	0.8
Foreign-born Mexican	19,313	2.8	80,591	7.1	95,532	7.3
Foreign-born Indian	1,770	0.3	6,730	0.6	7,134	0.5
Foreign-born Vietnamese	2,253	0.3	6,777	0.6	6,909	0.5
Foreign-born Chinese	939	0.1	4,043	0.4	5,621	0.4
Foreign-born Canadian	1,255	0.2	3,127	0.3	3,194	0.2
Foreign-born other	22,512	3.2	46,162	4.1	68,105	5.2
Total population	695,000	100.0	1,133,774	100.0	1,311,234	100.0

Source: Authors' calculations using 5 percent PUMS data from 1990 and 2000 and 1 percent PUMS data from 2005 (www.ipums.org).

a. Group-quarters population was removed from the analysis. The METAREA variable is used to delineate Austin metro (Hays, Travis, and Williamson counties only).

persons a year during the 1990s. More than 74 percent of the Austin metropolitan area's foreign-born population arrived after 1990.

These trends place Austin squarely in the category of a pre-emerging immigrant gateway, according to this book's typology.[7] Table 10-1 illustrates how quickly Austin's population has changed. Even though the majority of residents in Austin continue to be native-born, non-Hispanic whites, their percentage of the total population has decreased significantly, to 56.9 percent in 2005, down from 66.9 percent in 1990. The next largest group, Hispanics born in the United States, has increased rapidly, especially since 1990. Currently, one in five residents in Austin is a U.S.-born Hispanic, up from 16 percent in 1990.

Meanwhile in 2005 Mexican immigrants became the third-largest group, composing 7.3 percent of the total population, supplanting U.S.-born blacks, who are now the fourth-largest population group in Austin. Demographers predict that the metropolitan area will continue to lose black residents, and that by 2015 the Asian population (including both native- and foreign-born) will outnumber the U.S.-born black population.[8]

The increase in the Asian population over the past twenty-five years is noteworthy. Austin is by no means a prime magnet for Asian immigration, but the Asian population's growth is considerably higher in the Austin metro area than the national average.[9] The majority of this growth stems from Vietnamese, Indian, and Chinese immigrants. Although each of these groups represents less than 1 percent of the total population, the absolute numbers of immigrants from Vietnam, India, and China have risen from 4,962 in 1990 to 19,664 in 2005, a nearly 300 percent increase. Recent estimates from the 2005 American Community Survey indicate that the Korean immigrant population has also sharply increased. Although not shown in table 10-1, there are now nearly as many Koreans living in the metropolitan area as there are Vietnamese. Many of these foreign-born Asians are enrolled as students in undergraduate, graduate, or professional schools, which is important in understanding the particular socioeconomic characteristics of this immigrant population (for example, 12 percent of the foreign-born population from India was enrolled in undergraduate, graduate, or professional school in 2000). The increase in the native-born Asian population has also been significant. Now making up 1.3 percent of Austin's total population, the number of U.S.-born Asians grew from 3,259 in 1990 to 17,284 in 2005, an increase of 430 percent (see table 10-1). Interestingly, a large proportion of these native-born Asians (21 percent in 2000) are also enrolled as students in undergraduate, graduate, or professional schools, which provides an important clue when one interprets the socioeconomic status of this group compared to other native-born groups.

Figure 10-1 provides further evidence that the vast majority of immigrants arrived in the United States between 1980 and 2000. Of course, caution is in order given that the data include only those immigrants residing in Austin at the time of the 2000 U.S. census (other immigrants may have moved in, moved out, or died before or since the sample was taken). Although Mexican immigrants have been coming into the Austin area for several years, more than one-half of Mexican immigrants living in Austin in 2000 arrived in the United States after 1990. This is also true of Indian and Chinese newcomers; nearly 64 percent of both Indian and Chinese immigrants in 2000 arrived in the United States after 1990. At the same time, the Vietnamese, many of whom came to the United States as refugees, constitute a special population in Austin. Nearly 21 percent of those living in Austin in 2000 arrived in the area between 1970 and 1979 (the ten-year period during and following the Vietnam War); the rest arrived after 1980 as either secondary migrants from other parts of the United States (especially the Gulf region of Texas) or through family reunification programs.

That a slight majority of Chinese, Indian, Mexican, and Vietnamese immigrants in 1990 were male is another indicator of how recent immigration

Figure 10-1. Period of Entry to Austin Metropolitan Area for Top Five Immigrant Countries of Birth, 2000

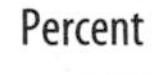

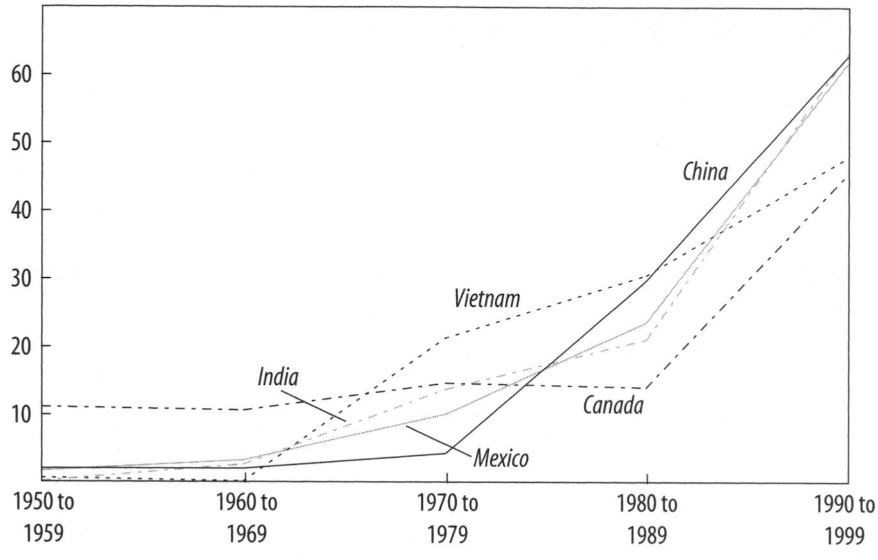

Source: Authors' calculations from 2000 Census using 5 percent PUMS data (www.ipums.org).

from these countries to Austin has been (table 10-2). Single males are often first to arrive, attracted by jobs.[10] In the case of the Vietnamese, the male-female percentages are fairly equal, which is quite common among refugee flows, since refugees often arrive in families.[11] By 2000 the percentage of males among the foreign-born population from Mexico and India in particular remained relatively high, indicating the important role of specific labor demands in community composition. The role of the labor market will also become evident later in this chapter. Mexican men tend to take the low-skill service jobs, while Indian males are recruited to fill white-collar, high-tech positions.

In summary, although small numbers of immigrants, especially from Mexico, have been living in Austin throughout the twentieth century, the 1990s saw major growth in the foreign-born.[12] Mexican immigrants are the most significant contributors in the ever-shifting social fabric in Austin. When combined with U.S.-born Hispanics, they compose 27.7 percent of Austin's population. What is also apparent is that Asians represent a newly emerging, and noteworthy, group in the metropolis.

Table 10-2. Percent Male among Top Foreign-Born Populations in the Austin Metropolitan Area, 1990 and 2000[a]
Percent male

Year	*Mexican*	*Vietnamese*	*Indian*	*Chinese*	*Canadian*
1990	57.5	54.1	59.8	51.2	39.1
2000	58.9	52.6	58.4	49.5	55.6

Source: Authors' calculations using 1990 and 2000 5 percent PUMS data (www.ipums.org).

a. Group-quarters population was removed from the analysis. The METAREA variable is used to delineate Austin metro (Hays, Travis, and Williamson counties only).

Socioeconomic Status of Austin's Immigrant Population

Austin's robust labor market is the major force attracting most immigrants. Indeed, Austin's reputation as a top creative center has attracted immigrants who vary considerably in education levels, English proficiency, and income. Much of this variation has less to do with the immigrants themselves and is more a function of recent U.S. immigration policies and the intrinsic labor demands of the globalizing economy, which requires a flexible labor force to fill specific occupational voids. Thus, less-educated, unskilled, and poorer Mexican migrants have been recruited to fill the lowest and least desirable jobs while the large majority of migrants from India and China arrive with high levels of education, professional training, entrepreneurial skills, or financial resources needed in the burgeoning creative-based economy.

As table 10-3 indicates, this dualism is readily apparent. Among Mexican immigrants, 67.2 percent of those twenty-five and older have not graduated from high school. At the other extreme are Canadian, Chinese, and Indian immigrants, with only 1.8 percent, 6 percent, and 8.1 percent of each population, respectively, lacking a high school diploma. At the same time, only 6.8 percent of Mexican immigrants are college graduates, in stark contrast to Indian immigrants, 83 percent of whom have college degrees. More than three-quarters of Chinese immigrants and more than one-half of Canadian immigrants are college graduates, which are considerably higher proportions than the 46.4 percent of U.S.-born whites in Austin (although even this percentage is noteworthy, given that nationally, only 27 percent of U.S.-born whites have a bachelor's degree or higher). Foreign-born Vietnamese represent a special case, given that many arrived in Austin as refugees, and with more wide-ranging socioeconomic characteristics. Just over one in five (21.6 percent) lack a high-school diploma, while 31.9 percent had a bachelor's degree or higher.

Table 10-3. Socioeconomic Indicators for the Austin Metropolitan Area, 2000[a]

	Native-born					*Foreign-born*					
Indicator	*White*	*Hispanic*	*Black*	*Asian*	*Other race*	*Mexican*	*Indian*	*Viet-namese*	*Chinese*	*Can-adian*	*Total popu-lation*
Educational attainment [b]											
Percent without a high school diploma	5.3	27.6	18.3	6.3	11.2	67.2	8.1	21.6	6.0	1.8	14.3
Percent with a BA or higher	46.4	19.6	23.0	53.9	34.5	6.8	83.0	31.9	78.1	58.7	38.8
English ability[c]											
Speaks English only	95.5	37.1	95.9	51.8	90.1	4.9	13.0	6.7	4.1	76.9	74.1
Speaks English well or very well	3.7	57.9	3.9	45.3	9.4	41.0	79.2	69.3	78.3	21.5	19.9
Speaks English not well or not at all	0.4	5.0	0.2	2.9	0.5	54.0	7.6	24.0	17.7	1.5	6.0
Socioeconomic status											
Median household income ($1,000s) in 1999	55.0	40.8	37.7	30.0	45.0	34.4	65.1	60.4	46.0	65.6	49.8
Mean household size (persons per household)	2.3	2.9	2.7	2.0	2.3	4.4	2.7	3.3	2.4	2.3	2.6
Percent of individuals living in poverty	6.8	15.0	14.5	18.4[d]	7.7	23.0	13.0[d]	7.0	7.7	5.5	10.4

Source: Authors' calculations using 2000 5 percent PUMS data (www.ipums.org).

a. Group-quarters population was removed from the analysis. The METAREA variable is used to delineate Austin metro (Travis, Hays, and Williamson counties only).

b. For the population ages twenty-five and over.

c. For the population ages five and over.

d. When the population enrolled in universities is excluded, the native-born Asian poverty rate drops to 6.8 percent and the foreign-born Indian poverty rate drops to 8.9 percent.

Another important indicator of the types of skills immigrants possess is English proficiency. We collapsed the four response options to the census question "How well does this person speak English?" into two categories: 1) not at all, and not well; and 2) well, and very well.[13] With the exception of Mexican immigrants, nearly two-thirds of every immigrant group reports being able to speak English at least well (see table 10-3). Yet 54 percent of Mexican immigrants do not speak English well or at all. This is an extreme example of Mexican immigrant disadvantage relative to other groups. The second-highest percentage who cannot speak English well or at all is the Vietnamese, at 24.0 percent. On the other end of the continuum, 76.9 percent of Canadians speak only English, and of those whose primary language is not English, 21.5 percent consider themselves able to speak English well or very well. Many Indian immigrants also have a mastery of the

English language. Thirteen percent of Indian immigrants speak only English, and another 79.2 percent speak English well or very well—not surprising given that English is an official language in India, and many Indian immigrants attended schools where English was a required course.[14]

Of course, household income is also important to socioeconomic integration. Mexican immigrant households in Austin fare less well than other immigrant households. The median total household income in Austin was $49,800 in 1999. Mexican immigrant households earn only a median income of $34,400 a year, while the median for Indian and Canadian immigrant households is $65,100 and $65,600, respectively, the highest of any immigrant group and also higher than U.S.-born whites in Austin, whose median household income is $55,000 in 1999 (see table 10-3).

Clearly, Mexican immigrants are arriving in Austin under circumstances much different from those facing other immigrant groups. Twenty-three percent of Mexican immigrants lived below the poverty threshold in 2000 (see table 10-3). Canadian, Chinese, and Vietnamese immigrants all have poverty rates below the average rate (10.4 percent) for Austin overall. Indian immigrants represent a unique case; individual poverty rates are higher largely because of the high percentage of both undergraduate, graduate, and professional students, who often have incomes below official poverty thresholds.[15] Excluding these students in poverty calculations drops the poverty rate among Indian households to 8.9 percent.

Disparities between Mexicans and other immigrant groups are likely to have repercussions not only for the immigrants themselves but also for their children. Indeed, when the 21 percent of native-born Asian undergraduate, graduate, and professional students are excluded from the analysis, the inequality of those living in poverty among U.S.-born Hispanics and U.S.-born Asians indicates that assimilation is likely to be uneven for the second generation.[16] The poverty rate for native-born Asians drops to 6.8 percent when enrolled students are excluded, well below the 23 percent of native-born Mexicans living in poverty in Austin in 2000.

Nonetheless, the burgeoning knowledge economy in Austin has kept unemployment low, even during the slow growth period of the early 2000s. As a result, both unskilled and skilled Latino and Asian newcomers have found a variety of jobs. The rise of high-tech industries in the United States and the function of science and technology as sources of growth and productivity have generated a demand for highly skilled laborers, creative and risk-taking entrepreneurs, and capital-rich investors.[17] Many of these workers arrive from overseas, as the need for employees trained in specialty occupations has often outstripped the current supply among native-born

Figure 10-2. Occupational Class of Workers Ages Sixteen and Over in the Austin Metropolitan Area, 2000

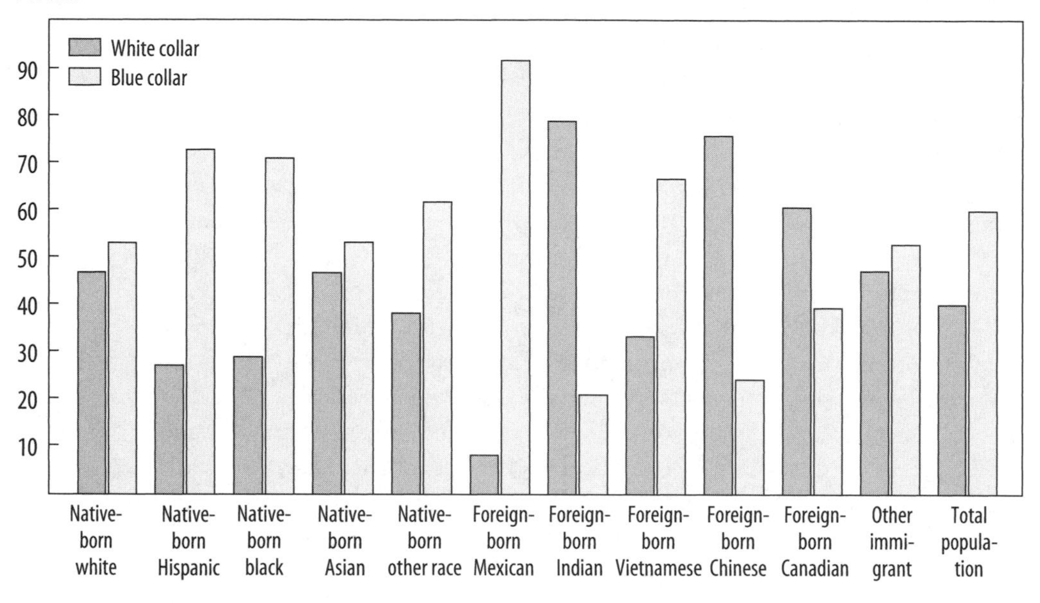

Source: Authors' calculations from 2000 Census using 5 percent PUMS data (www.ipums.org).

workers. The increase in high-level professionals also opens up a huge demand for service workers such as cashiers, food preparers, health aides, and clerical or administrative support. The boom in the economy means a rise in construction, roadwork, and manufacturing, which creates even more demand for cheap, unskilled labor.

Thus, immigrants in Austin are being funneled into different kinds of employment, as figure 10-2 suggests (see also Oberle and Li on Phoenix and Fennelly and Orfield on the Twin Cities in this volume). In this analysis, white-collar workers include those in management and professional occupations, while blue-collar workers include those in service, sales and office, construction, extraction, maintenance, production, and transportation and material moving occupations. Overall, Mexican immigrants are least likely to be employed in white-collar jobs (8.3 percent), with the remaining 91.7 percent working in blue-collar occupations. Indeed, Mexican immigrants have the highest percentage of blue-collar workers among all groups. Two-thirds of Vietnamese immigrants work in blue-collar jobs.

By contrast, the other immigrant groups are more concentrated in the better-paying, more prestigious white-collar jobs. For example, 78.8 percent of Indians, 75.7 percent of Chinese, and 60.6 percent of Canadian immigrants are white-collar workers.

Patterns of Immigrant Settlement

The Austin metropolitan statistical area encompasses five counties: Travis in the center, bracketed by Williamson to the north, Hays to the southwest, and Bastrop and Caldwell to the southeast (although as stated previously for data consistency purposes, only Travis, Williamson, and Hays are included in most of this chapter's analysis). Because the entire metro area includes more that 4,200 square miles, understanding the geography of immigrant settlement patterns can be quite complex, although there are some striking points. More "classic" ethnic enclaves in the downtown (some of which are more than one hundred years old) continue to figure prominently in immigrant settlement in Austin, but these sites are now being threatened by urban revitalization and smart growth policies, which have led to increased gentrification in the downtown area. As a result, rapidly changing suburbs are becoming new sites of diversity and immigrant settlement.

In 2000, 71 percent of the foreign-born population lived in the city of Austin, while the remaining 29 percent resided outside city limits in other parts of the metro area (map 10-1). This divide at first might seem surprising given the overall trend toward suburbanization among immigrants nationwide. However, the city of Austin is different.[18] Austin city limits cover much more land area than is typical of other metropolitan areas. The city of Austin covers more than 250 square miles, extending largely north and south along the I-35 corridor (Washington, for example, covers only 61 square miles, and Atlanta covers 131 square miles). This pattern is largely the result of massive annexation by the city, especially in the mid-1990s, when dramatic population increase combined with a new "smart growth" initiative to change urban planning policies. These processes pushed city planners to extend municipal services, regulations, voting privileges, and taxing authority to new territory in the name of sustainability and environmental protection. As a result, much of the land within Travis County (along with a few developed areas in Hays and Williamson counties) now falls under the jurisdiction of the city.

Because of this unique urban geography, it is difficult to interpret statistics on residential patterns of various immigrant and racial-ethnic groups

Map 10-1. Foreign-Born Population in the Austin Metropolitan Area, by Census Tract, 2000

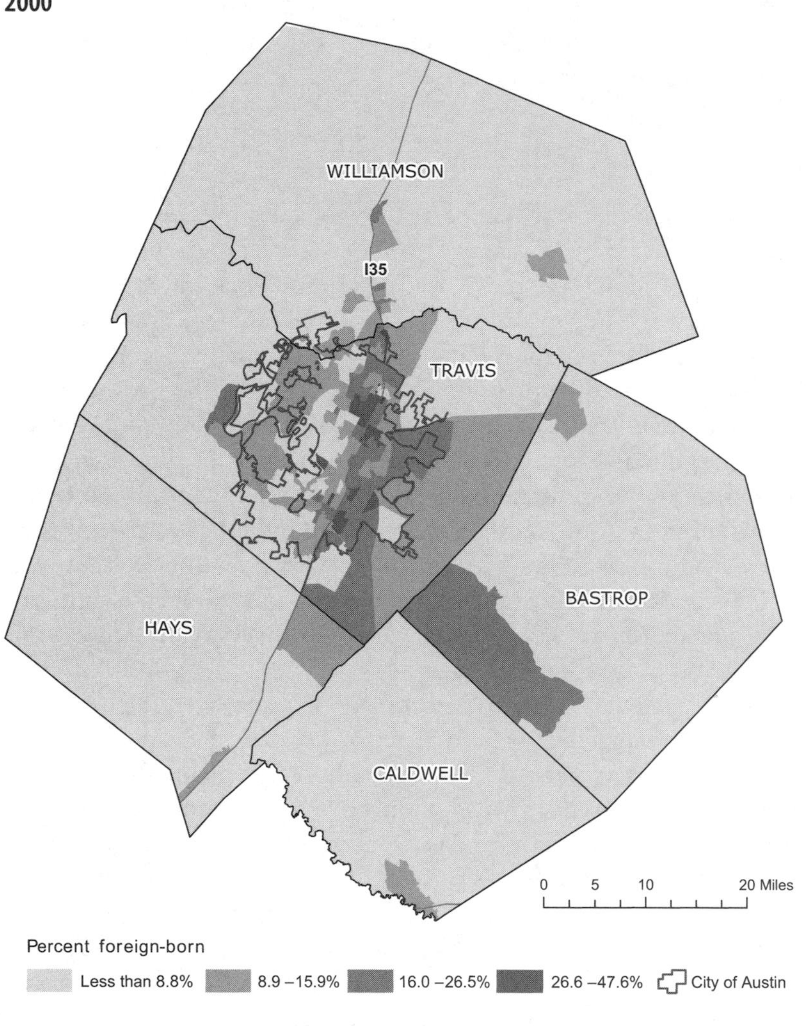

Source: U.S. Census Bureau, *Census of the Population 2000,* SF3.

using conventional census categories. For example, the "metro" variable in IPUMS, which indicates whether the housing unit is within a metropolitan area's central city (or cities), provides a very skewed interpretation of Austin's geography, since central city boundaries are so expansive. This becomes readily apparent in table 10-4, which shows the geographic distribution of both native- and foreign-born groups by county within the Austin MSA. Table 10-4 is based on summary statistics from the *American*

Table 10-4. Geographic Distribution of Native- and Foreign-Born, by County in the Austin Metropolitan Area, 2000[a]

	Native-born				*Foreign-born*					
County	*White*	*Hispanic*	*Black*	*Asian*	*Mexican*	*Indian*	*Vietnamese*	*Chinese*	*Canadian*	*Total population*
Travis	64.6	72.2	82.3	83.2	85.3	83.0	86.6	83.5	78.6	70.0
Williamson	26.3	15.9	13.8	15.1	10.3	15.9	12.1	13.9	18.8	21.6
Hays	9.1	11.9	3.9	1.7	4.4	1.1	1.2	2.7	2.7	8.4
Total	100.0	100.0	100.0	100.0	100.0	100.0	100.0	100.0	100.0	100.0

Source: U.S. Census Bureau, *American FactFinder County Fact Sheets* by race-ethnic group (for native-born groups) and Census 2000, SF3 (for immigrant groups).

a. The Austin Metropolitan Statistical Area includes two counties, Bastrop and Caldwell, in addition to the three shown above. However, these counties are not included here to maintain consistency with the rest of the analysis, which is limited to the three core counties.

FactFinder website. Most people live in Travis County, although 26.3 percent of the metro's native-born white population lives in Williamson County, which points to the increasing role of urban sprawl and suburbanization in this area. Nearly three-fourths (72.2 percent) of native-born Hispanics, 82.3 percent of native-born blacks, 83.2 percent of native-born Asians, and the vast majority of foreign-born Mexicans (85.3 percent), Vietnamese (86.6 percent), Indians (83.0 percent), Chinese (83.5 percent), and Canadians (78.6 percent), live in Travis County.

These statistics, however, fail to reflect the urban or suburban form of Austin's neighborhoods. Nor do the conventional categories used by the U.S. census to designate central cities and suburbs work in the Austin context, again because the city limits are so vast (encompassing many neighborhoods that by most measures would be considered suburban), while the "outside central city" category covers vast, suburban and quasi-suburban areas in surrounding counties. Even the conventional inner-ring versus outer-ring classifications do not work because highways and ring roads, which typically circle and divide the urban core from the suburban periphery, do not exist in Austin.

Nonetheless, some important immigrant settlement trends are occurring in Austin. For many, especially native- and foreign-born Hispanics (most of whom are Mexican American and Mexican), the East Austin enclave (located just east of downtown) is home, largely the result of external factors imposed by those with more power.[19] Despite being on "the wrong side" of the city, or more likely because of this, the East Austin enclave has become a place of pride for Hispanic residents. Institutions such as Our

Lady of Guadalupe Church, restaurants such as Juan in a Million, and the A. B. Cantu Pan-American Recreation Center, have made the east side home. In East Austin, Spanish-speaking residents visit restaurants, cantinas, and mobile food vendors that cater to them. They choose from various Spanish-language newspapers and radio stations. They mix with people from back home in any number of informal social clubs. Local bus companies offer service to destinations throughout Mexico, and public art and murals provide venues to embellish the barrio landscape and also serve as vehicles for political and social expression.[20] Residents draw on these internal resources and networks to create protected niches in which immigrant entrepreneurs find much success (even as certain business and community leaders sometimes exploit fellow newcomers by providing low wages, minimal benefits, and few opportunities for advancement).

Although the east side has been a traditional Mexican enclave, with a majority-minority resident population, recent pressures are changing that.[21] From 1990 to 2000 the non-Hispanic white population in East Austin increased by 31 percent, while the Hispanic population increased by only 16 percent.[22] Thus, a community that has traditionally been majority Mexican is now becoming increasingly white. Although the absolute number of white residents is still small, their increasing presence is likely to continue given the growing gentrification trends begun in the mid-1990s.

Gentrification on the east side began in the mid-1990s largely because of the workings of local government and developers to revitalize the downtown and encourage environmentally friendly smart-growth policies.[23] Increasingly, as city planners designate residential areas of East Austin as part of a desired development zone, the area is undergoing marked change.[24] To many residents, as the accompanying photograph attests, this is unfortunate because the east side enclave has generally been a key site and source of strength for Mexicans at the bottom of the economic hierarchy, especially for those working their way up to equality and integration in Austin.

As the gentrification process accelerates, many current—and most potential—Mexican homeowners are being squeezed out of the property market in the East Austin enclave. Mexicans (both native- and foreign-born) are beginning to move (or are being forced) to lower-density suburbs outside the downtown area, many to suburbs southwest of the city. At the same time, many Mexicans seek out apartments and single-family residences in the suburbs because these areas provide a variety of jobs and housing. Lower-rent apartments in particular allow recent immigrants from Mexico to share living quarters with others.[25] These kinds of high-density living arrangements are quite common and are the result of the

The process of gentrification in East Austin has resulted in a tremendous amount of resistance from local residents, who feel disenfranchised and disempowered by the change occurring in their neighborhood. Around 2005, these spray-painted signs appeared overnight in visible spots throughout the neighborhood.

"immigrant infill" that is taking place in the metropolis (see also Susan Hardwick's chapter on suburbanization in this volume). At the same time, some of the recent newcomers do not consider the often crowded and run-down neighborhoods in the central city their ideal place to live, and so they move to suburban neighborhoods where they can find decent housing, nicer neighborhoods, and better schools.[26]

Although many, including both native- and foreign-born Hispanics and Vietnamese immigrants, are finding homes in more affordable subdivisions, some recent immigrants, especially those from India and China, have the financial resources to afford the neighborhoods that offer the best and newest housing, the highest-performing schools, and superior living conditions and public amenities.[27]

Meanwhile, informal housing subdivisions have begun to appear primarily in sparsely populated, unincorporated areas outside the city limits but still within the metropolitan area.[28] Most of these subdivisions have emerged in the south and southeast areas, particularly in Bastrop and Caldwell counties. They are distinct from other more formal suburban subdivisions because of their low density, larger individual lots, idiosyncratic dwellings, irregular placement on lots, and unpaved streets.[29] These settlements may best be described as commuter "pockets" within largely rural areas, since most residents living in these communities commute to Austin. At the same time, these homestead subdivisions are usually not quite poor, nor are they necessarily dominated by one racial or ethnic group, although Hispanics, especially second-generation households, sometimes compose more than 70 percent of residents in certain informal settlements, including mobile home and trailer parks.[30] These informal housing arrangements are an important part of Austin's emerging landscape, given that they provide a key portal through which homeowners with fewer resources break into the property market.

The suburbs have traditionally served as both symbolic and material spaces of whiteness, yet more suburban neighborhoods throughout Austin are becoming increasingly multiracial, multiethnic, multilingual, multicultural, and multinational. Immigrants have begun to claim space in suburban Austin, establishing religious institutions, retail outlets, and other services. Strip malls of immigrant-owned stores and restaurants have developed along main thoroughfares, and more are being built every year. Latino, Vietnamese, Chinese, and Indian bakeries, grocery stores, clothing stores, travel agencies, video stores, and nail shops have emerged. Indeed, these developments have become the most visible symbols of the increasing numbers and economic clout of recent immigrants in Austin.

Homeownership, Quality of Housing, and Affordability

Owning a home is widely regarded as the keystone to achieving American middle-class status and is often treated as a chief indicator of minority and immigrant groups' levels of social integration. Of course, not everyone (poor or not) aspires to homeownership, and others might be sending remittances "back home" as an alternative, more transnational, form of property acquisition.[31] Nonetheless, homeownership is a principal source of wealth and financial security and thus has enormous consequences for Austin's residents. Although homeownership does indeed translate into increasing rewards and many returns for some, it also means mounting debt and few benefits for others.[32]

Table 10-5 shows the percentage of persons age twenty-five or older in each population group who own their own homes. Substantial numbers of

Table 10-5. Homeownership Rates for Population Groups in the Austin Metroplitan Area, 2000[a]

	Native-born					*Foreign-born*					
Category	*White*	*Hispanic*	*Black*	*Asian*	*Other race*	*Mexican*	*Indian*	*Viet-namese*	*Chinese*	*Can-adian*	*Total popu-lation*
Share who own homes	68.3	55.5	49.7	45.1	48.7	43.0	45.9	65.3	43.9	59.9	62.8
Of those											
Share who own free and clear	25.1	24.5	22.9	10.5	22.5	27.6	3.7	5.7	12.0	16.2	24.3
Share who own with mortgage or loan	74.2	74.1	75.7	89.4	76.1	63.8	96.4	86.0	86.1	83.8	74.5
Share with contract to purchase	0.7	1.4	1.4	0	1.4	8.6	0.0	8.3	2.0	0.0	1.2

Source: Authors' calculations from 2000 5 percent PUMS data (www.ipums.org).

a. Data are for persons ages twenty-five and over. Group-quarters population has been removed from the analysis. The METAREA variable is used to delineate Austin metro (Travis, Hays, and Williamson counties only).

the foreign-born own their own homes: 65.3 percent of Vietnamese, 59.9 percent of Canadians, 45.9 percent of Indians, 43.9 percent of Chinese, and 43 percent of Mexican immigrants. The rate of homeownership for Austin as a whole is 62.8 percent. Given that most of these immigrants only recently arrived in Austin, these comparatively high levels point to the critical role of human (education and income) and social (personal and business networks and organizational ties) capital in homeownership. At the same time, as refugees, the Vietnamese have access to a variety of government programs (including financial assistance and educational programs), which may facilitate homeownership for a group otherwise lacking resources. It is also noteworthy that similar percentages of Mexican immigrants and more wealthy Indian and Chinese newcomers are homeowners, considering that nationwide only 38.4 percent of Mexican immigrants own their own homes.[33] These relatively high homeownership rates are surprising given the lower-than-average median household incomes, and higher-than-average poverty rates characteristic of this group.

Even more interesting, of those who do own homes, the percentage of Mexican homeowners who own their homes "free and clear" (27.6 percent), meaning their mortgages or loans are paid in full, is slightly above the overall population in Austin (24.3 percent). In fact, Mexican immigrants have the highest percentage of free and clear ownership among all immigrant groups. In contrast, fewer than 3.7 percent of Indian or 5.7 percent of Vietnamese homeowners have fully paid for their homes.

There are several potential reasons why Mexican immigrants apparently do well in the housing market. The most obvious is because Mexican immigrants have been in Austin, on average, the longest of any foreign-born group, and as a result they have had more time to purchase and build equity in their homes. Another potential reason that Mexican immigrants vary from other foreign-born groups is their choice of housing—the "bungalow-style" homes that new, young, wealthy, and highly educated transplants now find so appealing.[34] Although not shown here, results based on our calculations of IPUMS data indicate that Mexican immigrant homeowners have the lowest median home values and that more Mexican immigrants than any other group have homes worth 50 percent or less of the citywide median house value. At the same time, Mexican immigrants have the smallest homes of all groups in Austin, the highest numbers of families per household, and the highest numbers of persons per bedroom. In fact, Mexicans are the only population group, besides Vietnamese, with an average of less than one room for each person living in the house. Although preference might, in part, explain the variability, restrictions on housing supply, housing affordability, low incomes, and immigrant concentrations are also possible explanations.[35] Whether this is an indication of inferior housing quality is questionable, however. The issue of quality exemplifies the difficulty of imposing a more traditional, middle-class, majority-white standard in an evolving society, where varying groups define their households, their housing quality, and overcrowding differently.[36]

Consequences of Immigrant Settlement in Austin

In the last twenty years, as Austin has gained the national spotlight as a mecca for local entrepreneurship and transnational business development, the metropolis has experienced incredibly high levels of migration, both domestic and foreign. As a result, the geographies of migration to and settlement within Austin are being reworked, at the same time that immigrant issues are beginning to unfold. Not only is the metropolis seeing the number of newcomers increase, but immigrants in this pre-emerging gateway are far more likely to live in suburban-like communities rather than central city enclaves. There are also some important disparities between Mexican immigrants and other immigrant groups that are likely to persist well into the next decade, if not longer. Foreign-born Mexicans are much more likely than the other immigrant groups to hold blue-collar jobs and be disadvantaged in terms of education, household income, poverty, and other measures. Asian immigrants (with the exception of undergraduate, graduate, and professional students), in contrast, generally have much higher human and social capital, job prestige, and incomes, and more expensive homes.

The potential ramifications of this bifurcation are significant. Clearly, achieving the white, middle-class standard is no longer the only way to assimilate: while some of Austin's immigrants are moving up in society, others are moving down or somewhere in between.[37] In many ways, then, the processes unfolding in Austin reflect the outcomes outlined in segmented assimilation theory, which argues that individual factors, such as education, place of birth, and length of stay, as well as contextual factors, including nature of migration, social capital, the presence of a co-ethnic community, and context of reception, combine to determine the incorporation of immigrants into the United States.[38] Thus, most Asian Indian, Chinese, Canadian, and even Vietnamese newcomers appear to be emblematic of the immigrant success story in the United States, but Mexican immigrants are generally treading a different and more difficult course.

These divergent paths among immigrant parents will have significant effects on the incorporation of their children. Indeed, as the second generation of the post-1965 new immigration begins to come of age in Austin, Asian American youth are diverging from their Hispanic counterparts (especially when undergraduate, graduate, and professional students are taken into account). In a variety of socioeconomic measures (see table 10-3), U.S.-born Asians appreciably outrank U.S.-born Hispanics. Consider, for instance, the fact that U.S.-born Hispanics in Austin rank highest among the native-born in the percentage lacking a high school degree, while U.S.-born Asians rank lowest (27.6 percent versus 6.3 percent). This disparity has innumerable implications for how members of the second generation come to define their identities, self-esteem, ambition, and achievement, and how they will experience family and social life in the years to come.

Nevertheless, the future is not set in stone. Clearly, there are some complicating factors to be considered in the Austin case, especially when it comes to homeownership. Even though foreign-born Mexicans and native-born Hispanics live in smaller houses with more people per room, they own homes at similar rates as most other native-born or foreign-born groups. The question that remains is whether current homeownership can translate into future wealth and financial security.[39] Given the overpowering forces of the smart-growth movement aimed at slowing urban sprawl and protecting environmentally sensitive areas, urban redevelopment is having tremendous effects on both long-time, newer, and future Hispanic homeowners in East Austin. Although some are reaping the benefits of gentrification, many are losing out to higher property taxes. As lower-income homeowners, many cannot afford the rapid increases in housing values that are currently taking place in the community; thus, foreclosures are on the rise and residents are being squeezed out.[40] Whether they can purchase similar quality homes in comparable neighborhoods remains to be seen—and will certainly be the subject of future research.

As a metropolis that has frequently heralded itself as a highly tolerant place, where keeping things "weird" and promoting creativity is the talk of the town, Austin is now being put to the test. The increasing numbers of domestic and international migrants who have begun to call Austin home place the city at a moment of transition, when the nature of belonging and membership will be redefined and patterns of inclusion or exclusion will be institutionalized.

Obviously, local public policy can play a formative role in ensuring that all newcomers who so desire are able to develop a sense of belonging and seize opportunities for success. Policies that protect long-established neighborhoods, through property tax freezes and stronger rent control in rapidly gentrifying areas, can ensure the psychological benefits of privacy, stability, and well-being that are associated with homeownership. Policies that also focus on prospects for upward mobility—including opportunities for legal status, secure employment, the establishment of credit, and capital accumulation—ensure the integration of newcomers and promote their overall well-being and the future welfare of their children. One notable innovation initiated by Austin's police department is a banking program started in 2000 called *Banca Facil,* which allows immigrants to open bank accounts using alternative forms of identification. The police were aware that Hispanic immigrants were often the target of robberies because they were unlikely to use banks and carried large sums of cash, particularly on payday. Although most financial institutions required a state-issued identification card and a social security card, the police were able to convince several banks to accept alternative forms of identification. This collaboration between the police and the banks brought in other institutions such as the Hispanic Chamber of Commerce and the Texas Secretary of State to promote the program, which has since been replicated in other localities across Texas.[41]

Unfortunately, although the city government has implemented some policies that are helpful for the newly arrived foreign-born, current rhetoric and discriminatory local policies suggest that the numbers of overt and subtle barriers against immigrants are increasing.[42] An antisolicitation ordinance is but one example. When day laborers started to congregate in the parking lots of local Home Depots in the early 2000s, nearby residents and owners of surrounding businesses complained that they deterred potential customers and home buyers.[43] Combined with increasing attention by the media both locally and nationally, the local government decided that it should take action.[44] During 2006 and 2007, the city council of Austin crafted an antisolicitation ordinance that essentially criminalized the process by which many immigrants, documented and undocumented, seek employment.

A variety of other exclusionary city policies have also emerged, including increased property taxes, fewer public and affordable housing programs, and aggressive central city revitalization measures such as historic zoning incentives and mobile food vendor regulations. Combined with the threat to dismantle Austin's "sanctuary" statute (a city council resolution passed in 1997 that forbids city agencies and the police from asking people's immigration status), these policies suggest a growing backlash against immigrants, even when the policies are not overtly anti-immigrant in nature.[45]

As local intolerance combines with the more generalized and widespread anti-immigrant sentiment nationwide, it is clear that the recent and dramatic change in the social and cultural landscapes of the city has not come without some signs of strain and unease. Despite being touted as a liberal and tolerant city by a variety of measures and magazines, Austin can also be characterized by discriminatory local policies that work against those who already lack access to power and resources. Whether the host community will rise to the challenge and reduce the number of barriers that are currently in place, or whether immigrants themselves will have to organize and demand fair treatment, remains to be seen. If current trends continue, the future may be bright for those immigrants with a wealth of human and social capital, but it will be less secure for those with fewer resources.

Notes

1. Kurt Badenhausen, "Wide Open for Business," *Forbes,* May 26, 2003, pp. 3–4.

2. Richard Florida, "Cities and the Creative Class," *City and Community* 2, no. 1 (2003): 3–19.

3. These data were obtained through the Minnesota Population Center's Integrated Public Use Microdata Series (IPUMS) website (usa.ipums.org) for each of the three time periods. See Steven Ruggles and others, *Integrated Public Use Microdata Series: Version 3.0* [Machine-readable database] (Minneapolis: Minnesota Population Center, 2004).

4. For further information, see (usa.ipums.org/usa-action/variableDescription.do?mnemonic=RACESING).

5. Constance Forbes Citro, Daniel L. Cork, and Janet Lippe Norwood, *The 2000 Census: Counting under Adversity* (Washington: National Academies Press for the National Research Council, 2004).

6. William Frey, *Metropolitan Magnets for International and Domestic Migrants* (Brookings, 2003); Joseph Cortright, *The Young and Restless in a Knowledge Economy* (Portland, Ore.: Impresa Consulting, 2005).

7. Audrey Singer, *The Rise of New Immigrant Gateways* (Brookings, 2004).

8. Suzannah Gonzales, "In North Austin, Asian Community Is Blooming," *Austin American Statesman,* September 30, 2006, pp. A1, A8-9.

9. Emily Skop and Wei Li, "Asians in America's Suburbs: Patterns and Consequences of Settlement," *Geographical Review* 95, no. 2 (2005): 167–88.

10. Douglas S. Massey and others, *Return to Aztlan: The Social Process of International Migration from Western Mexico* (University of California Press, 1990).

11. Audrey Singer and Jill H. Wilson, *From "There" to "Here": Refugee Resettlement in Metropolitan America,* (Brookings, 2006).

12. Anthony Orum, *Power, Money, and the People: The Making of Modern Austin* (Portland, Ore.: Resource Publications, 2002).

13. Although it would have been ideal to preserve all four categories, collapsing them simplified the analysis and conforms to other analyses of the same variable. See Richard Alba and Victor Nee, *Remaking the American Mainstream: Assimilation and Contemporary Immigration* (Harvard University Press, 2003); and Suzannah Gonzales and Emily Skop, "¿HABLA UD. INGLÉS? The Linguistic Assimilation of Mexican Immigrants in Texas," *Southwestern Geographer,* forthcoming.

14. Emily Skop, *The Saffron Suburbs: Lessons Learned from an Asian Indian Community* (Columbia College Chicago, Center for American Places, forthcoming).

15. Nick Werner, "Poverty Statistics Include College Students," *Star Press* (Muncie, Ind.), (www.thestarpress.com/apps/pbcs.dll/article?AID=2007709020356 [September 23, 2007]).

16. Alejandro Portes and Min Zhou, "The New Second Generation: Segmented Assimilation and Its Variants," *The Annals of the Academy of Political and Social Science* 530, no. 1 (1993): 74–96.

17. Wei Li, ed., *From Urban Enclave to Ethnic Suburb: New Asian Communities in Pacific Rim Countries* (University of Hawaii Press, 2006).

18. Singer, *The Rise of New Immigrant Gateways.*

19. See Emily Skop, "Austin City Limited: Race, Ethnicity and Place in a Dynamic Migrant Metropolis," unpublished manuscript, University of Colorado at Colorado Springs, 2007, for more explicit details about how Jim Crow–like city policies and regulations of the early twentieth century forcefully relegated nonwhite groups to the east side of Austin, a pattern that was reinforced again in the mid-twentieth century with the building of I-35.

20. Daniel D. Arreola, "Mexican American Exterior Murals," *Geographical Review* 74, no. 4 (1984): 409–24.

21. Ben Chappell, "The Barrio Moves: Lowriders and the Performance of Space," Paper presented at the American Anthropological Association Annual Meeting, Washington, 2006.

22. Susana Almanza, "Gentrification and Land Use in Austin" (www.podertexas.org [Oct. 2006]).

23. Skop, *Austin City Limited.*

24. Almanza, "Gentrification and Land Use in Austin."

25. Monica Bosquez, "El Hombre Masculino: Reexamining Patriarchal Constructs of Masculinity in Austin's New Immigrant Community," Paper presented at Age of Migration seminar, University of Texas, 2006.

26. Emily Skop and Wei Li, "From the Ghetto to the Invisiburb: Shifting Patterns of Immigrant Settlement in Contemporary America," in *Multicultural Geographies: Persistence and Change in U.S. Racial/Ethnic Patterns,* edited by John W. Frazier and Florence Margai (New York: Academic Publishing, 2003), pp. 113–24.

27. Skop and Li, "Asians in America's Suburbs." Also see Wei Li and Emily Skop, "Enclaves, Ethnoburbs, and New Patterns of Settlement among Asian Immigrants," in *Contemporary Asian America: A Multidisciplinary Reader,* 2nd ed., edited by Min Zhou and James V. Gatewood (New York University Press, 2007).

28. Peter M. Ward and Paul A. Peters, "Self-Help Housing and Informal Homesteading in Peri-Urban America: Settlement Identification Using Digital Imagery and GIS," *Habitat International* 31, no. 2 (2007): 205–18.

29. Ibid.

30. Ibid.

31 Brad D. Jokisch, "Migration and Agricultural Change: The Case of Smallholder Agriculture in Highland Ecuador," *Human Ecology* 30, no. 4 (2002): 523–50.

32. Also see Tara Buentello, "Homeownership Rates and Housing Quality among Mexican Immigrants in Austin, Texas," Paper presented at the annual meeting of the Southern Demographic Association, Durham, N.C., 2006.

33. George J. Borjas, "Homeownership in the Immigrant Population," Working Paper W8945 (Cambridge, Mass.: National Bureau of Economic Research, 2002).

34. Skop, *Austin City Limited.*

35. Dowell Myers, William C. Baer, and Seong-Youn Choi, "The Changing Problem of Overcrowded Housing," *Journal of the American Planning Association* 62, no. 4 (1996): 66–84.

36. Ibid.

37. Min Zhou, "Growing Up American: The Challenge Confronting Immigrant Children and Children of Immigrants," *Annual Review of Sociology* 23, no. 1 (1997): 63–95.

38. Alejandro Portes and Rubén G. Rumbaut, *Legacies: The Story of the Immigrant Second Generation* (University of California Press, 2001).

39. Lauren J. Krivo, "Immigrant Characteristics and Hispanic-Anglo Housing Inequality," *Demography* 32, no. 4 (1995): 599–615. See also Emily Rosenbaum, "Racial/Ethnic Differences in Home Ownership and Housing Quality, 1991," *Social Problems* 43, no. 4 (1996): 403–26; and Lori Latrice Sykes, "Income Rich and Asset Poor: A Multilevel Analysis of Racial and Ethnic Differences in Housing Values among Baby Boomers," *Population Research and Policy Review* 22, no. 1 (2003): 1–20.

40. Almanza, "Gentrification and Land Use in Austin."

41. Anna Paulson and others, *Financial Access for Immigrants: Lessons from Diverse Perspectives* (Chicago Federal Reserve Bank and Brookings, 2006).

42. Skop, *Austin City Limited.*

43. Erin Miller, "The Right to the Street: A Geography of Exclusion in Austin, Texas," Paper presented at Age of Migration seminar, University of Texas, 2005.

44. Steven Greenhouse, "Front Line in Day Laborer Battle Runs Right Outside Home Depot," *New York Times,* October 10, 2005.

45. See also Richard Schott, "Ethnic and Race Relations in Austin, Texas," paper, LBJ School of Communications, Austin, 2002.

11

The "Nuevo South"

Latino Place Making and Community Building in the Middle-Ring Suburbs of Charlotte

HEATHER A. SMITH and OWEN J. FURUSETH

For most of its 225-year history, Charlotte—in Mecklenburg County, North Carolina—was the quintessential southern city. Its economy was based on textiles and local and regionally focused business services, its development patterns were structured around a suburban-focused Sun Belt model, and class and economic status were shaped by black-white social relations framed largely by segregation and social distance. In 1990 the city's population was roughly two-thirds white and one-third black, with a small number of Asians (1.6 percent of the total city population) and Hispanics (1.4 percent).[1] Other ethnoracial minority groups were even less visible, with Native Americans, Pacific Islanders, and those in "other" categories representing substantially less than one-half of 1 percent of the population. In terms of immigrant representation, only 3.8 percent of Charlotte's 396,003 residents in 1990 were foreign-born. Indeed, until very recently, the city was defined and shaped by its overwhelmingly native-born black and white communities.

The last two decades have been a period of dramatic change. Traditional industrial and commercial sectors have been transformed by new technologies and expanding banking and finance. Charlotte, in turn, has emerged as a national, if not global, financial center. Charlotte was ranked twenty-second among all U.S. cities by size in 2005, yet it is headquarters to two of the country's largest banks and ranks second behind only New York City in bank-held assets. Associated urban development has transformed Charlotte's skyline, pushed suburban growth farther into exurbia, and ignited a newly discovered interest in older, traditional, pre–World War II suburbs as desirable residential places for upper- and upwardly mobile middle-class residents.

The city has also become an attractive destination for internal migrants from the North and West seeking new-economy employment and amenity-rich residence in a booming "New South" city. In the minds of many long-time observers, Charlotte is striving to reinvent and distance itself from traditional regional constructs and join the elite cluster of globalizing cities and urban regimes.[2]

Charlotte is located in a state with a laissez-faire approach to annexation. Incorporated municipalities are largely free to add new territory to their boundaries even before an area is fully developed. As a consequence, the city limits of Charlotte have nearly kept pace with the outward push of suburbanization. Therefore, throughout this chapter, our references to Charlotte address the incorporated city and not larger census or political multijurisdictions. Whenever the discussion addresses areas or jurisdictions beyond the city boundaries, we provide geo-referencing.

In the midst of the city's dramatic economic transition, Charlotte's immigration story has been rewritten. Charlotte's status as a welcoming and economically advantageous destination quickly gained the attention of migrants across the global and economic spectrum. In 2000 the census reported that 59,849 immigrants had settled in the city of Charlotte, representing 11 percent of its total population. Nearly two-thirds had arrived since 1990, with 45.2 percent arriving since 1995. Eight percent of the city's immigrants came from Africa, 12.5 percent from Europe, 26.3 percent from Asia, and 50 percent from Latin America. Given the labor market's focus on finance and technology, well-educated and financially established immigrants are a significant component of those drawn to the city.[3]

Many of the new immigrants are from Asia. Between 1990 and 2005 the number of Asian immigrants to Charlotte grew by almost 16,500. Between 2000 and 2005 alone, their numbers grew by 5,100, a growth rate of nearly 28 percent. Asian Indians and Chinese experienced the highest growth, 76.9 percent and 41.4 percent, respectively. The most significant new ethnic group in Charlotte, however, is Latinos, who dominate the immigration stream. A full 50 percent of international immigration to the city between 1990 and 2000 was from the collective nations of Latin America. The pace and scale of immigrant growth in the city and surrounding metropolitan region are key factors in Charlotte's designation as a *pre-emerging* immigrant gateway.[4] Like other pre-emerging gateway

Figure 11-1. Race and Ethnicity, City of Charlotte, 1980–2005

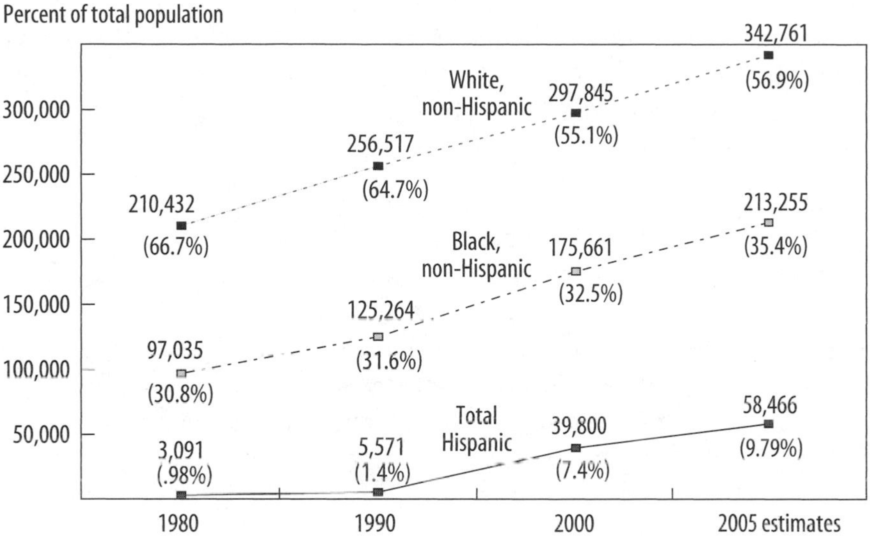

Source: U.S. Census Bureau, *Census of Population 1990, 2000;* American Community Survey 2005.

cities, Charlotte's immigrant population is characterized by its recent arrival, accelerated growth, and Latino skew.

Between 1990 and 2000 the Hispanic population in Charlotte increased to 39,800, a dramatic 614 percent gain (figure 11-1). Indeed, Roberto Suro and Audrey Singer labeled the Charlotte metro area as the fourth-fastest-growing "Hispanic hypergrowth" region in the United States during the last decades of the twentieth century.[5] Since 2000 Latino migration has continued unabated, growing by more than 18,500 persons, or 46.9 percent between 2000 and 2005. Although there are no reliable data on the census undercount for Hispanics, informal estimates within the Latino community and among service providers suggest that Charlotte's Latino population is currently between 70,000 and 80,000.[6] The 2005 *American Community Survey* (ACS) estimates there are 58,466 Hispanics in Charlotte, or 9.8 percent of the total city population. The Hispanic population in Charlotte is also overwhelmingly foreign-born. According to the ACS estimates, 38,809, or 66.4 percent, of Charlotte's Hispanic residents were foreign-born, with approximately one-half born in Mexico and the remainder born in the various other nations of Latin America.

It is not only the city of Charlotte that has a fast-growing Latino population; growth in Mecklenburg County and the larger six-county Charlotte-

Gastonia-Concord metro area has mirrored that in the city. The 2005 ACS estimates there are 71,904 Hispanic residents in Mecklenburg County and 112,637 in the metro region. This represents 9.2 percent of the county population and 7.6 percent of the metropolitan population. The proportion of foreign-born Hispanics is modestly lower than the Charlotte city estimate, with 62.1 percent in Mecklenburg County and 60.1 percent in the Charlotte-Gastonia-Concord metro area. Of the approximately 40,000 Hispanic residents in the city in 2000, 70 percent were foreign-born, and 99 percent of those were born in Latin America.

The release of Census 2000 figures, coupled with the growing visibility of Latinos across Charlotte, contributed to a widespread awareness of Hispanic migration and settlement in the city. This, however, did not translate into a common understanding of why Latinos were coming to Charlotte in such numbers, who they were, and what impact their presence was having on city structure, process, and identity. Indeed, the media and public discussion that flowed from the release of the census data, and from subsequent discussions of its undercounting, created a powerful mythic image that failed to capture the population's true complexity and, in turn, fostered misunderstanding of Latino migration and settlement dynamics in the city.[7] This image has been fueled by growing anti-immigrant sentiments in the city and state and rising tensions within Charlotte itself on issues of documentation status, resource allocation, and neighborhood transition.

One of the most powerful myths to evolve suggests that Hispanics in Charlotte have settled predominantly in a single, homogeneous, disadvantaged, and overwhelmingly Latino barrio, with stereotypical crime, illegality, and poverty. Fueled by media hyperbole and uninformed public discussion, this misperception has created backlash and, most critically, policy and planning missteps.

The reality is that Latino settlement has led to multiple segmented neighborhoods with distinctive class and ethnic composition and development trajectories. Indeed, a distinctive feature of Latino settlement in Mecklenburg County is that, unlike earlier immigrants in other gateway metropolitan areas and similar to cities discussed in the other chapters in this volume, Charlotte's new Latino residents have bypassed central-city neighborhoods and are moving directly into older, middle-ring suburbs. In the context of quintessential southern urbanism (car-dependent sprawl and discontinuous, leap-frog residential and commercial growth at the ever expanding urban fringe), Charlotte's Latinos are shaping three distinctive suburban clusters, as illustrated in map 11-1.[8]

This chapter, drawing from an array of both qualitative and quantitative data, explores these clusters and the varied processes that have shaped

Map 11-1. Mecklenburg County Hispanic Settlement Clusters, 2000

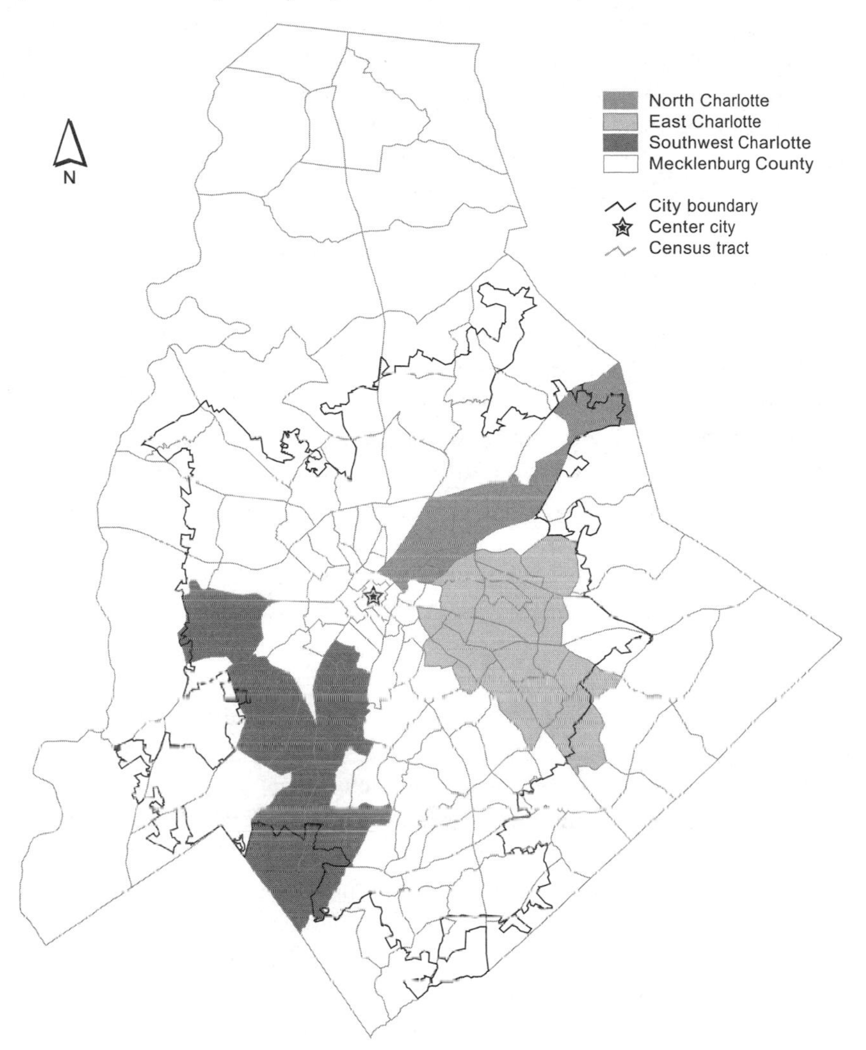

Source: U.S. Census Bureau, *Census of Population 2000,* SF1.

Note: Clusters comprise contiguous census tracts that have above-average Latino representation and expand out from a centralized core of Hispanic residential concentration. These clusters have been reviewed for accuracy by Latino community leaders.

them. Our discussion begins with an overview of selected immigrant settlement models and their intersection with the Charlotte experience, paying particular attention to why Latino settlement and place-making activities in this city have been concentrated in geographically disparate middle-ring suburban corridors. This is followed by a descriptive and statistical overview of each of the three clusters and an exploration of three key questions: How and why have settlement patterns and community building taken different trajectories than in the past and in such short order? What role does a rapidly maturing Latino migration stream play in creating new Latino-centered clusters in suburban districts? And what lessons might be learned from the Charlotte experience for community leaders and policymakers in other immigrant gateway cities?

Settlement Models

As noted in chapters 1 and 2, the classic Chicago School assimilation settlement model is structured around the presumed availability of low-cost housing in or near the central city and key links between home and work. These factors effectively steer new immigrants into inner-city residential districts. The presence of other immigrant populations, especially co-ethnics, in these neighborhoods helps to foster and sustain an urban landscape where transnational immigrants shape and make places, move on, and are replaced by new immigrants. Most of the widely reported examples of this model are drawn from European immigrants settling in traditional gateway cities in the late nineteenth century.

Recent investigations of immigrant settlement indicate that this once classic pattern is increasingly atypical, even in cities with long immigration histories. In his work on Chicago, Richard Green illustrates how processes of employment decentralization and edge-city development have redirected first-wave immigrants toward peripheral suburban sites of job opportunity for the semi- and unskilled. As he explains: "The old port of entry neighborhoods and low rent areas, close to the urban center, are not attracting new immigrants at a rate sufficient to offset recent population declines incurred there by the outward migration of African Americans to the suburbs. As a result, these old bypassed neighborhoods are becoming the locus of the region's indigenous poor who are economically disadvantaged by location."[9]

In 102 of the largest U.S. metro areas, John Logan shows that the percentage of minority residents in suburban communities grew from 19 percent in 1990 to 27 percent in 2000, with Hispanics leading the way (12 percent), followed by blacks (9 percent) and Asians (5 percent). In Charlotte, Logan reports, as Hispanics increased their proportional representation in the suburbs from 0.6 percent in 1990 to 3.4 percent in 2000, levels of Latino segregation in the city decreased. Although the "index of dissimilarity" (which gauges segregation) between whites and Hispanics in the

Charlotte-Gastonia-Rock Hill metropolitan statistical area (MSA) was 48.2 in 1990, it had dropped to 43.7 ten years later. In contrast, Logan shows that the suburbs may be seeing a growing trend toward Hispanic enclave development. Whereas an average Hispanic suburban resident in 1990 Charlotte could expect 1.8 percent of his or her suburban neighbors to also be Hispanic, by 2000 that number had risen to 10.4 percent.[10] In this regard, it is not insignificant that in 1990 most Latinos in Charlotte were middle class, came from Mexico, Puerto Rico, Cuba, or Colombia, and identified themselves as white (European ancestry).

The growing diversity of American suburbs is also a focus of William Frey's analysis of the 1990 and 2000 censuses, which indicates that minorities accounted for a significant proportion of population gain across the country's largest metropolitan areas. Emphasizing the role played by particular groups in this growth, Frey stresses that those suburbs with the largest proportion of minorities overall tended to be located in areas in which the "impact of rising Hispanic and Asian populations . . . is most evident."[11] In what Frey labels the melting pot suburbs, Hispanics were responsible for more than one-half of the population growth during the last decade of the twentieth century. For Frey, the fact that minority growth is increasingly responsible for overall suburban growth in U.S. cities necessitates a rethinking of the assumed dynamics between race and place, especially in regard to issues such as ethnic enclave formation, sociospatial mobility, and suburban resegregation. The Latino experience will necessarily inform this endeavor.

As others in this volume have pointed out, Wilbur Zelinsky and Barrett Lee identify a new, *heterolocal* pattern of settlement among many immigrants. They argue that immigrants are no longer bound on arrival to cluster in immigrant enclaves. However, ethnic networks and social capital are not entirely lost. Rather, spatial concentration is replaced by telecommunications, ethnic networks, and institutional community structures (for example, churches, clubs, and associations) empowered with Internet technologies. Consequently, ethnic groups living throughout a city or region can effectively maintain strong connections and common identity. Nonetheless, Zelinsky and Lee readily acknowledge that the least advantaged segments of the immigrant or minority population continue to settle in ethnic clusters.[12]

Recent research by Roberto Suro and Sonya Tafoya complements Zelinsky and Lee by finding that "rather than clustering in ethnic enclaves . . . most Latinos live scattered through neighborhoods where they are a small share of the population" and that this is so across the immigrant and socioeconomic spectrum.[13] Still, when the characteristics of Latino-majority neighborhoods are assessed, low-income, Spanish-speaking, and foreign-born Latinos often represent a large share of the population. An aspect of Suro and Tafoya's study that is particularly relevant to Charlotte is the significant differences they find between the census tract distributions of Latinos in traditional versus new settlement locations. Although Hispanics in traditional settlement states such as California, Florida, and Texas divide themselves between majority- and minority-Latino tracts, in new destination states such as Georgia and North Carolina, they overwhelmingly gravitate toward minority-Latino neighborhoods, a practice that "runs contrary to the classic model of ethnic clustering in which new arrivals in an area seek out each other's company."[14]

Latino Settlement Geography in Charlotte

As noted earlier, until the 1980s Charlotte had very limited experience with immigrant settlement and adjustment. At a minimum, the arrival of more than 56,000 Latinos since 1980 has ushered in a new multicultural era for the city. Consider that between 1990 and 2000, Hispanics contributed almost one-quarter of Charlotte's overall new population growth. Before the rapid and large-scale insertion of Latinos in the city, Charlotte had never before experienced a culturally distinct, non-English-speaking, and largely immigrant group making a significant imprint on the city's growth and urban character. Although job decentralization, suburban sprawl, and the lack of strong ethnic enclaves in Charlotte have shaped Latino settlement patterns, the availability and geography of affordable and flexible housing options are especially critical factors in molding these patterns.[15] Contextually, the Charlotte housing market, like many cities that saw the bulk of new housing built in the latter part of the twentieth century, is characterized by mass-produced, single-family residential subdivisions and apartment complexes. As new housing production moved continually outward, older suburban districts became less attractive to middle-class families.

By the 1990s Charlotte's middle suburbs, many of which were built in the post–WWII era, were slipping into decline. Strung along major thoroughfares, these communities were built largely to satisfy the city's expanding middle-class white housing market.[16] Small-scale businesses serving residents occupied nearby strip commercial centers, and large multifamily apartment complexes were located along the major thoroughfares or tucked in between the single-family developments. These middle suburbs, however, have struggled to maintain their middle-class status and economic vitality.

In Charlotte's sprawl-themed environment, the rental housing market, especially large-scale older apartment complexes, offered an attractive housing option for newly arriving Latino migrants. Having lost market status to high-end rental properties in the gentrifying center city and newer suburban locations, middle-suburban apartment agents began aggressively to court immigrants with affordable and flexible housing. New Latino migrants, especially those with limited English skills, viewed apartment rental as easier and less discriminatory than renting single-family housing.[17] Apartment sharing, with multiple roommates or families living together, was common and often overlooked by landlords pleased to have vacancies filled by tenants who paid rents on time (often in cash) and who required few services. There was also a perception in the Latino community that apartment complexes provided a less intrusive and socially restrictive environment. The latter issue was especially salient if undocumented immigrants were residents or guests in a home. Employment opportunities for the semi- and unskilled workers in the construction trades and building and grounds maintenance are plentiful and distributed fairly evenly across Charlotte's urban and suburban landscape. For the many Hispanics laboring in these industries, a centralized residential location accommodates the frequently changing worksite if, as is the case in Charlotte, that location is comparatively well served by public transportation or a freeway network.

What follows are descriptive and statistical overviews of the three main clusters in which the majority (68 percent) of Charlotte's Latinos live: the Eastside, the Southwest, and the North. Although 68 percent is a clear majority and substantive proportion, in keeping with Suro and Tafoya's argument about the lack of concentration of Latinos in new settlement destinations, more than 30 percent of Charlotte's Latinos live elsewhere across the city.[18] Before discussing the specific details of suburban settlement patterns, we want to stress that, unlike many studies, which tend to use the broadest of all possible urban scales (often the MSA) and conflate various suburban types, we focus on one suburban type, the aging post–WWII, middle-ring suburb. Also, although we speak of Latino clusters, we do not equate these with ethnic enclaves. Indeed, in our clusters, Latinos are a minority, representing, at the time of the analysis, only between 12 and 15 percent of each area's total population.

The Eastside Cluster

Although Eastside Charlotte (map 11-2) has hallmarks of becoming the most stable Latino community in Charlotte, it is a district that has witnessed multiple phases of transition. In this context, the arrival and settlement of

Map 11-2. Eastside Cluster

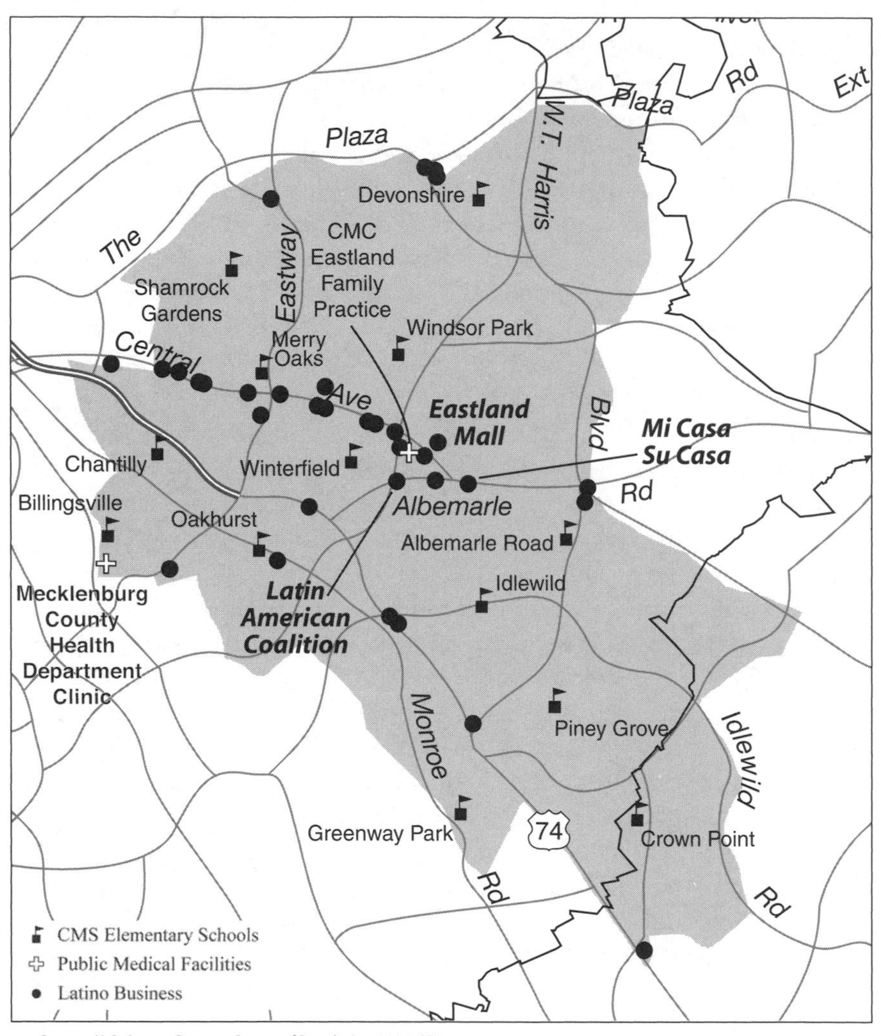

Source: U.S. Census Bureau, *Census of Population 2000,* SF3.

Latinos is only the most recent. Much of the area's modest single-family housing was built for middle-class whites in the 1960s, and the Eastside largely retained its homogeneity until the 1980s. Tucked in behind these low-density, single-family homes, and frequently lining the area's main thoroughfares, are multifamily, walk-up rentals, often adjacent to strip malls hosting an array of retail, commercial, and other services.

As the city's outer suburbs began to develop in the early 1980s, whites began to find newer housing in large-scale, amenity-driven subdivisions at the urban fringes. Replacing them were middle- and working-class blacks, who purchased or rented the single-family and apartment housing. The service and business landscape likewise changed to meet the needs and preferences of the area's new constituents.

Throughout the 1990s both whites and blacks continued to move to the periphery, with businesses and services following. As a result, the socioeconomic characteristics of Eastside neighborhoods became more solidly working and lower class. Strip malls experienced a growing number of store closures and vacancies, and property values began to stagnate or fall in the face of competition from newer housing on the periphery and revitalized housing in the city center. Apartment vacancies climbed as well. Into this landscape came the first wave of Charlotte's contemporary Latinos. Predominantly young men looking for work in the city's booming construction and landscaping industries, these trailblazing immigrants found a receptive community in Eastside Charlotte. As noted, landlords, eager for renters, were willing to take tenants on without documents and for flexible time periods. Among the three clusters examined here, only 34 percent of Latinos in the Eastside in 2000 experienced moderate to severe housing cost burden (the lowest of the three clusters examined).[19] This compares to a citywide burden of 36.1 percent and to 37.2 percent for Latinos citywide. In the area's vacant strip mall units, entrepreneurial efforts quickly yielded *tiendas* (small general stores), restaurants, recreational centers, and other commercial enterprises to meet the specific needs of the youthful, largely foreign-born population. Today, Charlotte's Eastside is home to the largest number of the city's Hispanic residents and is arguably evolving to become the city's most stable Latino cluster (table 11-1).

Part of this stability comes from the ethnoracial and demographic structure of the Latino community resident here. Although the Eastside cluster has the lowest proportion of Hispanic residents among the three clusters, it has the highest numbers. As table 11-1 shows, the 14,783 Hispanics who officially resided in this cluster in 2000 represented 13 percent of the area total.[20] Non-Hispanic whites were the proportionally dominant group, and non-Hispanic blacks represented 37 percent of the area's population. In terms of economic status, the median household income of Latino householders was $36,662, or just slightly lower than the cluster's overall median ($38,433). Black householders in this cluster fared slightly less well, with a median household income of $35,382. The citywide median is

Table 11-1. Selected Characteristics for Latino Clusters in Charlotte
Percent unless specified

Characteristic	*Eastside*	*Southwest*	*North*
Latino population (number)	14,783	9,678	5,995
Proportion of citywide total	29.0	23.0	12.0
Proportion Latino	13.0	14.2	15.9
Proportion non-Hispanic black	37.0	40.0	51.0
Proportion non-Hispanic white	44.0	45.0	29.0
Demographic characteristics			
Mexican origin	62.4	48.7	69.8
Central American origin	11.8	18.9	11.5
South American origin	3.7	9.7	2.2
Male/female ratio	65/35	62/38	68/32
Foreign-born	73.1	72.8	80.2
Foreign-born arriving after 1990	85.0	84.2	90.1
Citizen/noncitizen	36/64	39/61	31/69
Social characteristics			
Speaks English "not well" or "not at all"	52.1	43.5	63.3
Male householders	76.0	74.9	80.9
Proportion Latino children under 6	60.7	39.7	54.4
Proportion Latino children 6–17	39.3	60.3	45.6
Proportion city's Latino children	32.9	31.0	12.4
Poverty rate	24.0	22.7	31.5
Median Latino household income ($)	36,662	37,239	32,084
Ratio Latino household income to total cluster household income	95.4	86.2	88.9
Housing characteristics			
Latino homeownership	19.1	11.3	12.9
Overcrowded Latino households	45.1	34.2	48.2
Latino renters with "moderate" to "severe" housing cost burden	34.6	39.8	37.6

Source: U.S. Census Bureau, *Census of Population 2000.*

$46,975. The comparative strength of Latino incomes is another contributor to the evolving stability of this cluster.

Among the cluster's Latinos, 62 percent were Mexican, with the next highest group claiming Central American origin but accounting for only 11.8 percent of the Latino total (see table 11-1). Seventy-three percent of Latinos in the cluster were foreign-born, and the overwhelming majority (85 percent) of the newcomers arrived after 1990. Just shy of one-fourth in the cluster are living in poverty, and a little more than one-half (52.1 percent) do not speak English well or at all. Clearly, the Latino population in the Eastside is still in the early stages of integration and acculturation processes. Despite the recent arrival of the majority of the Latino population here, their impact on the community and the area's landscape and identity has been profound. Latino-owned and -oriented businesses have helped to reverse the economic decline and malaise of the Eastside. These thriving businesses are anchored in both the small and more substantive shopping districts along major roadways, most notably Central Avenue, the Plaza, and Albemarle Road. This highly visible and well-known commercial and service landscape attracts Latinos as residents and consumers from across the city, other parts of Mecklenburg County, and the region more broadly.

Perhaps not unexpectedly, the Eastside hosts important Latino human services. The region's two primary Latino service outreach and advocacy agencies, the Latin American Coalition and Mi Casa Su Casa, are located in the area. Both organizations offer a wide array of services and immigrant assistance. They are particularly oriented to serve the indigent and newly arriving non-English-speaking clients.

Three of the Charlotte-Mecklenburg public schools with the highest proportion of Latino students serve the Eastside. These elementary schools—Winterfield, Windsor Park, and Merry Oaks—enrolled 49 percent, 43 percent, and 41 percent Hispanic students, respectively.[21] These proportions are poised to rise substantially, given the age structure of the cluster's Latino children. Just over 60 percent of Latino children in the Eastside were under age 6 in 2000 (see table 11-1). Of the city's Latino clusters, the Eastside housed the highest percentage of preschool-aged Latino children and accounted for the greatest proportion of all the city's Latino children (32.9 percent).

The presence of children and the Eastside's growing Latino student enrollments indicate an expanding, family-structured, Latino residential community. Our interviews with school officials, service providers, and community advocates confirm this, despite census data that suggest a pioneering immigrant profile as of 2000. Anecdotal evidence from service providers indicates that the community has seen a rise in the number of women and children and significant growth in the number of traditional and extended families.

Another critical measure of the cluster's evolving stability is the degree of homeownership. Compared with the overall proportion of Latino homeownership across the three clusters, Latino homeownership rates in the

Eastside are the highest (19.1 percent) and nearest the citywide Latino average of 22 percent (see table 11-1). That said, another feature of this cluster is a Latino household overcrowding rate of 45.1 percent.[22] This compares with rates of 36 percent for Latinos across the city and of 5.3 percent for all Charlotte residents. Although we are speculating, it may well be that Latinos in this cluster, following the strategies of many other immigrant groups, obtain access to homeownership by pooling their resources and doubling up families or friends, which translates into what is considered statistical overcrowding.

The Southwest Cluster

Although the Eastside is evolving into stability, the Southwest cluster is currently the most long-standing and established Latino district (map 11-3). Indeed, the average Latino household income in this cluster is $37,239, or 86.2 percent of the cluster's overall median. As with the Eastside, Latinos in the Southwest are faring better than their black neighbors (whose median household income is $31,760). The cluster is also home to a substantial number of Latino newcomers (72.8 percent of Latinos in the cluster are foreign-born, with 84.2 percent arriving since 1990). Many are of very modest means, with poverty rates at 22.7 percent (see table 11-1).

Southwest is home to the city's second-largest and oldest Latino residential district. Just over 9,600 Latinos lived in this cluster in 2000, representing 23 percent of the city total and 14.2 percent of the area's total population. Non-Hispanic whites composed 45 percent of the total population and non-Hispanic blacks, 40 percent. The Southwest cluster is the most culturally diverse Hispanic, multiethnic suburb in Charlotte. Of its Latino residents, 49 percent are of Mexican origin; 19 percent, Central American origin; and 10 percent, South American origin. The percentage of Latinos from South America in the cluster is a significant marker of the area's more established character. As noted above, before the Latino boom in the city in the 1990s, Charlotte was home to a small Hispanic population, many of whom were Latinos of European descent. This group assimilated quickly into the mainstream social, economic, and cultural structures of the city, and many found residence in the solidly middle-class (in some cases upper-middle-class) suburbs surrounding the South Boulevard corridor. That this cluster has the highest proportion of Latino citizens of the three areas (38.5 percent), the highest proportion by far of children between the ages of six and seventeen (60.3 percent), and the lowest proportion of Latino residents with very limited English skills (43.5 percent) points to its more established nature. Increasing Hispanic school enrollments in the

Map 11-3. Southwest Cluster

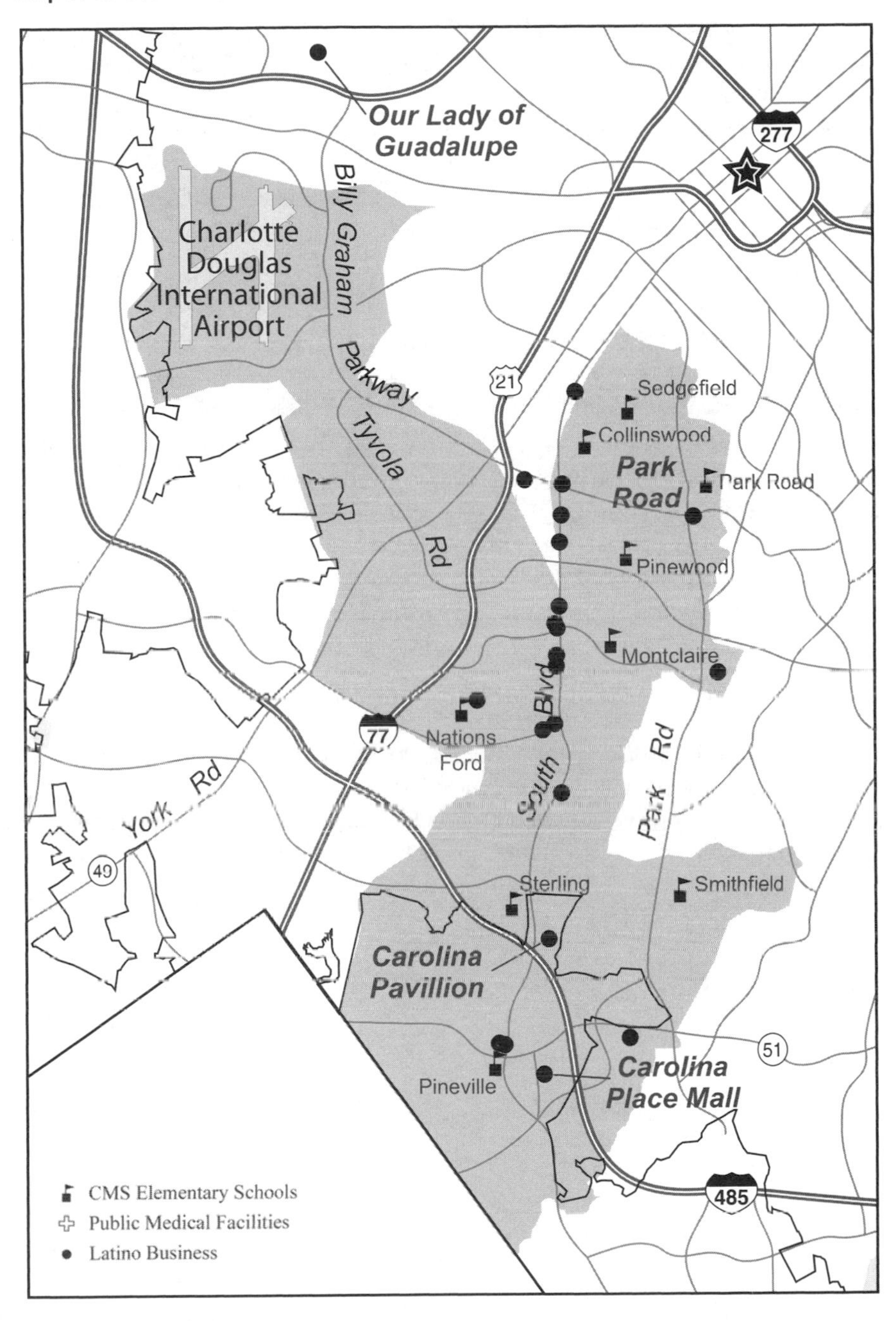

Source: U.S. Census Bureau, *Census of Population 2000*, SF3.

Charlotte-Mecklenburg school campuses serving this area also offer evidence of maturing settlement. Indeed, the Southwest encompasses the city's first two Latino-majority elementary schools (Montclaire and Collinswood) and some of the city's highest Hispanic-enrollment high schools.[23]

Like Eastside Charlotte, Southwest Charlotte was developed in the 1960s as a series of suburban neighborhoods for middle-class whites. Mirroring the Eastside neighborhood developmental model, single-family subdivisions are tucked in behind the major road, South Boulevard, which is lined with strip malls and larger shopping and commercial centers. Today, these many centers have been remodeled and are occupied by a growing number of Latino-oriented businesses and entrepreneurs, who serve a growing local and regional Latino and non-Latino market. In contrast to those in the Eastside cluster, however, Latino businesses and services are a less visible and defining aspect of the environment. The same is true of the residential landscape. Although the main roadways in the Southwest cluster have some visible multifamily apartment complexes immediately adjacent to main roadways, most such housing is scattered throughout the area and in many cases is located behind commercial areas or embedded within single-family residential communities. Compared with the Eastside, the Southwest cluster has many more multifamily apartment units, and this plays an important part in the lower rates of homeownership and limited overcrowding among Latinos in this particular area.[24]

Another factor likely responsible for lower rates of Latino homeownership in this cluster (see table 11-1) is the transitioning nature of the Southwest's development and socioeconomic trajectories. At the northern tip of this cluster are some of the most aggressively gentrifying districts in Charlotte (Dilworth and South End, for example). As property values in these areas rise beyond the reach of all but the very affluent, gentrification pressure creeps southward into the Latino core of this district. Not surprisingly, therefore, the costs of single-family homes are, on average, much higher than in either of the other two clusters examined. Burdens of affordability in the rental sector are also greater in this area. Among Latino renters, 39.8 percent experience moderate to severe housing burden—the highest among the clusters and higher than both the citywide (36.1 percent) and overall Latino figures (37.2 percent).

Along with gentrification pressure, the South Boulevard corridor is the first leg of the Charlotte Area Transit Authority's light-rail line. Under construction for two years, the line is scheduled to open in late 2007. In the wake of light-rail development, real estate investments, including mixed-use, transit-oriented developments along this artery have spurred significant upscale market pressure on both residential and commercial property in the area. Consequently, the sustainability of Latino settlement activity in the midst of this real estate boom along the South Boulevard corridor is questionable.

The North Charlotte Cluster

Downward pressure is the issue facing the North Charlotte Latino cluster (map 11-4). This is the smallest Latino residential district in the city, officially housing only 5,995 Hispanic residents (see table 11-1). However, in this district, Latinos compose the highest proportion of total residents (almost 16 percent) and are the most ethnically homogeneous. Just under 70 percent of Latinos in the North cluster are Mexican. Equally important, North Charlotte has the highest concentration of newly arrived, international immigrants. Eighty percent of Latino residents in the area are foreign-born, and slightly more than 90 percent have arrived since 1990.

The Hispanic population in this suburban area fits the classic "pioneering" migrant model. The male-female ratio is 68:32; the proportion of Latinos that are male householders is 80.9 percent, with almost 21 percent of Hispanic residents living in nonfamily households. Latino children in this district represent only 12.4 percent of the citywide total. Families are less evident here than in the Eastside and Southwest. Social and economic profiles also indicate a population that is in the early stages of assimilation and acculturation. Sixty-three percent of Latinos in this cluster are limited in their ability to speak English well or at all, raising questions of linguistic isolation. Fewer than 13 percent of Latinos in this cluster own their own homes, and 48.2 percent live in overcrowded conditions. The Latino median household income in this cluster is $32,084 (the lowest among the clusters) and the poverty rate, at 31.5 percent, is notably higher than in either Eastside or Southwest. The comparative income gap between Latinos and other major ethnoracial groups is also of significance. Indeed, the North cluster is the only one in which Latinos are economically less well-off than blacks. Whereas the median household income for blacks is 96.4 percent of the cluster mean, for Latinos it is only 88.9 percent.

The impoverished nature of this district is visible. Portions of the major arteries in North Charlotte are derelict. North Tryon Street, the most significant roadway, is lined with auto and mobile-home dealers, scrap yards, struggling small businesses, pay-by-the week motels, with a mix of aging and new strip malls, many of which have vacant storefronts. Where Latino businesses are present, they tend to be small *tienda*-type stores focused on serving only the local Hispanic population. Two exceptions are the city's

Map 11-4. North Charlotte Cluster

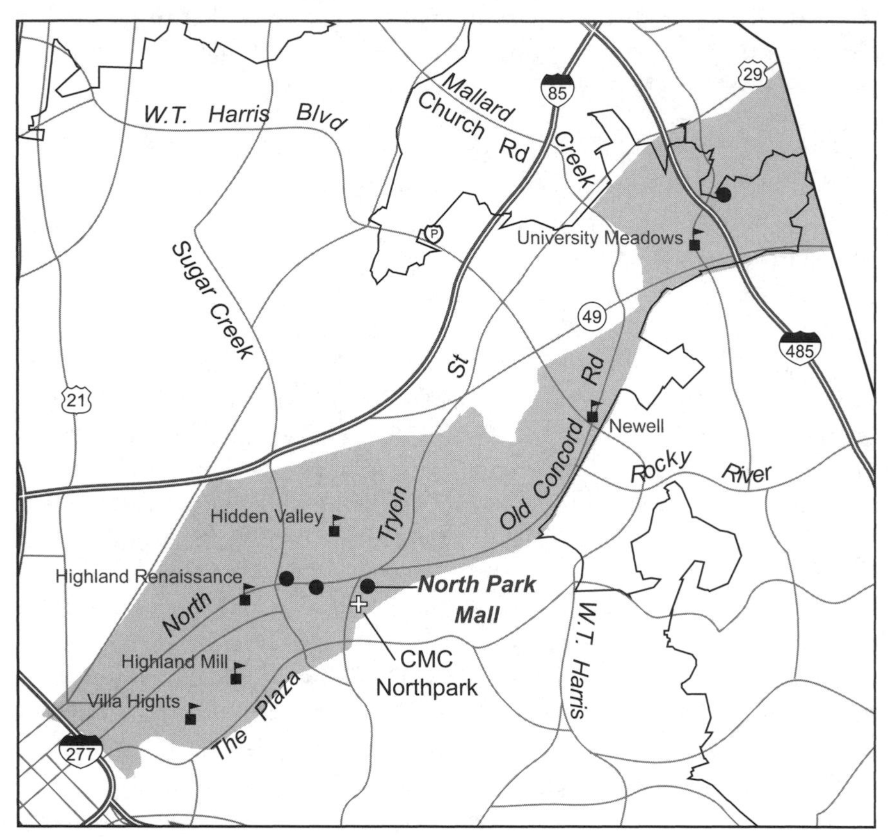

Source: U.S. Census Bureau, *Census of Population 2000,* SF3.

two transnational bus lines, regularly transporting people back and forth between Mexico and Charlotte; both have their depots in this cluster.

Support agencies serving Latinos are rarer in this district than in the other two, although it should be noted that services for the indigent and a growing stock of publicly subsidized housing are on the rise in the area. Nonetheless, residential opportunities are more infrequent compared with the other two clusters and are often oddly positioned several blocks behind main thoroughfares. The residential landscape is blurred and disjointed. Aging walk-up apartment complexes are mixed with small single-family subdivisions or town home complexes and the occasional mobile home park. The high proportion of Latino residents in these mobile-home parks is significant in two ways. First, it marks a form of transience and instability that is characteristic of the area, and, second, of all housing forms, mobile homes are the most invisible. The properties are rarely monitored by landlords or neighborhood associations and are frequently unknown by all but those who live in the area. Community leaders and service advocates interviewed for this study emphasized that of all of the clusters, North Charlotte was the one that likely housed the greatest proportion of undocumented immigrants and also presented the greatest gap between census reported and actual numbers of Hispanic residents.

One of the other distinguishing features of the North cluster is its ethnic-racial profile. Although in the other two clusters, whites were the proportionally dominant group, in North Charlotte, blacks represent 51 percent of the residents and non-Hispanic whites account for only 29 percent. Although processes of succession-replacement occurred in the Eastside and Southwest clusters, with Latinos stepping into residential and commercial landscapes vacated by middle-class blacks and whites, a more traditional pattern of invasion-succession may be occurring here.[25] The evidence is anecdotal, but informants claim that black and white middle-class homeowners in the area are selling their properties and moving out as property values fall, the commercial landscape declines, and the population of pioneering Latino immigrants grows. The sequencing of these processes and the degree to which they feed into one another is very much a matter of interpretation and debate. Nevertheless, our interviews indicated that tensions between long-time black residents and their new Latino neighbors are beginning to surface. According to the police and health-related social service agencies, immigrant-centered crime and victimization, as well as other indicators of social distress, are also on the rise.

In short, the North cluster is the most pioneering and the most fluid of the Hispanic suburbs in Charlotte. It is also the newest Latino settlement district. Our interviews suggest that Latinos began arriving in the late 1990s. Most important, North Charlotte has clearly emerged as the first stop for many single, predominantly male immigrants coming to the city for work and opportunity. The cluster also has an uncertain future. Although Latino children are a growing presence in the local schools, interviews suggest that the family or household circumstances of these children are highly transitory. Clearly, more research is needed to ascertain which processes are at work here. However, one possibility is that shortly after children and their mothers join their male partners, they quickly move again to more traditional, more supportive communities, such as the Eastside or Southwest districts.

Our Lady of Guadalupe Church in the suburbs of West Charlotte, a symbol of an incipient Latino community whose members are seeking relatively uncontested ground for housing and services.

Finally, there is evidence of an incipient Latino settlement district in West Charlotte, one not captured in the 2000 census data. During the later stages of our community interviews (summer 2006), several respondents spoke about a newly evolving, predominantly family-oriented Latino community in West Charlotte tied to a Spanish-language parish, Our Lady of Guadalupe Catholic Church. Built in 2002 on a vacant field surrounded by light industrial and airport-related businesses, Our Lady of Guadalupe is located at a distance from the other clusters. Moreover, the church campus is not easily accessible by public transit or highways. Still, an embryonic Latino community seems to be taking shape near the church. In this case, factors other than those identified above are driving settlement choices of newly arriving Latinos. Rather than the centrality of housing economics or other "traditional" influences, the proximity to a cultural icon providing faith-based and other outreach services seems a dominant factor. For some Latinos, location here may also represent the promise of uncontested space and protective anonymity at a particular moment in time when anti-immigrant sentiment appears to be fueling challenges in the other three settlement clusters. As we noted earlier in this chapter, today's climate in

Charlotte is increasingly hostile and unwelcoming for Hispanics, particularly those who are newly arrived, foreign-born, and without formal documentation. In that context, residence in a new and self-forming residential area that is adjacent to a Spanish-language church offering unconditional and comprehensive support, as well as anonymity of place and person, is highly attractive. Exploring the rationale, dynamics, and process of carving out this Latino community from unclaimed urban space is a critical next step for our ongoing research project.

Understanding Settlement Patterns

Research exploring the suburbanization of immigrants in U.S. cities tends to focus on the decentralization and diversification of job opportunities and the location of affordable housing as key reasons for location choices. The Charlotte example illustrates additional and reinforcing forces at work. Charlotte's aggressive center city revitalization and gentrification have resulted in significant declines since 1990 in affordable and available central-city housing.[26] Similarly, the rapid development of the suburban fringe, with large-scale, amenity-driven, single-family housing subdivisions, has also played a critical role in fostering new middle-class settlements and continued migration by whites and blacks from aging middle-ring suburbs. They leave in their wake a surplus of high-quality and affordable housing for newcomers, much of which is multifamily apartment housing located near major traffic arteries with comparatively well-integrated public transit routes. In addition to affordability, the apartments offer flexibility and anonymity to immigrant newcomers.[27] In turn, the centralized locations of these middle-ring suburbs, especially the Eastside and Southwest, facilitates easy access to frequently changing worksites in landscaping, construction, and personal services.

Although housing geography and the local economy are key factors helping to explain the initial residential choices of many Latinos in the city, one should not overlook the influence of networks, particularly once a core group of households becomes established and word of mouth attracts local and transnational arrivals. Thus, the story of Charlotte's Latino immigrant settlement is a complex layering of family and community networks that has incrementally attracted and then hosted men, women, and families. Even in the aftermath of 9-11 and despite the anti-immigrant rhetoric, these resilient networks continue to function and expand.

In this context, landscapes offer cultural cues to potential settlers. Many of those interviewed emphasized the importance of visible indicators of a

Latino presence in their decisions of where to live. For example, Spanish-language signs advertising vacant apartments, grocery stores, restaurants, laundromats, and other necessary services for daily life are important factors drawing migrants to particular neighborhoods over others. In Charlotte the visibility of immigrant support systems and Latino social networks explains why the Eastside and Southwest clusters were established first. Although the presence of Latinos in these districts was minimal before 1990, other immigrant populations were present, and services and commercial ventures meeting their needs were embedded in the landscape. The Eastside, for example, had a small, primarily Asian immigrant community, and the South Boulevard corridor was a dominant residential site for the city's early Euro-Latino population. In the case of Our Lady of Guadalupe, the presence and support network of the church has undoubtedly acted as an institutional magnet for settlement.

The varying levels of services and institutional infrastructure also help explain Latino settlement and place making in these varied middle-ring suburbs. As noted previously, when compared with the other clusters, Eastside Charlotte has a more fully integrated Latino service infrastructure, with the widest range of Latino-oriented businesses in the city and a complete range of Spanish-language services. In Southwest Charlotte Latino retail and services are more broadly scattered across the area and interspersed among the larger mainstream commercial and service landscape. A similar situation exists in North Charlotte, where Latino businesses and services are localized and scattered amid the area's many declining strip malls and small retail and commercial centers. A 2006 Mecklenburg County Latino Community Needs Assessment identified sharp differences in service providers, with sizable portions of the Southwest and the most suburban section of the North cluster having few or no services.[28] Moreover, significant portions of all three clusters had only average or below average accessibility to services identified as important to integration and acculturation for the Latino community.

Given the importance of public transit to low-income immigrants, a critical component of the needs assessment was public transit service in each of the clusters, as measured by the distribution of Charlotte Area Transit bus lines and stops. Public transit services offer enhanced accessibility to underserved portions of Southwest Charlotte, especially along South Boulevard. Conversely, large areas in North Charlotte had no bus services. Among the three Latino residential districts, the Eastside was the best served by public transit. The large Latino services, institutions, and transportation on the Eastside are significant factors in its designation as the cluster most likely to maintain its Hispanic presence through continued Hispanic population growth, institutional completeness, and targeted commercial development.

Although the above discussion offers insight into why settlement occurred in these clusters as opposed to other areas of the city, it is important to say more about why settlement, place making, and community building have, in short order, taken different trajectories and expressed varied ethnic neighborhood typologies across the different clusters. In addition to the differing service landscape detailed above, the characteristics and dynamics of the Latino population resident in each cluster play roles in this regard. The Southwest cluster is the most established and ethnically diverse Latino area; the North is overwhelmingly Mexican, with very high proportions of its male migrants arriving in the city and country since 1990. In comparison, the Eastside is more family oriented with significant numbers of children. Its ethnic makeup is predominantly Mexican but with higher proportions of Central Americans than the North and fewer South Americans than the Southwest.

Taken together, the distinctive population characteristics, the varied housing and business landscapes, and the differing development trajectories suggest very divergent immediate and long-term futures for each cluster. Southwest Charlotte's more established Latino cluster is situated near one of the city's most desirable inner-city neighborhoods. The impending start-up of the city's first light rail line has stimulated widespread real estate upgrading and residential gentrification in and around the district. Will the current Latino community benefit from this land development, or will it be displaced? The lessons from other cities embarking on light rail do not bode well for the sustainability of the Latino community in the Southwest cluster. North Charlotte, home to the pioneering immigrant stream and the most impoverished Latino immigrant group, is an area increasingly overlooked and marginalized in the local development realm. Indeed, North Charlotte is absorbing more than its fair share of low-rent and public housing as well as services for the indigent and is largely ignored as a place for city-funded investment and improvement. This raises a perplexing policy question: to what extent does the growing presence of Latino immigrants here, many of whom are thought to be undocumented, feed into decisions to disinvest from the area?

Historically, East Charlotte has been the first reception center and residential community for Charlotte's small transnational immigrant population. Latinos are the largest and dominant immigrant group. Thus, in addition to Latino-oriented services, the area also has the highest concentration of immigrant-focused services in the city. As the increasingly stable Latino community in the area grows, to what extent will other migrant populations become subsumed or obscured by the Latino presence? And, in that regard, given the rapid pace of Latino place-making processes in the Eastside and its regional identity as Latino space, will the area become the Latino barrio many already identify it to be?

As Charlotte's Latino settlement clusters continue to grow and become more permanent, they will take on an increasing role in shaping the city's definition of, and response to, the middle-ring suburban landscape. Already, the growing number of Latino families and the burgeoning entrepreneurial and business class have begun to advocate and speak out on a variety of issues, most notably, educational opportunities as well as crime and safety. These early efforts toward civic engagement and activism are likely to be expanded and to play out on a variety of fronts, including increasing community involvement on key quality of life issues beyond education and crime; growing articulation of the unmet needs and expectations of the Latino population; increasing visibility in the broader community; and the appropriate use of public space for festivals, sporting events, public meetings, and protests.

The public realm of middle-ring suburbs is also likely to experience tensions around a "sense of belonging" in a place. As noted earlier, in all of Charlotte's Latino settlement clusters the majority is non-Hispanic. In this context, the growth of the Latino population in largely white or black neighborhoods has generated some resentment and tension. In particular, tensions between blacks and Latinos in all three clusters have been ongoing, with the most serious challenges in North Charlotte and, to a lesser degree, Southwest. In the contested spaces of residential, commercial, and public areas, these tensions are likely to be exacerbated.

Finally, what lessons can be taken from the Charlotte experience to inform community leaders and policymakers in other emerging immigrant gateways? First is the need to recognize both the diversity of the Latino population itself and the diversity of spaces and places in which they settle. Charlotte has, in fact, multiple Latino communities: at the broadest cut, Mexican, Central American, South American, Cuban; established versus newcomers; documented versus undocumented. Careful consideration should also be given to the varied benefits and drawbacks of residence in different suburban settings. Immigrants living in aging middle-ring suburbs require different support, services, and representation from those in gentrifying "streetcar suburbs" or the expanding and more affluent suburban periphery. Questions of heterolocalism and enclave development should also be addressed. Charlotte's Latino communities are both socially and spatially diverse, yet one can see the evolution of three distinctive clusters with significantly different population profiles. To what extent are Latinos living and experiencing daily life beyond these clusters? To what extent are they using the tools of transportation and communication to create intricate heterolocal networks extending between and beyond the clusters? At what point do these clusters become enclaves? In their work on multiethnic suburbs, Phelan and Schneider argue that a 15 percent threshold indicates an ethnocultural influence substantive enough to affect community character, experience, and identity.[29] As of 2000 each of Charlotte's Latino clusters was nearly at or slightly above this threshold.

The suburbanizing trends of Latinos and immigrants should be explored more frequently at a variety of scales. Specifically, scholars, policymakers, and community leaders should recognize that the experiences of middle-ring suburban dwellers—Latino or not, immigrant or not—are being overlooked as studies assess the suburban experience along broad and sweeping scales. There is also a need to narrow the lens even further and take a much closer look at the internal dynamics of distinctive suburban areas, even closer than we have done here. As an example, field visits to our clusters combined with interviews and focus groups suggest that the spatial clustering of certain groups in certain areas also occurs at smaller scales of analysis. As one of our interviewees noted: "The other thing I see in the Hispanic community is [that it in] itself is very divided. . . . A good example here in Charlotte is that [in] certain apartment complexes, you will see a certain nationality there, be it Central American, Salvadoran, Guatemalan, even a certain part of Mexico in one apartment complex or one building . . . they kind of cluster together."

Studies of the suburbanizing trend among immigrants must take on a diversified, multiple-scale, and on-the-ground approach. Only then will there be a full and nuanced understanding of the causes, consequences, and complex dynamics of suburban settlement in pre-emerging and other nontraditional immigrant gateway cities.

Notes

1. Although the U.S. Census of Population and other government sources use "Hispanic" for persons of Latin American origin, members of this community prefer the term "Latino." In this chapter, we use the terms interchangeably.

2. See, for example, Heather A. Smith and William Graves, "Gentrification as Corporate Growth Strategy: The Strange Case of Charlotte, North Carolina, and the Bank of America," *Journal of Urban Affairs* 27, no. 4 (2005): 403–18; and

Heather A. Smith and William Graves, "The Corporate (Re)Construction of a New South City: Great Banks Need Great Cities," *Southeastern Geographer* 43, no. 2 (2005): 213–34.

3. David Reimers, "Asian Immigrants in the South," in *Globalization and the American South,* edited by James C. Cobb and William Steuck (University of Georgia Press, 2005).

4. Audrey Singer, *The Rise of New Immigrant Gateways* (Brookings, 2004).

5. Roberto Suro and Audrey Singer, *Latino Growth in Metropolitan America: Changing Patterns, New Locations* (Brookings, 2002).

6. Personal interviews with Christine B. Bolling, staff writer, *The Charlotte Observer* (July 30, 2004); Angeles Ortega, executive director, Latin American Coalition (July 27, 2004); and Theresa Villamarin, program supervisor, Catholic Social Services, Diocese of Charlotte (August 3, 2004).

7. Heather A. Smith and Owen J. Furuseth, "Making Real the Mythical Latino Community in Charlotte, North Carolina," in *Latinos in the New South: Transformations of Place,* edited by Heather A. Smith and Owen J. Furuseth (Burlington, Vt.: Ashgate Publishing, 2006).

8. Clusters are composed of contiguous census tracts that have above-average Latino representation and that expand out from a centralized core of Hispanic residential concentration. These clusters have been reviewed for accuracy by local Latino community leaders.

9. Richard P. Greene, "Chicago's New Immigrants, Indigenous Poor, and Edge Cities," *Annals of the American Academy of Political and Social Science* 551 (1995): 190.

10. John R. Logan, "The New Ethnic Enclaves in America's Suburbs" (Albany, N.Y.: Lewis Mumford Center for Comparative Urban and Regional Research, 2005), pp. 1–15.

11. William H. Frey, *Melting Pot Suburbs: A Census 2000 Study of Suburban Diversity* (Brookings, 2001), p. 3.

12. Wilbur Zelinsky and Barrett A. Lee, "Heterolocalism: An Alternative Model of the Sociospatial Behaviour of Immigrant Ethnic Communities," *International Journal of Population Geography* 4 (1998): 281–98.

13. Roberto Suro and Sonya Tafoya, *Dispersal and Concentration: Patterns of Latino Residential Settlement* (Washington: Pew Hispanic Center, 2004), p. 1.

14. Ibid., p. 11.

15. Heather A. Smith and Owen J. Furuseth, "Housing, Hispanics, and Transitioning Geographies in Charlotte, North Carolina," *Southeastern Geographer* 44, no. 2 (2004): 216–35.

16. Thomas W. Hanchett, *Sorting out the New South City: Race, Class, and Urban Development in Charlotte, 1875–1975* (University of North Carolina Press, 1998).

17. Drawn from author interviews with Charlotte-based service providers and advocates working with Latino communities.

18. Although the focus of this chapter is Latinos, other immigrant groups in Charlotte also show distinctive patterns of residential settlement. Asian immigrants to the city experienced a 27 percent increase between 1995 and 2000, and their distribution yields a very different pattern from that of Latinos. While Latinos are

clustered in three aging middle-ring suburbs, Asian immigrants cluster, albeit to a far lesser extent, in the outer and newly developing suburban periphery. Areas proximate to the University of North Carolina at Charlotte, and the University Research Park in the city's northern suburbs, as well as areas characterized by affluence and high-performing public school districts in the far south of the city, are those with the highest degree of Chinese clustering. Asian Indians show a similar pattern with an even more marked presence (although still only representing less than 4.1 percent of tract residents) in the northern university and research communities. In many ways, these patterns intersect with studies showing the strong presence of highly educated Asians in new immigrant destinations, especially those with growing professional and service-based economies. See, for example, William Frey and Kao-Lee Liaw, "Internal Migration of Latinos and Asians," in *Migration and Restructuring in the United States,* edited by Kavita Pandit and Suzanne Davies Withers (Lanham, Md.: Rowman and Littlefield, 1999); and Reimers, "Asian Immigrants in the South."

19. The measure of housing burden used in this chapter is derived from the Joint Center for Housing Studies, *The State of the Nation's Housing 2005* (Harvard University). This report defined a severe housing cost burden as an expense of more than 50 percent of pretax income, and a moderate housing cost burden as an expense of 30 to 50 percent of pretax income.

20. Again, these are official U.S. census statistics and likely grossly undercount the real number of Latinos living in the cluster.

21. Data provided by Charlotte-Mecklenburg Schools Diversity office.

22. This research applied the U.S. Census Bureau's measure for residential overcrowding. This standard uses the ratio of persons to rooms in a housing unit. A residential structure is considered overcrowded if it has more than one person to a room. U.S. Census Bureau, *American Community Survey, Housing Fact Sheets* (U.S. Department of Commerce, 2003), p. 2.

23. As of 2006, Montclaire Elementary School was 65.7 percent Hispanic and Collinswood was 57.1 percent Hispanic.

24. Smith and Furuseth, "Housing, Hispanics, and Transitioning Geographies in Charlotte, North Carolina."

25. Mark E. Reisinger, John W. Frazier, and Eugene L. Tettey-Fio, "Patterns and Issues in the Latinization of Allentown, Pennsylvania," in *Race, Ethnicity, and Place in a Changing America,* edited by John W. Frazier and Eugene L. Tettey-Fio (Binghamton, N.Y.: Global Academic Press, 2005).

26. Declines in affordable housing in Charlotte are occurring in both the private and public sectors. In the case of public housing, central-city development and the influence of the new federally directed public housing model, widely known as Hope VI funds, have accelerated losses in recent years.

27. Altha Cravey, "Transnationality, Social Spaces, and Parallel Worlds," in *Latinos in the New South,* edited by Smith and Furuseth.

28. Jana Harrison, Owen J. Furuseth, and Heather A. Smith, *Latino Community Needs Assessment for Mecklenburg County* (University of North Carolina, Urban Institute, 2006).

29. Thomas J. Phelan and Mark Schneider, "Race, Ethnicity, and Class in American Suburbs," *Urban Affairs Review* 31, no. 5 (1996): 659–80.

Afterword

Coming to Terms with Federal and Local Immigration Reform

AUDREY SINGER, SUSAN W. HARDWICK, and CAROLINE B. BRETTELL

In July 2007 a federal judge ruled unconstitutional a local ordinance in Hazleton, Pennsylvania, that targeted illegal immigrants and those who did business with them. One of the first of its kind, the Hazleton "Illegal Immigration Relief Act" was passed in the summer of 2006.[1] The law received nationwide attention for launching a local crackdown on immigrants. It also served as a model for other places looking for ways to discourage immigrants from settling in local areas.[2]

The Hazleton ordinance is emblematic of the frustration that many local public officials feel about the lack of federal guidance in reforming federal immigration policy. Congress has vigorously debated what was called comprehensive immigration reform in its 2005–06 session and again in 2007, but in the face of strong opposition from legislators of both parties, the reform was defeated. A growing intolerance toward illegal immigration—and a growing frustration with the federal impasse on immigration reform—have driven local officials to propose laws that serve to deflect immigrants elsewhere and hence show that they are responding to public pressure.

These new policies result in part from the new geography of immigration that has been discussed in this book and from the rapidity with which immigrants are appearing in new communities across the country. Coupled with fairly widespread economic and political insecurity, and spurred on by the larger and acrimonious national debate swelling around illegal immigration, the public is wary about changes happening around them. City, county, and municipal officials are pressured to "do something" about immigration. The result is that local governments are creating their own immigration policy—generally considered the exclusive purview of the federal government—using a variety of approaches.

The National Conference of State Legislatures reports that as of November 2007, all fifty states are considering immigration-related bills—more than 1,560 pieces of legislation, or nearly three times the number they considered in the preceding year.[3] States have already enacted 244 bills, more than triple the number passed into law in 2006. Bills under consideration include those that focus on employment, IDs and driver's licenses, law enforcement issues, and education:

—244 bills (in forty-five states) are related to employment, most of them restricting the employment of unauthorized workers or addressing eligibility for workers' benefits.

—257 bills in forty seven states address IDs and licensing, including driver's licenses. Many of these bills restrict licensing qualifications to citizens and legal residents, some determine acceptable forms of documentation for proof of identity, and some add penalties for false documents. Several propose to extend driver's licenses to unauthorized immigrants.

—165 bills in thirty-seven states deal with law enforcement issues, either those that would authorize local law enforcement to work with federal immigration authorities or the opposite: those that prohibit local law enforcement from doing so.

—131 bills in thirty four states address education-related issues, some restrictive, some inclusive, including bills around eligibility for in-state reduced tuition costs.

In addition to state-level reforms, countless local jurisdictions have introduced laws to address day-labor sites, language, employment, rental housing, and local law enforcement, all with immigrants in mind. Other communities are using existing laws, such as ordinances on residential zoning and occupancy, to curb the increase of immigrants or force them out. The local decisionmaking discussed in some of the chapters in this book reflects these new trends. Farmers Branch in the Dallas-Fort Worth metroplex recently voted into law an ordinance that makes it illegal for landlords to rent to unauthorized immigrants. Several suburban Washington, D.C., jurisdictions have put into place measures regulating immigrant day-labor sites as well as resolutions to deny local services to unauthorized immigrants. Several of Atlanta's suburban communities have tightened their housing occupancy codes and passed English-language ordinances that affect public signage. The sheriff of Mecklenburg County, North Carolina, where Charlotte is located, has enrolled in the federal program that allows local police to work with federal immigration authorities.

As several chapters in this book point out, however, not all of these local policy changes are restrictive or punitive. Nationwide, some places have developed new policies and passed ordinances that accommodate immigrants, such as publishing material in languages other than English, implementing language and other "assimilation" programs in local libraries and schools, or maintaining local services for all immigrants regardless of legal status. Notably, New Haven, Connecticut, has begun issuing municipal identification cards to provide access to city services to all residents, U.S.-born and foreign-born alike, an act that embraces immigrants regardless of legal status. Many mayors have declared their cities to be "sanctuary cities" and have active policies that forbid their police to report illegal immigrants to federal immigration authorities, even if arrested or convicted of crimes.[4] However, many of the most restrictive measures have been developed in areas with little or no prior experience with immigration but where the foreign-born population has grown rapidly in the span of ten or fifteen years.

Although many of these new laws may be legally challenged and eventually struck down, they stir up local debate and create an uncomfortable environment for immigrants, even those who are here legally. The ruling striking down the Hazleton law will give some municipalities pause; however, it also may stimulate some places to fine-tune restrictive policies in a way that maintains their constitutionality.[5] As this book goes to press, the city of Hazleton has filed an appeal of the ruling in the hope that a higher court will rule in its favor. City officials have vowed they will appeal to the U.S. Supreme Court if necessary.

With the lack of federal leadership on immigration issues, we cannot predict when new legislation will pass or what it ultimately will look like. However, in August of 2007, the White House announced twenty-six new immigration initiatives that bolster the enforcement of existing laws. At the center of these new policies are strict guidelines for employers to follow to avoid prosecution for employing unauthorized immigrants when they receive a "no match" letter from the Social Security Administration, indicating that ten or more employees have a social security number that does not match government records.[6] Among other new reforms are newly published regulations that will reduce the number of documents that employers are permitted to accept to establish the identity and legal status of workers. In terms of border enforcement, the administration announced plans to increase U.S. Border Patrols to 20,000, and add more fencing and other security measures by the end of 2009. It also is providing more resources for supporting state and local law enforcement in addressing illegal immigration in local communities.

In the absence of any comprehensive federal policy reform, state and local officials are likely to continue to develop their own strategies for dealing with immigrants and refugees, particularly undocumented immigrants. At the root of this conflict is the idea that new immigrant populations are not "assimilating." But this notion is in turn related to new anxieties about what it means to be an American and about the core values and symbols of American identity including the flag, the English language, and even the rule of law. Regardless of how the current immigration reform debate is resolved, local places are the ones that assume most of the day-to-day responsibility for helping to integrate immigrants into neighborhoods, local labor markets, and schools. In this charged atmosphere, it has become essential to devise effective measures that can more successfully incorporate immigrants socially, economically, and civically at the local level.

Immigrant Integration: A "New Americans Initiative"

Immigrant integration is an overlooked aspect of the immigration policy landscape. Immigrant integration is the long-term process by which immigrants become incorporated into U.S. life. It means immigrants' learning the English language and embracing American ways of life. It also means that American institutions must adapt to newcomers over the long run and combine diverse origins and perspectives into one people, the "motley" American people, as it has done for more than two hundred years. Ultimately, immigrant integration fosters social inclusiveness and economic mobility as immigrants and their offspring become full members of U.S. communities. Therefore, integration refers to changes immigrants undergo as they adapt, but it also refers to the effect immigrants have on local institutions and communities as well as on the nation.

For the U.S. immigration system to work, it must address the social, political, and economic integration of immigrants who arrive with a multitude of national origins, languages, religions, customs, and skills. The current system of integration involves little formal aid or guidance from the federal government. Historically, immigrants turned to mutual aid societies, settlement houses, churches, and synagogues. Today, alongside state and local governments are religious congregations, ethnic community organizations, and a host of nonprofits that develop programs and practices that aid in the integration of immigrants. Some of these institutions have developed within the immigrant communities themselves.

At the forefront of integration are our local public schools, which historically have offered a path to integration and what it means to be an American. Schools can provide the children of immigrants with the human capital, basic education, knowledge of English, and civic education that will allow them to become successful American citizens.

We, like other scholars of immigration across the country, are optimistic about the second generation, although the public schools cannot succeed in their missions without support. This is particularly important for those schools in twenty-first-century gateways and other new destinations, large and small, where the burden of educating the children of immigrants is felt most dramatically. As some of the authors in this book point out, initiatives are already under way in public and charter schools in twenty-first-century gateways such as Atlanta, Dallas, and Minneapolis. But more can be accomplished.[7]

For working adults, the workplace can be a place of adult integration. Recently geographers have emphasized that work segregation is much lower than residential segregation, suggesting that the workplace is where people of different backgrounds come together and interact.[8] Often, when asked in what situations they "feel most American," immigrants respond "at work."[9] Workplaces are also often the venue for diversity training and diversity seminars, forums that attempt to foster a broad understanding of a multicultural America.[10] Not all work experiences offer a diversity of social contacts, however. Latino women often work in isolation as domestics in private homes or as part of largely immigrant crews that clean hotel rooms during the day or office buildings at night. Latino men often work solely with other immigrants on construction sites, for landscaping firms, or in agricultural jobs.

Although there is evidence of proactive local responses—many of them unique to immigrant communities—we must ask what a more coordinated effort to advance immigrant integration would look like? How might local areas—the context where integration plays out—using a sober and grounded approach, work with immigrants and longer-term residents to ease the process for both? More established destinations, where state and local governments and nonprofits already work together to meet the needs of and integrate new immigrants, have much to offer. However, states and localities in new immigrant destination areas would also benefit from intentional, strategic, and coordinated public policy directed explicitly at immigrant integration and, just as important, the funding to carry it out. Funding for private-public partnerships would be an appropriate avenue to pursue.[11]

To begin to lay out what such an effort would look like nationally, we draw attention here to some initiatives that are under way in a few states. One model is an Illinois initiative, which has been organized through a state executive order signed in 2005 and is built around public-private partnerships. An appointed task force, which includes high-level state agency and department officials, has been charged with examining how the state government can systematically address its changing population.[12] The work of this task force is augmented by a policy council, which includes Illinois leaders with experience managing immigration in the business, community, philanthropic, faith, labor, and government fields. The recommendations from these two groups prioritized programs that would help immigrants learn English, put legal immigrants on a path to citizenship, establish state welcoming centers as a first point of contact for immigrants arriving in Illinois, and provide better access to services that state agencies provide.

Another model comes from the Colorado Community Trust's Supporting Immigrant and Refugee Families Initiative, which supports nineteen Colorado communities in their efforts to encourage immigrants and established residents in working together for healthy communities. Specific needs and strategies are identified through a planning process that involves members from a wide range of perspectives: health care, education, business, banking, law enforcement, local government, and various nonprofit and faith-based organizations. Current projects include strengthening the ability of local health care providers to offer competent care to people from different cultures, helping immigrant parents to become more involved in their children's schools, improving access to English classes for immigrants, and developing mentoring opportunities among foreign- and native-born families.[13]

We highlight several recommendations from the Illinois experience that may be universally applicable. However, we recognize that each place has its own set of economic and social circumstances, migration history, and motivations for changing policy or practice. And indeed they should tailor responses to local needs and situations.

—*Implementing an English-Learning Campaign.* Gaining English proficiency is fundamental if immigrants are to participate fully in American society. This recommendation calls for a coordinated effort among the state community college board, businesses, educators, and immigrant advocates to create, fund, and implement a campaign to offer English instruction where immigrants live and work.

—*Ensuring That Immigrants and Refugees Can Access State Services.* While immigrants are building their English skills, they should have good access to services and information about state offerings, even if it must be provided in their own languages. Many local governments across the country already offer services and material in languages of local immigrant groups, provide translation services, and hire multilingual staff. Implementing this recommendation will make language access a foundational method of doing business with local governments.

—*Helping Eligible Legal Permanent Residents Attain U.S. Citizenship.* When immigrants naturalize, they take on the rights and responsibilities of being a full member of U.S. society: they can vote, hold public office, serve on juries, and participate in other civic activities. The program should support community-based organizations that help immigrants prepare for the naturalization exam and guide them through the formal process.

This last element is especially timely and important and reflects an issue raised by several authors in this book in the conclusions to their individual chapters. They point to incorporation in the political process, which includes naturalized citizens' running for local office. On August 1, 2007, the *New York Times* reported the story of an Indian American of Sikh heritage, Harvinder Anand, who was elected mayor of Laurel Hollow, New York, a village of multimillion-dollar homes on Long Island with a population that is 95 percent white.[14] And elsewhere, members of other Asian groups have been elected to important state and local offices—individuals like Hubert Vo, a Vietnamese American currently serving in the Texas State legislature; Indian-born Swati Dandekar, a member of the Iowa State Legislature; and Korean-born Jun Choi, who was elected mayor of Edison, New Jersey, in 2005. This kind of involvement signifies deep commitment to a local community and full participation in America's political, socioeconomic, and cultural life.

Conclusion

Anthropologist Takeyuki Tsuda recently observed that "cities remain important in a globalized world, not only as sites where the financial management and support structures for global capital are concentrated but also as places where global migrants are incorporated as local citizens." It is local places, he continues, that have been "drawn into the governance of the local diversity introduced by globalization."[15] Many of the chapters in this book have documented the entrée of local governments into the management of diversity, particularly in the suburban communities surrounding twenty-first-century metropolitan gateways. Building on the findings reported in each of the preceding chapters of this book, we strongly recommend federal assistance to states and localities to help manage the diversity wrought by immigration. As Robert Putnam has recently stated, "Immigration policy is not just about numbers and borders. It is also about fostering a sense of shared citizenship."[16] And in her comparison of Canadian and U.S. policies of political incorporation, Irene Bloemraad demonstrates clearly how important explicit policies and structures of integration are in making immigrants citizens in the full sense of the word—Canada's national immigration policy emphasizes integration much more explicitly than does the United States.[17] Dowell Myers makes the case that enlightened self-interest among an aging native-born population should precipitate the investments necessary for this generation of immigrants and their children to advance for the benefit of both parties over the long term.[18]

Federal immigration policy all but ignores the fact that immigrants settle in particular places and live in local communities. Big picture policy issues like border enforcement and the visa allocation system are national-level concerns. But immigrants are not evenly distributed across the nation, and they live in cities, counties, towns, and neighborhoods. They attend local schools; work in local firms, shops, and factories; join local religious congregations; and use state and local services. Municipalities have no control over who enters the country or who lives in their communities. But as suggested in the case studies presented here, the locus of immigration and subsequent integration is the local community; this is where the social, economic, and civic incorporation of immigrants happens.

Notes

1. This was the first of several local ordinances intended to prohibit the employment and "harboring" of undocumented immigrants in Hazleton.

2. Another local place recently well-covered by the media is Carpentersville, Illinois, a suburb of Chicago. Two members of the Carpentersville Board of Trustees, Judy Sigwalt and Paul Humpfer, directly reference Hazleton as a frame for their own ordinance proposals. See Alex Kotlowitz, "Our Town,"*New York Times Magazine,* Sunday, August 5, 2007, pp. 30–37, 52–57.

3. National Conference of State Legislatures, "2007 Enacted State Legislation Related to Immigrants and Immigration" (www.ncsl.org/2007immigrationfinal.htm).

4. Sanctuary cities include long-standing large gateways such as Los Angeles, San Francisco, Houston, and New York. But the list of sanctuary cities also

includes some of the twenty-first-century gateways, including Austin, Minneapolis, Portland, Seattle, and Washington, D.C. See Lisa M. Seghetti, Stephen R. Viña, and Karma Ester, "Enforcing Immigration Law: The Role of State and Local Law Enforcement" (Congressional Research Service, Library of Congress, October 13, 2005).

5. There are arguments about federal preemption that seem unresolved, that is, many state and local initiatives are preempted by the federal government's exclusive authority to regulate immigration. See Monica Guizar, "Facts about Federal Preemption," National Immigration Law Center, June 2007 (www.nilc.org/immlaw policy/LocalLaw/federalpreemptionfacts_2007-06-28.pdf [July 18, 2007]).

6. In October of 2007, a federal judge in San Francisco blocked the implementation of the federal "no-match" plan on the basis that it "would result in irreparable harm to innocent workers and employers" and that the unions that filed the suit demonstrated that legal workers and their employers stood to lose more by swift implementation of the law than the federal government would by a delay. This injunction is in effect until the case goes to trial some months away.

7. For a discussion of responses to immigration in schools in the New South, see William A. Kandel and Emilio A. Parrado, "Hispanic Population Growth and Public School Response in Two New South Immigrant Destinations," in *Latinos in the New South: Transformations of Place,* edited by Heather A. Smith and Owen J. Furuseth, pp. 111–34 (Burlington, Vt.: Ashgate Publishing Company, 2006).

8. Mark Ellis, Richard Wright, and Virginia Parks, "Work Together, Live Apart? Geographies of Racial and Ethnic Segregation at Home and at Work," *Annals of the Association of American Geographers* 94, no. 3 (2004): 620–37.

9. Brettell has found this to be a common response in research on citizenship and civic engagement that she is currently undertaking with funding from the Russell Sage Foundation.

10. For further discussion, see Pawan Dhingra, *Managing Multicultural Lives; Asian American Professionals and the Challenge of Multiple Identities* (Stanford University Press, 2007).

11. See Audrey Singer, "The Impact of Immigration on States and Localities," testimony presented before the Subcommittee on Immigration, Citizenship, Refugees, Border Security, and International Law, House Judiciary Committee, U.S. House of Representatives, Washington, D.C., May 17, 2007 (www3.brookings.edu/views/testimony/asinger/20070517.pdf); and Doris Meissner and others, *Immigration and America's Future: A New Chapter,* Report of the Independent Task Force on Immigration and America's Future (Washington: Migration Policy Institute, 2006).

12. Illinois Coalition for Immigrant and Refugee Rights, *For the Benefit of All: Strategic Recommendations to Enhance the State's Role in the Integration of Immigrants in Illinois: Joint Executive Summary, Year One* and *Report of the New Americans Policy Council, Year One* (Chicago: Illinois Coalition for Immigrant and Refugee Rights, 2006).

13. Susan Downs-Karkos, "Immigrant Integration in Colorado" (Denver: The Colorado Trust, 2004).

14. Paul Vitello, "This 'Harry' Stands Out From the Crowd," *New York Times,* August 1, 2007.

15. Takeyuki Tsuda, *Local Citizenship in Recent Countries of Immigration: Japan in Comparative Perspective* (Lanham, Md.: Lexington Books, 2006), p. 12.

16. Robert Putnam, "*E Pluribus Unum*: Diversity and Community in the Twenty-First Century," the 2006 Johan Skytte Prize Lecture, *Scandinavian Political Studies* 30 (2007): 137–174.

17. Irene Bloemraad, *Becoming a Citizen: Incorporating Immigrants and Refugees in the United States and Canada* (University of California Press, 2006).

18. Dowell Myers, *Immigrants and Boomers: Forging a New Social Contract for the Future of America* (New York: Russell Sage Foundation, 2007).

Contributors

Caroline B. Brettell
Southern Methodist University

Tara Buentello
University of Texas–Austin

Robin Datel
California State University
Sacramento

Dennis Dingemans
University of California–Davis

Katherine Fennelly
University of Minnesota

Owen J. Furuseth
University of North Carolina–Charlotte

Susan W. Hardwick
University of Oregon

Wei Li
Arizona State University

James E. Meacham
University of Oregon

Alex Oberle
University of Northern Iowa

Myron Orfield
University of Minnesota

Mary E. Odem
Emory University

Marie Price
George Washington University

Audrey Singer
Brookings Institution

Emily Skop
University of Colorado–Colorado Springs

Heather A. Smith
University of North Carolina–Charlotte

Index

BROOKINGS The Brookings Institution is a private nonprofit organization devoted to research, education, and publication on important issues of domestic and foreign policy. Its principal purpose is to bring the highest quality independent research and analysis to bear on current and emerging policy problems. The Institution was founded on December 8, 1927, to merge the activities of the Institute for Government Research, founded in 1916, the Institute of Economics, founded in 1922, and the Robert Brookings Graduate School of Economics and Government, founded in 1924. Interpretations or conclusions in Brookings publications should be understood to be solely those of the authors.